# POLITICAL IDEAS IN THE ROMANTIC AGE

*Also by Isaiah Berlin*

✳

KARL MARX
THE AGE OF ENLIGHTENMENT

*Edited by Henry Hardy and Aileen Kelly*

RUSSIAN THINKERS

*Edited by Henry Hardy*

CONCEPTS AND CATEGORIES
AGAINST THE CURRENT
PERSONAL IMPRESSIONS
THE CROOKED TIMBER OF HUMANITY
THE SENSE OF REALITY
THE ROOTS OF ROMANTICISM
THE POWER OF IDEAS
THREE CRITICS OF THE ENLIGHTENMENT
FREEDOM AND ITS BETRAYAL
LIBERTY
THE SOVIET MIND
LETTERS 1928–1946

*Edited by Henry Hardy and Roger Hausheer*

THE PROPER STUDY OF MANKIND

✳

*For more information on Isaiah Berlin visit*
*http://berlin.wolf.ox.ac.uk/*

# POLITICAL IDEAS IN THE ROMANTIC AGE

## Their Rise and Influence on Modern Thought

ISAIAH BERLIN

Edited by Henry Hardy
With an introduction by Joshua L. Cherniss

Princeton University Press
Princeton and Oxford

Published in the United States and Canada in 2006 by
Princeton University Press, 41 William Street, Princeton, New Jersey 08540

In the United Kingdom and European Union, published by Chatto & Windus in 2006

Library of Congress Control Number 2006922242
ISBN–13: 978–0–691–12687–6
ISBN–10: 0–691–12687–9

Printed on acid-free paper

pup.princeton.edu

Typeset by Deltatype Ltd, Birkenhead, Merseyside
Printed in the United States of America

2 4 6 8 10 9 7 5 3 1

In memory of Solomon Rachmilevich

# CONTENTS

# ABBREVIATIONS AND CONVENTIONS

The following abbreviations are used in this volume for the titles of books by Isaiah Berlin:

| | |
|---|---|
| AC | *Against the Current* (1979) |
| CC | *Concepts and Categories* (1978) |
| CTH | *The Crooked Timber of Humanity* (1990) |
| FIB | *Freedom and its Betrayal* (2002) |
| KM | *Karl Marx* (1939; 4th edition 1978) |
| L | *Liberty* (2002) |
| L1 | *[Flourishing:] Letters 1928–1946* (2004) |
| MN | *The Magus of the North* (1993; incorporated in TCE) |
| PI; PI2 | *Personal Impressions* (1980); 2nd edition (1998) |
| PIRA | *Political Ideas in the Romantic Age* (2006) |
| POI | *The Power of Ideas* (2000) |
| PSM | *The Proper Study of Mankind* (1997) |
| RR | *The Roots of Romanticism* (1999) |
| RT | *Russian Thinkers* (1978) |
| SM | *The Soviet Mind* (2004) |
| SR | *The Sense of Reality* (1996) |
| TCE | *Three Critics of the Enlightenment* (2000) |

References to PIRA in the introduction are given by page number alone.

Curly brackets – {} – identify Berlin's handwritten marginalia (mostly notes pointing to further revision), here presented as footnotes. Square brackets mark editorial comment or intervention, except that such brackets have not been used to identify exact references to published works, almost all of which have been supplied by the editor.

Any corrections needed in this volume will be posted at *http://berlin.wolf.ox.ac.uk/* under 'Published work' as soon as they come to the editor's notice.

# EDITOR'S PREFACE

## A Tale of a Torso

... in accepting the invitation to become President of Iffley College in 1965 Berlin was acknowledging that he was incapable of writing a big book.

Maurice Cowling[1]

275 printed pages! *Quel horreur!*

Isaiah Berlin[2]

*Political Ideas in the Romantic Age* may be seen as Isaiah Berlin's *Grundrisse*,[3] the ur-text or 'torso',[4] as Berlin called it, from which a great deal of his subsequent work derived, but which also contains much that is distinctive and not to be found elsewhere in his writings. It was first composed between 1950 and 1952, and is based on a distillate of his early work in the history of ideas, itself informed and to a considerable extent constituted by the enormous amount of background reading he did for his Home University Library biography of Karl Marx[5] in the 1930s, when he was a Fellow of All Souls College, Oxford. It is the longest continuous text he ever wrote, at over a hundred thousand words.[6] The prologue was written somewhat later, and Berlin revised the main

---

[1] *Spectator*, 17 October 1998, 38.

[2] Letter to Henry Hardy, 10 March 1992, on being told the approximate length of the present book: see p. xiv below.

[3] Karl Marx's *Grundrisse* ('Foundations') is the name given to his rough drafts of 1857–8 for his lifetime project, a 'critique of the economic categories', part of which was later published as *Das Kapital* (1867). *Grundrisse* was first published in German in 1939 and 1941 in a rare, two-volume Soviet edition, reprinted in German for general circulation in a one-volume edition in 1953, and first translated into English in 1973.

[4] The metaphor became less appropriate as time went on: instead of adding missing limbs to the torso, Berlin quarried it for shorter pieces. I look forward to reading someone's *The Torso as Quarry: The Intellectual Auto-Parasitism of Isaiah Berlin*.

[5] *Karl Marx: His Life and Environment* (London and Toronto, 1939).

[6] Originally it was perhaps up to half as long again: see p. xii below, note 2.

text in his own hand – particularly heavily in the earlier chapters – after it had been typed from his initial dictation.

I have already recounted the story of this text briefly in my preface to Berlin's *Freedom and its Betrayal*,[1] an edited transcript of a set of radio lectures that derive from it. But let me expand on this a little here.

On 21 April 1950 Katharine E. McBride, President of Bryn Mawr College, Pennsylvania, wrote to Berlin, inviting him to give the Mary Flexner Lectures. The letter reached him at an opportune moment, as he was about to return to All Souls to become a full-time historian of ideas. He accepted with alacrity, in the first place provisionally, and six weeks later definitely. In his second letter[2] he proposed a topic:

> As for the subject of my lectures; I am wondering whether you would find the political ideas of the late eighteenth and early nineteenth century a suitable topic. What I should like to talk about is the different fundamental types of approach to social and political problems – e.g. the Utilitarian; that of the Enlightenment (rational and sentimental) from the Encyclopaedia to the French Revolution; the Authoritarian-Reactionary (de Maistre and his allies); the Romantic; the Technocratic-Scientific (Saint Simon and his followers), and perhaps the Marxist.[3] These seem to me to be the prototypes from which our modern views in their great and colliding variety have developed (only stated, it appears to me, with much more clarity, vigour and dramatic force by the founders than by their modern epigoni). My lectures, while occupied with the history of ideas, would have a very direct bearing upon our present discontents. I don't know what I ought to call this subject – it is part of a work on the history of European ideas from 1789 to 1870 which, in any case, I must at some time write for the Oxford History of Europe,[4] but perhaps the title could be thought of later. Perhaps something quite simple, 'Six (or however many) Types of Political Theory', or perhaps something a

[1] *Freedom and its Betrayal: Six Enemies of Human Liberty* (London and Princeton, 2002), xii–xv.

[2] Dated 2 May 1950.

[3] In the end Berlin did not discuss Marxism, though he did include a chapter on Marx's historicist precursors – Vico, Herder and Hegel.

[4] A contract for Berlin's contribution to this series (the Oxford History of Modern Europe, edited by A. C. L. Bullock and F. W. Deakin) survives among many that were offered, agreed to or signed for books he never wrote. The book was first discussed with him at dinner in Wadham College, Oxford, in 1948, and was to be entitled *Ideas in Europe 1789–1870* (though the end-date varies).

little more arresting. However, if this kind of subject is suitable I could set to work and prepare some lectures.

[ ... ] I hope you will have no hesitation in rejecting my suggested lectures if for some reason they are not what you desire, but I am pre-occupied with the thought of the early nineteenth century and its antecedents, and should find it difficult to turn my attention to something very different; but that is no reason why you should allow this to be foisted upon you if some other plan would suit you better. If, on the other hand, my suggestion is acceptable to you, I have no doubt that I shall myself vastly profit by the experience.

Naturally, Berlin's suggestion was accepted. And he was right to predict that giving the lectures would serve his own purposes, because the invitation proved to be the catalyst for the preparation, over the next two years, of the present work, which can for once rightly be described as 'seminal'. I say 'preparation' rather than 'writing' advisedly, since in December 1951 he is still 'in process of hysterical dictation of the rough draft'.[1]

The only other surviving detailed evidence of Berlin's thinking as he worked towards the typescript, so far as I know,[2] appears in a letter to Bryn Mawr written in November 1951, sent in reply to a request for an overall title under which to announce the series, and for titles for the individual lectures:

I am not sure what the best title of my lectures would be, perhaps 'Political Ideas in the Romantic Age' would be best, and you can put in '1760–1830' if you think well of that. I have been looking for some title denoting what I really want to talk about; i.e. the particular period during which modern political and social beliefs really came to be formulated and the controversies acquired their classical expression, in the sense that present-day arguments still deal in concepts and even terminology which crystallised during those years. What I wanted to avoid was a term like 'origins' or 'foundations', since this would

[1] Letter to Anna Kallin of 11 December 1951: see p. 279 below.
[2] There is also an undated sheet (MS. Berlin 570, fo. 23) in the Berlin Papers in the Bodleian Library, Oxford, on which Berlin has written what seems to be an intermediate version of his plan: 'The Rise of Modern Political Thought / 1. Nature, Rights & the new scientific spirit (The philosophes & the Encyclopaed-ists) / 2. The Problem of Freedom (Rousseau & Kant) / 3. Idealism & Romanticism (Vico, Herder, Fichte & the Romantic movement) / 4. The organization of Society (St. Simon & the beginnings of socialism) / 5. The revolt against Reason (De Maistre & Görres) / 6. History & the Individual (Hegel & Marx)'.

commit me to talking about people like Machiavelli, Hobbes, Locke etc., who may be the fathers of all these things, but are definitely felt to be predecessors and precursors and, certainly as far as mode of expression is concerned, altogether obsolete. I had therefore thought of as an alternative title 'The rise and crystallisation of modern political ideas'. If you can think of something more elegant than either, I should be grateful. Perhaps the first might be the title, the second a subtitle. I leave that to you.

As for the individual lectures, I should like to suggest the following: (1) 'The Concept of Nature and the Science of Politics' (Helvétius and Holbach); (2) 'Political Liberty and the Ethical Imperative' (Kant and Rousseau); (3) 'Liberalism and the Romantic Movement' (Fichte and J. S. Mill); (4) 'Individual Freedom and the March of History' (Herder and Hegel); (5) 'The Organisation of Society and the Golden Age' (Saint-Simon and his successors); (6) 'The Counter-Revolution' (Maistre and Görres).[1]

His mood as he finished the draft typescript was characteristically unselfconfident. As he wrote to a close friend at New College, David Cecil:

here I am trying to write this book on political ideas, & it is coming out all awry – sentimental, vague, clumsy, soft, unscholarly, a mass of verbiage & dough unseasoned, no sharp points, only occasionally little gleams of what I thought I said, what I thought I wanted to say. However I persist. I don't know what the lectures will sound like, but there *will*, unless I fall ill or die, be a book. Not very good, less so than I can do on the Russians. But I must get the circulation of blood going: I accepted the lectures because I knew they wd lay the foundations of a book. – & having dictated 150.000 words, I suppose there is.[2]

The lectures were duly delivered in the spring of 1952 – the first on 11 February and the last on 17 March – after a good deal of characteristic administrative flimflam into which we do not need to enquire here. As usual, the act of lecturing caused him terrible self-doubt. Between the second and third lectures he wrote to Marion

---

[1] Letter of 20 November 1951 to Mrs Samuel H. Paul, Bryn Mawr.

[2] Letter of 29 January 1952. The word-count is not necessarily reliable, but may indicate that he did draft the whole work (see p. xiv below, note 3). IB continues: 'I shd rather like Cole's professorship at Oxford: perhaps the book will help with that: I am being quite frank.' He always said afterwards that the BBC version of the lectures was instrumental in winning him that very professorship in 1957.

Frankfurter: 'The lectures are an agony, of course, I seem to myself to be screaming meaningless phrases to a vaguely discernible, half darkened, audience; & feel terrified before, hysterical during & ashamed afterwards.'[1]

Berlin certainly intended to publish a book based on the typescript he had prepared for the lectures, and to do so within a year or two of their delivery. As he told A. L. Rowse during the last phase of preparation, 'I am even now in the throes of the most awful agony of writing lectures for Bryn Mawr to be given in February & then printed, I suppose next year.'[2] On 25 November 1952 he wrote to Arthur Schlesinger, Jr, that he would have 'finished the politics – Bryn Mawr book' in 1953. The following January he remained optimistic in a letter to President McBride:

> This brings me to the subject I am trying to evade and avoid, the question of the manuscript, which I really do hope to be able to send you by about May. Heaven knows what its condition will be, whether it will be 140,000 words or 60,000 words or both – but let us turn away from this bleak and distasteful topic.[3]

He never did complete the necessary work, and the torso was laid aside and forgotten, despite the fact that he had revised much of it extensively.

It is hard to say at what precise juncture hope of a book was lost, but the last reference I have seen in the Bryn Mawr files occurs in March 1956, when President McBride gamely hopes for a manuscript by that July;[4] and in 1959 Berlin still writes to Oxford University Press as if the book was on his agenda; at any rate, it provides an excuse to explain the delay in writing his book for the Oxford History of Modern Europe, from his commitment to which he then proceeds to extricate himself.[5]

In 1992 I produced a fair copy of PIRA, incorporating all Berlin's myriad handwritten alterations, and the prologue that he had written subsequently, but I do not believe that he ever looked at it, at any rate seriously. Here is the relevant part of the covering letter I sent with the typescript:

[1] Letter of 23 February 1952.     [2] Letter of 20 January 1952.
[3] Letter of 22 January 1953.       [4] Letter of 27 March 1956.
[5] Letter to Dan Davin of 11 November 1959.

With somewhat bated breath I enclose my provisional rendition of what is by far your longest unpublished work (about 110,000 words, or 275 printed octavo pages), the 'long version' of the Flexner Lectures. Don't panic! I'm not asking you to do any work on this – not even to look at it in any detail. But since it now exists, it seemed reasonable to show it to you, if only so that you might admire its bulk. Perhaps you had no idea you had in fact written such a long book?!

I have inserted after the contents page a note on the text[1] which you might find of interest. It raises one or two questions, such as: Was there ever a corresponding 'long version' of the last two lectures, or did you never have time to draft this? Why did you never publish the lectures with OUP, as you were under contract to do? Was it indeed Anna Kallin's plan that the Third Programme version should be the 1952 Reith Lectures, and if so, when and why was this notion scotched? Was there a recording of the lectures as delivered in the USA?[2]

Berlin replied:

275 printed pages! *Quel horreur!* I don't know about the last two lectures – the BBC texts are in their own way surely complete? I have no recollection of a contract with OUP (remember, I shall be eighty-three in June). Anna Kallin did indeed wonder whether they might make Reith Lectures – I was only too ready. She put it up, I had a letter inviting me to do them, followed by a letter two days later countermanding. That was that. I was asked to do the series seven or eight years later, and by that time said that I had nothing to say. That was before I thought of Romanticism.

Even though I have still found no trace of the last two chapters, there is some evidence that they were drafted, though one cannot be certain.[3] In any event, for Maistre he could make use of a

---

[1] Reproduced on pp. 279–83 below as 'Note from the editor to the author'.

[2] Letter of 3 March 1992.

[3] In November 1951 he writes to his parents: 'I stay at Harvard anyway till Xmas. Then I have a month or so to finish the Bryn Mawr lectures. [ . . . ] Then I shall go on working – correcting all the six chapters of the book which the Bryn Mawr chapters will become.' At this stage, of course, the later chapters might have been planned rather than actually dictated, but by 21 February 1952 he writes (again to his parents): 'I *have* written the first draft of a *book*. Which is an event. It will take about another 6–8 months of polish but shd appear, in 1953.' And on 7 November of the same year he writes to T. S. Eliot apropos the BBC Lectures: 'I possess the MS. of the text on which the talks are based, even longer, fuller, duller, with an apparatus of notes.' He is perhaps unlikely to have

typescript prepared some years before. He was right about the
BBC texts, and his views on Saint-Simon and Maistre appear in
*Freedom and its Betrayal*. A longer version of his treatment of
Maistre is the centrepiece of *The Crooked Timber of Humanity*. I
have not repeated these accounts in this volume, but the reader
may wish to turn to them after finishing the present text, to
complete the journey begun within these covers.

Readers familiar with Berlin's *oeuvre* will hardly need to be told
where in his later work the ideas of PIRA reappear, in a more or
less altered form; those less well travelled in his writings may
welcome some brief preliminary guidance. At one stage I contem-
plated an exhaustive concordance of parallels, but once I began
compiling this it quickly became clear that a complete listing would
be more confusing than helpful, since so much of Berlin's work
consists of journeys across similar terrain. The context and the
purpose of the enquiry often differ; nor does Berlin ever exactly
repeat himself, even when he is ostensibly recapitulating discussions that have appeared elsewhere, which means that one needs to
read all his discussions of a topic to be sure that one has squeezed
out every drop of what he (not always consistently) has to say
about it. Nevertheless there is a good deal of overlap in his work
taken as a whole, and readers who tackle it systematically will
recognise a number of previous acquaintances – eventually old
friends – as they travel onward.

   A striking example of Berlin's avoidance of repetition is provided by his multiple treatments of what he sometimes calls the
'three-legged stool' or 'tripod' of key assumptions (for him mistaken) on which Western philosophy has, in his view, rested for
some two thousand years. In his usual account, these assumptions
are that in ethics and politics, as in science, all genuine questions
have unique answers, that these answers are in principle discoverable, and that they all fit together into a coherent whole. This
leitmotif is implicit in the first chapter of PIRA, though not set out
there in a single coordinated passage.[1] It becomes explicit in
Berlin's later work, for example (among many other instances) in
'The Romantic Revolution' (1960; SR), in the second lecture – 'The

---

expressed himself thus if two chapters remained unwritten, however great an
exaggeration he committed in referring to 'an apparatus of notes'.
[1] See, for example, pp. 21, 23, 28, 54–5 and 77–8 below.

First Attack on Enlightenment' – of *The Roots of Romanticism* (1965), and in 'The Divorce Between the Sciences and the Humanities' (1974; AC).

These accounts are broadly similar. However, if we turn to other treatments of the trope, differences appear. In 'The Birth of Greek Individualism' (1962; L)[1] we find that the usual first and third legs have become legs 1 and 2, and that there is a new leg 3: 'The third assumption is that man has a discoverable, describable nature, and that this nature is essentially, and not merely contingently, social.' Though this substitution is obviously motivated by the topic of the lecture, made clear in its title, one does wonder if there is a certain arbitrariness about the selection of legs for the tripod, indeed about the number of legs this supportive piece of furniture is said to possess. In chapter 4 of 'The Magus of the North' (1965; TCE) we find the Enlightenment tradition resting on 'three pillars' of faith – 'in reason', 'in the identity of human nature through time and the possibility of universal human goals', and 'in the possibility of attaining to the second by means of the first'.[2] The cake is recognisable, even if the recipe is subtly different. In any event, as Berlin wrote in another context, 'like all over-simple classifications of this type, [it] becomes, if pressed, artificial, scholastic and ultimately absurd', though it can certainly offer 'a starting-point for genuine investigation'.[3]

Let me now mention a few of the other principal correspondences between PIRA and later works that may strike the reader who comes to the former when familiar with the latter, or indeed vice versa. The first and most straightforward of these, of course, is between the four chapters of PIRA, the first four Mary Flexner Lectures, and the first four BBC Lectures published in *Freedom and its Betrayal* (reckoning the introduction to that volume together with its first chapter – on Helvétius – as the single item they originally constituted). Next in line is the use of the second and third chapters in 'Two Concepts of Liberty', and of the fourth in 'Historical Inevitability'. These are the reworkings that George Crowder has in mind when he sums up the main thrust of PIRA in these terms: 'In the torso Berlin sketched the outlines of what would become his mature position in many areas, but three in particular: the complex political legacy of Enlightenment rationalism

---

[1] L 290 ff., 319.    [2] TCE 278.
[3] 'The Hedgehog and the Fox', PSM 437.

and its critics, the contrast between negative and positive liberty, and the vulnerability of positive liberty to corruption.'[1]

This brings us to more local echoes of individual chapters or passages from PIRA in later writing. Here one should first strike a note of caution: there is not necessarily a straightforward one-to-one correspondence between the subject-matter of earlier and later passages, since different topics, or different aspects of the same topic, appear in different combinations at different times. So, for example, the earlier pages of 'The Divorce Between the Sciences and the Humanities' echo the depiction of Enlightenment scientism in the first chapter of PIRA – the idea that cumulative progress is possible in all areas of enquiry if one applies the scientific method (allegedly the only rational method there is) – while the later part of the essay, with its focus on Vico, is more closely related to PIRA's chapter 4. Conversely, chapter 1 points forward in some ways to 'The Divorce . . .' and in other ways to 'The Concept of Scientific History' (1960; CC, PSM); indeed, chapters 1 and 4 themselves overlap a good deal. So the specification of parallels is a necessarily inexact science.

That said, some rough signposting is possible. The prologue to PIRA contains Berlin's well-known definition of philosophy as a third way, different from both empirical and formal disciplines.[2] This resurfaces in fuller form in several places, including the introduction to *The Age of Enlightenment* (1956; POI), 'The Purpose of Philosophy' (1961; CC, POI), 'Does Political Theory Still Exist?' (1961; CC, PSM), and 'An Introduction to Philosophy', a television interview with Bryan Magee.[3]

The prologue and the first chapter of PIRA, 'Politics as a Descriptive Science', set out the avowedly oversimplified view of the Enlightenment that Berlin rehearsed many times throughout his writings, refining it to some degree as time went by. Notable later instances are the chapter on 'The Enlightenment' in *The Magus of the North* (1965), described by John Gray as canonical,[4] and the relevant part of 'The First Attack on Enlightenment', the second lecture of *The Roots of Romanticism*, delivered in the same

---

[1] George Crowder, *Isaiah Berlin: Liberty and Pluralism* (Cambridge, 2004), 56–7.

[2] See pp. 11–12 below.

[3] Published in Bryan Magee (ed.), *Men of Ideas: Some Creators of Contemporary Philosophy* (London, 1978), 14–41.

[4] John Gray, *Isaiah Berlin* (London, 1995), 136.

year. As noted above, all these works include accounts of the variously triform bedrock on which Berlin saw the Enlightenment as being founded.

In addition, Berlin begins the first chapter by raising the problem of obedience as fundamental to political philosophy: 'Why should anyone obey anyone else?' This question also inaugurates the first Flexner/BBC Lecture, and 'Two Concepts of Liberty'.[1] One of the main themes of the same chapter, namely the difference between the logic of enquiry in science as opposed to the arts, and the linked rejection of methodological monism, reappears in 'The Divorce Between the Sciences and the Humanities'.

The discussion of Rousseau and Kant in the second chapter, 'The Idea of Freedom', is recognisable in a condensed form in 'Two Concepts of Liberty'. And the section on Kant that ends the chapter is developed in 'Kant as an Unfamiliar Source of Nationalism' (1972; SR).

The material on Fichte in 'Two Concepts of Freedom', the third chapter of PIRA, is used not only in 'Two Concepts of Liberty', but also in the fourth lecture, 'The Restrained Romantics', of *The Roots of Romanticism*. In chapter 3, too, we find intimations of the extended treatment of historical realism that Berlin provided in 'The Sense of Reality', written soon afterwards (1953; SR), though here he calls it the 'sense of history'.[2]

The final, fourth chapter, 'The March of History', after a recapitulation of much of chapter 1, includes not only the material (on Hegel, for instance) that is reworked in 'Historical Inevitability', but also sections on Vico and Herder that can be seen as the germs of Berlin's later work on those two thinkers (1960 and 1965 respectively), represented especially by the studies of them incorporated into *Three Critics of the Enlightenment*. In this chapter too we see the beginning of Berlin's preoccupation with pluralism and the Counter-Enlightenment, and also the main origin of the discussion of historicism and of differing views of the nature of history in 'The Concept of Scientific History'.

Some later resonances of the appendix on 'Subjective versus Objective Ethics' are identified in Joshua Cherniss's introduction.[3]

---

[1] FIB 1, L 168. It appears, too, in 'Does Political Theory Still Exist?' (PSM 64) and in 'The Birth of Greek Individualism' (L 293).

[2] See p. 200 below (the 'sense of reality' appears on pp. 192 and 259).

[3] See pp. xlii–xlvi below.

Once again, I emphasise that the echoes catalogued here comprise only a small selection, chosen more or less at random, and should not be taken as any kind of comprehensive guide to the ubiquitous presence of ideas from PIRA in Berlin's later work. Nor, on the other hand, should their existence be allowed to obscure the fact, alluded to at the outset, that there is a great deal in PIRA that is not said at all – or not said as fully and/or as well – in Berlin's later writings. Some dimensions of the thinkers Berlin discusses receive much more detailed treatment than he ever gave them subsequently. More importantly, as Joshua Cherniss explains, PIRA uniquely draws most of Berlin's main themes together, exhibits them as a coherent overall thesis, and shows how the debates discussed are prototypes of many of our current preoccupations. In this context I should like to quote Ian Harris,[1] who has pointed out that PIRA

> reveals the unity in Berlin's thought much better than anything published hitherto. In particular, it shows very clearly that like Cassirer, Croce, Lovejoy, Oakeshott and Collingwood, Berlin wrote a history that was formed by, and which was a vehicle for, his philosophical views. That is also what makes it intellectually interesting, and puts it in a different category from any number of specialised works published in the intervening half century.

As compared with the other works I have reconstructed from Berlin's *Nachlass* – chiefly *The Magus of the North*, *The Sense of Reality*, *The Roots of Romanticism*, *Freedom and its Betrayal* – PIRA presented a rather special problem of intellectual archaeology. Those other works were in a sufficiently completed state for me to turn them into books that needed no special explanation or apology beyond making clear what their origins were, so that they would not be judged by inappropriate standards. PIRA, however, was in a far more rough-hewn condition, like the massive sculptures for the tomb of Pope Julius II left unfinished by Michelangelo, or the colossal *kouros* that lies, a moment of arrested history, on a hillside near the sea at Apollonas on the Greek island of Naxos. This lent it a certain mystique and grandeur, but meant that it couldn't be brought to completion in the same way as its predecessors were, especially since it lacks its final two chapters. I and Berlin's other Literary Trustees therefore decided to give it the

[1] Personal communication.

rather different treatment that this volume constitutes. PIRA, that is, is offered to the public not as any kind of forgotten though essentially finished work, but as the 'torso' Berlin knew it to be, without artificial prostheses attached where limbs are missing, and without excision of his unimplemented notes for revision, or concealment of other signs of incompleteness.

I am most grateful to Joshua Cherniss, whose introduction skilfully places PIRA in context in the development of Berlin's thought and of his subject. Joshua has generously helped, besides, with the above sketch of later parallels. I should also like to thank Robert Wokler for invaluable contributions from his expert knowledge over a long period; Alan Ryan, one of my fellow Literary Trustees, for his indispensable support and guidance during the preparation of the volume; and James Chappel for timely and efficient research in the Berlin Papers on PIRA's history. Help on individual points was given by George Crowder, Steffen Gross, Jennifer Holmes, Michael Inwood and Serena Moore, whom I warmly thank, as I do all those whose input I have carelessly failed to keep track of.

I hope and believe that Isaiah Berlin would have approved of the dedication of this book to the memory of Solomon Rachmilevich. As Berlin said to his biographer, 'He was the first person who gave me a taste for ideas in general, interesting ideas *tel quel*.'[1] 'Rach' died in 1953 in his early sixties, at about the same time as the PIRA project, and it seemed right to bring them both back to life together.

Wolfson College, Oxford                  HENRY HARDY
May 2005

---

[1] See L1 141 note 1.

# ISAIAH BERLIN'S POLITICAL IDEAS

*From the Twentieth Century to the Romantic Age*

## Joshua L. Cherniss

A study of the history of opinion is a necessary preliminary to the emancipation of the mind.

J. M. Keynes[1]

The use of the word 'freedom' is one of the surest indices of the user's general ultimate ideal of life, of what to want and what to avoid [ . . . ] one of the most faithful indicators of where a man stands.

Isaiah Berlin[2]

I

ISAIAH BERLIN was a fundamentally unsystematic thinker. His work ranged across many disciplines – principally the history of ideas, political theory, analytic philosophy, Russian literature, Soviet politics, and the philosophy of history and the social sciences – and embraced a varied cast of characters. Berlin produced no great synthesis or magnum opus; temperamentally, and stylistically, he was an essayist. Value pluralism and liberalism formed the leitmotifs of much of his mature work;[3] but his writings cannot be reduced to a systematic statement or comprehensive exposition of either of these doctrines. Yet while Berlin's thought did not constitute a centripetal system or converge on a single solution, it did form a cohesive whole, consisting of a set of recurring, overlapping, interrelated concerns and convictions. The themes that he pursued across many years and pages ultimately fit

---

[1] Keynes 1926, 16. For full references, see p. viii above, and the bibliography at the end of this essay (pp. lv ff.).

[2] See p. 207 below. Subsequent references to PIRA in this introduction are given by page number alone.

[3] For the relationship between these two concepts – a topic of considerable controversy in recent literature on Berlin – see Gray 1995, Galston 2002, Crowder 2002, and particularly Crowder 2004.

into a pattern; but they are held together by his intellectual personality, rather than by a single master idea, or guiding principle, or preordained plan.

*Political Ideas in the Romantic Age* (PIRA) is not a summation of Berlin's career as either intellectual historian or political theorist. It is by no means the best, most original or most interesting of his historical works. It is not a characteristic example of his approach to the history of ideas, largely lacking the psychological insight and focus on individual thinkers that mark his best historical essays; nor does it provide a comprehensive statement of methodological principles. And it contains no major ideas that cannot be found – often more fully and coherently worked out – in his other writings.

Yet PIRA occupies a central place in Berlin's intellectual life; and read properly, it reveals much about the development and nature of his thought and career. For it contains, often in embryonic form, most of the ideas, and encompasses most of the concerns, that would dominate Berlin's work over the next three decades. Here we find early manifestations of his conceptualisation of liberty, his analysis of the philosophy of history and critique of determinism, and his accounts of the Enlightenment and its varied critics and successors – romantic, reactionary, historicist and socialist. Furthermore, we find all these, which Berlin would develop in separate essays over many years, laid out side by side. PIRA helps us understand the development, and appreciate the unity, of Berlin's thought, and reminds us how venturesome a thinker he was. For this reason it is an important document for those who wish to understand, and learn from, Berlin's work.

II

Berlin began his career as a professional philosopher, absorbed primarily by questions in the theory of knowledge. Although this field of interest is still in evidence in his later work, his intellectual attention shifted to other areas. While working on his biography of Karl Marx in the 1930s, Berlin became fascinated by Marx's precursors and exegetes, and by the problems of social and political theory and the philosophy of history that they forcefully raised. The looming threat of totalitarianism, which cast a shadow over the 1930s, and his first-hand experience of both political administration in the USA and the suffering of the Russian intelligentsia under Stalinism during and immediately after the Second World War, further turned his mind towards politics. He returned to Oxford in 1946 more engaged with the political events of his day than previously, and determined to turn his attention from analytical philosophy to the history of ideas.[1]

This conjunction was not coincidental. For Berlin the history of ideas was not only a subject of intrinsic fascination, but also a means to self-understanding. Berlin interpreted contemporary political conflicts in the light of the history of ideas, and he turned to history to make sense of the concepts that dominated the politics of his day: he sought to make past ideas speak to present problems. 'Political words and notions and acts', he declared, 'are not intelligible save in the context of the issues that divide the men who use them [ . . . ] our own attitudes and activities are likely to remain obscure to us, unless we understand the dominant issues of our world.'[2] Social, political and moral problems arise in every age. But ideas are especially powerful at moments of particularly rapid change and acute confusion. In his inaugural lecture as Chichele Professor of Social and Political Theory in 1958, Berlin pronounced his own age to be such a time: 'there has, perhaps, been no time in modern history when so large a number of human beings [ . . . ] have had their notions, and indeed their lives, so deeply altered, and in some cases violently upset, by fanatically held social and political doctrines'. Some professors and intellectuals could wield immense and destructive power; it was up to other professors and intellectuals to understand their influence, expose their errors, and provide a clearer and truer understanding of reality.[3] This was the task that Berlin undertook.

But why approach political ideas *historically*? Because, Berlin replied, such ideas were historical phenomena. 'Political theory is an aspect of thought (and sometimes feeling) about men's relationships to each other and to their institutions, in terms of purposes and scales of value *which themselves alter as a result of historical circumstances of varying types*, not least in terms of new models derived from other fields of experience.'[4] To understand past ideas required knowledge of the circumstances, social and intellectual, out of which they arose. But it also depended on some

---

[1] For the latter, see his letters to Herbert Hart, early October 1944 and 23 February 1945, and to Sir Anthony Rumbold, 11 January 1945, L1 498, 518, 534.
[2] L 168.        [3] L 167.        [4] 12, italics added.

features of human experience remaining the same, so that the
problems of the past continued to be absorbing, and the responses
to them comprehensible, to the men and women of the present.
'[E]ach political philosophy responds to the needs of its own times
and is fully intelligible only in terms of all the relevant factors of its
age, and intelligible to us only to the degree to which (and it is a far
larger one than some modern relativists wish to persuade us that it
is) we have experience in common with previous generations.'[1]
These successive and competing political philosophies 'are not
commensurable, any more than novels, or histories, which spring
out of a given world and sum up each experience, can be ranged in
some strict order of merit or "progress", as if there were a single
goal which all these works of art were seeking to attain'.[2] To
contribute to human self-understanding, the historian of ideas
should seek not to rank the belief-systems of the past, or portray
the inevitable progress from one to another, but rather to describe
the dominant models which have shaped human experience over
time, and continue to underlie the outlook of the present. Berlin's
approach to the history of ideas was thus consistent with his
pluralism and his anti-teleological philosophy of history.

Berlin regarded the period surrounding the French Revolution
as a political and intellectual watershed. The ideas that emerged at
that time continued to 'form the basic intellectual capital on
which [ ... ] we live today'; the political discourse of Berlin's age
depended on 'the concepts, the language, indeed the images and
metaphors which were generated during that period'. During those
years 'the issues debated were literally identical with those which
stir individuals and nations' in the present.[3] While he disavowed

---

[1] ibid. For a later statement of Berlin's conception of the nature and importance
of ideas and their relation to history, fully consistent with the points made in
PIRA, see Jahanbegloo 1991, 24.

[2] 13.

[3] 1–2; cf. PSM 86–7. Such passages reflect the gulf separating Berlin's view of
the relationship between the history of political ideas and the present from that of,
for example, J. G. A. Pocock, Quentin Skinner, and their followers. Without
seeking to make any claims for either approach, it should nevertheless be noted
that the contention that the incendiary political issues of the 1950s were 'literally
identical' to those of the 1800s is extremely difficult to take seriously. Such an
assertion is also a notable departure from Berlin's essay of a year or two earlier,
'Political Ideas in the Twentieth Century' (Berlin 1950b), in which he had argued
that there was a fundamental difference between the outlook of the twentieth
century and that of the nineteenth.

the practice of attributing blame to past thinkers, or seeing the ideological tree fully grown in the philosophical acorn,[1] Berlin was at pains to draw links between the ideas of the past that he discussed, and the political assumptions and ideological movements of the present. He linked the rationalism and humanitarianism of the Enlightenment, as well as the Utilitarianism of the more radical *philosophes* and of Bentham, to the later liberalism of Mill, Morley, Wilson, the architects of the League of Nations and the UN, and to liberal opponents of Communism. Berlin identified with this tradition; yet he was also critical of many of the *philosophes'* assumptions, and especially those of the physiocrats and early Utilitarians. And if he traced the influence of the Enlightenment to liberalism, he also saw it feeding into one of liberalism's most treacherous ideological rivals: Communism. Thus what Berlin saw as the central ideological struggle of the times in which he was writing, that between Communism and liberal democracy, was a conflict not so much between the Enlightenment and its critics, as between different dimensions and implications within, and successors to, the Enlightenment.

Berlin expressed a similar ambivalence towards Rousseau's place in the history of ideas, the value of his thought, and his legacy. Rousseau is here identified both as an adherent, and as a passionate critic, of the Enlightenment. He is portrayed as the intellectual progenitor both of radical individualism and of authoritarianism, of nationalism, with all the good and evil that it entailed, and of all movements of 'resistance to foreign and domestic oppression', with their noble ideals and often destructive means. Rousseau broke with the materialism and scientism of the radical Enlightenment, but not with its rationalism, or its conviction that liberty could be reconciled with order; he thus both went too far, and not far enough, in his intellectual revolt.

Berlin saw the influence of Hegel at work all along the political spectrum, affecting Fascists, Communists, imperialists (all of whom Berlin strongly opposed), as well as liberal republicans and constitutional monarchists. He claimed that social scientists (of many of whom, as his letters of the period show, he had a low opinion),[2] as well as 'planners and technocrats', of whom he was

---

[1] 2.

[2] e.g. Berlin to Lady [Shirley] Anglesey, 9 May 1949.

much afraid,[1] and 'New Dealers', whom he admired and sympath-
ised with, and with many of whom he was on the warmest personal
terms, had all had their outlooks shaped by Saint-Simon. The
opponents of these groups – reactionary irrationalists, and existentialists and other intellectual exponents of 'anti-intellectualism' –
were the (sometimes unwitting) epigoni of Maistre and Fichte,
respectively. For Berlin, to paraphrase Faulkner, past ideas were
not dead; they weren't even past.

## III

Political commitment was a source of tension and unease for Berlin
(and one which he explored in his works on Russian intellectuals
of the nineteenth century).[2] Berlin was at once engaged and
disengaged, politically committed and politically cautious. He was
a lifelong and passionate anti-Communist, and an intellectual guru
to the anti-Communist left; yet he was wary of becoming a
propagandist or crusader.[3] He intensely admired political courage,
and liked and respected political activists; but his temperament and
outlook were too moderate, tentative and ironical for him to be
capable of activism himself. Berlin's work was decisively influenced
by the moral conflicts and quandaries inherent in politics; yet he
usually shrank from making direct pronouncements on current
events. He was a political theorist who rarely wrote directly about
political theory, and ignored many of its central, perennial topics –
the basis of political legitimacy, the demands of citizenship, the
nature and functioning of political institutions. Of the thinkers
discussed in PIRA, only two are generally recognised as major
political thinkers – Rousseau and Hegel. Moreover, Berlin's
interpretations of these decisive figures are among the weakest
parts of the book; and his account of Hegel focuses on his philosophy of history far more than his theory of the State. Finally,
Berlin sought to avoid political partisanship in his writings, offering

[1] Although he remained deeply wary of F. A. von Hayek's attacks on all forms
of State control as posts along the 'road to serfdom'.

[2] e.g. Berlin 1962a and 1972.

[3] See the insightful account by Ignatieff 1998, 199–200, 231, 237. This tension
between commitment and aloofness, enthusiasm and irony, is reflected in the
conflicting estimations that Berlin continues to inspire; see e.g. the differing
reactions to the first volume of Berlin's letters in Lee 2004 and Kirsch
2004.

sympathetic accounts of deeply anti-liberal thinkers, and pointing to the dark sides of the ideas of the founders of liberalism, despite his own firm commitment to liberal values.

Yet, for all this, Berlin's writings on the history of ideas – particularly those dating from the period surrounding and succeeding PIRA's composition – were inspired by moral convictions and political fears. He was often ambivalent, but he was not uncertain. His judgements were complex and qualified; but he was constantly judging, even as he sought to understand.

Central to these commitments and judgements was his distinctive vision of human liberty. Although PIRA is not explicitly focused on the idea of liberty, this idea is central to Berlin's account: for, as he first wrote here, and would repeat in 'Two Concepts', the central question of political philosophy was that of liberty and obedience: 'Why should any man obey any other man or body of men?'[1]

Berlin's anxieties regarding liberty were, unsurprisingly, influenced by the looming shadow of totalitarianism. Both the recently vanquished threat of Nazism, and the surviving spectre of Communism, were much on the minds of liberal intellectuals in 1951–2. They devoted their works to trying to explain the origins, appeal and evils of totalitarian ideologies and regimes, and to advancing a defence of what was best in the liberal tradition of political thought and practice.[2] This appalled response to totalitarianism, which took the form of a desire to understand as well as a determination to fight, led many intellectuals to look at their own societies with anxiety. An interest in the psychological roots of Nazi and Soviet rule gave rise to the fear that social life and individual character in the Western democracies were increasingly dominated by a toxic mixture of conformism, obedience, dependency, mediocrity and resentful aggression.[3] The study of politics in this period was also marked by the rise of positivism and behaviourism in the social sciences, and the more general quest for a 'value-neutral', fully scientific study of individuals and society – an intellectual trend that was accompanied, probably not accidentally, by a similar emphasis on neutrality and technocratic administration in political life.

[1] 17, 19; cf. FIB 1, L 168.
[2] See e.g. Arendt 1951, Aron 1957, Hayek 1944, Niebuhr 1945, Popper 1945, Talmon 1952.
[3] See e.g. Adorno et al. 1950, Fromm 1942, Hoffer 1951, Riesman et al. 1950.

There was, then, an increasing tendency towards consensus, social cohesion and a non-partisan, 'objective', managerial approach to social and political problems, which bred anxiety about conformity and coercion – whether the 'hard' coercion of totalitarianism, or the 'soft' coercion of propaganda and pacifying, integrating socialisation in Western society – and provoked an insistence on the value of liberty, personal experience and non-conformity.

One of Berlin's first mature statements of the meaning of liberty derived, like PIRA, from a lecture at an American women's college. This was 'Democracy, Communism and the Individual', a talk given at Mount Holyoke College in June 1949. Berlin claimed that the 'basic proposition' of Communism and other totalitarian ideologies was that, if one knows how human beings should live and society be ordered, 'one can, in the name of reason, impose [this knowledge] ruthlessly on others, since if they are rational they will agree freely; if they do not agree, they are not rational'. The totalitarian position asserted that 'there is only one healthy or efficient condition for the soul': harmony with the laws of historical necessity. Those who failed to adjust to necessity were 'not worth listening to, and indeed a nuisance [ ... ] to be swept away as an obstacle to progress'.[1]

The totalitarian proposition that the 'pronouncements of the individual soul are valuable only if that soul is in a position to discover the true path' utterly denied the liberal, democratic belief that all individuals are of equal worth, so that there is no élite with the right to 'guide and govern' everyone else; that 'individual experience' is more valuable than 'the impersonal needs of society'; that 'different ideals of life, not necessarily altogether reconcilable with each other, are equally valid and equally worthy'; and that the State should have 'as little power as possible' over the lives led by its citizens, who should be free to decide 'each [ ... ] in accordance with his own lights, what he should do, and how he should live', since 'the ultimate and only source of authority for the rightness or wrongness of legislation and wider social action is the moral sense of the individual'.[2] Liberal democrats were committed to 'a

[1] Berlin 1949b, 1, 5, 4.

[2] ibid., 4, 3, 5, 5, 1, 1, 4, 3. This account of Communism may have been inspired by Berlin's encounter with a woman during his visit to Moscow in 1945, who declared that 'if there is no room for free thinking in physics – a man who questions the laws of motion is obviously ignorant or mad – why should we,

necessarily precarious balance between incompatible ideals based on the recognition of the equal or nearly equal validity of human aspirations as such, none of which must be subordinated to any single uncriticisable single principle'.[1] Here we find the first stirring of what would solidify into Berlin's doctrine of pluralism – and the linkage of this pluralism to a liberal commitment to safeguarding an area of personal freedom, which would be central to the argument of 'Two Concepts of Liberty'.

In his article in the *Time and Tide* series 'Notes on the Way' (1949), and in 'Political Ideas in the Twentieth Century' (1950), Berlin warned of the rise of a belief that tormenting psychological and intellectual problems were a disease to be cured by 'so treating the patient that the problem no longer troubles him', that is, by removing the problem 'like an aching tooth': 'Instead of unravelling you cut. Instead of answering the question you remove it from the questioner's consciousness.'[2] The distinctive political movements of the twentieth century – Fascism, Communism and Nazism, but also managerialism, whether progressive or corporate – regarded independent thought with hostility as the source of 'too much disquiet', and the 'troublesome questions' that it might raise as 'a form of mental perturbation, noxious to the mental health of individuals and, when too widely discussed, to the health of societies'.[3] The trend of modern political thought was to 'reduce all issues to technical problems', attempting to produce social contentment by suppressing 'whatever in the individual might raise doubt or assert itself against the single all-embracing, all-clarifying, all-satisfying plan'.[4]

Berlin feared that 'free self-expression, the infinite variety of persons and of the relationships between them, and the right of free choice', which he identified with 'the area within which the

---

Marxists, who have discovered the laws of history and society, permit free thinking in the social sphere? Freedom to be wrong is not freedom [ . . . ] Truth liberates: we are freer than you in the West' (PI2 212). As Berlin remembered remarking at the time (provoking a response of stony silence), this statement came directly out of Comte; hence, in part, his linkage of Soviet Communism to nineteenth-century positivism. It also echoes Lenin's scriptural (for Soviet Communists) declaration that 'those who are really convinced that they have advanced science, would demand not freedom for the new views to continue side by side with the old, but the substitution of the old views by the new ones'. Lenin 1937, 14.

[1] Berlin 1949b, 3.        [2] Berlin 1949a, 1188.        [3] L 78, 61.        [4] L 81.

individual may commit blunders', were in danger of being sacrificed in the name of 'an efficiently working order, untroubled by agonising moral conflict'.[1] Against this, he emphasised the need for 'more room for the attainment of their personal ends by individuals and by minorities whose tastes and beliefs find (whether rightly or wrongly must not matter) little response among the majority [ ... ] a loose texture and toleration of a minimum of inefficiency' so as to allow for 'more spontaneous, individual variation', which will 'always be worth more than the neatest and most delicately fashioned imposed pattern'.[2] Berlin declared himself 'more concerned with making people free than making them happy', and preferred 'that they choose badly than not at all'.[3] He was most horrified by the spectacle of 'one set of persons who so tamper [with] and "get at" others that the others do their will without knowing what they are doing; and in this lose their status as free human beings, indeed as human beings at all'. What he found unbearable was

> the getting [of the victims] into one's power, the twisting them this way and that in accordance with one's whim, the destruction of their personality by creating unequal moral terms [ ... ] whereby the gaoler knows what he is doing, and why, and plays on the victim, i.e. treats him as a mere object rather than as a subject whose motives, views, intentions have any intrinsic weight whatever.[4]

Such passages express an overwhelming opposition to manipulation and degradation, founded on a moral vision of human beings as ends in themselves, whose dignity derives from their capacity to choose freely. At this point, Berlin had yet to distinguish between this positive view of human self-rule, influenced by Kant's moral philosophy, and the 'negative' political programme that it inspired. The realisation that the Kantian moral principle to which he was devoted had fed into the very political doctrines to which he was opposed, and the distinction that he would draw between the 'positive' dimension of this view of liberty and a more modest 'negative' one, had yet to emerge in Berlin's work. It was here that his study of the history of ideas was decisive; and PIRA represents this key moment in the development of his political thought.

The two central chapters of PIRA are explicitly focused on

---

[1] L 91–2.    [2] L 92–3.    [3] L 342.    [4] L 339–40.

freedom, and would form the basis for 'Two Concepts of Liberty'. In 'The Idea of Freedom', Berlin defines the desire for freedom as the desire not to be interfered with by others; freedom is primarily a negative concept. He distinguishes this from the idea of freedom as self-fulfilment, individual or collective, which (according to proponents of this conception) depends on an understanding of, and submission to, one's purpose as dictated by the rational pattern of the universe. To understand is to accept, and to accept is to rule out alternatives. Freedom, paradoxically, in this view involved the narrowing, rather than widening, of choice.[1]

A central figure in this account is Rousseau, who, Berlin claims, sought to reconcile a belief in the importance of individual freedom defined as self-mastery with the conviction that there is a correct way of ordering society, which justifies, and requires, obedience to authority. Rousseau's resolution of the conflict between freedom and authority rests on the idea of the 'real' will, according to which man has two natures, one higher, one lower; suppression of the lower liberates the higher.[2] Rousseau's insistence on the necessity of freedom to morality was taken up by Kant, who occupies a pivotal point in Berlin's account of the development of the idea of liberty, paradoxically standing as the progenitor both of modern liberal humanism and of its most formidable opponents. Kant stressed that individuals were ends in themselves, because they were the 'sole authors of moral values'; and, as the source and repository of all values, were 'the only absolutely good, absolutely valuable things in the world'. To deprive them of the ability to make decisions following the dictates of their own consciences, through deception or manipulation, was a negation of the essence of morality.[3] This view was at the ethical heart of nineteenth-century liberalism, with its protest against 'any form of despotism, however benevolent and rational [ . . . ] [as] intrinsically degrading, a falsification of what [ . . . ] relationships between equal and independent [ . . .] beings ought to be'.[4]

Here a complication in Berlin's account of the idea of liberty begins to emerge. The Kantian position, defining liberty as freedom *to* make decisions, *to* 'develop one's individual capacity', is what Berlin would later refer to as positive liberty. Berlin depicted this Kantian commitment to individual liberty as central

---

[1] 88–92, 94–5, 155–6.    [2] 112, 116–18, 121, 123–5, 134–6, 140–3.
[3] 151–3; FIB 58–9, 61–2.    [4] 153–4.

to later versions of liberalism (his own included), even though, elsewhere, he described the 'liberal' concept of liberty in the nineteenth century in 'negative' terms. For such liberals as Constant, Tocqueville and Mill, liberty was a 'fundamentally negative concept', consisting of the protection of individuals against encroachment. This view held that 'the individual has certain tastes [ . . . ] desires [ . . . ] inclinations, and wishes to lead his life in a certain fashion', and that therefore a certain 'vacuum' around the individual, within which he is allowed to fulfil 'reasonable wishes' – namely, those which don't conflict with the similar liberties of others – must be maintained.[1] Berlin thus suggests that the liberalism of the nineteenth and twentieth centuries had at its heart *both* positive *and* negative conceptions of liberty, deriving both from earlier Western liberalism and from German romanticism.

However, Berlin begins the third chapter of PIRA, significantly called 'Two Concepts of Freedom: Romantic and Liberal', by asserting that the 'nuclear, central, minimal meaning' of liberty is the absence of restraint or coercion on the part of other human beings. *Political* liberty is a negative concept, to be conceived of as a sphere within which individuals are not forbidden to do whatever they might wish. Freedom is freedom *against*; liberty *to* do something, 'upon analysis', means freedom *from* obstacles. For liberals subscribing to this view, liberty is a central, but instrumental, ideal, a means necessary to prevent positive goals from being frustrated, but not an end in itself.[2]

The liberal position set out here is essentially the view of liberty that Berlin would endorse in 'Two Concepts'. Yet in PIRA Berlin associates this position with an instrumentalist view of freedom as valuable only as a means to, or condition for, achieving other ends, while he ascribes to Rousseau and Kant the view that freedom is an intrinsic good, an end in itself. Although Berlin harshly criticised what in PIRA he calls the romantic conception of liberty (which he later identified with positive liberty),[3] he was sympathetic to Rousseau and Kant's contention that freedom was 'an absolute end [ . . . ] needing no justification in terms of any other purpose, and worth fighting for [ . . . ] for its own sake, independent of its

---

[1] FIB 50–2.    [2] 156, 160–1, 163, 165–6.
[3] PIRA thus clears up the misapprehension, voiced in some accounts of Berlin's thought, that associates positive liberty with the Enlightenment, and negative liberty with romanticism.

value in making people happy or wise or strong'.[1] Berlin, in seeking to combine a 'negative' conception of liberty with a non-instrumentalist understanding of liberty's value, placed himself between the liberal and romantic camps he portrayed as irreconcilably opposed.[2]

At the conclusion of his discussion of freedom in PIRA, Berlin makes another distinction between two opposed conceptions of liberty – in this case, 'humanistic and non-humanistic'. The former consists of the traditional liberal position, holding that freedom consists in the lack of, or protection against, interference from others, fortified with Kant's emphasis on the importance of choice to human moral dignity. It holds that individuals should be regarded as valuable as ends in themselves, since they are 'the source of all morality, the beings for whose sakes alone whatever is worth doing is worth doing', and therefore should not be sacrificed to larger principles.[3] The humanistic conception of liberty differs from the romantic, and is at one with the liberal, in resting on an empirical rather than a metaphysical conception of the individual, whose freedom consists in 'pursuing such ends as he pursues for whatever reasons', and therefore requires 'a certain area protected from invasion by others'. But while the humanist conception of liberty leads to liberal conclusions – the need for the protection of an area of non-interference within which individuals can act as they wish – it does so at least in part on the basis of a Kantian insistence that the importance of the freedom to make choices for oneself is in itself an essential element in a fully human life. In other words, it holds that freedom is good, not only as a means to the pursuit of the ends the individual chooses to pursue (whatever these may be), but also because it is simply and intrinsically good to be free.

The 'non-humanist' conception, on the other hand, defines

---

[1] SR 54.

[2] This was, at least, Berlin's view in the earlier 1950s; later, as pluralism became increasingly important to his work, and he became more and more fascinated with the anti-rationalist thinkers of the Counter-Enlightenment, the views of Kant that he expressed in his writings would become more critical. Yet a commitment to the Kantian principle of treating human beings as ends in themselves, as well as an emphasis on the importance of conceptual categories derived from Kant and later, neo-Kantian philosophers, continued to mark Berlin's work throughout his life. Towards Rousseau, he was considerably, and unjustly, far less generous.

[3] 206–7.

liberty as self-realisation through the union of the individual with some larger group or movement, or the dedication of the individual to some higher ideal. The 'humanistic' conception of liberty, with its particular, empiricist conception of the self, combining a commitment to negative liberty with a non-instrumental respect for freedom of choice and individual dignity, is recognisable as the basis for Berlin's position in 'Two Concepts'. Berlin's political thought would come to be associated with the conceptual distinction between negative and positive liberty, and has often been taken to advocate the former and attack the latter. In fact, as his writings of the early 1950s suggest and PIRA reveals, for Berlin the crucial moral or evaluative distinction was the related but distinct one between humanistic and non-humanistic conceptions of liberty; and his political thought was devoted to championing the former against the latter.

IV

Despite the political preoccupations which lay behind its composition, PIRA sets out to be a historical account, covering political thought during a particular period of intellectual history, focusing on the questions at issue between the exponents of the Enlightenment and its critics, the conflict between whom would continue to form the centre of Berlin's work on the history of ideas for the rest of his life. This account is interesting primarily for what it tells us about how Berlin saw the world, what it reveals of the concepts and categories that lay behind and structured his own thinking, and for the substantive philosophical issues it raises. These issues, the differing responses to them, and the impact that they have had on modern thought, experience and action, are real, even if Berlin's accounts of the Enlightenment and its critics, and of individual thinkers, are often at best flawed and over-simplified, at worst decidedly misleading. The reader searching for scrupulously and exactly accurate historical reconstruction should not consult Berlin. But then Berlin was not trained, and did not practise, as a professional historian; and his historical works, while deficient in some respects, have been, and remain, richly rewarding in others.

Berlin's historical work is marked by an ever-present tension between the goals of understanding the past in its own terms, and of drawing on the past to explain how the present came to be as it is, so as to gain perspective on the issues that are most important to us, now; between identifying what was unique about the past, and revealing what makes it still relevant; between the past as something intrinsically interesting in its own right, and as something interesting because of its relationship to the present. Related to this is the tension between Berlin's interest in the history of ideas and his interest in their content. Alan Ryan has put it well: Berlin was 'not interested in the quotidian history that lay behind the ideas by which he was fascinated. It was bold ideas and original, quirky, and imaginative thinkers that interested him', rather than the derivative or second-rate, however historically prominent or significant they may have been.[1] Berlin was too much the intellectual – that is, in his own definition, someone who was interested in ideas, and wanted ideas to be as interesting as possible[2] – to be a completely diligent and accurate intellectual historian. His knowledge should not be underestimated;[3] but it was not employed with rigorous discipline for the purpose of careful reconstruction. If it had been, Berlin's readings of history would be far less controversial, and far more reliable. But it is unlikely that they would have so powerfully expressed so important and original an intellectual agenda; or that they would still be read, as Berlin's works are, by scholars and general readers alike, decades after their composition and years after Berlin's death.

Berlin was, in short, not so much an intellectual historian, as an intellectual who was deeply knowledgeable about and engaged with history (intellectual and otherwise), and who drew on it in all of his work. At the same time, his contribution to the practice of intellectual history should not be forgotten or underestimated. Berlin wrote during a period when intellectual history was deeply out of fashion in Britain (even if it was flourishing in the USA). It

---

[1] Ryan 2004. This judgement, like all statements about Berlin, needs to be qualified. The focus of Berlin's work was certainly not on the quotidian history behind ideas. But while Berlin excelled at the depiction of ideas and personality, he saw these as arising from particular historical contexts, and all of his intellectual portraits are set against a sharply and surely sketched historical background. This is particularly true of *Karl Marx* (significantly subtitled *His Life and Environment*), with its vivid and extensive recounting of life among German university students and revolutionary exiles in Paris in the 1830s, and European socialist politics following 1848; but it is also a notable feature of his accounts of romanticism, which stress the social backgrounds and political concerns of the early German romantics.

[2] Jahanbegloo 1991, 183.            [3] As attested to by Wokler 2003, 20.

is perhaps difficult to remember how marginal, how foreign, Berlin's historical interests were in those distant days before John Pocock, Quentin Skinner, John Burrow and others won the history of ideas a central place within the British historical profession.

Berlin excelled, above all, at portraiture; this is why PIRA, the closest to a large-scale, panoramic landscape that he ever sketched, is one of his less satisfying historical works. He was at his best when his personal responsiveness and sensitivity were called into play. So powerful were these that he sometimes gave the impression – to himself as well as to others – that he knew the subjects of his writings at first hand.

Berlin's own intellectual personality was strong and distinctive and coloured all that he wrote. Whether or not Herder's doctrine of expressivism is true about human language and activity in general, as Berlin seemed to believe, it was certainly true of him. And yet this personality that was so singular was also elusive and protean. This was in part because one of his most marked traits was his ability to feel and think his way into other perspectives. This ability did not stem from a Keatsian 'negative capability';[1] it was a positive capability. Berlin's receptivity and empathy reflected no lack, no empty space waiting to be filled, but rather an excess, an overflowing of thought and feeling.

This quality of Berlin's, which made him such an attractive human being, was both a strength and a fault in a historian of ideas. It allowed him to enter into the outlooks of others; but it also meant that, whenever he sought to depict outlooks other than his own, something of himself coloured his account, and often distorted it. In some of his essays it seems as if Berlin begins to become those he writes about – Herder or Vico or Sorel or Herzen or Hess; but they, on the other hand, often seem to become Berlin.[2] In his writings on these figures Berlin was engaged in a

---

[1] John Keats, in a letter of 27 October 1818 to his brothers George and Thomas Keats, used this term to describe the gift that operates 'when a man is capable of being in uncertainties, mysteries, doubts, without any irritable reaching after fact and reason'. This is often glossed as a process of emptying out one's own personality and preconceptions, which is consistent with, but perhaps goes somewhat further than, Keats's words. Some have argued further that Keats's conception of negative capability included a capacity for empathy; but this is a step which Keats himself seems not to make in this passage.

[2] As Ernest Gellner has put it: 'Machiavelli, Vico, Herder, Tolstoy [ . . . ] come out looking suspiciously alike – Niccolo Berlini, Gianbattista Berlino, Johann

task that was as much artistic and political-philosophical as historical, or more so; in Borges's phrase, he created his precursors.[1] At his best, Berlin's own personality and intellectual concerns exist within his writing alongside those of his subject, producing a complex interaction between the two. The end result is often dazzling, and it is not a matter of mere projection of Berlin's assumptions and agenda; but it also isn't history as it is written or conceived by most historians.

Berlin's deeply 'personal' approach to the history of ideas made his work uniquely convincing and lively, but it did not always conduce to accurate analysis or reconstruction, and indeed sometimes impaired it. Berlin's very gifts, perhaps, sometimes led him to underestimate the sheer unknowability of past persons and their ideas, and the need to rely on exact factual detail, careful textual analysis and reconstruction of intellectual contexts where firsthand or 'internal' knowledge is insufficient, or impossible. Berlin had a tendency to form vivid personal impressions of the thinkers about whom he wrote, and subtle and plausible explanations of their thoughts, their behaviour, their responses to ideas and events, and then offer up the resulting portraits to his audience. Sometimes his imagination ran away with him. And sometimes his sense of knowing those about whom he wrote as human beings – of being able to hear them talk[2] – got in the way of his being able to perceive accurately what they had actually said – which was very often less incisive, penetrating, cogent or humane (in the case of Berlin's heroes), or less simplistic, monolithic and ill-conceived (in the case of butts of his criticism, such as Rousseau or Hegel), than what he presented. Berlin sought to serve both his own ideas and insights, and the history of ideas. These goals were not the same, and were often not compatible; and when they diverged, Berlin often got things at least partly wrong.

If the most marked and appealing feature of Berlin's historical

---

Gottfried Berliner, and Lev Nicolaievich Berlinov.' Gellner 1995, 56. This is perhaps more witty than accurate; Berlin's Machiavelli, Vico, Herder and Tolstoy are all certainly filtered through his own perceptions, but they do not, in fact, look very much alike – indeed, they are all (with the exception of Machiavelli) portrayed as vividly individual and lifelike human beings. Furthermore, while Berlin encounters each of these thinkers on his own terms, he also makes clear the ways in which their beliefs and temperaments differed sharply from his own.

[1] Borges 1962.

[2] See Cassidy 1991.

work as a whole is his portrayal of individuals, while his accounts of larger contexts and currents are often too brief and impressionistic not to be seriously oversimplified, and are therefore unsatisfying, PIRA displays inverse qualities, being faulty in its details, but powerful in its broad sweep. Berlin's depiction of individual thinkers may be contested.[1] But he also makes claims about the larger shape of intellectual history in the period he discusses, about the evolution of European thought in a period which he regarded, plausibly, as particularly momentous and turbulent. Here, too, his account may be faulted – and that he was aware of its shortcomings is reflected by the fact that, throughout his career, he modified his claims about the developments he traced, and never produced a final or comprehensive account of the subject. But then Berlin was always wary of final accounts, both because they can never capture the full complexity and open-endedness of reality, and because they put a stop to conversation – that is, to the project of learning about and making sense of the world. The historical account presented in PIRA should be taken as one among many possible ways of interpreting not only the phenomena it describes, but the nature, course and fate of modernity more generally (if one may use a portentous turn of phrase which Berlin himself would have neither deployed nor trusted). It is penetrating, but it is not complete. It should be taken as a provocation to further reflection, a spur to think about the influence of ideas and the larger implications of the course of history, to engage with the issues that Berlin identifies and states so forcefully and accessibly, rather than as a textbook, or an authoritative scholarly reconstruction, or a final synthesis. To fault Berlin for not writing, or PIRA for not being, such a careful or exact work of scholarship is perfectly fair and just; it is also, however, to miss the point.

As well as being contentious in many of its interpretations, PIRA represents an approach to the history of ideas, and makes

---

[1] It should be added that contestation and refutation are two different things. The accounts of Rousseau and Hegel contained in PIRA seem to this author to be incomplete and unjust, and inordinately influenced, like so much of Berlin's work in the history of ideas, by the ideological oppositions and assumptions of the period in which he wrote. Yet they are not implausible in every respect. While Berlin neglects many of those complex and ambiguous insights that make Rousseau and Hegel such fascinating subjects of study, he does identify genuinely important elements in the thought of each, which were recognised by, and deeply impressed, each thinker's contemporaries and successors.

assumptions about the period which it covers, which were either widely accepted or refreshingly unfamiliar in 1952, but are very much out of fashion today. Recent scholarship has tended to break the large movements which Berlin characterises so confidently and vividly into smaller, more concrete, more varied phenomena. Thus Berlin's depiction of the Enlightenment may seem too simplistic even to other scholars who accept the idea of a single and unified movement that goes by that name.[1] But the very idea of 'the' Enlightenment has, in recent years, come to be rejected by many historians in favour of a variety of 'Enlightenments', divided and differentiated from one another by national, cultural, religious and chronological borders.[2] An even more marked change has occurred in the historical profession as a whole, in the form of a move away from the sort of intellectual history Berlin practised in favour of social and cultural history – and this has been matched by an eclipse of the history of ideas in many English and American universities.[3]

However, Berlin cannot be easily grouped with the intellectual historians and historians of literature and philosophy from previous generations who wrote general accounts of the Enlightenment. His exposition is far less systematic and more selective; it is more concerned to convey a particular philosophical message – and at the same time, ultimately, less partisan in its treatment of the Enlightenment than the accounts offered by many historians.[4] In

[1] See, for instance, the robust objections to one of Berlin's later narratives of the Enlightenment and its critics in Gay 1999.

[2] See e.g. Porter and Teich 1981, Outram 1995, Pocock 1999a and 1999b, Porter 2000, Schmidt 2000 and Himmelfarb 2004. For recent defences of the idea of a single Enlightenment, see Israel 2001, Robertson 2003 and Robertson 2005.

[3] This shift has shaped recent scholarship on the Enlightenment as well as other historical subjects: see e.g. Darnton 1971a and 1971b, Jacob 1991, Goodman 1994, Roche 1998, Munck 2000. An excellent application of this approach to Berlin's favourite topic of the Counter-Enlightenment is McMahon 2001.

[4] The most obviously editorialising among the great histories of the Enlightenment are probably the short and elegant critique of Becker 1932 and the monumental, vigorous and sympathetic work of Gay 1966–9. More Olympian in tone are Cassirer 1932 and Hazard 1946. Berlin's forceful critique of the English translation of Cassirer's still standard work offers one of the most revealing statements of how to practise the history of ideas that he ever penned: see Berlin 1953c. A notable recent attempt to return to the sort of examination carried out by Cassirer, Gay and others – which, like them, presents a view of the Enlightenment decidedly different from Berlin's – is Dupré 2004. The most important works on romanticism to follow in Berlin's footsteps – though they

this respect the interpretation contained in PIRA is also difficult to assimilate entirely, for all the resemblance between them, to the more partisan and teleological narratives of Horkheimer and Adorno or Talmon.[1] Berlin's work, once again, proves difficult to categorise. This is in part because the intellectual concerns behind his historical enquiries, as well as the personality that shaped and coloured them, were very different from those of most of his predecessors, successors or even peers.

v

As a historian of ideas and political theorist Berlin was concerned with two types of political ideas: normative political concepts, such as liberty or equality, and the ideas about morality and human nature on which they were founded; and theories about how politics should be understood or studied, and the metaphysical and epistemological assumptions on which they were built. He was interested in the way that politics were understood both in the past and in the present, and in the relationship of this understanding to action – that is, how the study of politics affected practice, and how the practice of politics was understood, or misunderstood, by students of politics.[2] Berlin reacted against the vision of a fully scientific, value-neutral study of political behaviour, which was in the ascendancy in the 1950s, and which he traced back to the Enlightenment. He sought to bring to light the misunderstandings of politics that bedevilled his contemporaries, and to offer an alternative conception of political understanding, by returning to the roots of modern social science, just as he sought to combat anti-liberal ideologies and defend liberalism by returning to the ideological conflicts and political aspirations of the period surrounding the French Revolution.

cover the ground far more carefully – are those of Frederick Beiser; see e.g. Beiser 1987, 1992, 2003. Other important recent studies to take a broad look at romanticism as a philosophically and politically important intellectual movement are Riasanovsky 1992 (which is dedicated to Berlin) and the concise Larmore 1996.

[1] Horkheimer and Adorno 1944; Talmon 1952. For Berlin on Talmon, see Berlin 1980.

[2] For a fuller discussion of this facet of Berlin's thought, see Hanley 2004. Berlin addressed these themes most directly in Berlin 1954b, 1957, the opening section of 1958, and 1961.

PIRA's intellectual architecture is constructed on a set of overlapping, but distinct, dichotomies between opposing intellectual positions, which are set out in a letter to the President of Bryn Mawr quoted in Henry Hardy's preface,[1] as well as in Berlin's Prologue. The first of these positions is that of the 'lucid and passionate' rationalists of the Enlightenment, with their faith that scientific method could solve all questions of both ends and means, and discover a harmonious scheme of social organisation that would for ever end injustice, misery and conflict, and their belief that human beings were 'infinitely malleable', and may have their emotions 'canalised' by enlightened experts so as to promote happiness, security and efficiency. To this he opposes the 'liberal Kantian protest' against treating people as children, with its insistence on the sacredness of the act of individual choice, its commitment to liberty as an end in itself, and its fear of any form of social control, however wise and beneficent it may be. Related to this dichotomy, but not quite identical, was that between the optimistic Utilitarianism of Helvétius and Bentham, seeing the rational pursuit of happiness as the best form of life, and Rousseau's rebellious vision of 'socially and emotionally emancipated beings', uncorrupted by self-interest and sophistication, simple, spontaneous and governed only by conscience.

Another conflict concerned the proper way to understand human nature and society. One side of this debate was dominated by those rationalists who sought to apply Cartesian logic, or the inductive methods of the natural sciences, to human affairs. They were opposed by conservative and Christian critics who embraced a historicist and organicist view of society, emphasising the uniqueness of human life, its dynamic change over time, the importance of tradition and emotional bonds, and the need to understand human institutions from the inside.

Finally, Berlin intended to discuss the clash between the faith in the benevolence or malleability of human nature on the part of liberals and rationalists who cherished visions of perfection and liberation, and a dark reactionary pessimism that regarded men as neither good nor malleable, but as inherently and irredeemably weak, vain and vicious, and held that they must be governed by fear of authority and blind faith.

Berlin would later attribute romanticism's historical significance

---

[1] See pp. x–xi above.

to its profoundly radical break with the monistic assumptions that had dominated earlier Western thought. In PIRA he identifies a different but related doctrine as romanticism's central contribution. This held that values were not, as previously believed, 'ingredients of the universe' to be discovered, but human creations. This view, and the new scale of values and set of ideals it generated, was for Berlin 'the largest step in the moral consciousness of mankind since the Middle Ages, perhaps since the rise of Christianity'.[1]

Berlin takes up this theme in his note on 'Subjective versus Objective Ethics' (SVOE). Here, as in his later work advocating pluralism, Berlin identifies as the source of intellectual error the desire for certainty and security, and tries to overcome this delusive aspiration by identifying and correcting the confusions underlying it – without falling into the opposite extreme of cynicism and exaggerated scepticism about morality. In this case, Berlin insists that the urge to found ethics on a firm 'objective basis', and the fear that, if this is not done, a slide into subjectivism is inevitable, stems from a basic misunderstanding of the nature of statements about value. Normative statements are 'in principle different in the way they are used from logical or descriptive statements'. This being the case, the objective/subjective opposition, which applies to logical or descriptive statements, simply doesn't apply to normative statements. Berlin hopes, by this method of argument – which he presents as an explanation of Hume's ethical theory – to save ethics from the dead-end debate over subjectivism, from the futile quest for objectivity on the one hand and from cynicism and dismissal on the other.

Berlin's interpretation of Hume was influenced both by German neo-Kantianism and by the concerns and style of Oxford analytical philosophy.[2] In particular, it probably reflects a response to logical positivism, which asserted that all meaningful statements are empirically verifiable. Those statements that are not empirically

---

[1] 11; cf. Berlin 1960b, 1975; RR 119–46.

[2] The claim that the objective/subjective opposition simply didn't apply to ethics was asserted from a Kantian perspective by Heinrich Rickert, whom Berlin praised both early and late in his life (Berlin 1932; Hausheer 2003, 49 note 8); see e.g. Rickert 1902. The nature of moral values and statements, and their relations to facts and factual statements, was a major theme in twentieth-century British philosophy; see e.g. Moore 1903, Ayer 1936, Hare 1952, Weldon 1953, Warnock 1960, Foot 1978, MacIntyre 1967, 1981. Berlin's reading of Hume, and its intellectual context, are examined in Wokler forthcoming.

verifiable – including normative statements – are strictly meaning-less, and should be viewed only as statements of subjective preference or taste confusedly expressed. Thus, the statement 'Cruelty is evil' and the statement 'I like my coffee black' are of the same, subjective sort, as opposed to verifiable statements such as 'The cat is on the mat' or '$E = mc^2$.' Berlin argued against this that normative statements, while not verifiable statements of objective fact, are also not merely statements of subjective preference, but *sui generis*. The impact of Oxford philosophy is further evidenced by his emphasis on the way that different sorts of terms are used (in this case, the way that ethical terms and factual terms do essentially different work) and his attempt to overcome time-worn problems by dismissing them as category-errors.

Such an approach is markedly different from that exemplified by most of Berlin's writings. This is fortunate; for SVOE is not, ultimately, successful. Berlin asserts that statements about value are neither subjective nor objective, but he doesn't explain just what normative statements are, or why the objective/subjective distinc-tion, which applies to two other, quite distinct, sorts of statement (about empirical fact, and logical rules) doesn't apply in the normative realm. Berlin's account is therefore frustratingly incom-plete, even if the basic intuition to which he appeals is plausible. The piece does however shed light on Berlin's thinking about ethics at the time, as well as on the connections between his writings on the ethical revolution of romanticism, and his early immersion in Oxford philosophy.

Berlin's insistence on the *sui generis* nature of normative statements and concepts manifests his lifelong conviction that different methods and standards are appropriate to different fields of human experience and thought, and that one of the most common and dangerous of intellectual errors is the inappropriate application of a single model to all facets of life. Berlin first articulated this view – which Jonathan Allen has termed 'anti-Procrusteanism' – in his early essay 'Some Procrustations', and would continue to emphasise it in his later writings on the distinction between the sciences and the humanities.[1]

PIRA also suggests that for Berlin the idea that values are facts was connected to the belief that goals aren't freely chosen, but given, that there are truths about human nature to be discovered,

---

[1] Allen 1998, Berlin 1930, 1953b, 1960a, 1961, 1974; see also L 167.

which, once discovered, should govern our thought and behaviour. Berlin was particularly averse to the idea of a 'true self', the nature of which dictates the choices that should be made and the ends pursued by the individual; this notion first assumes prominence in PIRA, and would be the centrepiece of 'Two Concepts of Liberty'. But he sometimes seems to go beyond this attack on the 'metaphysical' idea of the self, suggesting that any form of essentialism regarding human nature – the view that human nature (whether individual or collective) is something natural and unalterable, and that values are not human creations, but rather follow from the necessities of, and can be discovered through knowledge of, human nature – poses a threat to human liberty.

Although SVOE reflects some continuities in Berlin's thought, it also reveals at least one significant change. Here, and in the main text of PIRA, Berlin emphasises claims about the origin of human values: the crucial point is the contention that values are created by human beings, rather than discovered – that they are not facts, but something quite different. While Berlin would continue to identify this in his later writings as one of the most original, significant and indeed revolutionary philosophical contributions of romanticism,[1] his account of romanticism's significance, and his writing about the nature of values, shifted their focus to pluralism. Berlin came to stress, not the origins of values, but the way that values appear to us – that is, he moved from noumenal claims about where values come from or reside, to phenomenal claims about our experience of values.

While Berlin's conception of the nature of values as expressed in SVOE and PIRA was central to his work, it also points to a major tension in his thought. Berlin disputed the view that ends are given rather than chosen, that there is both a general human and an individual, personal nature which dictates the ends that individuals choose and pursue. But he also often seems to appeal to the idea that there are indeed inherent and unalterable truths about human nature as well as individual selves, complex and protean as they are, which should not be forced to conform to standards and demands that are unnatural to them.[2] Berlin's concern about the deformation

---

[1] See for instance RR 118–20; CTH 28–30, 32, 40–43, 181–4, 199; these instances come from pieces published or delivered as lectures in 1959, 1965 and 1978.

[2] I am indebted to Jonathan Allen for the characterisation of Berlin's view of the self as 'protean' (in an unpublished paper on Berlin).

of human personality by attempts to 'mould' it to conform to ideological blueprints suggests that there is something there that won't fit, or will be violated by, the mould. 'Procrusteanism', after all, derives its horror from the fact that it involves the cramping or vivisection of something that is there; Proteus, the shape-shifter, would presumably be in no danger from Procrustes, since he would be able to conform to whatever shape Procrustes might demand of him. If human beings are characterised only or primarily by their capacity for change, their malleability, what is wrong with moulding them to have more harmonious values and lives?[1] Berlin's pluralism suggests that the reality of complexity is itself a 'brute fact' about human character which should be recognised and respected, and which is ignored at moral and intellectual cost. There are limits to the extent to which human beings can transform themselves, at least if they are to remain human – which, Berlin implies, they should.[2] Berlin's apparent acceptance of the distinction between facts and values needs to be qualified. The values that people pursue are facts about them, and the facts of human character – both of individual character and those of groups and humanity as a whole – while flexible, have normative implications.

SVOE may also be seen as a response to the instrumentalist view of human beings that Berlin attacked in his earlier writings, and in this way related to the critique of historical determinism that figured prominently in his work throughout the 1950s.[3] Berlin saw the doctrine of determinism as an assault on the human capacity for moral judgement, and on the faculty of self-determining choice that confers moral dignity on individuals. He charged both historical determinism and the modern vision of human beings

---

[1] One possible response to this is that there is a difference between being forcibly moulded by others and freely moulding oneself, and that it is the former that is objectionable. This is part of what Berlin maintained (it is also an example of the way in which Berlin's thought includes an element of positive liberty, since the point at issue in such a claim is a question not merely of interference or non-interference, but also of who exercises control over me, and one of the principal values to which the claim appeals is that of self-mastery). But he also seems, at least sometimes, to go beyond it, and to claim that all forcing of human aspirations and perceptions into straitjackets dictated by dogmatic and simplistic beliefs about what human beings 'should' be like is objectionable, even if self-imposed.

[2] For Berlin's assertion of this, see e.g. CTH 203–4.

[3] The classic statement is Berlin 1954a; this theme also features in 1953a, 1953b and 1960a.

that he diagnosed in 'Democracy, Communism and the Individual' and 'Political Ideas in the Twentieth Century' with a denial of the worth of individuals' self-perceptions, moral judgements and actions by viewing them as 'subjective', and therefore without validity or value.[1] Berlin was as concerned to defend values against being dismissed as subjective, and therefore unimportant, as he was to reject the belief that values could be derived from, or known with the same certainty as, facts, a belief which led to the condemnation of disagreement and variety, and to faith in the rule of moral experts. SVOE, for all its failings, brings into focus this delicate two-sided intellectual effort, which was central to all of Berlin's work – his critique of determinism, his advocacy of pluralism, his excavation of romanticism and his condemnation of authoritarianism, conformity and 'Procrusteanism'.

VI

It was largely his association of the Enlightenment (with whose political and moral commitments he felt considerable sympathy)[2] with a 'Procrustean' attempt to understand all human experience systematically, from a single perspective (generally, that of empirical natural science), that led to Berlin's fascination with its critics.[3] His conviction that Hume and the romantics had expressed important insights about the nature of human values as things that are created rather than discovered, and which derive their importance from their role in individual human lives rather than their existence as ingredients in an objective order, also fostered this involvement with romanticism. So did his historical approach to ideas and human experience in general: Berlin tended to associate the Enlightenment with the hostility to history of both scientism and the analytic philosophy in which he had earlier engaged, but from the aridity of which he eventually drifted away.[4]

[1] e.g. 'praise and blame are subjective attitudes put to flight by the advance of knowledge', L 154; cf. L 138. For an excellent discussion of this topic, see Hanley 2004, especially 329.

[2] See Berlin 1956; Jahanbegloo 1991, 68–76; Berlin 1992.

[3] In this respect his position was similar to that of Horkheimer and Adorno; see e.g. Horkheimer and Adorno 1944, 7–8. For a typical expression of this view of the Enlightenment following the composition of PIRA, see e.g. AC 148.

[4] On this point, see Bernard Williams, Introduction to CC, and Roger Hausheer, Introduction to AC; for Berlin's association of logical positivism with the Enlightenment, see Berlin 1937b.

A final reason for Berlin's sympathy towards romanticism was its emphasis (often, he acknowledged, terribly exaggerated in the forms it took) on the force of human emotions and personality, and the significance of individual character and actions. Berlin's writings in the years preceding and succeeding the composition of PIRA make it clear that he saw 'romantic humanism' – with its sympathy for dissenters, minorities and the 'irregulars of civilisation', its emphasis on quality of personality rather than worldly success, the premium it placed on dignity and choice as against efficiency, order and correctness – as closely connected with the revolutionary reconceptualisation of the nature of values as human creations, the worth of which derived from the worth of the human beings to whom they were important, and of whose lives they were essential ingredients.[1] These 'romantic humanist' values, and the view of the nature and importance of human personality to which they were connected, were close to Berlin's heart, and shaped both his conception of history and his historical practice.[2]

This raises the question of Berlin's attitude to the historical movements and ideas he discusses in PIRA and elsewhere. A debate has been going on for some years about where Berlin stood in relation to the Enlightenment and its critics – whether he is best regarded as a latter-day *philosophe*, or as a profound and committed, though not unsympathetic, critic and even opponent of the Enlightenment.[3]

Here, too, PIRA sheds considerable light, representing Berlin's first extended and recorded attempt to come to grips with the Enlightenment and its critics. The work lends credence to the picture of Berlin as critical of the Enlightenment, which he here associates with a belief in the indivisibility of reason, fostering an either/or mentality.[4] Its representatives regarded all true knowledge as factual, failed to emancipate themselves from the teleological assumptions of earlier ages, and built their theories on a false belief in the natural harmony of human life.[5] PIRA makes clear that Berlin traced back to the Enlightenment the belief in the

[1] See e.g. L 337–43; Berlin 1959.

[2] See 10–11, as well as Jahanbegloo 1991, 201, and the essays collected in PI, particularly those on Churchill, Roosevelt and Weizmann.

[3] For contributions to this debate, see Arieli 1990, Galipeau 1994, Lilla 1994, Lukes 1994, Siedentop 1994, Gray 1995, Margalit 1995, Steinberg 1996, Garrard 1997, and the essays collected in Mali and Wokler 2003.

[4] 33–4, 40–2, 48–50, 113.          [5] 38–9, 57–8, 61–5, 73–82.

permissibility and even desirability of rational planning by experts, about which he was particularly worried.[1] But it also reveals that Berlin associated the perversion of the concept of liberty with romanticism, and saw the Enlightenment as the origin of the liberal tradition to which he was committed, as well as of the technocratic vision he deplored.

As a pluralist, Berlin realised that in the conflicts within the Enlightenment, and between the Enlightenment and its critics, each side represented genuine values – and each side was also misguided in failing to recognise this fact. Berlin's pluralism led him to see the strengths and failings of duelling monisms.[2] Thus, he begins his account of political ideas in the romantic age by enumerating dichotomies, not to construct a simple tale of heroes and villains, but to highlight the ways in which different facets of the Enlightenment and the reactions against it embodied genuine values – and, in some cases, how the pursuit of these values embraced errors and produced evils. In this account, modern liberalism and its most dangerous opponents were alike heirs to a complex, divided inheritance in which Enlightenment and Counter-Enlightenment currents combined with and opposed one another. Berlin wrote the history of ideas with a moral purpose in mind; but his account is no simplistic morality play.

This pluralist perspective prevented Berlin from being partisan, but it did not make him neutral. Alongside the pluralism that allowed him to see that not all values are compatible, so that contending ideologies and *Weltanschauungen* may divide and share truth and merit among them, was a liberal humanism which enabled him to discriminate between value-systems.[3] These were further joined to a deep-seated, if refined, empiricism, which led

---

[1] 68–71, 78–80, 122, 126–7, 130.

[2] Elsewhere, reviewing the battles between clashing monisms that made up much of the history of philosophy, Berlin likened proponents of each position to the man who offers cogent demonstrations of the lunacy of another who claims to be Napoleon, only to add as a clinching argument that he is himself Napoleon. CC 69. Cf. Berlin's remarks on Rousseau below, 47.

[3] By 'liberal humanism' I mean an ethical outlook that assigns moral priority to the dignity and well-being of individual human beings, which associates human dignity with the capacity for choice and self-development, and defines well-being, at its most basic, in terms of freedom of thought and behaviour (at least in so far as the behaviour in question does not harm others), physical safety, and protection against pain, fear and humiliation.

Berlin to trust the particularity of human experience. Those elements within each world-view that recognised the complexity, irreducibility and open-endedness of reality, respected liberty and dignity and allowed for variety and happiness, he embraced; those which excused or encouraged cruelty, dogmatism, coercion, simplification, intolerance, smug paternalism, brutal cynicism, small-mindedness and moral and emotional meanness, he opposed.

PIRA reflects an important stage in the development of Berlin's thinking about pluralism. The early roots of the idea are visible in Berlin's writings as far back as the 1930s, but his criticisms of monism become explicit only in the notes for 'Democracy, Communism and the Individual'.[1] PIRA expands this account, without yet explicitly expounding value-pluralism. Berlin here identifies the monistic assumption that all genuine questions are in principle answerable, and that there is one true solution, which is factual. The 'rich variety' of answers to all genuine and significant problems itself suggested to Berlin that this belief was problematic. Even more problematic were the consequences to which this belief had led: the search for the sage or expert who could discover the truth and realise it, and the belief that, if there was one correct way to live or believe, all other ways were wrong – at best to be tolerated as deplorable but ineradicable error, at worst to be extirpated.

Berlin's pluralism was shaped both by his moral beliefs and by the sharp awareness of disagreement and variety that his historical perspective on ideas, and his experience as a Russian Jew living and flourishing in England, allowed. But these were not the only influences that led Berlin to pluralism. Philosophical convictions also came into play. Berlin's 'anti-Procrusteanism' made him wary of all claims to comprehensiveness or universal validity on the part of any theory; such a belief, he thought, was not compatible with a genuine and scrupulous empiricism, which would do justice to the uniqueness of every facet of reality. Berlin was suspicious of the 'Ionian fallacy', the belief in the unity of all the sciences, and thus the intelligibility of all experience in terms of, and the deducibility of all knowledge from, 'one single integrating law or principle'. It was the challenge that it posed to this belief – as well as his own proclivity towards taking a historical approach – that attracted Berlin to the founders of historicism.

[1] Although some of the main claims of Berlin's critique of monism are advanced in Berlin 1937a.

Berlin had been aware of historicism from early on, thanks to the lectures of R. G. Collingwood (who introduced him to Vico by way of Croce), and the more informal, eccentric and inspiring tutelage of the Russian Menshevik émigré Solomon Rachmilevich, who may have introduced the young Berlin to neo-Kantian ideas about the differences between the sciences and the humanities.[1] His attention seems to have been truly riveted to this topic, however, by his study of Marx: following Plekhanov, Berlin would see Hegel's historicist challenge to earlier naturalist theories of society as decisive for Marx's development and significance. Although Vico and Herder were given brief cameos in Berlin's early writings, it was only in PIRA that they emerged as protagonists. At the same time, Hegel retained a significance in PIRA that he would lose in Berlin's later work; or at least he would cease to figure as prominently by name. In fact, Berlin's opposition to what he took to be Hegel's philosophy remained decisive throughout his intellectual career. Berlin objected to what he saw as the teleological and theodic dimensions of the Hegelian system, which, he charged, justified whatever came to pass as being rational and necessary. Hegel, in Berlin's mind, was on the side of the victors and dismissed the victims; his thought provided a justification for bullying and a glorification of strength. Hegel's brand of historicism seemed to Berlin to share one of the greatest deficiencies of Enlightenment progressivism: an exultant faith in the march of progress which ignored its costs, and a denial of the reality of suffering and loss which encouraged its callous infliction.[2]

---

[1] For Rachmilevich (to whose memory this volume is fittingly dedicated), see Ignatieff 1998, 42–4, 80–1.

[2] This perception was clearly influenced by later Communist theoreticians, leaders and activists, with their praise of progress and consigning of opponents to the 'dustbin of history'. This is not surprising, given the tremendous impact that Berlin's personal encounters with Russian Communism had made on him, and the fact that he had come to the study of the Enlightenment and Hegelianism through his early work on Marx. He thus tended to think of these earlier thinkers in light of later ones – ironically, his critique of teleological thinking itself involved a form of teleological thinking. Also decisive for Berlin's perception of Hegel, and of the history of ideas and those thinkers who formed it more generally, was the influence of nineteenth-century Russian thought; and as he himself acknowledged, and indeed stressed, the ideas of Western thinkers tended to be exaggerated and simplified in the hands or minds of their ardent Russian disciples and antagonists. Berlin's Hegel (for all its resemblance to Popper's, by which Berlin was surely influenced) is the Hegel of Belinsky, Bakunin and Herzen rather than the historical Hegel.

Hegelianism also fell into the error of confusing statements about fact with statements about value: just as earlier thinkers had mistakenly located the source of value in nature, the historicists located it in the forward movement of history. Hence Berlin's preference for Vico and Herder, who were both more marginal figures themselves, and in Berlin's eyes more sympathetic to minorities and eccentrics.[1]

The historical account offered in PIRA thus reflects the philosophical preoccupations and moral convictions that motivated Berlin's work at the time, and which would give rise to his later work on both political theory and the history of ideas. PIRA represents the point at which the major strands of Berlin's thought came together; out of the confluence of these historical, philosophical, moral and political concerns would grow the ideas and works which made Berlin's reputation and dominated his intellectual career.

VII

The preceding discussion has sought to situate PIRA within the development of Berlin's thought, and in so doing explain its interest to students of Berlin's work. However, even when this is understood, a more fundamental question remains: Why is this intellectual development, and the thought it yielded, worth studying?

The first part of this question can, for the purpose of this essay, be disposed of summarily. If we wish to learn from Berlin, we should try to get his ideas right, to understand what he actually said and thought. If we are to do this, and not misunderstand Berlin and miss the point of his work, we must understand where his ideas came from, how they developed, what his work was meant to accomplish, and why he was so anxious that it should be accomplished. The purpose of studying a thinker of the past should be, at least in part, to learn something new, to expand our own mental horizons, by coming into contact with a mind other than

---

[1] See e.g. L 113 (and elsewhere in Berlin 1954a), 340–3; Berlin 1950a, 1962b; CTH 179–80; TCE 350. On Berlin's anti-Hegelianism, see Chamberlain 2004, 282–3.

our own, and coming to understand that mind. It is this widening of intellectual horizons that makes the history of ideas one of the most challenging, and potentially enriching, of intellectual pursuits.

But why is Berlin in particular worth studying? The interest of Berlin's intellectual career is, in the first place, historical. Berlin was a representative and influential member of a significant generation of intellectuals, who lived through, and sought to respond to, a momentous epoch in political and intellectual history. He was deeply impressed by the events, and acutely sensitive to the currents, of his time. He was also utterly *sui generis*, moving sure-footedly through disparate mental worlds and uniting them in a unique personal synthesis. Berlin uncovered forgotten and unfamiliar heritages and communicated them to a wide audience; drawing on these resources, he enriched and revitalised the important but strained tradition of Western liberalism. In the process, he made important contributions to the intellectual life of his times, which also offer lessons for our own.

Berlin's contribution to liberalism was at once one of restoration and innovation. He returned to the ideas of earlier liberals, such as Constant, Tocqueville and Mill, and supplemented the resources of liberal theory with the insights of sympathetic non-liberal thinkers such as Herzen, and even the lessons of anti-liberal thinkers such as Hamann, Maistre and Sorel. But Berlin also brought something that was wholly his own and of his own time to liberalism. This consisted in part of his value pluralism, in part of the scepticism and anti-Utopianism that pervaded his work, in part of his epistemological anti-Procrusteanism, and in part of something more personal than theoretical: his interest in human personality, his recognition of variety as an intrinsic good and complexity as at once an inescapable burden and a source of dignity. In this he went beyond earlier liberal thinkers; and his liberalism, with its opposition to myths of progress and perfection, its awareness of the limitations and tragedy that haunt human life, and its combination of a commitment to individual liberty with appreciation of deep diversity and the difficulties it engenders, remains a compelling vision for today's world.

Berlin's work also remains relevant to students of politics. Berlin is instructive as a theorist and practitioner of the human sciences, warning against the limitations of scientific paradigms and the neglect of the particular and irreducible in human experience, and

setting a contrasting example with the imaginative scope, psychological insight and emotional zest of his own work. He reminds us
of the importance of avoiding inhumanity in thought as well as in
practice, of restoring the uniquely human to the study of the
human sciences, of placing individual well-being at the centre of
our ethical considerations and of putting the person back into
political studies and political theory.[1]

Berlin was hardly alone in attacking scientism, totalitarianism or
ideological dogma. Yet his liberal, pluralist, anti-Procrustean
humanism remains distinctive in the way that it embodies the
virtues it extols, and puts into practice the lessons it urges. Berlin
summarised the thrust of his work as a whole as distrust of all
claims to the possession of incorrigible knowledge about human
behaviour.[2] He advocated an intellectual ethic and a moral
sensibility based on humility, scepticism and sympathy. His was a
forceful and passionate, but non-ideological, non-reductionist and
non-simplistic critique of ideology, reductionism and simplicity, a
complex defence of complexity, best represented by his own
description of human nature:

> Man is incapable of self-completion, and therefore never wholly
> predictable; fallible, a complex combination of opposites, some
> reconcilable, others incapable of being resolved or harmonised; unable
> to cease from his search for truth, happiness, novelty, freedom, but
> with no guarantee [ . . . ] of being able to attain them; a free, imperfect
> being capable of determining his own destiny in circumstances
> favourable to the development of his reason and his gifts.[3]

Berlin warned against the pitfalls of thought in order to vindicate
thought. He cautioned against the characteristic errors of intellectuals, but was not himself an anti-intellectual (as his hostile reaction
to what he regarded as Rousseau's anti-intellectualism in PIRA
attests). He argued that reason's limitations should be recognised;
but so should its virtues, and its importance, indeed necessity, to
human life. Our attempts to make sense of the world will always be
imperfect and incomplete; and we should acknowledge this. But we

---

[1] For an expansion on this, see Hanley 2004 and Cherniss 2002. For a similar
contribution to the study of history, see Berlin 1960a and Cracraft 2002.
[2] RT viii.          [3] L 250.

must still continue striving to understand. 'We cannot speak without incurring some risk [...] the only way of being absolutely safe is to say absolutely nothing.'[1] We must be aware of these risks, and exercise caution; but we should not let this caution become stifling. 'Men cannot live without seeking to describe and explain the universe to themselves [...] The goal of philosophy is always the same, to assist men to understand themselves and thus operate in the open, and not wildly, in the dark.'[2] Even as, with his work on PIRA, he became a historian of ideas, Berlin remained a philosopher in that he continued to strive towards this goal; even as he criticised the Enlightenment, he continued to work on behalf of light, and against darkness.

## ACKNOWLEDGEMENTS

I am grateful to Ryan Hanley, Steven B. Smith, José Harris, Luca Cuneo, Chris Brooke, John Burrow and Arthur M. Schlesinger, Jr., conversations with whom have contributed to my thinking about Berlin and his work; to Michael Hughes and James Chappel for providing me with information culled from their scrupulous and energetic work on Berlin's papers; to Jonathan Allen and Ryan Hanley for sharing their work on Berlin, from which I've learned much, with me; to Cary and Deborah Cherniss and Bradley and Marcia Marcus for their stylistic suggestions and encouragement; to Chiansan Ma for a fruitful remark about Borges; to Cary Cherniss, Alan Ryan, and especially Ryan Hanley, for reading various drafts of this piece, and offering helpful comments; to Robert Wokler, for sharing his own work on PIRA with me and reading and commenting on this essay, as well as for many acts of kindness and stimulating conversations about this project and others; and, most of all, to Henry Hardy, without whose painstaking editorial labours, judicious advice, searching questions and unfailing encouragement, this introduction would either be far worse than it is, or not exist at all. I remain, of course, solely responsible for the interpretation offered, and the errors and idiosyncracies contained, in this piece.

---

[1] CC 78. This last is probably an allusion to Wittgenstein's declaration in the *Tractatus* that 'What we cannot speak about we must pass over in silence.' Wittgenstein 1922, proposition 6.57.

[2] POI 34–5.

## BIBLIOGRAPHY

The place of publication is London unless otherwise specified. Citations of Berlin's works in the footnotes are in the form 'Berlin 1954' when a whole essay is referred to, 'Berlin 1949b, 1' for a specific passage from an unpublished work posted in *The Isaiah Berlin Virtual Library* (see Hardy 2000– below), and 'L 168' for a specific passage from a collection of Berlin's essays or letters. References to works by other authors take the form 'Allen 1998', but the entries for these works given below do not give the date directly after the name except where more than one work by the same author is listed.

### Books by Isaiah Berlin

As listed on p. viii.

### Other works by Isaiah Berlin

1930: 'Some Procrustations', *Oxford Outlook* 10 (1930), 491–502

1932: review of Leonard Woolf, *After the Deluge*, *Oxford Outlook* 12 (1932), 68–70

1937a: 'Utilitarianism', unpublished lecture, in Hardy, under 'Unpublished work' (full URL *http://berlin.wolf.ox.ac.uk/lists/nachlass/utilitarianism.pdf*)

1937b: review of Julius Weinberg, *An Examination of Logical Positivism*, *Criterion* 17 (1937–8), 174–82

1949a: contribution to the series 'Notes on the Way', *Time and Tide* 30 (1949), 1133–4, 1157–8, 1187–8

1949b: 'Democracy, Communism and the Individual', notes for a talk at Mount Holyoke College, in Hardy, under 'Unpublished work' (full URL *http://berlin.wolf.ox.ac.uk/lists/nachlass/demcomind.pdf*)

1950a: 'Soviet Beginnings' (review of E. H. Carr, *A History of Soviet Russia*, vol. 1: *The Bolshevik Revolution, 1917–1923*), *Sunday Times*, 10 December 1950, 3

1950b: 'Political Ideas in the Twentieth Century', L 55–93

1953a: 'The Hedgehog and the Fox', RT 22–81

1953b: 'The Sense of Reality', SR 1–39

1953c: review of Cassirer 1932, *English Historical Review* 68 (1953), 617–19

1954a: 'Historical Inevitability', L 94–164

1954b: 'Realism in Politics', POI 134–42

1957: 'Political Judgement', SR 40–53

1958: 'Two Concepts of Liberty', L 166–211

1959: 'European Unity and its Vicissitudes', CTH 175–206

1960a: 'The Concept of Scientific History', PSM 17–58

1960b: 'The Romantic Revolution', SR 168–93

1961: 'Does Political Theory Still Exist?', PSM 59–90

1962a: 'Artistic Commitment: A Russian Legacy', SR 194–231

1962b: 'Mr Carr's Big Battalions' (review of E. H. Carr, *What is History?*), *New Statesman* 63 (January–June 1962), 15–16

1972: 'Fathers and Children: Turgenev and the Liberal Predicament', RT 261–305

1974: 'The Divorce Between the Sciences and the Humanities', PSM 326–58

1975: 'The Apotheosis of the Romantic Will', CTH 207–37

1980: 'A Tribute to my Friend', *Forum* (Israel) No 38 (Summer 1980), 1–4

1992: Letters to Conor Cruise O'Brien, in Conor Cruise O'Brien, *The Great Melody: A Thematic Biography and Commented Anthology of Edmund Burke* (1992), 612–15, 617–18

*Works by other authors*

Adorno, Theodor W., et al., *The Authoritarian Personality* (New York, 1950)

Allen, Jonathan, review of SR, *South African Journal of Philosophy* 17 No 2 (1998), 173–7

Arendt, Hannah, *The Origins of Totalitarianism* (New York, 1951)

Arieli, Yehoshua, 'Sir Isaiah Berlin: Humanism and the Romantic Experience', in Avishai Margalit, ed., *On the Thought of Isaiah Berlin: Papers Presented in Honour of Professor Sir Isaiah Berlin on the Occasion of his Eightieth Birthday* (Jerusalem, 1990)

Aron, Raymond, *The Opium of the Intellectuals* (1957)

Ayer, A. J., *Language, Truth and Logic* (1936)

Becker, Carl, *The Heavenly City of the Eighteenth-Century Philosophers* (New Haven, 1932)

Beiser, Frederick (1987), *The Fate of Reason: German Philosophy from Kant to Fichte* (Cambridge, Mass., 1987)

—— (1992), *Enlightenment, Revolution, and Romanticism: The Genesis of Modern German Political Thought, 1790–1800* (Cambridge, Mass., 1992)

—— (2003), *The Romantic Imperative: The Concept of Early German Romanticism* (Cambridge, Mass., 2003)

Borges, Jorge Luis, 'Kafka and his Precursors', in *Labyrinths: Selected Stories and Other Writings*, trans. D. A. Yates, J. E. Irby, A. Kerrigan, L. A. Murillo, D. Fitts, J. M. Fein, H. de Onás and J. Palley (New York, 1962)

Cassidy, Suzanne, ' "I think I hear them talk" ', interview with Berlin, *New York Times*, Book Review section, 24 March 1991, 30

Cassirer, Ernst, *The Philosophy of the Enlightenment* (1932), trans. Fritz C. A. Koelln and James P. Pettegrove (Princeton, 1951)

Chamberlain, Lesley, *Motherland: A Philosophical History of Russia* (2004)

Cherniss, Joshua, ' "A Cautious, Sober Love Affair with Humanity": Humanism in the Thought of Isaiah Berlin' (2002), in Hardy, under 'Publications about Berlin' (full URL *http:// berlin.wolf.ox.ac.uk/writings_on_ib/cherniss.doc*)

Cracraft, James, 'A Berlin for Historians', *History and Theory* 41 No 3 (October 2002), 277–300

Crowder, George (2002), *Liberalism and Value Pluralism* (2002)

—— (2004), *Isaiah Berlin: Liberty and Pluralism* (Cambridge, 2004)

Darnton, Robert (1971a), 'The High Enlightenment and the Low-Life of Literature in Pre-Revolutionary France', *Past and Present* 51 (1971), 81–115

—— (1971b), 'In Search of the Enlightenment: Recent Attempts to Create a Social History of Ideas', *Journal of Modern History* 43 (1971), 113–32

Dupré, Louis, *The Enlightenment and the Intellectual Foundations of Modern Culture* (New Haven, 2004)

Foot, Philippa, *Virtues and Vices and Other Essays in Moral Philosophy* (Oxford, 1978)

Fromm, Erich, *The Fear of Freedom* (1942)

Galipeau, Claude J., *Isaiah Berlin's Liberalism* (Oxford, 1994)

Galston, William A., *Liberal Pluralism: The Implications of Value Pluralism for Political Theory and Practice* (Cambridge, 2002)

Garrard, Graeme, 'The Counter-Enlightenment Liberalism of Isaiah Berlin', *Journal of Political Ideologies* 2 (1997), 281–96

Gay, Peter (1966–9), *The Enlightenment: An Interpretation*, 2 vols (New York, 1966, 1969)

—— (1999), 'Intimations of Partiality', *The Times Literary Supplement*, 11 June 1999, 3–4

Gellner, Ernest, 'Sauce for the Liberal Goose', review of Gray 1995, *Prospect*, November 1995, 56–61

Goodman, Dena, *The Republic of Letters: A Cultural History of the French Enlightenment* (Ithaca and London, 1994)

Gray, John, *Isaiah Berlin* (1995; Princeton, 1996)

Hanley, Ryan P., 'Political Science and Political Understanding: Isaiah Berlin on the Nature of Political Inquiry', *American Political Science Review* 98 (2004), 327–39

Hardy, Henry (ed.), *The Isaiah Berlin Virtual Library*, website of The Isaiah Berlin Literary Trust, *http://berlin.wolf.ox.ac.uk/* (Oxford, 2000–   )

Hare, R. M., *The Language of Morals* (Oxford, 1952)

Hausheer, Roger, 'Enlightening the Enlightenment', in Mali and Wokler 2003

Hayek, Friedrich, *The Road to Serfdom* (1944)

Hazard, Paul, *European Thought in the Eighteenth Century* (1946), trans. J. Lewis May (1954)

Himmelfarb, Gertrude, *Three Roads to Modernity: The British, French, and American Enlightenments* (New York, 2004)

Hoffer, Eric, *The True Believer* (New York, 1951)

Horkheimer, Max, and Theodor W. Adorno, *Dialectic of Enlightenment* (1944), trans. John Cumming (1972; original German title *Philosophische Fragmente*)

Ignatieff, Michael, *Isaiah Berlin: A Life* (1998)

Israel, Jonathan, *Radical Enlightenment: Philosophy and the Making of Modernity 1650–1750* (Oxford, 2001)

Jacob, Margaret, *Living the Enlightenment: Freemasonry and Politics in Eighteenth-Century Europe* (Oxford, 1991)

Jahanbegloo, Ramin, *Conversations with Isaiah Berlin* (New York, 1991)

Keynes, John Maynard, *The End of Laissez-Faire* (1926)

Kirsch, Adam, 'Letters of an Aloof Young Man: Philosopher of Perennial Dissatisfaction', review of L1, *New York Sun*, 7 July 2004, 1, 15

Larmore, Charles, *The Romantic Legacy* (New York, 1996)

Lee, Hermione, 'Swerving Berlin', review of L1, *Guardian*, 1 May 2004, *Saturday Review*, 9

Lenin, Vladimir Ilich, *What is to be done?* (1937)

Lilla, Mark, 'The Trouble with the Enlightenment', review of MN, *London Review of Books*, 6 January 1994, 12–13

Lukes, Steven, 'The Singular and the Plural: On the Distinctive Liberalism of Isaiah Berlin', *Social Research* 61 (1994), 687–718

MacIntyre, Alasdair C. (1967), *A Short History of Morals* (1967)

—— (1981), *After Virtue: A Study in Moral Theory* (1981)

McMahon, Darrin, *Enemies of the Enlightenment: The French Counter-Enlightenment and the Making of Modernity* (Oxford, 2001)

Mali, Joseph, and Robert Wokler (eds), *Isaiah Berlin's Counter-Enlightenment* (Philadelphia, 2003)

Margalit, Avishai, 'The Philosopher of Sympathy: Isaiah Berlin and the Fate of Humanism', *New Republic*, 20 February 1995, 31–7

Moore, G. E., *Principia Ethica* (Cambridge, 1903)

Munck, Thomas, *The Enlightenment: A Comparative Social History 1721–1794* (Oxford, 2000)

Niebuhr, Reinhold, *The Children of Light and the Children of Darkness* (1945)

Outram, Dorinda, *The Enlightenment* (Cambridge, 1995)

Pocock, J. G. A. (1999a), 'Enlightenment and Counter-Enlightenment, Revolution and Counter-Revolution: A Euroskeptical Enquiry', *History of Political Thought* 20 (1999), 125–39

—— (1999b), *Barbarism and Religion*, vol. 1, *The Enlightenments of Edward Gibbon* (Cambridge, 1999)

Popper, Karl R., *The Open Society and its Enemies* (1945)

Porter, Roy, *Enlightenment: Britain and the Creation of the Modern World* (2000)

Porter, Roy, and Mikuláš Teich (eds), *The Enlightenment in National Context* (Cambridge, 1981)

Riasanovsky, Nicholas V., *The Emergence of Romanticism* (Oxford, 1992)

Rickert, Heinrich, *The Limits of Concept Formation in National Science* (1902), ed. and trans. Guy Oakes (Cambridge, 1986)

Riesman, David, with Nathan Glaser and Reuel Denney, *The Lonely Crowd* (New Haven, 1950)

Robertson, John (2003), 'The Case for the Enlightenment: A Comparative Approach', in Mali and Wokler 2003

—— (2005), *The Case for the Enlightenment: Scotland and Naples, 1680–1760* (Cambridge, 2005)

Roche, Daniel, *France in the Enlightenment* (1993), trans. Arthur Goldhammer (Cambridge, Mass., 1998)

Ryan, Alan, 'Berlin, Sir Isaiah (1909–1997)', *Oxford Dictionary of National Biography* (Oxford, 2004)

Schmidt, James, 'What Enlightenment Project?', *Political Theory* 28 (2000), 734–57

Siedentop, Larry, 'The Ionian Fallacy', *The Times Literary Supplement*, 23 September 1994, 8

Steinberg, Jonny, 'The Burdens of Berlin's Modernity', *History of European Ideas* 22 (1996), 369–83

Talmon, Jacob L., *The Origins of Totalitarian Democracy* (1952)

Warnock, Mary, *Ethics since 1900* (Oxford, 1960)

Weldon, T. D., *The Vocabulary of Politics* (1953)

Wittgenstein, Ludwig, *Tractatus Logico-Philosophicus* (1922), trans. D. F. Pears and B. F. McGuinness (1961)

Wokler, Robert (2003), 'Isaiah Berlin's Enlightenment and Counter-Enlightenment', in Mali and Wokler 2003

—— (forthcoming), 'A Guide to Isaiah Berlin's *Political Ideas in the Romantic Age*', *History of Political Thought*

# PROLOGUE

THIS BOOK is an attempt to deal with some of the social and political ideas of certain leading thinkers of Western Europe towards the end of the eighteenth and at the beginning of the nineteenth century. Some of these ideas are intrinsically interesting; almost all had a marked influence in generating, or alternatively in counteracting, the impact of what is still the greatest upheaval of modern times, the great French Revolution. But they have a further interest for us today, since, new and old, revolutionary and counter-revolutionary, in their particular sphere they form the basic intellectual capital on which, with few additions, we live to this day. Social, moral, political, economic discussion has ever since occurred in terms of the concepts, the language, indeed the images and metaphors which were generated during that period, in the minds and feelings of these truest founders of the modern outlook.

Plato and Aristotle, Dante and Aquinas, Epicurus and Augustine, Machiavelli and Hobbes, Grotius and Locke were in some respects bolder and more original thinkers than those with whom this volume is concerned, but their concepts and language are at best half alien to us. They need translation and interpretation; to try to state the crucial issues which divide us, and have divided the Western world during the last century, in terms of the philosophy of Aristotle, or even of Hobbes, or Montesquieu, is an artificial proceeding justified only as a *tour de force* intended to show the continuity of European thought. But the language and the thought of Helvétius or Condorcet is a great deal more like that of Mill than it is like that of Locke or Bayle or Leibniz, not very different from that of Morley, or Woodrow Wilson, or those who framed the Charter of the United Nations, or those who took and take part in the debates between the Western powers and the Asiatic or Communist worlds about the rights of individuals or of classes or of peoples.

Similarly, we do not today literally speak in terms of social contract or general will or civil society. Nevertheless, it is the words and the imagery of Rousseau that have shaped the language of nationalism, of resistance to foreign and domestic oppression, both sincere and specious, for well over a hundred years: Mazzini and Michelet, Lincoln and Masaryk, the Spanish Republicans and Nehru, who use its formulae, believe in its principles, and there are conspicuous echoes of it in Carlyle, in Nietzsche, in Lawrence, in the sense in which, say, St Augustine or Pascal, whose thoughts are a great deal profounder and more original than those of Rousseau, do not directly sound in anyone's speech.

Fascists and Communists, imperialists and totalitarians, liberal republicans and constitutional monarchists too, to this day, speak the language not merely of Burke but of Hegel; social scientists of all brands, planners and technocrats, New Dealers and social and economic historians use, without knowing it, the notions and terminology of Saint-Simon virtually unaltered. And it is not only the traditional irrationalists and enemies of democracy and the disciples of Charles Maurras who inhabit a violent world brought into being, almost single-handed, by Joseph de Maistre. Nor should it cause as much surprise as perhaps it might to find so much of modern anti-intellectualism and existentialism (particularly of the atheistical type), and much of 'emotive' ethics, not merely in Kierkegaard or Nietzsche or Bergson, but in the writings of Fichte and in forgotten treatises by Schelling.

This is not merely a question of tracing sources and attributing responsibilities. Few activities are more dangerous to the cause of historical truth than the attempt to find a fully grown oak in the acorn, or the attempt to stigmatise (or praise) thinkers living in and speaking to a society remote from us for the transformation, and often degradation, which their ideas have often undergone at the hands of demagogues and popular movements which have taken what they needed from such doctrines and put them to their own cruder uses, and have as often as not totally perverted, or at best violently oversimplified, the original vision of a great man whose name they place upon their banners. But during the years of which I speak, the issues debated were literally identical with those which stir individuals and nations in our own time.

The years in question were ones in which ideas were particularly influential. They constituted what the Saint-Simonians called a critical epoch, during which the old order is in visible decay, its institutions no longer serve its needs, and are indeed being used by those whom they oppress against themselves – as lawyers and 'subversive' writers of dangerous ages use the laws and the principles of the established order as the most effective weapons to destroy it. In this atmosphere ideas play a very crucial part, whether or not it is held that they are the direct product of forces other than ideas – economic or social or biological.

The collision of ideas during this period (and its results) is very familiar to us. On the one hand are the most lucid and passionate opponents: the notions of the Encyclopaedists and their nineteenth-century disciples, the Saint-Simonians and the positivists. According to these, scientific method can solve all questions, of ends as well as of means. Patient and disinterested research can establish what are the fundamental needs of all men as such; these needs are not irreconcilable. Provided one sets about formulating and satisfying them in a rational manner, a harmonious scheme of existence can be developed which will put an end, for ever, to all injustice, misery, conflict and frustration of every type. Human ills are caused not by nature, nor by some incurable imperfection in the human soul, but by ignorance, idleness, prejudice and their exploitation by some – the minorities who are in power – and an inability to resist them effectively on the part of the vast majority of mankind. Where some men failed, other men can succeed. Men are infinitely malleable. Education, and above all legislation, conducted by enlightened élites – who will canalise human persons into productive channels, turn drones into working bees, and by a rational system of rewards and punishment, as well as the elimination of vested interests in human vice, provide irresistible incentives to efficiency, benevolence, justice and enlightenment – will guarantee a harmonious and perpetual happiness for all men.

And on the other hand, against this, and even before the Jacobins and Napoleon, stands the liberal Kantian protest against treating human beings as children or docile sheep, even though it be to promote their happiness and peace; reiterated insistence upon rights, including the right to stray from the proper path even though it lead to sin, suffering and punishment; the sacredness of the act of choice on the part of the individual human being, and the notion of liberty as an end in itself, whatever its consequences; the fear of control, however benevolent and wise, beyond an essential socially necessitated minimum, as being likely to lead to the destruction of that which alone makes everything else worth pursuing – the unhampered individual will; unhampered, that is, at any rate by other human beings – in short, the notions of liberty and equality as against those of security, happiness, efficiency, however disinterested, however just – even the most humane and attractive forms of what Karl Popper has well called 'the closed society'. Surely these priorities have become not less but more relevant and immediate to us as time has passed.

Another party to this collision is Rousseau's world of socially and emotionally emancipated beings: 'natural' men, uncorrupted by institutions designed to serve, at best, the needs of sectional interests, at worst, obsolete and oppressive relics of ancient errors, so effectively blown up by Bentham and his followers; men living simple, spontaneous lives following the dictates of their consciences, which, provided original virtue has not been destroyed in their hearts by destructive institutions or unscrupulous education by wicked or corrupt men, will always vote in a manner likely to lead to a communal life that will fulfil all its members' legitimate needs and desires. There is a suspicion of too much wealth, too much sophistication, too expansive an economy, too undiscriminating an encouragement of all talents, useful and dangerous alike; the feeling that the poor are somehow nearer the heart of things than the rich, the simple than the clever, common men than officials or aristocrats, or intellectuals. There is a Tolstoyan passion for what existentialists of our day like to describe as 'authenticity', perpetual warnings against the self-deceived will that rationalises and too easily persuades its owner that its selfish or sectional interest is identical with that of the common good, in which alone individuals can find fulfilment; a general analogy, not often stressed, with the notion of a community of fervent, simple believers, a Church of which the members are parts of one another rather than a society founded for the protection of the minimum rights of its members, or for power or glory or the maximum of production of material and spiritual goods. Opposed to this is the optimistic utilitarianism of Helvétius and Bentham, convinced that the pursuit of happiness (which is in any case psychologically inevitable) and the use of the most rational means thereto (which will bring it about most efficiently, swiftly and universally) do not entail a return to the restrictive economics and discipline of Sparta as against the richer civilisation of Athens, but, on the contrary, the development of all human resources and faculties under the beneficent guidance of enlightened rulers, whether individual or collective, that will open up as yet undreamed of possibilities of human felicity.

Helvétius believed in planning and the control of experts; Bentham, situated in different social and historical circumstances, feared bullying and interference by institutions more than by arbitrary individuals, and said that every man was the best judge of his own happiness, which it is the sole business of institutions to make it possible for him to pursue. But both, in company with Turgot and Adam Smith, Voltaire and Diderot, Holbach and Hume, looked upon Rousseau's attack on the arts and sciences (much as later intellectuals looked upon D. H. Lawrence's hatred of the civilisation of his day) as being subversive of the civilised and tolerant society for which they were fighting; nor had they any taste for the language of rights or other metaphysical abstractions, which seemed to them to derive from a discredited, pre-scientific theology, although they seldom attacked it with the violence of Bentham and his English followers. Nor did they have overmuch confidence in the judgement of the simple and pure in heart, still less of majorities, which, like liberals of a later day, they suspected of being the repositories of prejudice, philistine hatred of what they most cared about themselves – truth, liberty, the rightness of truth [sic] and of culture – potential sources of oppression a great deal more difficult to check or reform than individuals, despots or oligarchies. They judged measures by their consequences and cared little for sincerity or innocence, if these led to results destructive of individual or social happiness, and were in this respect wholly alien and indeed antagonistic to the ethical views of Kant or Rousseau or the German romantics, with their emphasis on purity of motives, nobility of character, the quality of the inner vision as alone conferring value on men's lives or actions.

This conflict – which was destined to come into the open in the nineteenth century, especially in the form of the triumphant materialistic romanticism of Saint-Simon, with his vision of a frictionless, self-maintaining social and economic system, ceaselessly generating material and spiritual benefits under the guidance of men of creative genius, as against the neo-puritanism of Proudhon, Tolstoy, Sorel and the strong element of positivism in both the liberal and socialist outlooks, connected as in part it is with the contrast between delight in the ever-expanding triumph of the industrial and scientific revolution of our time and a fundamental emotional rejection of its advance – this collision of values found its classical expression during the period in question, immediately before and immediately after the French Revolution. This is never so clear and so simple again.

But whatever might be the deep-rooted differences which divided Helvétius from Rousseau, Holbach and Diderot from Rousseau and Mably, or Kant from Helvétius, or Fichte and his followers from all of these, or those who believed that nature had a purpose and saw in her at once the goal and the teacher of man, the source of natural rights, the corrector of errors, as against those who merely believed in the rule of mechanical and repetitive causality, or those who believed in nature not as an ideal to be followed, a schoolmistress to be feared and venerated, but as so much raw material to be moulded, dead matter, a challenge to creative activity, not a model but a stimulus and an obstacle – yet all these stand together against two other schools of thought whose doctrines came to the fore also, as so many others, only in their own day: in the first place of those who, whether inspired by Herder or by Burke, claimed that the new rationalism, the application of scientific method and Cartesian logic to human affairs, had failed even as a respectable instrument of social analysis, let alone as a guide to life. Vico, who had originally enunciated boldly original views against the rationalists of his time, was unread and forgotten. Hamann, who alone preached about the inadequacy of reason during the height of German enlightenment, wrote too obscurely to be widely read, but Burke was one of the most eloquent and widely admired writers of his time, and Herder wrote with infectious passion and eloquence. Their followers, in their various fashions, maintained that the analysis of society into homogeneous human atoms, on the analogy of the physical sciences, led to gross distortion of the facts; that the spiritual and social cement which held men together in associations, communities, Churches, nations, cultures had little to do with rational self-interest; that the sense of solidarity, of belonging to a given unit, with conscious and unconscious roots continuously stretching into an infinite past, the great society of the quick and the dead and those yet unborn,[1] with which every member of a society or a nation in some sense knew himself to be involved, could not be

---

[1] [A reference to Edmund Burke's description of society as 'a partnership not only between those who are living, but between those who are living, those who are dead, and those who are to be born'. *Reflections on the Revolution in France*: p. 147 in *The Writings and Speeches of Edmund Burke*, ed. Paul Langford (Oxford, 1981–    ), vol. 8, *The French Revolution*, ed. L. G. Mitchell (1989).]

represented as a conscious association for mutual profit; that the new scientific analysis gave no account of that sentiment of loyalty not towards specific individuals but towards tradition and the past of one's community, towards impersonal institutions whose characteristics could not be analysed without residue into those of the hosts of anonymous human beings who compose them, nor do justice to the springs of action, conscious and unconscious, rational and irrational, in the name of which men were prepared to sacrifice themselves and rise to untold heights of heroism, which inspired their art and penetrated their modes of life in a manner incapable of being described, let alone accounted for, in the terminology of the new sciences, which made the fatal blunder of assuming human beings to be psychophysical mechanisms capable of total dissection, and societies to be mechanical combinations for the sake of ascertainable and finite purposes, instead of organic growths, the cells of which were connected by impalpable strands which men felt and acted upon even if they could not give an account of them in chemical or mathematical or psychological terms, or those of the new science of political economy. The historical development of the patterns of human experience, the inner, only half-articulate, ideals, the difference between which gave a character and unique flavour, quality of feeling, to cultures, nations, historical periods – these were the characteristics with which men, whether they were conscious of it or not, were far more familiar, because their thoughts and feelings were inescapably impregnated by them, than with the facts brought to their attention by the absurd simplifications of the new sciences of man. Anyone who does not build upon his understanding of the impalpable connections which tie men to each other and to the generations that precede them, and does not allow for the unanalysable and infallible datum, that which can be conveyed only by images and examples – of which no generalisations (which are alone admissible in a science) will hold – builds upon sand. Their reforms must fail, since they are an attempt to pulverise society into the imaginary constituents of their false societies. This was the heart of the revolt against eighteenth-century rationalism in the name of history and of the Christian tradition. It grew in strength in the nineteenth century and is almost the dominant social philosophy of the present.

In the second place there was an even more violent onslaught upon the premises of the Enlightenment. It came from the school of Maistre in France, and Görres and his followers in Germany.

Everything that the philosophers of the Enlightenment asserted, they denied. Man was neither naturally good, nor neutral and infinitely malleable: he was born in sin, weak, vain, vicious and, if left to himself, unable to resist his self-destructive impulses. It needed all the discipline and all the faith and all the wisdom of the Church of Rome to create even a tolerable life for him on earth, and when he threw off its yoke and rebelled against it in the eighteenth century, his unbridled savagery and bestial violence provoked the great revolution which destroyed the foundations of its traditional culture.

Man cannot be governed without authority. To enquire perpetually for the reasons for things, to dig into the foundations, to see whereon the building stands, can only destroy it. Analytical reason is by nature destructive and must be held in bounds by blind faith. What the Enlightenment denounces as superstition and prejudice is merely that accumulated traditional knowledge of the generations which has stood the test of experience. Science must not be allowed to progress freely but must be repressed artificially, if need be, before it starts to undermine the faith which alone holds societies and men together against a return to the primal chaos – the jungle from which man has painfully emerged. What reason constructs reason unmakes. Only institutions whose origins are concealed in impenetrable darkness possess sufficient hold upon human imagination. It is said that men come together for mutual profit: it would be truer to say that one of the great passions which holds men together is the desire for self-immolation on the altar of some ideal, religious, national, historical. And that is why wars, which are the most irrational of activities, plainly and undeniably contrary to the individual's interests, will never cease; that is why hereditary monarchy, the most absurd of institutions by rational standards, is so much more successful and permanent than democracies or liberal republics, or elective monarchies, and why the papacy will last for ever.

The ways of God are inscrutable and human claims to be able to understand them, whether in the workings of nature or those of history, are a pitiful farce. Those who seek to guide their actions by the feeble light afforded by human science will inevitably suffer shipwreck. The ancient wisdom of the race, or of the Church, through which alone the voice of God speaks, this alone can secure the foundation of a life which at best must remain painful, precarious, shrouded in ignorance; blind obedience alone on the part of the subject, self-sacrificing duty on the part of the rulers, who know how little they know and will never explain, and severely repress all attempts at the examination of their credentials, these alone will save human society from total destruction. The alternative is a return to nature – foolishly apostrophised by the shallow prophets of the Enlightenment as a divine harmony and a source of wisdom and strength. If these men made the objective, disinterested observations which they advocated, they could see easily enough that nature, so far from being benign and peaceful, is a blood-drenched field in which every animal, every plant is occupied in the destruction of the species, and that man is exceptional only in that he, unlike other animals, destroys the members of his own species as well as those of others. Only faith, humility and resignation – and the collective wisdom of the Church – can prevent this war of nearly all against all and everything from depriving man of his last comforts on earth.[1]

Enough has been said to indicate that the issues which faced each other in the eighteenth century, whether derived or new-born, are among the profoundest which have divided the historical period of which we are among, perhaps, the latest inhabitants. But there is one further thesis which is perhaps even more revolutionary – as it is certainly far newer and more original – than the other doctrines of this time. This is the doctrine which lies at the heart of the romantic movement, and which, so far as I know, has not been adequately presented in the literature of the subject.

In the past, human values – the ends of life, that for the sake of which other things were worth creating or promoting or destroying, for the sake of which whatever is worth doing and being is regarded as being so – these ends or purposes or ultimate values were believed to be ingredients of the universe, to be found in it by whatever faculty it was with which investigators had classified the inventory of the world. To say that a thing was good or bad, right or wrong, beautiful or ugly, noble or ignoble, worth fighting for or discovering or making, was regarded as a descriptive statement – and recorded that the things in question possessed these properties. What a value consisted in depended, no doubt, upon the general

---

[1] This black and ferocious irrationalism, particularly in its secular forms – *révolté* poetry and 'black' literature – as well as the equally fierce nihilism and obscurantism of the anti-liberal extremists, whether in their Fascist or existentialist or anarchist form, were regarded in their time as peculiar contributions of the nineteenth century to political thought.

philosophy adopted. Some meant by it objective qualities existing in the world, whether perceived or not, like natural properties, or the ordinary characteristics discerned in everyday experience – colours, tastes, sizes. Others might think that a value consisted in being part of the general purpose of life in the world, created by God or self-created. Or else it might be that which satisfies some need on my own part, or that of my society, a need which is to be identified by means of psychological introspection or sociological observation; that which I like, or approve of, or think likely to give me pleasure or conduce to my glory – in short, whether the value could be analysed in terms of subjective inclinations or those of bodies of men, at a given point in time or throughout a period. But whatever view is taken, objective or subjective, absolute or relative, naturalistic or metaphysical, a priori or a posteriori, individualist or social, a statement of value or purpose described facts and represented reality. It was obviously crucial – literally a matter of life and death – to discover what the truth in matters of conduct was, that is, what the true values were. Men died and wars were fought because of differences about this.

It is during the period of which we are speaking that, for the first time, there begins to emerge the notion that perhaps value judgements are not descriptive propositions at all, that values are not discoverable, that they are not ingredients of the real world in the sense in which tables or chairs or men or colours or past events are, that values are not discovered but invented – created by men like works of art, of which it is senseless to ask where they were before they were conceived. Whereas philosophers from Plato onwards seemed agreed that such questions as 'What is good?', 'How should I live?', 'What makes acts right?', 'Why should I obey?' had answers which special wisdom could discover, although opinions might differ widely as to where the answer was to be found, and therefore wherein the wisdom consisted, the new doctrine held, or implied, that this was as senseless an approach as one which set itself to discover where the symphony was before the composer conceived it, where the victory was before the general won it. Ideals and goals were not found, they were created.

The revolution which ensued from this point of view – the transformation of values, the new admiration of heroism, integrity, strength of will, martyrdom, dedication to the vision within one, irrespective of its properties, veneration of those who battle against hopeless odds, no matter for how strange and desperate a cause, as against previous reverence for knowledge, skill, wisdom, success and truth, virtue, happiness, natural endowment – was the most decisive in modern times. It was certainly the largest step in the moral consciousness of mankind since the ending of the Middle Ages, perhaps since the rise of Christianity. No step of comparable magnitude has occurred since – it was the last great 'transvaluation of values' in modern history.

It is one of the purposes of this book to draw attention to its consequences – the degree to which it modified existing attitudes, the reaction against itself which it stimulated, and the degree to which it marks a chasm between the generations – those that came after, who have accepted these changes, sometimes scarcely conscious of how great and startling they must have seemed to the more self-conscious and acute observers of their times, and those whose words and thoughts, merely because they came before, seem antiquated or shallow, sometimes for that reason alone. Our own thought is to a large extent the product and the battlefield of the old, 'pre-revolutionary', and the new, 'post-revolutionary', points of view; no true synthesis between them has been effected by the mere process of time or the mere process of change. Present controversies, both in morals and politics, reflect the clash of values initiated by the romantic revolution. The time has perhaps come to assess its intrinsic importance and its vast consequences.[1]

Unlike the history of natural science or mathematics, or even to some degree history itself, the history of moral and political ideas does not constitute a cumulative story of steady progress, not even of progress broken by occasional moments of regression. Political thought is not a form of knowledge in the sense in which the sciences or common sense contain knowledge, or facts, or in which formal disciplines – mathematics or logic, or even heraldry or the art of chess – can be said to embody knowledge of formal relationships. Political philosophy is a branch of thought which deals neither with empirical matters of fact nor with formal relationships governed by identifiable rules and axioms. Its task is to explain, elucidate, classify, make clear what a given doctrine asserts, entails, whether it is internally consistent or not, of what vision of the universe it forms a part. But these visions – the general

[1] Vast consequences, not least influential where they form an ill-assorted combination of the new and the old, fitting equally ill into the categories provided by either side and so constituting typical philosophical problems.

outlook of which political theory is but an aspect, a coherent, articulate expression – are themselves not forms of knowledge, if this is a continuous growth of information about a relatively unchanging subject-matter, in which errors of the past are corrected, techniques can be learned and applied by men themselves not gifted enough to invent them, and knowledge of the past period is not required to make it possible to use the methods of the present with success. Political theory is an aspect of thought (and sometimes feeling) about men's relationships to each other and to their institutions, in terms of purposes and scales of value which themselves alter as a result of historical circumstances of varying types, not least in terms of new models derived from other fields of experience, scientific or historical, or religious, which bind their spell upon the imagination of the most impressionable and socially conscious men of their time, and transform their vision. But the expression of such a vision does not constitute progress, only the history of successive attitudes towards their predicament on the part of human beings, attitudes which, precisely because the presuppositions of one age and culture are sometimes so difficult to grasp for those brought up in a different one, require for their understanding the exercise of a specific kind of moral imagination to a very unusual degree.

It is a platitude to say that each age has its own problems, its own experience, its own imagery and symbolism and ways of feeling and speaking. It is a lesser platitude to add that political philosophy derives its intelligibility solely from the understanding of such change, and that its perennial principles, or what seem to be such, depend on the relative stability and unchanging characteristics of human beings in their social aspect. If the supersession of eighteenth-century doctrine, which evaluated everything unhistorically, by a more historical or evolutionary point of view has any value, it should teach us that each political philosophy responds to the needs of its own times and is fully intelligible only in terms of all the relevant factors of its age, and intelligible to us only to the degree to which (and it is a far larger one than some modern relativists wish to persuade us that it is) we have experience in common with previous generations. But to the extent to which this is so, it is idle to expect progress in this enterprise; the conclusions and problems and agonies of each age are what they are, and the attempts at solutions and answers and nostrums can be judged properly only in terms of them.

The great political philosophers have made their mark by projecting some great pattern which has uncovered hitherto concealed characteristics of experience (the more permanent and constant such experience, the greater the penetration of the philosopher's contribution) and, in the course of so doing, probably inevitably concealed other aspects which did not fit into the great analogy. We can do no better than to try to describe what some of these models, which have affected our own age most deeply, consisted of. They are not commensurable, any more than novels, or histories, which spring out of a given world and sum up each experience, can be ranged in some strict order of merit or 'progress', as if there were a single goal which all these works of art were seeking to attain.

Bertrand Russell rightly said that the ingenuity of philosophers, the great intellectual virtuosity which they show in piling argument upon argument to support a given doctrine, is often no more than the outworks of the citadel which they are defending, weapons to protect it against attack, defence against actual and possible objections, and that all the subtlety and complications, which are indeed admirable, often enough, as monuments of human genius and skill in reasoning, conceal an inner vision which is comparatively simple: coherent, harmonious and not difficult to grasp. But unless the central vision is perceived, the great constructions of reason piled up to protect it seem often enough mere exercises in intellectual power, impressive but ultimately not convincing. For the only thing which convinces in matters not capable of proof, in the sense in which the propositions of mathematics or logic, or even those of empirical science, can be said to be so, is a direct appeal to experience, a description of what we think right or true which varies with what our audience has itself in some sense, however inarticulately, known or felt. This is the sense in which some models are more revolutionary, more convincing and more transforming than others, and solve difficulties and answer problems in the sense in which no argument or proof could hope to do.

During the great ferment of ideas which preceded and followed the French Revolution, experience altered what Collingwood used to call the 'absolute presuppositions' of experience. Those categories and concepts which were taken for granted and had been taken for granted before, and seemed too secure to be shaken, too familiar to be worth inspection, were altered, or at any rate severely shaken. The controversies of our age are the direct product of this 'transformation of the model', which alone makes the period and its thinkers worthy of our attention. We shall be told that one must not exaggerate the role of ideas, that ideas are created by 'social forces' and not the other way about, that while, no doubt, the ideas of Locke and Montesquieu played their part in the American Revolution and the constitutional document that followed, this was only so because the social or economic structure of colonial American society resembled that European order of which Locke and Montesquieu were the 'ideological representatives' – heralds or spokesmen, but not creators. There is no doubt a good deal of truth in this, but those who maintain it with partisan favour seem to me to be breaking in through open doors: they are saying something which is true but too obvious to be arresting. Of course, the founders of the American republic were unlikely to be influenced in their ideas by Bossuet or Bolingbroke, or the Jesuits – where there is no soil receptive to it the seed will not grow. But the soil can remain fertile and yet no seed fall, or else some plant suitable to some very different climate be planted and wither away or fail to grow to maturity. And there is no social law yet discovered which guarantees that demand creates supply inevitably, and that where conditions are mature human genius is bound infallibly to respond to human needs. The Americans were only too ready to be influenced by Montesquieu's doctrine of the division of powers, but this doctrine is a product of individual genius, and if Montesquieu had died at birth or confined himself to writing elegant satire and books of travel, this idea might never have seen the light in the form in which it could have so profound an effect. The great Heine cannot be accused of lack of historical sense, for his hypotheses, particularly with regard to Germany and Communism, have come only too literally true. He was a Hegelian, a Saint-Simonian, the admired friend of Marx. Few men understood their age better, and when he said that 'implacable Kantians [ ... ] with sword and axe will dig up the soil of our European life in order to tear out the last roots of the past [ ... ] armed Fichteans will enter the arena [ ... ] restrained neither by fear nor by self-interest [ ... ] like the first Christians, whom neither physical torture nor physical pleasure could break',[1] he

---

[1] *Zur Geschichte der Religion und Philosophie in Deutschland*, book 3: p. 228, lines 16–24, in *Heines Werke*, Säkularausgabe, vol. 8, ed. Renate Francke (Berlin/Paris, 1972).

spoke of what he knew. Robespierre behaved as he did because he was filled with the ideas of Rousseau and Mably, but Rousseau and Mably might not have written, and Helvétius and Montesquieu might have taken their place, and in that event the course of the French Revolution might well have been different and Robespierre might have lived and indeed died differently from the way in which he in fact did. The greatest event of our own day was certainly the Russian Revolution, and yet it is difficult to conceive that it would have taken the turning it did if Lenin had been shot by a stray bullet in 1917, or had not come across, during his impressionable years, the works of Marx or Chernyshevsky.[1]

Individuals do affect events. Their genius – their historical greatness – is in part defined by their ability to bend events to their will; the force of the 'logical facts' can be exaggerated to a point at which it explains everything which happens as inevitable and regards all rejected courses, indeed all possible courses other than that which was adopted, as foredoomed from the beginning. We possess no science which justifies this view to us, or even renders it probable. History, so far as it teaches anything, does not show this, and the notion which dominated the historians of the eighteenth century, that history is but 'philosophy teaching by examples',[2] and shows us merely that in analogous circumstances the consequences are similar too, and that laws of social behaviour are easily derivable from this, has, for lack of evidence, rightly become discredited among historians and lingered only among those who look in history for a theodicy. Ideas are born in circumstances favourable to their emergence, although it is so difficult to specify what the circumstances, in specific cases, are, that such laws amount almost to tautologies. Sometimes these ideas result in little practical effect; at other times the organising genius of those who

[1] If Mussolini had remained a Marxist, Italy might have become Communist and the fate of Germany might well have been different; it is at least as plausible to argue that it was the absence of a Lenin which caused the Spanish Revolution to fail as that his presence was not indispensable to the success of the revolution which he did make.

[2] [Henry St John, Viscount] Bolingbroke, *Letters on the Study and Use of History*, letter 2: vol. 2, p. 177, in *The Works of Lord Bolingbroke* (London, 1844). [Bolingbroke says that he thinks he read the remark in Dionysius of Halicarnassus, and he is right (see *Ars rhetorica* 11. 2), except that the *Ars rhetorica* is no longer attributed to Dionysius. Pseudo-Dionysius attributes his version – 'History is philosophy from examples' – to Thucydides, but it is in fact a creative paraphrase of what Thucydides says at 1. 22. 3.]

generate them or identify themselves with them makes it possible to conceive of men and their relationships in terms of some single pattern, and to transform the vision of their contemporaries – and sometimes of their opponents – by means of it.

Patterns of this kind sometimes, like Frankenstein's monster, acquire a reality of their own, and pursue careers in other men's minds independent of their originators or first propagators. Rousseau can hardly have anticipated that totalitarian 'democratic centralism' which derived, indeed, from his doctrine of the general will, but which neither he nor his early followers in the French Revolution had been conscious of. Nor had Helvétius perceived – nor could he have perceived – the goal to which the road to technocracy might ultimately lead. Nor was Fichte responsible for the Byronic romanticism and nihilism which he had, in a sense, originated. It is one thing to blame individual thinkers and another to trace the development and effects of their ideas once they are afloat. Saint-Simon probably came nearest to the truth when he maintained that ideas of genius are fruitful only when circumstances are appropriate (and by circumstances he meant all that the most faithful Marxists could demand in the way of class relationships and economic structure), but that if no genius arose the age remained fallow, the arts and sciences declined, and a retrogression occurred of which no one could predict the duration or the depth. The age of which we speak was singularly rich in original conceptions; they transformed our world, and the words in which they were formulated speak to us still.

# 1

# POLITICS AS A DESCRIPTIVE SCIENCE

I do not care if men be vicious so long as they are intelligent [ . . . ]
Laws will do everything.[1]

Claude-Adrien Helvétius

[ . . . ] le tribunal suprême & qui juge en dernier ressort & sans apel
de tout ce qui nous est proposé, est la Raison [ . . . ][2]

Pierre Bayle

The people [ . . . ] are cattle, and what they need is a yoke and a
goad and fodder.[3]

François Marie Arouet de Voltaire

I

THE CENTRAL ISSUE of political philosophy is the question 'Why
should any man obey any other man or body of men?' – or (what
amounts to the same in the final analysis) 'Why should any man or
body of men ever interfere with other men?'

Political thought has, of course, occupied itself with many other
topics: such as the actual behaviour of individuals in and out of
society, their purposes, their scales of value and their own beliefs
about the character and aims of their social conduct; as well as the
motives and causes which, whether they know it or not, affect the
lives, acts, beliefs and feelings of human beings. It includes, as it
grows more analytical, the examination of the concepts and
categories involved in the thoughts and the words of men
concerning their relations to one another, and to their institutions

---

[1] 'Peu importe que les hommes soient vicieux; c'en est assez, s'ils sont éclairés
[ . . . ] Les lois font tout.' *De l'homme* 9. 6.

[2] 'The supreme tribunal, the final arbiter of all that is set before us, against
which no appeal is possible, is Reason.' *Commentaire philosophique* (1686), part
1, chapter 1: vol. 2, p. 368, col. 1, in *Oeuvres diverses de Mr Pierre Bayle* (La
Haye, 1737).

[3] 'À l'égard du peuple [ . . . c]e sont des boeufs, auxquels il faut un joug, un
aiguillon et du foin.' Letter to Jean François René Tabareau, 3 February 1769. Cf.
*Oeuvres complètes de Voltaire* [ed. Louis Moland] (Paris, 1877–85), vol. 19, pp.
208, 623, vol. 24, p. 413.

past and present, actual and imaginary, and seeks to elucidate such notions as liberty and authority, rights and obligations, justice and happiness, State and society, equality and oppression, rules and principles, and many other familiar terms of political discourse. At its best and sharpest it deals with questions that are still more general and fundamental, such as the logic of political argument or deliberation, and asks how such crucial links in human thinking as 'because' and 'therefore', 'obviously' and 'possibly', as well as such notions as 'true' and 'false', 'convincing' and 'implausible', 'valid' and 'invalid', are employed in thinking about political issues, as compared to the ways in which they function in the thought of logicians, or mathematicians, or historians, or chemists, or archi- tects or lawyers or literary critics.

There is much else that political thought, in the largest sense, has embraced. It speculates about the possibility – and discoverability – of general laws governing human behaviour and the limits of their application. At times it offers practical advice for both rulers and ruled. At other times it explains why this is not, and should not be, part of its province, and prefers to discuss the relations of political theory and practice to other fields of human activity, religion, or economics, or natural science, or ethics, or law. And while it may be readily conceded that it is pedantic or stupid to draw absolute distinctions between these activities, and to pretend that these fields can be insulated from one another and be made subject to wholly separate disciplines, yet not to discriminate between them at all, to treat these topics as they suggest themselves, as the spirit moves one, is a free exercise of the intellect which is bought at too high a price. Such methods may stimulate thought, excite the imagination, and lead to interesting and valuable *aperçus*, but they tend to increase the prevailing rich confusion of a subject which more, perhaps, than any other needs discipline and dry light if it is to be an object of serious study.

Political philosophy is what it is and not identical with every other form of reflection about human affairs. Its frontiers may have grown indistinct, and it may be arid scholasticism to erect artificial barriers, but it does not follow from this that it has not a province of its own. As things stand at present, it seems to me a greater service to the cause of lucidity and truth to try to indicate what this province is, however provisionally, rather than to pretend either, as some have done, that it is a province of epistemology or semant- ics – that nothing useful can be said unless and until the ways in which words are used in political argument have been properly compared and contrasted with other ways of using words (valuable and indeed revolutionary as this analysis, in the hands of a man of genius, could be); or, as others tell us, that politics is part of a larger whole (the whole of human history or the material evolution of society or some timeless order), and can and must be studied only within that whole or not at all. And it is because so much has been urged in favour of these ambitious schemes that I propose more modestly to assume, at any rate by way of a tentative initial hypothesis, that at the heart of political philosophy proper is the problem of obedience, and that it is, if nothing else, convenient to view the traditional problems of the subject in terms of this problem.

To put the question in this way is to be reminded of the rich variety of the answers to it. Why should I obey this or that man or group of men, or written or spoken enactment? Because, says one school of thought, it is the word of God vouchsafed in a sacred text of supernatural origin; or communicated by direct revelation to myself; or to a person or persons – king or priest or prophet – whose unique qualifications in such matters I recognise. Because, say others, the command to obey is the order of the *de facto* ruler or his chosen agents, and the law is what he wills and because he wills it, whatever his motives or reasons. Because, say various metaphysical Greek and Christian and Hegelian thinkers, the world has been created, or exists uncreated, to fulfil a purpose; and it is only in terms of this purpose that everything in it is as it is, and where and when it is, and acts as it does and is acted on as it is; and from this it follows that a particular form of obedience to this rather than that authority, in specific circumstances and in special ways and respects, is required of a being such as I am, situated in my particular place and time: for only by obeying in this way will I be fulfilling my 'function' in the harmonious realisation of the overall purpose of the universe.

Similarly other metaphysicians and theologians speak of the universe as the gradual unfolding in time of a 'timeless' pattern; or of human experience as a reflection, less or more fragmentary or distorted, of a 'timeless' or 'ultimate' reality, itself a harmonious system, wholly concealed, according to some, from the gaze of finite beings such as men; partially or progressively revealed, according to others. The political arrangements – and in particular those of obedience – derive from the degree of perception of social facts that the depth of understanding of this reality affords. But again there are those who have said that I must obey as I do because life would be intolerable to me unless a minimum of my basic needs are fulfilled, and a particular form of obedience is either a wholly indispensable, or else the most convenient and reasonable, method of securing this necessary minimum.

There is the celebrated school which affirms, still in answer to the same question, that there exist laws universally binding on all men, whatever their condition, called natural law, in accordance with which I am obliged to obey, and, alternatively, to be obeyed, by certain persons, in certain situations and respects. If I infringe this law (which according to Grotius even God cannot abrogate, since it flows from the 'rational', that is, logically necessary, 'nature of things' like the laws of mathematics or physics) I frustrate my own deepest wants and those of others; cause chaos; and come to a bad end. It is a corollary of this view that these basic require-ments – and the laws which make possible their satisfaction – neces-sarily spring from the purposes for which I was created by God or nature; hence the natural law is the law which regulates the harmonious functioning, each in its appointed fashion, of the components of the universe conceived as a purposive whole.

Closely related to and historically connected with this view is the doctrine that I possess certain rights, implanted in me by nature, or granted to me by God or by the sovereign, and that these cannot be exercised unless there is an appropriate code of laws enjoining obedience by some persons to others. This doctrine too may form part of a teleology – a view of the world and of society as composed of purposive entities in a 'natural' hierarchy – or it may be held independently, where 'natural rights' are conditioned by needs which spring from no discernible cosmic purpose, but are found universally as inescapable and ultimate parts of the natural world and the system of cause and effect, as Hobbes and Spinoza thought.

There is the equally famous doctrine that I am obliged to obey my king or my government because I have of my own free will promised, or because others have promised for me, that I shall obey and be obeyed according to certain rules, explicit or implicit; hence not to do so would be equivalent to going back on my undertaking, and that is against the moral law which exists independently of my undertakings. And there are many more answers with a long tradition of thought and action behind them. I obey because I am conditioned to obey as I am doing by social pressure, or by the physical environment, or by education, or by material causes, or by any combination or by all of these. I obey because it is right to do so, as I discern what is right by direct intuition, or moral sense. I obey because I am ordered to do so by the general will. I obey because to do so will lead to my personal happiness; or to the greatest happiness of the greatest number of other persons in my society; or in Europe; or in the world. I obey because in doing so I am fulfilling in my person the 'demands' of the world spirit, or the historical destiny of my Church or nation or class. I obey because I am spellbound by the magnetism of my leader. I obey because I 'owe it' to my family or my friends. I obey because I have always done so, out of habit, tradition – to which I am attached. I obey because I wish to do so; and stop obeying whenever I please. I obey for reasons which I feel but cannot express.

What all these celebrated historical doctrines, which are here set forth in an oversimplified form – almost in a Benthamite caricature – have in common is that they are answers to the same fundamental question, 'Why should men obey as, in fact, they do?' Some are also answers to the further question, 'Why *do* men obey as they do?', and some are not; but the answers to the former are not necessarily answers, or parts of the answers, to the latter question as well – their *raison d'être* is that they are answers to the first, the 'normative' question, 'Why should a man obey?' If the question had not presented itself in this way in the first instance, the answers, and the battles about them which are so great a part of the history of human thought and civilisation, would scarcely have taken the form they have. Hence its unique importance.

I have called the question normative, that is, a question requiring an answer of the form 'ought' or 'should', rather than descriptive, that is, answerable by '*x* is' or '*x* does this or that', but this distinction, now so deeply rooted as not to need elaboration, is scarcely noticeable before the middle of the eighteenth century. This fact is of crucial importance. For it rests on an assumption that is universal, tacit, scarcely questioned in all the centuries that preceded Kant, namely that all genuine questions must be questions about matters of fact, questions about what there is, or was, or will be, or could be, and about nothing else. For if they are not about the contents of the world, what can they be about? The perennial issues with which the great thinkers occupied themselves –

How was the world created? What is it made of? What are the
laws that govern it? Has it a purpose? What, if any, is the purpose
of men in it? What is good, what is permanent? What is real and
what is apparent? Is there a God? How does one know him? What
is the best way of living? How can one tell that one has discovered
the correct answers to any questions? What are the ways of
knowing what are the criteria of truth and error in thought, or of
right and wrong in action? – all such questions were, as often as
not, regarded as resembling one another in that they were all
enquiries about the nature of things in the world; and, furthermore,
as being of the same kind, ultimately, as such quite obviously
factual questions as: How far is Paris from London? How long
ago did Caesar die? What is the composition of water? Where were
you yesterday? What are the most effective means of becoming
rich, or happy, or wise?

Some of these questions seemed easier to answer than others.
Any well-informed person could tell you the distance between two
towns, or indicate how to set about answering the question for
yourself, or how to check the answers of others. It required more
knowledge and more technical skill to analyse water; perhaps still
more to discover how to make yourself or your community
prosperous; and only the greatest sages, armed with an immense
range of knowledge, and very exceptional moral and intellectual
gifts, perhaps special faculties – 'insight', 'depth', 'intuition',
'speculative genius' and the like – were thought capable of
acquiring even so much as a glimpse of the true answers to the
great but dark problems about life and death, about the vocation of
man, about the true purposes of human society, about truth and
error in thought and the right and wrong goals of action – the great
questions which had tormented thoughtful men in every generation. But no matter how unattainable the required range of
knowledge, or rare the special faculties without which these crucial
truths might remain for ever shrouded in darkness, the task was
assumed to be fundamentally similar to that of any other factual
enquiry, however humble. The questions themselves were more or
less intelligible to anyone with an enquiring turn of mind; the
answers might be enormously difficult to discover, but the
necessary data existed somewhere – laid in the mind of God, or in
the mysterious arcana of physical nature, or of some mysterious
region to which only a small number of privileged persons – seers
or sages – had access; or perhaps they might, after all, be

discoverable by systematic and coordinated labour conducted in accordance with the principles of this or that discipline – say, mathematics or theology or metaphysics – or perhaps of some empirical science.

However wide the disagreements about the attainability of such knowledge, or about the correct methods of investigation, one common assumption underlay the entire discussion; namely that no matter how complex a riddle might be, if it was genuine, and not simply a form of mental or verbal confusion, the answer to it – the one true answer – lay in a region in principle attainable, if not to men, then to angels; if not to angels, then to God (or to whatever omniscient entities atheists, or deists or pantheists, might appeal). The assumption entailed that every genuine question was genuine precisely in the degree to which it was capable of a genuine answer; the answer, to be 'objectively true', must consist in facts – or patterns of things or persons or other entities – which are what they are independently of thoughts, doubts, questions about them. At worst, being but finite, fallible, imperfect creatures, we may be doomed to eternal ignorance on the most essential issues; but the answers must be knowable in principle, even though we shall never know them; the solutions exist, as it were, 'out there' in the unknown regions, though we may never be allowed to see them: otherwise what is our enquiry *about*? What limits our knowledge? Of what does it fall short?

The issue on which for centuries, indeed since the Greeks had first raised it, everything turned was how to be sure where true wisdom lay. And wisdom, however gained – whether by learning or revelation or innate genius for obtaining the truth – consisted above all in comprehending the nature of the world – the true facts – and of man's place – and prospects – in it. The possessor of such knowledge was looked up to with hope and awe and placed high above the heads of conquerors or heroes, for he alone held the keys of the kingdom – could tell men how to live, what to do, and what would be their fate hereafter. Human and divine – Pythagoras, Socrates, Plato, Aristotle; the Stoics and Epicurean sages; Moses, the Buddha and Jesus, Muhammad, their apostles; and more lately Bacon or Descartes, Leibniz or Newton and their disciples – they knew the true facts.

It was like the search for the philosophers' stone in spiritual as well as material matters. There was no agreement about where the expert was to be found. Some looked for him in the Church, others in the individual conscience; some in metaphysical intuition, others in the simple heart of the 'natural' man; some in the calculations of mathematicians, others in the laboratory or in worldly wisdom or the mystic's vision. Somewhere the sage, the man who knew, was, at any rate in principle, capable of existing; if his views were true, those of his rivals were necessarily false – if only about what mattered most – and thus deserving of extermination by every possible means.

The great controversies of the seventeenth and eighteenth centuries between Catholics and Protestants, theists and sceptics, deists and atheists, intuitionists and empiricists – and within these camps themselves – for the most part derive from differences of view about where true knowledge was. Political wisdom was, above all, a matter of expertise, skill, the proper method of acquiring and applying the relevant information. The Jesuits taught, for example, that only the Roman Church could provide the true answer to the question whether it was right to obey a given government or sovereign, because it followed from the larger question of why man was created, by whom, and for what purpose, and what his duties were at any given point of his historical career; and that these questions – which were questions of theological fact – could be answered only by those who had expert knowledge of this province of human knowledge – in this case divinely appointed persons who, in virtue of their sacred office, were endowed with special knowledge inherited from their predecessors as well as unique powers of discriminating the truth in these matters.

Against this, various Protestant sects maintained that the proper solutions were not confined to the minds of a set of experts, linked by continuous historical tradition, but could be discovered in the heart of any Christian man attuned properly to hear the voice of God. Bossuet held that national traditions had a special part to play in the attainment of that state of mind in which men of various countries and ways of life had been vouchsafed by God a vision of the true facts of the case – each in the peculiar light with which their traditions irradiated the central single truth – and that the wills and actions of individual monarchs, in virtue of the peculiar functions with which they were endowed by God, were if anything surer indications of the divine will than the pronouncements of theological experts in the service of the Pope.[1] Spinoza,

[1] Referring to kings in a sermon on their duties delivered on 2 April 1662,

on the other hand, supposed that only individual human beings had wills and purposes, whereas the universe as a whole, not being a person, could have none; nor had it been created to serve God's purpose, for no personal creator, and so no divine tactic, knowable or inscrutable, existed. But men, being endowed with reason, could, if they patiently exercised it, and kept it unobscured by passions, presently perceive the connections which exist between everything that exists in the world; connections called 'necessary' because to be aware of them was not merely to be face to face with what there is, but also to grasp why everything was necessarily what it was, and where and as it was, in relation to everything else – not merely seemed to be, but really was. If you wished to know whom you should obey, and when, and under what circumstances and why, this could be discovered, like everything else, only by examining the facts in the light of reason. The faculty whereby we convinced ourselves of the truths of arithmetic and geometry, and realised not merely that $2 + 2 = 4$, but also that this could not be otherwise, would solve such other questions, also, as 'What is the life of reason?' and, *eo ipso*, what part obedience played in it.

Politics, like physics, was a matter of discovering the necessary connections between the components of the universe; and theological methods which disdained the use of logic and rational insight into the world of experience had led to much avoidable error. It was a factual enquiry; to be pursued not indeed by means of mere empirical observation, and precarious generalisation thereon, but by the superior weapon of that same rational insight which guaranteed the axioms from which followed the truths of mathematics. So Grotius thought, combining this notion of rational investigation with Roman and medieval and indeed biblical

Bossuet quoted 'Vous êtes des dieux!' ('You are gods!': Psalm 82: 6; cf. Exodus 22: 28): *Oeuvres complètes de Bossuet*, vol. 1 (Besançon, 1836), p. 507, col. 2. Louis XIV turned to the East, but his courtiers turned towards him. Authority, hierarchy, blind discipline, blind obedience and, to avoid bleak despair, renunciation – there was no other way to live in the vale of tears. If the King of France sells lands to the King of England or the King of Spain, what should his subjects think? They should say nothing and think nothing; they have no right to think. The King does as he wills with his own. This is the view of Jacques Esprit, who represents, admittedly, the extreme position. My point is that both this doctrine and the criticisms of it by defenders of the claims of natural law or the authority of the Church and of the Bible or men's desire for happiness are equally founded on an appeal to 'data'. There is disagreement about what the 'data' are, but not about the principle that only the evidence of facts can settle the issue.

traditions, that the reasons for obedience could be found in the existence of a law of nature – a set of axioms – rules – timeless and binding upon all men, which they might occasionally and for long periods forget, or misinterpret, or otherwise violate. But, whether observed or not, these axioms existed 'objectively', independently of human thought. It followed that the task of legislation was to make the existence of the natural law indubitably clear to the nations, and in particular to those who ruled them. Once the existence of this law had been recognised, the reason for obeying it required no further demonstration. Grotius, and for that matter Althusius and Pufendorf and the other great theorists of the natural law, Catholic and Protestant, speak as if it was self-evident that political rules and the rights and duties flowing therefrom were no less an actual ingredient of the world than other ingredients of it. What is required is the power of discovering their existence, and their definitive, authoritative description by reliable experts: as physicists and mathematicians were engaged in defining and describing the relations of entities in the physical world – which would make for a vast improvement of material life by invention and exploitation of nature – so jurists and political thinkers should be engaged in defining and describing the furniture of their politico-legal world. That 'Murder is wrong' (or 'Every man has the right to defend his life against attack') is as true a proposition about the world as that the earth is round. If the discovery and demonstration of the latter transforms navigation and geographical discovery and thereby provides for the necessities and amenities of material existence, there is no reason why the placing of political rules on an equally secure rational foundation should not similarly transform the social lives of men and societies. We must always seek for the facts. Facts are what they are: and when the truth about them has been discovered it must be formulated clearly. This alone will do much to secure us from the blunders due to previous ignorance or vanity. At best the application of the new knowledge will open rich, new kingdoms for our use and pleasure: physical knowledge will secure physical satisfactions; knowledge of moral and political facts, moral and political felicity on earth and rewards in heaven. Facts; generalised knowledge derived from them; accuracy – is all.

Indeed this seemed to flow quite naturally from the very notion that questions of morals and politics were genuine questions, as surely they were. For if they were genuine, then answers to them could be found only by the techniques of discovery proper to them. Opinions, as we have noted, conflicted as to what these techniques were. Thomists and Jesuits might differ from Occamites or Jansenists about the degree of reliance to be placed on the Aristotelian rationalism expounded by the doctrine of the Church: and still more with Calvinists or Lutherans about traditional interpretation as against the literal inspiration of sacred writings. But there is agreement about the major premiss from which all true demonstrations must begin: the undemonstrated and indemonstrable first axioms themselves rest ultimately on the testimony of faith in the word of God, as revealed in sacred texts to which a properly illuminated spirit – a properly instructed reason – gives 'natural', unforced, assent. Whereas Descartes or Grotius, or Leibniz and, at times, Locke too when dealing with the foundations of morality and political obligation, spoke of some species of intuitive insight into rational connections – 'necessities' whereby everything in the universe was held together and behaved as it did. Still others – very audacious spirits, Machiavelli or Hobbes – dared to ignore the theological implications, and suggest that the answers, concerned as they were, after all, primarily with the welfare of men in this world, were obtainable neither by faith nor by special insight but empirically; that is, by surveying, with such faculties of sense perception as we possessed, the actual behaviour of individuals and communities, together with such knowledge as might be obtained by introspection and imagination of the passions which moved them (and in the case of Hobbes, evidence gleaned from the discourse of physicists), and that no more was required to provide both sufficient knowledge (as certain as such information ever could be) of how things happen, and what was the proper course for a rational individual, who knew what he wanted, and observed how others had fared in the past and present.

It is natural enough that such wide divergences about the nature of man and the world, and above all about the right direction in which to look for answers to problems of behaviour, should have led to violent controversies, and indeed long and bitter wars, and caused deep and permanent divisions in Europe. But the most significant aspect of this situation for us is not the respect in which they disagreed but, on the contrary, that on which even the fiercest antagonists seemed agreed – the common basis which alone made the controversy possible. This common basis is that all true knowledge is descriptive: and depends for its validity upon correspondence with objectively existing 'facts'.

Ignorance, curiosity, doubt can be fully satisfied only by knowledge. Knowledge (it seemed plausible to suppose) must take the form of true propositions about the real world; moreover if the world was a harmonious system – and to suppose otherwise was 'contrary to reason' – the propositions must form a harmonious system too, and be (at least by an omniscient mind) capable of being inferred one from another, no matter where one begins. The 'rationalist' thinkers of the seventeenth century and their successors in the eighteenth believed precisely this. The science of sciences of that age of reason – mathematics – claimed to be able to achieve this great synthesis. It claimed to record real 'necessities' – the objective relations that constituted the structure of reality, of which the senses gave but a blurred, capriciously coloured, often delusive picture. To describe reality was the ambition of all human enquiry. A true account of things, truly to deserve that name, must in the first place be wholly intelligible: expressed in terms transparently clear, that is, definable in terms of those ultimate constituents of the world which can be inspected directly by a rational being, and, being simple – incapable of being further analysed – unable to delude or mislead. Secondly it must be capable of proof and not consist either of axioms so self-evident that to reject or doubt them would itself be a symptom of mental incapacity or derangement, or else of propositions deducible from those axioms by rules which are universally recognised as the laws of thought as such: the criteria of rational reflection. Thirdly it must be comprehensive – consist of propositions both general and necessary and equally applicable to all realms of enquiry; capable of leading the mind by logically rigorous, unassailably valid steps from any point in the system to any other.

Tested by these criteria empiricism lacked precision, rigour, system: and was at best a collection of loose impressions and rules of thumb, lacking exactness and logical connection, that could not reflect the nature of a systematic and harmonious reality; at best a first approximation to its inessential, fleeting, superficial aspects. Theology and the scholastic metaphysics related to it used terms which, on analysis, failed to correspond to anything in the realm of reason: and proved at best a solemn rhetoric or poetry or mythology, at worst so much meaningless verbiage; where its statements were intelligible they were too often demonstrably false.

Mysticism merely stammered incoherently about the ineffable: its insights could not be incorporated in rational discourse. History too, lacking definitions, proof, demonstrable laws of universal validity, failed to be a science, and yielded no certain truth. The central questions of ethics and politics, than which none were more crucial, must be capable of solutions as certain as those of physics. To suppose that final truth was less attainable in the great moral issues than in such spheres as those of astronomy or chemistry was unthinkable – contrary to all reason.

## II

That virtue is knowledge is one of the oldest of human doctrines. It has dominated Western philosophical thought from Plato to the present: and was not seriously questioned until a comparatively recent age. Opinion might differ as to what was virtue and what was knowledge, but the proposition connecting the two was not subject to doubt. Yet on the face of it this is a paradox: why should knowledge – of the fauna of Central Asia – or of stereoscopic geometry – make a man morally good, let alone be identical with such goodness? The more a man knows, the more effectively he can carry out wicked designs: criminals are surely more knowledgeable than kindly fools? But this view, according to the central tradition of European thought, is superficial and delusive, as vulgar and false as the corollary that virtue does not always pay. The good is that which alone will satisfy my rational nature – which seeks truth, happiness, reality; for this is what I mean by 'good'. All men seek – cannot help seeking – those ends. Attainment of them depends directly on knowing how to seek them. The criminal seeks them too, but mistakenly supposes that he will attain them by causing suffering to others, against the rules of morality. Mistakenly, because only by obeying the rules can a man hope to attain to what his nature seeks after. This is so because the rules themselves flow from the nature of things: to understand the nature of reality is to understand the reason for these absolute moral rules and principles, to defy them is to fly in the face of the nature of things and thereby inevitably cause inner conflict, frustration and misery. To obtain what one wishes one must know the truth about oneself and the world in which one lives: this knowledge will inevitably – as one understands oneself and the world more profoundly – alter one's desires: omniscience alone can guarantee that what one desires is wholly in accord with the nature of the world and oneself as part of it. If one flouts what knowledge one possesses – or fails to seek it – one will inevitably be punished: for reality will destroy one in the end. Ends are not chosen freely but given, for one's nature is what it is; and the question of what alone will fulfil it – that is, what is truly good – is one which only rational knowledge of the nature of things can answer: true knowledge alone can answer questions, fulfil desires, tell me why I am as I am and what I am to do and be in order to fulfil my proper function. Only if I know this can I fulfil it, and to fulfil it is to be realised, wise, happy and good: for all these finally coalesce.

Physics, astronomy, chemistry, optics were true sciences in that they described the composition and movements of bodies in space in a manner to satisfy the new standard of knowledge. Mathematical sciences were the paradigm of rational knowledge. Crucial questions dealing with human behaviour – moral, political, legal – must submit to the same unique discipline. Physical science described the world of matter. There must be created sciences of jurisprudence, ethics, politics to describe and explain the world of the spirit. Somewhere there must be discernible legal, moral, political 'atomistic' entities whose properties and behaviour the new mental and social sciences would identify, describe, explain, that is classify in terms of the laws they obey, discerned by reason. This was, in the context of the new sciences of the seventeenth and eighteenth centuries, a perfectly reasonable ideal: psychology, anthropology, philology, sociology, economics owe their origins to it. The triumph of one activity stimulated, often with valuable results, the creation of similar disciplines in other fields.

This occurred in the case of the descriptive human sciences. But ethics and politics have this peculiarity, that they ask not so much what exists in the world, as what ought to or should exist: what I ought to do; why I *should* obey. What kind of objects in the world could correspond to the answers to such questions? The propositions of physics described, or were believed to describe, events or bodies in principle accessible to some human faculty – rational intuition or the senses, depending on whether one adhered to a rationalist or empiricist doctrine. The propositions of geometry were held, however erroneously, to describe the properties of a real receptacle called space. The propositions of history, geography, geology, botany described – or claimed to describe, however insufficient the claim in the eyes of Cartesians – the behaviour of men in space and time, the configuration of earth and water, the behaviour of plants or minerals. But when ethical and political statements took normative forms – spoke in terms of 'ought' and 'should' and held up this or that character or action for imitation or avoidance – what entities in the external (or mental) world did they claim to describe? Did the world, in addition to men, things and relations – 'contingent' and 'necessary' – in addition to particular 'substances' and their 'attributes' and 'modes', also contain 'de-ontological values' as objective ingredients? 'Ought-facts' as well as 'is-facts'? Obligations and duties beckoning men on, or thundering at them, imperiously demanding to be fulfilled, and their contra-ries – uncommitted crimes and sins, terrifying men into flight or clamouring to be suppressed? Yet what were objective 'rights' if not such claims or demands floating in an ethical realm? What were the objective correlatives of the correct answers to the question 'Why should I obey the King?' if they were not objective ethical or political principles and rules of this queer sort, inhabiting the world alongside men and trees and tables – objective goals, innate purposes, ideals, enjoying an independent status of their own, exerting an influence – a compulsive pull on normally sensitive human beings, similar to the cruder, more sensuous attraction and repulsion exercised by persons or things upon their senses and minds and emotions?

Not until late in the eighteenth century did the news that all genuine questions – and therefore also 'normative' questions – must be answerable by descriptive statements verifiable by the existence of appropriate entities in the world begin to be superseded by the dawning realisation that certain questions, about what men should be or do, might differ logically from questions of fact; and that the methods of obtaining answers to them were in principle not like scientific enquiries, voyages of discovery, however peculiar and unique. It might be that not all questions entailed a search after some kind of hidden treasure which, as it were, existed in its own proper place, whether it was ever found or not. Not every question was a question of fact: normative statements were not descriptive, and if they were to be called true or false, this did not entail the existence somewhere – in nature or the human heart or the mind of God – of an objective analogue which could persist unperceived. Yet during the period in question, the paradox had not emerged. The great mechanical model dominated thought on all subjects. The great physicists, above all

Newton, had created a body of clear and coherent generalisations which described and foretold the behaviour of the physical world with hitherto unexampled precision and comprehensiveness. Theologians might protest that false metaphysical inferences had been drawn from the new science, in the form of materialism or atheism or other forms of unorthodoxy, but whatever was thought of their fears and warnings and outright attacks, the triumph remained a triumph. What had been discovered could not be undiscovered. The new knowledge had made it possible to do what could not be done before, to make inventions and discoveries which transformed human lives in every sphere. The theological implications might be perilous, but nothing succeeds like success, and the proof of the new methods lay in the splendid achievements, universally acknowledged, which they had made possible.

It might be that there were excellent metaphysical or theological reasons for supposing that God had created the world in seven days; that he had divided it into natural, that is mutually insulated, uncombinable, kinds, and that to each kind he had appointed its own peculiar purpose or end; and that the world represented the gradual unrolling of the pattern in the vast universal carpet, wherein each natural kind pursuing its own prescribed purpose, implanted in it by its maker, represented some indispensable element in the general design. Again it might be that human beings can obtain full happiness only from a sense of free unobstructed self-realisation, which in its turn depends upon being in harmony with the grand design of the universe; and that this is enhanced by a perception, however dim, by some inner faculty implanted by God, of what this design must be, and of one's part in it, which prevents one, if only in sheer hedonistic self-interest, from setting oneself against the fulfilment of one's proper task, which is bound to end in frustration and misery: for the universe is stronger than individuals in it. All that might be very true, and be much admired as expounded in the calm and beautiful prose of persuasive and eloquent preachers such as Bishop Butler or Archbishop Fénelon, or the well-wrought and equally sensible philosophical verse of Pope and his imitators. But mere general belief in the existence of a design or pattern, or the conviction that God would not be so cruel as to leave man devoid of a faculty of detecting it, does not provide the seeker after moral or political truth with a specific answer to his query; nor that degree of rational certainty which the more enviable physicists or mathematicians, and increasingly the astronomers or chemists, and even the biologists, had a right to claim on the basis of the concrete achievements – the accurate predictions, the calculations verified in observation – of their sciences.

This new, victorious, infallible method – would it yield results equally certain and revolutionary in the realms of morality and social life? In every age there tends to be a particular branch of enquiry whose success is so spectacular as to make it, for the time being, the ideal, a model to the relatively less progressive activities of its time. The multiplicity and contradictoriness of the answers to what, after all, was the most serious of human problems – how to live, how to organise communal life – and the confusion, unreason, fanatical dogmatism that accordingly prevailed, with the resulting injustice and misery, had become a grave and growing scandal in the eyes of men who felt justifiable pride in the stupendous, rapidly increasing sum of their knowledge in other realms. The powerful stream of reason which had cleansed the Augean stable of natural knowledge of the accumulated rubbish of the Middle Ages must be directed to the field of social life. Reason was indivisible: what had driven the forces of darkness from the realms of natural science would, given enough energy, application, genius, settle the problems of politics too, once and for all. This opinion grew as the eighteenth century progressed. All problems were either obsolete and by now meaningless survivals of self-blinded scholasticism, or else capable of being stated in clear terms and soluble once for all by scientific method.

Newton's mechanical model of nature fascinated the entire educated world as no other construction – not even the worlds of Darwin or Marx or Freud – ever did again. It affected not merely the conscious but the semi-conscious and unconscious modes of feeling and thought of its time, until ordinary language acquired new metaphors, drawn from mechanical and gravitational hypotheses, which ceased to be felt as metaphors and became an intrinsic part of it, one of the surest signs of the transformation of an entire outlook within a society. The old dogmatic truths about the nature of the universe and its purposes, and the part that man played within it, were plainly incompatible with the findings of the new science. It was clear enough where victory would lie: 'le tribunal suprême & qui juge en dernier ressort & sans apel de tout ce qui nous est proposé, est la Raison'.[1] Bayle's celebrated words became

---

[1] loc. cit. (p. 17 above, note 2).

the battle cry of the entire century. Either the world was created in seven days or it was not. Either man possessed an immortal soul, a spark of the divine flame which would rejoin its source upon the death of its bodily dwelling – being an entity not subject to the laws which govern matter in space – or else no such thing existed. Either men were endowed with special spiritual faculties which afforded them knowledge – or at least a presentiment – of a world more real than the earthly scene of their daily lives, or they did not. Either they were fallen creatures, weak, vicious and purblind, capable of creating anything of enduring value not by their own unaided efforts, but only by the grace of God, whether at the hands of his Church, or by a direct relationship with him, or this was neither true nor, if properly considered, intelligible. Either the sole way to discover the difference between good and evil, between right and wrong, was to understand what part it was intended that men should play in the great drama of existence, conceived and executed in the timeless mind of the divine playwright, and imparted by myths and parables, as well as direct revelation and the evidences which could be gleaned from the observation of nature by sages with minds open to glimpses of the infinite; or it was enough to conceive of nature as a set of events occurring in repetitive patterns, which patient observation, supplemented by experiment and inspired conjectures, could unfold; such natural knowledge, systematised in the precise manner lately made possible by the advances in mathematics, would take the form of laws whereby the future could be predicted, the present summarised, and the past reconstructed – a picture in which the human body and its sensations obeyed mechanical laws and played no unique part in any irreversible, non-repetitive, purposive process given value or meaning by an omnipotent creator. Both sets of beliefs could not be true; and those who, like Descartes and his followers (not excluding Leibniz), attempted to have it both ways were led into obscurities and inconsistencies that a later age did not hesitate to expose.

Newton escaped, largely because he did not demand logical links between his theological speculations and his physical theories. Efforts were made to reach a reasonable compromise. Perhaps one could try, without positively denying such central tenets of Athanasian theology as original sin, or the prospect of eternal damnation, or the absolute difference between, and the mysterious union of, the immaterial soul and the material body, the infallibility of the literal inspiration of the Bible or of its authorised expounders, at any rate not to lay violent emphasis on them. One might, perhaps, without actually rejecting these beliefs, let them fall into the background, and stress those positive and optimistic aspects of rational Christian theology which offered least resistance to the new scientific picture, especially if its lines were not too sharply drawn. It was nature, rather than direct verbal revelation, that constituted the principal language through which God spoke to his creatures. His purposes could be discerned best by the study of his works, which are everywhere about us, and by listening to the dictates of the voice of God within us, two sources of knowledge which, if properly interpreted, can never return different answers. The sciences might tell us *how* things happened, but they could never say *why* – to serve what purpose, for the sake of what ultimate end – they were made to function as they did; and unless we knew this too, we were condemned for ever to be the blind playthings of forces the need for which we did not understand, when all the while a supernatural source of light (revealing the divine purpose and the relation to it of our faculties – and of the properties of beasts, plants and inanimate objects) was to be found both within and outside us, adding immeasurably to the scattered and broken information provided by the senses, and by deductive reason, and never in conflict with them, if only we did not perversely close our eyes to it.

This was the kind of compromise adopted in varying degrees by the philosophical Broad Church English divines – including men of authentic genius like Butler and Berkeley – the theological friends of reason, the enemies of violent enthusiasm and obscurantism and religious irrationalism, which had wrought destruction half a century before, leaving wounds some of which were not wholly healed yet. This, too, was the kind of conciliatory view propagated by the mild philosophers who followed Leibniz, and offered many a compromise between reason and faith. Thus Christian Wolff taught, for example, that miracles were due solely to a superhuman understanding of nature – of the familiar nature of normal life. Thus Christ converted water into wine because he was a greater chemist than Boyle (or any finite creature), and understood and used the unalterable laws of nature, and appeared to suspend them only to our limited intellects. By similar reasoning most of the seeming contradictions of faith and science could, it was hoped, be reconciled.

Something of the same tone is to be found among the Cambridge Platonists, and the intuitionists who followed Shaftesbury or Hutcheson. Grotius' natural law is sometimes a set of rules intuited by a species of metaphysical insight; sometimes discovered to exercise a universal sway by quasi-empirical observation of actual societies. Pufendorf's view of the sacredness of compacts is sometimes a dogma: at other times a utilitarian argument. Such hybrids, and two-faced concepts, on the border between the metaphysical and the empirical, are characteristic of an age which saw the slow passing away of theology as the queen of the sciences, and the real lawgiver and ultimate source of political as well as personal morality. Locke is perhaps the most characteristic of all those who, from the Renaissance to our own day, neither confront these incompatible principles nor deny them, but try to see them as different faces of the same truth, putting their trust, like Lessing and his friends, in the general effects of time, toleration and the good sense of men.

This precarious compromise was not destined to survive. In England and in Northern Europe in general the Protestant Churches, during the eighteenth century, in their very constitutions represented a triumph of moderation, a compromise between the ancient order and the demands of a new and therefore critical social class. But in France, the most civilised of European States, the Church did not temporise: it fought for its power and indeed increased it, at the cost of a precipitous fall in its moral and intellectual prestige; and the radical intellectuals, largely under the influence of Voltaire (whose life and writings probably liberated a greater number of human beings than those of any man in recorded history), proceeded at first to a cautious and moderate scepticism, and attacked only the more violently irrational superstitions and most glaring social and political injustices and absurdities; but gradually with growing originality and courage began to enquire whether the new science, which was proceeding from triumph to triumph, did in fact leave the doctrines of the Church either relatively unaffected, as its most full-blooded representatives still proclaimed, or, as its more moderate apologists so persuasively maintained, in need of no more than a mild series of reformulations to make a peaceful condominium with science possible.

The question was not, indeed, new. Hobbes had shown startling originality in the previous century, and had, in effect, before Hume, in all but name relegated metaphysics and theology to the rubbish heap, as either irrelevant or unintelligible; and had constructed his picture of society, its constituents, laws of development and needs, by analogy with the physical model of nature which the Cartesians had constructed. But if his approach was deemed correct, his conclusions seemed to the free spirits of the eighteenth century, in the light of common observation of mankind, and in particular of English political experience, too pessimistic. Perhaps even he had not emancipated himself quite completely from the Christian belief in original sin, which had led him to depict man as being by nature greedy, brutish and violent, restrained from injuring other men only by fear. Fear on the part of the weak many before the ambitious and powerful few had, in Hobbes's theory, led to the foundation of societies, in which by the conferring of absolute authority on the absolute ruler, and by his use of the threat of ferocious sanctions, the wild beast in man was caged and sufficiently tamed and trained, and his pride and fear harnessed, to make a minimum degree of social cooperation possible. But in the eighteenth century the rising faith in the speedy improvement of the human lot by the proper application of the new physical sciences – the march of reason which nothing seemed able to arrest – made Hobbes's grim estimate of human prospects seem perversely gloomy. The last years of Louis XIV had been filled with bigoted persecution of all heterodoxies; and the sense of relief which followed that monarch's death in France created a mood in which it seemed that all that was needed for a better life was the removal of the burdens and obstacles imposed by a fanatical cruel despot and an ignorant and rapacious Church. If only the Court, the priests, the corrupt nobility and oppressive bureaucracy would cease to stifle those mental and moral capacities whose liberation in England had led to such brilliant and beneficent results, a political, economic, moral and artistic renaissance would lift France high above the heads of other nations. It was hard to reconcile the existence and the power of natural human benevolence, and the persuasiveness of reason, once it is permitted to state its case clearly and openly, with Hobbes's black picture of human life in a state of nature, as having been 'solitary, poor, nasty, brutish and short';[1] for from something so devoid of humanity it was scarcely possible, by however many removes, to have reached that state of toleration and political freedom, that firm foundation

[1] *Leviathan* (1651), part 1, chapter 13.

for civil liberty and civic harmony, which was the glory of free English society in the eighteenth century. It was in England that the sciences had so notably advanced: in England that so little resistance to the advance of reason was offered by her national Church, in contrast to the fanaticism with which the Church of Rome was still repressing the efforts at enlightenment in France and Southern Europe and the Americas. Hobbes had surely proceeded upon a set of prejudiced assumptions; and while professing to observe nature, had made man too much in his own terror-stricken image. The example of Hobbes's own admirable compatriots, with their moderate and skilful constitution with its checks and balances, their sober and rational temper, their love of liberty, their civilised and tolerant outlook, their success in the arts of peace, had served to confute his psychological theory. It is not nature but vicious education – prejudice, superstition, poverty, ignorance, idleness of body and mind – that was responsible for Hobbes's subhuman creatures; an impartial study of men, with evidence from history, from the condition of the lately discovered natives of remote countries, untouched by the vices of Europe, might lead to very different conclusions.

How had Galileo, Kepler, Harvey, Newton, Boyle, Huyghens, Leuwenhoek, and lately Buffon, reached their indestructible conclusions? By observation, by the formulation of general laws and hypotheses, by the verification of these by experiment. This same method, then, whose application involves no occult faculties, and whose conclusions can be checked by any reasonably intelligent man who will take enough trouble, can be applied to the realm of politics. As physics tries to discover the laws of the empirically accessible external world, so morals and politics is the science of an equally accessible world of human relations: it must describe them, and find out the laws under which they operate. If politics is a form of knowledge it has precisely the same relation to social facts as chemistry has to molecules or atoms. Locke had preached this[1] but had not attempted to apply it systematically to the

---

[1] There is a marked reluctance among Locke's French and Italian followers to admit that in matters of morals and religion (and politics too) the master relied on those very intuitions of absolute a priori truths, such as natural rights, and the absolute difference between right and wrong, which it was his most notable achievement to have excluded from his theory of the knowledge of the external world. But since his conclusions were correct and led him to favour toleration and defend civil liberties, and since his position owed so much to Newton's reflected

analysis of morals and social life. His disciple Helvétius, who of all the social and political thinkers of the eighteenth century was the most honest, thorough, clear-headed and consistent – and with his reckless ally La Mettrie, and Holbach and his disciple Bentham, happily marched to the farthest lengths to which reason seemed to drive him – attempted to carry out precisely this programme. This conclusion was inescapably entailed by the unexamined assumption of the century: that all true knowledge is in some way descriptive; that politics and morals are a form of knowledge or they are nothing; and must consequently set out to look for – and isolate – specifically moral and political facts to verify their statements and their laws.

Man is an object in nature no less than plants or stones; whatever his differences from non-human species, they must be capable of being observed, classified and correlated in such a manner that it is possible to formulate general laws to describe and predict human behaviour. Unlike other species, man has purposes; will and intellect and emotions, and perhaps other faculties as well. How, then, can sciences adjusted to inanimate matter or the behaviour of non-rational animals be made to apply to him? The French thinkers of whom I am speaking did not consider this objection grave. If such purposive and elaborately organised communities as those of ants or beavers were susceptible to treatment by the sciences of zoology or physics, human society, merely because it is more complex, offers no insuperable obstacle. We must no longer ask why man is created, or for what purpose, for it is more than doubtful whether he was created for a purpose, or indeed created at all. The question of what was man's function or end, what instrument a man or a group of men was appointed to play in the cosmic orchestra, what part an individual or a Church, a country or a nation had had assigned to them in the divine drama, was senseless if there was neither play nor playwright, neither orchestra nor conductor – if, in fact, these notions were mere figments of poetical imagination, conceived during man's barbarian childhood, with no evidence in their support. And by a similar reasoning the question *why* a man should obey this or that State, this or that ruler, could not be formulated in terms of spiritual authority, to which unquestioning obedience had to be rendered for reasons

glory, the presence in his system of a large layer of the scholastic and Cartesian a priori metaphysics was, on the whole, politely overlooked.

independent of empirical observation or scientific, logically valid, methods. No supernatural sanction for anything could be admitted when the very concept of it, whether analysed in Cartesian or empirical terms, seemed devoid of clear meaning. Catholics had disputed with Protestants and with heretics in their own midst – and for that matter with Jews and Muslims and pagans too – the validity of their source of knowledge of the ways of God, and of men's duties towards him and towards each other 'in him' and 'under him'; and these disputes, which had involved the whole of the civilised world in almost continuous bloodshed and misery, turned out to be a dispute about nothing at all – nothing but the product of ignorance, fear and weakness and the unscrupulous exploitation of these by cunning and ambitious knaves, clad in royal or priestly garments.

Grotius had spoken in terms of the ancient Roman and medieval concept of the law of nature, *jus naturale*: a set of rules of conduct so powerful and authoritative that even God himself could not alter or abolish them. Montesquieu had laid it down that human laws should be 'les rapports nécessaires qui dérivent de la nature des choses',[1] 'necessary relationships which derive from the nature of things'. This 'nature', these 'things', are susceptible to empirical examination: they include such factors as climate and soil, local customs and psychological differences of national character, and other accessible data. But from these, laws must somehow be 'derived': if we understand the purpose for which men were created, we can so adjust the laws that they promote this purpose best in the given environment and applied to the given national or tribal characteristics; and because these environmental and social and psychological factors vary in the world, the laws will vary correspondingly.

But what is this purpose? How do we discover it? Is it, too, an empirical datum? And if so, where must we look for it? Descartes, Grotius, to some degree Montesquieu too, seem to believe in some 'rational' faculty which reveals it: reveals the absolute end or goal of man as such, whence *jus naturale* – an equally absolute set of rules – logically flows. And this seems identical with the theological doctrine that there are within man certain innate principles – that if only he will look within his heart he will find within it precepts of absolute validity which his maker has inscribed therein

[1] *De l'esprit des lois*, book 1, chapter 1.

for his guidance: that there is, in short, a faculty, unique, infallible, confined to rational beings alone and necessarily proof against any obstacles which empirical experience may throw up, which tells us how to live, what to do, what best satisfies the goal which we have not invented but discovered within ourselves, set for us by some agency in some sense outside ourselves: God or nature. This is the 'nature des choses', and the 'rapports nécessaires' are deducible from the way in which we fit into the system of ends or goals imposed upon us by the demiurge. We have, in effect, returned to the image of the orchestra, the play: the doctrines whether of Grotius or of Montesquieu, for all their non-teleological appearance, are unintelligible save in a world conceived as a purposive process; and no doubt in the hundred years which lie between Descartes and Condorcet it was only men of very exceptional capacity for independent thought – a Hobbes, or a Spinoza – who could even so much as conceive of a world which did not, albeit 'immanently', impersonally, embody a purpose – let alone the near-meaninglessness of this notion for empiricists of any order: for impersonal 'purposes', immanent or otherwise, are not the kind of data which observation or experiment discover. And yet, as we shall see, even the boldest materialists of the eighteenth century, who thought themselves completely emancipated from all the metaphysical and theological 'rubbish' of their fathers, had by no means freed themselves from their obsessively teleological categories, which mingle very queerly with their fierce empiricism.

But they begin bravely enough – the new, *révolté* followers of Newton and pure science, the generation whose faith was undermined by the mild scepticism of Bayle and Locke, and finally exploded by Voltaire. They begin by rejecting all save what the sciences guarantee as real: nothing that a man cannot observe, or infer from what he observes, or imagine in terms of what he observes, can be knowledge. Observation is the only criterion which can preserve us from the wild fantasies, the absurd doctrines, which have bedevilled our ancestors, for nothing should be believed without evidence, and all evidence comes from experience. Let us then observe the world in which we live with the cold, keen, unbiased eye of the natural scientist, who expects neither good nor evil from his data, and looks at them neither with hope nor fear, but solely as data, as collections within which he seeks to find an order; seeking to describe this order, not because it is good or bad, interesting or dull, but because it exists, and is the beginning and the end of knowledge. Individuals and societies must be studied like stones and trees, beavers or bees. And until we have discovered what men are like in their various species, why they do what they do, how they came to be what they are, what they can and what they cannot do, and how this comes about; until we have amassed observations and formulated the general laws similar to those of physics or biology – until then, all that we say, our theology and metaphysics, remain either worthless fantasy or haphazard guess-work, vague, crude, unreliable, unorganised; opinions founded on no scientific evidence, shot through with prejudice, superstition and emotion, casting at most feeble light, more often clouds of darkness, upon the subjects they touch.

This point of view is not wholly new. In earlier centuries, when nature was believed to be divided into separate realms – God and angels, man and beast, form and matter, body and soul – these heterogeneous orders clearly required wholly different methods of cognition. The supernatural realm was approached humbly, with the faltering steps of human theology; the human soul could be investigated only in the light of an inner sense, a kind of spiritual self-absorption, and the evidence of the physical senses was considered to be irrelevant to the vision within. It was the greatest and most grotesque of all errors and insults to man's divine origin to treat him as if he were a natural object wholly determined in his bodily behaviour, as well as in his thoughts and wishes and imaginative life, by forces which could be studied by the natural sciences. There had indeed existed ancient philosophers, Epicureans and other atomists, who had approached this position very nearly, but the light of Christian revelation and learning had made an end of them, it had been hoped, for ever. Yet this ancient heresy was very like the doctrine and methods which the new school of social thinkers were upholding. They did not merely maintain it as a principle, they applied it and they published their findings.

Let us consider two of its most vigorous and celebrated exponents. Helvétius, in his two most famous works, expounded this doctrine, which, since his day, has scarcely ever looked back; opposed, fought, 'refuted' over and over again, it has merely grown in influence, and that not merely in its later sophisticated form, but in the crude format of its creators. No setback but was followed by a longer advance, and today it is perhaps the most powerful single view which, though they may sometimes deny it, unites individuals and parties and nations who are otherwise in the most violent disagreement. Holbach was less concerned with the propagation of the positive doctrine than with defence of it against its enemies. He spent his long and dedicated life in trying, and stimulating others – the members of his celebrated salon, where such ideas were born and ceaselessly discussed – to destroy the adversaries of the new scientific truth: obscurantism, superstition, political and social prejudice, oppression of individuals, arbitrariness, distrust of the sciences, but above all, and first and foremost, religion in all its forms – every Church, every faith – which he regarded, more strongly perhaps than any man before or after him, as the source of almost all unhappiness and evil in the world.

The doctrine is clear and simple, but as it is expressed in published writings and in the recorded conversations of the *Holbachiens* perhaps too simple. Man is a combination of molecules – bones, blood, tissue, water – played upon by the selfsame physical forces as govern everything else in the world. He is by nature neither as good as theologians imagine him before the Fall, nor as bad as they maintain he has become after it, if by 'good' is meant what all rational men had always known it to mean – the tendency to seek by rational means the happiness of themselves and of others – and by 'bad' the opposite of this. Indeed the meaning of these central notions has been perverted by the bad men in power – kings, captains, priests – in order to dupe innocent human beings into piously accepting unhappy, and even brutish, forms of life, useful only to their masters and exploiters. All human misery, all injustice, all crime and folly spring from two sources only: ignorance and fear. And these can be destroyed in one way only: by the increase and dissemination of true knowledge. Vast strides have been made in the regions of the natural sciences by the application of Newtonian methods, and it is now the turn of the science of man. Locke has given us a very satisfactory psychological analysis of the working of the mind in its acquisition of knowledge about the external world and itself: the same method must now be applied to social problems. First the phenomena must be described; then analysed into their ultimate sensible constituents – those final atomic particles whose movement in space is responsible for all that is and occurs.

Helvétius claims to have done just this in his analysis of the behaviour of individuals in society: and reports that he finds that there is only one hypothesis which explains all human action in every possible circumstance; and this is the desire for pleasure and avoidance of pain. Everywhere and always men have sought and seek and doubtless will seek personal happiness; have avoided, avoid, will avoid all forms of pain: all human acts, institutions, habits, moral and political characteristics can be deduced from this single principle. If he has appeared to seek other things (or avoid them) it is because he has deceived himself or been deceived by others either deliberately, or as a result of their own ignorance and confusion. The constituents of happiness may differ for different peoples and individuals in accordance with their age or society or geographical or physical condition. Montesquieu was quite right to notice the differences of ideals and values and forms of life between different peoples, and to trace these mainly to differences in natural conditions such as climate, types of soil, or in national tradition, but he was mistaken in thinking that different groups of men seek radically different goods; there is but one thing that men seek – and call good when they seek it – and that is happiness. The means towards it, and therefore the kinds of states or objects thought good, will differ in accordance with temper, circumstances and historical development; but what is good about them is always one aspect of them and one only: they render – or are thought to render – those who seek for them happy and contented. Why they should do so is a matter for physics or biology or psychology. The moralist and political philosopher is concerned with establishing the nature of the good – what it 'really' is – as the physicists established the true nature of 'matter' or 'motion'. The enquiry is factual, and the answer, after many centuries of error and darkness and unnecessary suffering, clear at last. Good and bad are what a man fully cognisant of all the relevant facts would regard as such; and he would regard as such only what he supposed would make him happy or unhappy respectively. That is what he would call good and bad, and has always so called, despite all the disguises and distortions perpetrated upon him by ignorance and folly in their favourite disguises of theology, metaphysics and law. As for happiness, everyone knows to some degree what that is, at least in his own case; and if he does not know, the progress of knowledge can – and will – illuminate him.

This (whatever its disguises) naturalistic and utilitarian doctrine occurs in at least two distinct forms: a *de facto* mechanistic form, and one that appeals to the commandment of nature or 'nature's God'. The first form is modelled upon the physical description of the external world. Its laws are causal uniformities, and a rational being, being part of it, and seeking what he cannot help but seek – harmony, happiness – will reject the fictions of religion and metaphysics or unenlightened 'common sense' and use his new-found knowledge to devise the most effective means to secure his purposes. This is the view of Bentham, of his masters Helvétius and Hobbes, of Hume, on the whole; and of a good many nineteenth-century positivists and empiricists. But the majority of the *philosophes* sought to justify their doctrine by appeal to nature. Despite the extreme looseness and ambiguity with which the term is used – we are told by at least one painstaking researcher that no fewer than sixty senses of this most spellbinding of all symbols can be distinguished in the usage of the eighteenth-century thinkers – the general notion is not in doubt. Nature is more than the sum of things and the laws they in fact obey. It is also a harmonious system, each ingredient of which is designed by it – for it is conceived as an active force or principle – to play its own unique role in the fulfilment of the general design. Reason – natural light – is a synonym for insight into the design: its rules or command-ments are those which tell one how best to fulfil one's own proper part in the general design. Unlike mechanical laws, they can be disobeyed, but only at the cost of being defeated, sooner or later, by the natural order, which is infinitely stronger than those who seek to disturb it. All that we are – our flesh and spirit – our organs, faculties, ideas, feelings, actions – has been fashioned by nature (or the Deity, with which it is often identified) to fulfil her purposes: to use them in ways contrary to these purposes is to pervert them; in the end to bring ruin on oneself. Such notions as natural law, natural rights, the code of nature, the discovery of solutions, 'in accordance with natural principles', to aesthetic, economic, social, psychological problems, derive from an unques-tioned teleological assumption that all things belong to an unalterable order, some 'higher' than others in the hierarchy, and develop along lines, or in pursuit of inner purposes, 'implanted' in them from birth.

Natural law is the minimum of rules without observing which men cannot long continue to fulfil their proper ends as men – without which they would lose human semblance, lose those properties which alone make them men and alone enable them to survive, communicate, cooperate, achieve anything in common.[1]

[1] The difference between laws in the sense of inexorable regularities and laws in the sense of man-made enactments is necessarily blurred in any teleological

Natural rights are the minimum without which a man cannot fulfil his proper part in the design. The economic programme of the physiocrats claimed not to invent anything new, only to transcribe for all to see the system of economic relationships (and the actions designed to promote and maintain them) which nature had laid down: by adopting which men would readjust themselves into the general harmony to which they had been rendered blind by ignorance or prejudice or vice, and which could be discovered by watching nature at work. *Laissez-faire* is the invocation to let nature 'take her course' without artificial hindrance, and heal social ills as she more obviously does those of the human body: physicists (or economic experts) are needed only to rectify deviations from the proper natural path; to bring the organism back to its normal, that is natural, function – not to set it on some new path of its own.

Opinions differed very widely as to how nature's purposes were best discerned, for she seems to speak to different thinkers with such very different voices: saying to some (Voltaire, Montesquieu, Holbach) that inequality was part of her order, and ineradicable; to others (Rousseau) that inequality was a sin against her; preaching Spartan austerity to Mably, but rewards commensurate with abilities to Helvétius; strict communism to Morelly or Babeuf, but the sacredness of private property to Locke, Voltaire and Condorcet; *laissez-faire* to the physiocrats, but complete State control to Mably; the progress of the arts and sciences to Diderot and d'Alembert, their dangerous and degrading effect to Rousseau; democracy to Rousseau, but enlightened oligarchy to the Encyclopaedists; despotism and atheism to Holbach and republicanism to Robespierre. Indeed the tender-minded Rousseau no less than the tough-minded Bentham complained that no criteria for discovering the true desires of nature seemed to be in use: every social reformer claimed for his own pet scheme the authority of 'nature', whose inner purpose he claimed a unique capacity of divining. Bentham scoffed at the entire enterprise as dishonest metaphysical mystification. But Rousseau denounced the false prophets because they usurped a right that was his alone: nature did speak, but he alone heard her voice clear and strong; and could tell others how to learn to listen and obey. His polemic against the babel of voices all

system: laws of nature are both rules which we flout to our inevitable cost, and the causal uniformities which govern our behaviour and are therefore the basis for the rules.

claiming to speak for nature is acute, entertaining and convincing until one realises that he is like the lunatic who rejects the claims of other inmates of his asylum to be Napoleon because he himself is Napoleon.

But whichever form the doctrine takes – whether mechanistic or teleological or, as most often of all, an inconsistent mixture of the two – certain presuppositions are common to both: the true ends of life are given – either as a psychological compulsion ('One cannot help desiring pleasure and pleasure alone', 'All men desire power') or as the wish of God or nature; these ends are discoverable by the proper faculty – reason or instinct or observation; the ends of legislation and education are to cause men's lives to be lived in pursuit of these objectively discoverable ends; they and they alone justify coercion, establishment of rules of orthodox behaviour, eliminating heresy, for where true knowledge is obtainable, of universal validity for all men, error should be extirpated, and opinion be replaced by unquestioning certainty. Nature – whether in the form of scientific infallibility or a quasi-personified source of faith and illumination – can be a tyrant as crushing and ruthless as a Church or divine leader. This remains concealed only while her adherents remain a minority and an opposition.

If nature is a harmonious whole, why is it that one man's happiness often seems incompatible with that of another, that there is a struggle for wealth, power, existence itself in which the virtuous are often defeated and ruined? No doubt nature is at times niggardly of her goods, and endows her children with her blessings, whether material benefits or natural endowment, in very unequal degree; but she has also given them the very means to overcome such obstacles: reason, inventiveness, knowledge of good and evil. Man's own ignorance and folly are responsible for his misfortunes. It is true that men differ in physical and mental gifts, in the natural environment in which they live, in what they inherit from their predecessors. But the key to happiness does not necessarily lie in uniformity. The ideal condition of mankind is a complicated pattern into which very dissimilar components fit, each in its proper place and time, as dictated by reason – which is precisely the understanding of the parts and how and why they fit in the harmonious whole. Views as to what this pattern is may differ: but according to one view of it, at least, inequality is of the very essence of it. Unless the most gifted, those best equipped by skills, technical, political, psychological, moral, and by knowledge – sciences built on the reliable basis of observed facts – are set over others to rule them, society will founder: or at the very least be exposed to much preventable conflict and misery. There is a solution to social problems, as to all other real problems clearly conceived: tragedy, whether in personal or public life, is not an unavoidable consequence of man's imperfection, for man is infinitely perfectible, but to errors due to avoidable blindness about what happiness is and how to obtain it. Demand for unqualified equality as uttered by democrats, or insistence on the supreme virtue of altruistic self-sacrifice as advocated by Christian preachers, may turn out to be as irrational and productive of misery as the claims of obvious knaves or fools. The ideal society is a jigsaw puzzle and the problem is what it is, and how this or that person or group fits into it.

There were several celebrated solutions, all of which presuppose this doctrine. Thus Adam Smith maintained that all interests, if rationally pursued, automatically coincide; and fail to do so only when interfered with by clumsy, stupid or ill-intentioned persons or associations of persons (often incorporated in institutions) ignorant of the true laws of economic life. These laws are the laws of nature: if they are observed – that is to say, if men pursue their interests rationally – human activities will not frustrate but complement one another. Adam Smith's notorious 'invisible hand',[1] which harmonises all the apparent discrepancies, and guarantees that all individual felicities necessarily combine in a harmonious whole, is only a dramatic way of saying that to be rational is to want and be able to fit into the pattern offered by nature. This is natural law as transposed into the economic sphere by the physiocrats; the *laissez-faire* doctrine according to which the good of one man can, in principle, not clash with the good of another: for good cannot conflict with good. Such widely admired authors as Mercier de la Rivière and Le Trosne are perpetually intoning the formula that laws are not made but discovered: for they are given, eternal truths, waiting like the laws of physics only to be revealed and promulgated: that is why there exists legislation, not legisfaction.

[1] *The Theory of Moral Sentiments* IV 1. 10, p. 184 in the Glasgow Edition (Oxford, 1976); *An Enquiry into the Nature and Causes of the Wealth of Nations* IV ii 9, p. 456 in the same edition (Oxford, 1976). Cf. *Essays on Philosophical Subjects*, 'History of Astronomy' III 2, p. 49 in the same edition (Oxford, 1980).

Other variants of this view were very widespread: for example, (*a*) that one man's satisfaction can never be complete unless other individuals are happy too, since if they are not, this will breed social discontent, and thereby hamper, interfere with and generally distress him. Benevolence is part of the 'natural' constitution of rational man: and altruism, therefore, is the only dependable road to egoistic satisfaction. Or one might hold the slightly different view (*b*) that human beings are in fact endowed with an imaginative faculty – let us call it sympathy – whereby one human being is made automatically happy by the spectacle of the happiness of another; derives pleasure, in other words, from perceiving that others are happy, without deriving any other benefit from this. Hence altruism is itself a species of egoistic pursuit of happiness; for all pleasures are ultimately self-regarding. Hence the cement that binds society together is natural sympathy, solidarity and the calculation that my happiness cannot be achieved either in solitude or in the midst of the miseries of others, and not Hobbes's mutual suspicions and mutual fears. This optimistic premiss, shared by such diverse thinkers as Shaftesbury, Hutcheson, Holbach, and in some moods Hume, was not, however, universally held: and there were those who taught that even if the optimistic assumption is false, even if some men are intrinsically malicious – take pleasure in the pains of others – this can be eradicated by the application of scientific principles to the management of men. We know by empirical observation – the source of all light – what it is that man desires; all that is left is to find out how to satisfy him, and that is a matter of technological progress, scientific discovery, and invention in every realm of human existence.

There are three main forces, according to the leading materialists, that mould men: physiological structure, material environment and the influence of other human beings. By environment are meant all the physical, geographical, climatic and economic processes and objects that surround men from birth, and the results of the interplay of these with their physical and mental properties. The theologians of all faiths, and metaphysicians, whether they follow Aristotle or Leibniz, are equally mistaken: the new-born child has no 'spiritual propensities'; as for the immortal non-sensible soul with its own empirically unobservable constitution, that is a scarcely intelligible figment designed to obscure the problem, not to solve it. What a man becomes he becomes as a result of his environment and the influences of other men. Man is infinitely plastic: if you reproduce the conditions in which Newton was born and reared, you can create a second Newton; and if you could transform a Doctor of the Sorbonne into the physical shape of a dog (said Diderot, a little ironically), he would behave like one; and vice versa. The only innate tendency he has is to seek happiness. Education is responsible for the form which this natural passion takes. Education – conceived almost in its modern form of social conditioning – can make a man a hero or a traitor, a sage or a halfwit. But education alone is not enough in the existing state of society, where the educators themselves are not perfect, being themselves creatures malformed by so much ignorance, stupidity and vice on the part of the earlier generations. Moreover, until society is composed of persons of perfect wisdom and virtue and efficiency, environmental and human pressures will be too great for the results of mere education, however strict, to be sufficient to resist them. Hence legislation is required, firstly to cause men to want those things which are in fact good for them (that is, will make them happy), and to avoid those things which they may, indeed, desire, but which, science shows us, will in fact make them miserable; and secondly to integrate the conflicting purposes of differing individuals into a single social policy.

Virtue is the tendency to promote happiness; vice to destroy it. 'Whose happiness?', it may be asked; if interests clash how are they 'integrated'? Helvétius is quite clear: if at a great financial sacrifice to myself I get an assassin (who happens to be related to me) off the gallows, my family will bless me but the 'public good' is damaged; if I appoint the most deserving candidate to a public post and not my own kinsman, my family will blame me but the society is benefited. Why should I prefer the common good (assuming that there is such a thing and that it is easily discoverable)? Because not to do so will in the end lead to my own and others' greater misery. Conflicts between the common good and that of myself, my family, my class are not inherent in the natural order (that is, the life of men as it could be made to be). They are due to some earlier maladjustment between the interests of individuals and those of groups; or between those of smaller and larger groups; or between those of groups or classes within society, and society as a whole. In a perfect society all these interests would coincide, for a man is not many but one person: he has a fixed nucleus of attributes called his essential nature, and not many natures. I cannot simultaneously be hurt as a stockholder or a family man and benefited as a citizen; only bad, that is mistaken, education, bad legislation are responsible for such conflicts. Good education and legislation can prevent them. It is useless to *preach* morality to men: for men are psychologically incapable of following save what seems to them in their own interest; their minds rotted by the fantastical and pernicious nonsense in which they have been brought up, they are in no condition to understand the most enlightened advice. Hence two measures must be instituted: they must be re-educated in the truth as demonstrated by the sciences, and not, as hitherto, on a mixture of old wives' tales and moral principles useful only to their oppressors; and the laws must be so altered as to tempt them, by a nicely constructed system of rewards and punishments, to do and avoid those acts the doing and avoidance of which will in fact make for their highest and most durable happiness.

Helvétius, in particular, believed in the omnipotence of education and legislation: by education you made men aware of their true good – of what would make them truly contented; and prevented recurrence of medieval superstition, cruelty and injustice; by legislation – that is, by an appropriate arrangement of rewards and punishments, a policy of sticks and carrots – you caused men to behave in certain fashions which, in fact, would make them and others happy. It did not matter what their motives were: what mattered were the results. By playing on men's simplest hopes, desires, passions and fears you could set up in them useful habits, until no further coercion or persuasion was required. By substituting 'the language of interest' for 'the tone of injury'[1] of the moral preacher, you brought into play the fundamental human spring of action – self-interest. Without the passions, nothing would be done. Spinoza and many another philosopher had committed a grave error in advocating the elimination of passion: this was not desirable, and in any case impossible. Hume had correctly analysed the impotence of unsupported reason. Legislation must not attack prejudices, irrational impulses, the 'bad' instincts. It can do better: it canalises them, or harnesses them to promote that which gives happiness. Manipulation – social engineering – by means of rewards and punishments is all.[2] All this was duly repeated in more vigorous language by Jeremy Bentham.

---

[1] *De l'esprit* 2. 15 (beginning of penultimate paragraph).

[2] See the quotation from Helvétius at the head of this chapter (p. 17 above).

But it is already fully developed by Helvétius: not merely the theses of utilitarianism, which is an older doctrine, indeed as old as Plato; what is new is the explicit notion of social engineering: that legislation and education and whatever other reforms are needed – of language, of architecture, of whatever may influence human conduct – can transform society into a collection of beings who semi-automatically satisfy their own and others' wishes as fully as it is possible on earth.

There is no general agreement about the means for determining what will make men happy. Bentham thinks that every man is the best judge of his own happiness;[1] and that the task of legislation is therefore largely negative – to remove interference by obsolete or corrupt or inefficient institutions. So far as he gives thought to the matter at all, he seems to believe, like the physiocrats, in the ultimate coincidence or harmony of the self-regarding activities of a society of rational egoists. This makes for individualism and democracy, which indeed became inalienable elements in the political programmes of his liberal and radical followers in every country. Helvétius and the French *philosophes* in general are less confident about the capacity of an average human being to discover what he most needs: like all but the simplest problems this is a matter for scientific enquiry, careful anthropological and psychological investigation, to be conducted by trained experts. When these have discovered what is most likely to make for the greatest happiness of a society, every effort to obtain this must be made by placing such experts in authority: which leads to enlightened despotism, technocracy, social planning, the harmonisation of the conflicting activities of individuals, if need be, by State coercion. This in its turn entered permanently into the programmes of all the parties dedicated to the need for State control, in particular all the varieties of socialism and State capitalism. What was common to all the *lumières* from Voltaire to James Mill and Auguste Comte is the belief that men possess a basic and relatively unaltering constitution which is determined by natural causes; that this constitution – 'human nature' – and the causal laws that it obeys are wholly discoverable by scientific investigation; that such enquiry shows conclusively what the inevitably identical ends sought by all men,

---

[1] 'For no man can be so good a judge as the man himself, what it is gives him pleasure or displeasure.' *Introduction to the Principles of Morals and Legislation*, chapter 15, section 2. 4: vol. 1, p. 84, in *The Works of Jeremy Bentham*, ed. John Bowring (Edinburgh, 1843).

whatever their dissimilarities, are; and that human action – in particular education and legislation – can overcome or reconcile such differences, and fully satisfy the basic needs of mankind.

Certain obstacles, no doubt, will remain: the differences created by natural environments, for instance. However advanced science may become, it is unlikely that it will be able to alter the more constant and fixed physical factors: for example, right the axis of the earth and create a temperate climate everywhere; or put an end to earthquakes, droughts and floods. Even under a perfect utilitarian system of education and legislation, some imperfections may therefore remain. But Helvétius and his friends consistently played this down, and Montesquieu is much criticised for devoting his gifts to a dispassionate description of the irreconcilable variety of human character, institutions and their causes, rather than to the problem of how to improve them. There is an ironical essay by Diderot in which he compares his own views with those of Helvétius; and whenever Helvétius pronounces dogmatic opinions about the absolute power or total irrelevance of this or that factor in human affairs, Diderot politely offers qualifications. Climate is not *wholly* without influence, though Montesquieu doubtless exaggerated it. Legislation is not all-powerful, although possibly more so than has been supposed. Reason is not totally inactive, education is not all-transforming. But such scepticism is rare, even in Diderot's writings.

Yet while we may marvel at the excessive simplicity and baldness of the Encyclopaedists' programmes, we should not marvel too much: Helvétius was writing at a time when the horizon of technological possibilities was opening with astonishing and intoxicating rapidity; when advances in psychology, anthropology, ethnology looked as if they were about to rival those of physics and astronomy, and a multitude of points of light, growing in intensity and number, were scattering the medieval darkness. He and his contemporaries had a sense of living at a moment when the long night of ignorance began to lift, revealing the exquisite features of the beautiful hero of the fairy tale, too long concealed beneath the hideous disguise which had been laid upon humanity by the evil spirit of early Christianity and the medieval Church. The fashionable stories of 'natural man' in China, in the Pacific, in America, living innocently free from the miseries of European civilisation, added to this picture. At such a time it was natural enough to build the future upon the immense achievements which seemed within the power of human beings, if only enough champions of humanity, enough believers in his future, could be found. The number of obstacles was great, the enemy still powerful but in retreat, the work to be done vast and inspiring, the hands few, the rewards immeasurable. It was a moment of such optimism, seldom, if ever, attained before; it would have been surprising if the leaders of this movement had not been guilty of exaggeration both in their denunciation of the past, and in their bright dreams of the future. Science is all: and the best government is the most scientific – that which is most skilled at moulding men. To achieve social peace all friction can and should be eliminated from individual and social life; happiness is obtainable only through the full development of all our socially useful faculties, and the suppression of all disruptive tendencies. The best human beings are therefore those who fit best into the social pattern: all abnormality, eccentricity, oddity is a form of unsuccessful social adaptation; the harmony to be sought after is that of a perfectly functioning mechanism. In place of the old image of the human orchestra or the divine comedy, we now find the model of Newton's mechanical universe. As nature is, as a piece of man-made machinery is, so should society become: a smooth interplay of precisely fitting elements, each realising its proper function without hindrance, free from the frustrations of aimlessness or chance collision.

How can we be sure that all human wishes can in principle be combinable even under the maximum degree of social pressure? Whence this notion of an attainable harmony, which underlies the entire thought of the period? Wherever we look – from the deists and the believers in natural law or natural religion to the disciples of Quesnay or Adam Smith, from the German metaphysicians to the atheistic materialists in France, from the neo-classical aesthetic theorists to chemists and mathematicians and zoologists – we find the same common assumption: that the answers to all the great questions must of necessity agree with one another; for they must correspond to reality, and reality is a harmonious whole. If this were not so, there is chaos at the heart of things: which is unthinkable. Liberty, equality, property, knowledge, security, practical wisdom, purity of character, sincerity, kindness, strength, generosity, rational self-love, all these ideals to which Helvétius and Holbach call men, since they are constituents of the all-embracing ideal of human society, cannot (if they are truly desirable) conflict with one another; if they appear to do so it must be due to some misunderstanding of their properties. No truly good thing can ever be finally incompatible with any other; indeed they virtually entail one another: men cannot be wise unless they are free, or free unless they are just, happy and so forth.

Here we conspicuously abandon the voice of experience – which records very obvious conflicts of ultimate ideals – and encounter a doctrine that stems from older theological roots – from the belief that unless all the positive virtues are harmonious with one another, or at least not incompatible, the notion of the Perfect Entity – whether it be called nature or God or Ultimate Reality – is not conceivable. It is reliance upon this perennial dogma, and not at all the assumptions or the data or the laws of the natural sciences upon which they affect to ground them, that alone explains the method of argument and belief of Helvétius and the *philosophes*: and their conclusions possess as much validity as this major premiss and no more.

But this is not all. Not only must all the ultimate ends – the absolute values in terms of which all legislation, education, life itself must be organised – be in harmony: but – and this is very fundamental – they must all be discoverable by any man of normal ability if he goes about looking for them in the right way, with the right tools; as discoverable as the specific gravity of lead, as the cure for a disease; discoverable, that is, by the methods of the empirical sciences. They are there – objective facts – for rational man to find, and had always been within his grasp, if he had only known it. The reformers of the eighteenth century declared – and profoundly believed – that once the scales had fallen from men's eyes, the nightmare of ignorance and despotism would be lifted of itself. The problem was technological, the ideals had only to be translated into reality with the newly discovered methods that were the glory of the new enlightenment.

The golden age – the heavenly city – seemed very near. How did one, in fact, set about looking for the social panacea? One thing was clear: it is essential for any self-respecting study to have an 'objective' basis. Political thought remains a mere subjective set of personal preferences and caprices unless it, too, can be secured on such a basis. What is objectivity? What makes a science scientific? It must, at the very least, be such that the answers to its questions are to be sought in scientific observation of 'facts'. The difference between genuine physics and those earlier speculations or opinions which were now condemned as fanciful or subjective is that the

ultimate data which verify or confirm its theories are such as occur
in the ordinary human experience of the sensible world; as for the
reasoning that occurs in the course of the argument, it must be
such as any normal person who has had an adequate training and is
endowed with 'reason' can check for himself. The words 'normal'
and 'adequate', 'reason', 'experience' are no doubt question-
begging. Montesquieu, for example, had achieved fame by pointing out that what is 'normal' in Persia is not so in France.[1]
Nevertheless, there is a point beyond which the thesis that all
criteria of normality are conventional, artificial, and depend on
differing cultures, climates, temperaments, times and places,
becomes unplausible. The appeal of these empiricists is ultimately
pragmatic, to self-critical common sense whose guarantee is its
own satisfaction. Cartesian doubt is only a heuristic maxim. It may
often be a good thing to doubt. But not always. We may at times
be too confident of our findings, but we discover this only because
we compare such states with other situations when such confidence
is thoroughly justified. Whatever the situation with the odd or
borderline cases, we call them doubtful or borderline precisely
because they differ from those clear cases, nearer the centre, to
which we refer as examples of justified certainty. To mistake, if you
are flying in an aeroplane, clouds for mountain ranges, or vice
versa, may be not uncommon; to confuse mirror images with
material objects is a well-known illusion; to misidentify colours, or
see double, is possible; but if a man looks, as we should say, at a
table and takes it for a waterfall, we have no hesitation in
pronouncing his experience abnormal; if, despite the presented or
available data, and the arguments employed in connection with
them, a man still declares himself convinced that the earth is flat,
we say without much hesitation that something is wrong: his
powers of reasoning are defective or, in extreme cases, deranged. In
short, we do in fact recognise that there are interpersonal public

---

[1] [Here Berlin adds: ' – even Helvétius on sheep', a reference to the passage he
introduces in FIB in these terms: 'He asks us to imagine what the minute little
gnats or flies who live in the high grass must feel about other animals which occur
in their world. They see a large beast, to our eyes a sheep peacefully browsing in a
meadow, and they say: "Let us flee from this greedy and cruel animal, this
monster in whose voracious jaws we and our cities will be swallowed up. Why
can it not behave like lions and tigers? These kindly animals do not destroy our
dwellings; they do not batten upon our blood. Just avengers of crime, they punish
sheep for the cruelty sheep inflict upon us." ' De l'esprit 2. 2; FIB 22.]

criteria both for determining what kind of material objects there are in the world and what kind of arguments are valid, and in what contexts and for what purposes. The fact that much – more than is suspected by uncritical common sense – is obscure or vague or ambiguous; that daily language is not precise, and scientific language at times not clear or self-explanatory; the fact that mistakes can be and have been made, that mental capacities and outlooks and opinions differ, that communication and agreed results are more difficult to achieve than is sometimes naïvely supposed – these cannot be used to show that every empirical statement is in some degree incurably vague, ambiguous, doubtful, relative, subjective, not fully communicable, or to point to the possibility of another kind of knowledge, infallible, a priori, given to a special faculty of rational intuition or inspired supernatural vision. On the contrary, if that was so, there would be nothing in normal experience with which such words as 'dubious', 'ambiguous', 'subjective', 'arbitrary' as ordinarily used would be contrasted, and so they would lose their force and indeed their very meaning as descriptive or pejorative words.

This largely unconscious pragmatism, at once made articulate, questioned and reaffirmed by Hume and Reid in their very different fashions, underlies the whole of eighteenth-century empiricism as against the rationalism of the Cartesians and their scepticism about empirical knowledge. The triumphs of natural science were themselves so much testimony to the power of those normal and fallible faculties which Locke and his followers had correctly thought to be sufficient to explain and establish the validity of both scientific method and common sense. Authority, dogma, revelation led only to unintelligible mysteries, or pompous platitudes, or downright demonstrable falsehoods. It was true that even physicists spoke in terms of unobserved entities. But these were inferred from what was visible, and visible to any specialised observer, and inferred by methods not in principle different from those which occurred in ordinary, everyday thought. If this sufficed to raise the physical sciences to their unchallenged height, it was natural enough to assume that no less, but also no more, was required of any other discipline claiming to be objective. Hence, if propositions of political science were to be rendered 'objective', 'scientific' and so on, they too must, after however many removes, be able to come to rest upon generally recognised common data – facts, realities – to which the propositions of politics should have the same kind of relation as those of physics now had to those of sense or common experience. The observations and hypotheses of such considerable thinkers as Hobbes and Harrington and Locke, no less than those of Bodin and Montesquieu and the travellers from distant lands with their tales of happy Indians, claimed to rest upon the facts of social life as squarely as those of physics or anatomy upon the observable behaviour of molecules or living organisms.

So far, then, a large hope was held out of being able to construct a science or several sciences of how human beings behaved, both individually – this was the task of physiology and psychology – and in societies – the task of sociology, political economy, political science, or by whatever other names these new enquiries might be called. Here, too, facts must be gathered, laws discovered, hypotheses tested, and the whole of available knowledge organised into a coherent system, with fewer and fewer central generalisations of ever-increasing scope, logically entailing more and more embracing sets of more specific generalisations, which, fitting, as they ultimately and of necessity would, into the total structure of available human knowledge, would between them describe and account for all there is, was and will be, all that occurs or can occur. When as much was known about individuals and groups and societies as was already known about the behaviour of matter in space, vast areas of ignorance and error would be eliminated, the possibilities of the education of individuals, and the planning of social and political life, would be extended beyond the limits of anything as yet imaginable, and order and reason would be installed into spheres still alarmingly open to the play of prejudice, superstition, and irrational and subjective fancy. This is what Holbach and Helvétius claimed to have done, or at least begun: this too was to be taught in the schools and universities – the natural sciences, sociology, ethics, and not the useless lumber of dead languages or the dangerous gibberish called metaphysics and theology. This was the dream of every enlightened person in the eighteenth century, and Diderot is merely the most eloquent exponent of it, and La Mettrie merely the most deliberately shocking and paradoxical. The degree to which this idea has been, or can be, or should be realised is a matter of acute controversy in our day.

But whatever the legitimacy of this claim, it still left at least one question unanswered. The crucial issue which divided men was that of how a man should behave, whether in the privacy of his home, or as a citizen. Or, according to the new style, what was it reasonable, scientific, objectively correct, for a man to do? It is one thing to ask – and answer – the question 'How do men in fact behave? And what causes them so to behave?', and another to ask how they should or ought to behave. To the first question you replied, if you were a supporter of the new scientific programme, that men did what they did, not because of the peculiar essence of their inner soul, nor their relation to the author of their being, nor the purpose for which that author had created them, nor any other occult or impalpable factor. You echoed Montesquieu and spoke of climate or soil, or Helvétius and discussed the influence of education and legislation, or Holbach and denounced the cruelties or absurdities of religion, and the dust deliberately or innocently thrown in men's eyes by theologians or metaphysicians or other unscrupulous or self-deluded quacks, or poets, or preachers, or other unscientific, or anti-scientific, and therefore blind or wicked, persons. You pointed out the fact that with so great a revolution in your cosmogony your moral and political outlook would inevitably undergo a change.

All this was true enough; what remained unanswered was the old and crucial question 'How should men behave?', and, more specifically, 'Why should these persons or groups of persons obey those other persons or groups of persons?' Helvétius answered that you need obey only if it was reasonable to think that this would lead to a happier world, for yourself and others too; to which you might rejoin that if you were in fact a utilitarian, his programme might be a useful enough means of reaching the goal: but you were enquiring about goals. *Why*, you asked, should I work solely for happiness? I may in fact already do so. Helvétius and Bentham may be right: perhaps I cannot avoid even seeking this alone as my ultimate goal. But I was not asking for an analysis of my own character or prospects: I wanted to know *why* I should obey the king rather than rebel; and if you answered that if I rebelled I might find my happiness sensibly diminished by imprisonment or death, I could go on to ask, 'Why should I sacrifice all to happiness?' Why not some other goal? How can I tell which is the right one? And what do I so much as mean by asking this question? Where should I look for the answer to questions such as 'Why should I . . . ?' or 'What is the good of . . . ?' rather than 'What is there?' or 'What am I like?', 'How do I behave?'

In the old days the answer was 'God has ordered you to do so. Do it.' To say of an act that it was right was to say that it had been so commanded: but now that God had been relegated to the status of a First Mover, who, having wound up our world like a clock, took no further interest in it, this was no longer open. Whose wishes and orders were, then, to be regarded as relevant? What were the 'facts', the public data, to which the answers to these questions should relate? Was there a realm of political facts (or for that matter moral or aesthetic facts) in which the proposition 'Men should obey the majority' or 'Monarchy is the best form of government' or 'Every man has a natural right to life, liberty, property, security' or 'To tell a lie is always unconditionally wrong' could find their analogues, to which they corresponded or failed to correspond, as there plainly was a realm which physics purported to describe, which contained those entities and relationships by which the statements of physicists were verified or falsified, or rendered less or more probable?

It seems reasonably clear to us now, who live after Kant, that questions of fact are different in principle from questions of value, that the question 'What kind of thing is $x$?' or 'Where or when or how big is $x$?' is different from such questions as 'Why should I do what you say?' or 'Should I make others happy?', that the former questions are what we call questions of fact, answerable ultimately by inspecting the relevant state of affairs, which remains what it is, whether I ask the question or not, and possesses certain characteristics of its own, however inaccessible or difficult to describe. But when I answer questions of the form 'Why should I?' by explaining that I do what I do for the sake of this or that aim or purpose, it seems strange to say that aims or ideals or ends possess independent being, in some universe of their own, like tables or atoms, whether anyone takes an interest in them or not. If I ask whether I am to – should – obey the King or my conscience, where is it sensible for me, an enlightened adherent of a new, eighteenth-century, scientific view of life, to look for the right answer? If I was a believing Christian I understood the situation quite well: to say of something that it was right to do it was not so much to state a fact as to refer to an order, an order made valid for me by being derived from the commands of God or his prophets or his Church or the precepts contained in his sacred book. This was at least intelligible: the answer to my enquiry was not a proposition describing something, made true or false by this or that state of 'the facts', but an *order*, a *command*; and commands are not true or false, though they may be right or wrong, just or unjust; they are not something verified or falsified by their alleged relationship to an independent state of affairs of which they claim to be an accurate or true description. Why I should obey what God or his ministers order me to do is another question. Perhaps it is impious to ask, or perhaps I have my private reasons. At any rate the two types of statement were clearly quite different; physics, biology, history, common sense described less or more successfully both what there was, is, will be, might be, could have been, and could not have been; whereas political and ethical statements ordered me to do something but described nothing. A command was not a statement of fact, nor did it claim to be one. By now God had been abolished or reduced to irrelevance; his ministers and the sacred books were repositories of error and confusion.

Where then was I to look for the answer to the question 'Why should I obey the government?'? I might not wish to obey the order, and prefer to live a wicked, defiant or irresponsible life, but even the terms 'wicked' and 'irresponsible' implied that 'standards existed' in terms of which such behaviour was a deviation. Existed where? In what sense? Hobbes replied that I had better obey the State, else it would destroy me: but this was a reply only to the question 'Why do I obey?' – out of fear – and if I asked 'Why should I not seek destruction at the hand of the State? Savonarola did: why not I?', no factual answer could in principle satisfy me. Only one discipline existed which seemed to throw some light on the answer to this question; and that was the law. In the statutes and the judgements of courts, I found not descriptions or statements of fact, so much as instructions and directions as to how to behave. But then the law itself, unless it was issued by God or some other supernatural agency, and therefore beyond enquiry, could be called in question. *Should* the laws be obeyed or not? What did it mean to say that they *should*? To say that they should be obeyed because they were just might be to say only that they should be obeyed because they were formulated in accordance with principles which should themselves be observed; and what did it mean to say some principles were, whereas others were not, to be observed? When Montesquieu said that different principles were observed by different peoples, and gave naturalistic explanations for this, that was no doubt true and illuminating to those interested in the rich variety of social experience, but it did not help those who wanted to know *not* why men *did* obey, but whether they were right or even wise to do so, whether their example should – not merely would in fact – be followed or avoided.

It is here, as a bridge between fact and value, that the central and fatally ambiguous concept of nature made its appearance. It was not only the jurists of the Middle Ages or the seventeenth century who supposed that only those laws were just which in some way flowed logically from, were specific applications of, a set of imposed rules, binding on all men, existing in a queer world of their own – 'natural law'. They could be dismissed as still in the toils of a dark theology or metaphysics: but what are we to say when the hard-boiled representatives of the new behaviourism – the atheistic materialist Helvétius, the chemist and botanist Holbach – appeal to this dubious entity? To do right, we are told, to do what you ought, you must obey the laws of nature. Enlightenment in all spheres consisted in the discovery of the true natural laws. As there were the *natural* sciences of physics or biology or astronomy or botany, and latterly of political economy and history, so there was the natural science of how to live; and it applied equally to individuals and to groups. Nature is something real, which holds the answers to all questions; no less to those which ask what there should be, or what one should do, than to those which ask what there is. Much has been written about the concept of nature in the eighteenth century, but all that concerns us here is that even the toughest political radicals evidently held nature to be not only what there is – the sum of things – a living organism or an elaborate machine, but in some extraordinary fashion a source of purposes and orders and ideals – a semi-personal agency speaking to those with ears to hear, half governess, half dictator,[1] beckoning, persuading, cajoling and sometimes threatening or issuing indignant cries: always in language clear to those whose minds have not been darkened by metaphysical or priestly fantasies.

The notion that nature is a source not merely of information about what there is, and how it functions, telling us about what is practicable and about means and roads, but also in some sense a kind of repository of ends – of what should be done, or is worth

[1] {See Becker [Carl L. Becker, *The Heavenly City of the Eighteenth-Century Philosophers* (New Haven, 1932), e.g. p. 63; although Berlin's note is located as indicated above, Becker's treatment of the idea of nature in his second chapter is relevant to the whole sentence]}

doing for its own sake – is one of the oldest ideas in the history of thought. To know how we ought to live, whom to obey, and why, we must, according to Plato, understand the nature of 'reality' by a special intellectual process which he calls dialectical. To understand reality is to know what is one's 'natural' function in it. To have a function is not merely to be doing something, or to be acted upon in a certain way, but to realise that all that one does has a certain purpose or end or ideal for which one has been created, whether by a personal God or by an impersonal nature. All Aristotle's enquiries, whether he is arguing from empirical observation or from a priori premises, are in fact directed to the discovery of what is the 'natural function' of the entity under examination – a plant or an animal, an individual or a society. The happiness or satisfaction of those entities which are capable of such experience comes into consideration only in the sense that it must accompany, and indeed is part and parcel of – is intrinsic to – the unimpeded progressive realisation of the proper ends assigned by nature to each being. Rationality consists in the consciousness of the direction and method proper to each being in the hierarchy of nature. One's nature is one's function – the process of growth or development, less or more successfully, into the perfect entity which one potentially is from the first moment of one's existence. To know or understand something is to know what it must tend to become; to be able to define the essence of something is to state what the purpose of that thing is, such that the nearer it approaches that purpose the more 'real' it becomes. An empirical description of something, founded on observation, is rightly condemned as superficial – a catalogue of inessential properties – in that it omits to convey the unique *raison d'être* of the object, why it is as it is and uniquely individual – in principle distinguishable from everything else in the universe. At most it might be a report on what stage in its inevitable development an object or person has reached, what gap still obtains between it and its goal, between it and its perfect realisation. The definition of an object describes not so much its actual condition, as revealed to ordinary empirical observation, as the 'inner' formula in accordance with which it has changed from what it was in the beginning into what it is now, and what it is becoming, what, if it pursues its proper path, it will be.

Stoics, Peripatetics, Neoplatonists and Christians – all, in short, except those who believed that things happened through chance collisions of matter in space and had no purpose – took this for granted. The Christians, like the Jews before them, substituted for an impersonal nature of things the purposes of a personal God. To metaphysical insight or empirical observation they added, as a superior – indeed, as the only truly valid – source of knowledge, revelation, the voice of God speaking either directly to the soul of man or through his prophets or Church or his sacred writings. The assumption common to the classical and the Christian traditions was the view of every entity as occupying its own unique and specific place in the great order of nature or creation (whichever one happened to believe in). God or nature had divided everything into 'natural kinds', into genera and species, each of which was defined in terms of its function, that is, in terms of the kind of process which led to its particular kind of goal or perfection. To confound or pervert the genera or kinds was opposition to nature, revolt against natural order, mutiny against what was apportioned and therefore a form of failure due to ignorance or madness or wickedness; and this was involved, too, in the stunting of the 'natural growth' of anything – whether of a blade of grass or of a child or of human society. It might be that the perfect completion of the process was not here, on earth, where human beings were corroded by natural sin, but in another world where the soul was freed from its earthly trammels; and it might be that whatever had lost its way, whether through its own perversity or through misfortune, was destined never to reach its proper goal, but to wither on earth, or end in the torments of hell. Whatever metaphysical or theological view was taken of the destinies of things, animate or inanimate, one assumption ran through all these divergent views: that the attributes of a thing in some sense coincided or were identical with its value; that a true and complete description of it would identify the distance – the degree of perfection – which it had reached along the path proper to it. And, consequently, that natural law could be regarded as being at once that ultimate force which, in fact, regulated the movements of the stars in their courses, the lives of men, and the behaviour of the humblest thing in the universe, and, at the same time, not as mere causal machinery but as the system of rules in accordance with which the machine worked – as the constellation of purposes which its behaviour necessarily fulfilled.

To commit a crime was to offend against your own or someone else's proper purpose. For a short time this could be and, of course, had been done, but in the end the inexorable laws – of God or of nature – would assert themselves against such deviations, and the perpetrator would be punished if only by finding himself in disharmony with the universe; and this must inevitably be accompanied by – even consist in – bodily or spiritual suffering and sometimes total destruction. There was, of course, always the problem of evil – of how a beneficent deity or a harmonious nature could be compatible with the possibility of such discords – and to this there were many answers, many theodicies justifying the ways of God – or nature, or reality – to man; none of them wholly convincing, all intended to close the logical gap between the assumption that the universe was a harmonious system, and the apparent occurrence in it of purposeless or discordant elements. Be that as it may, this ancient difficulty was not by itself sufficient to undermine the general assumption that everything had a purpose – something in which law and fact ultimately coincided. Things or events which did not seem to obey laws were but imperfectly understood (for to understand was to understand the laws which governed things and events), while laws – moral and political, and social – which appeared to be so freely broken, were, if one saw the story through to its conclusion, never broken with impunity, but would sooner or later avenge themselves – reality would humble or destroy the perverse or presumptuous man, the malefactor, in the end. From this flowed the doctrine that crime was identical with folly, vice with error. Every creature, in so far as it has a nature at all – and to give it a name was to attribute to it a nature – must seek, whether it recognises it or not, its natural, proper end, the unique purpose which it has in the universe, in which nothing can be uselessly duplicated. To pursue this end, that is, to fulfil its proper function, is to realise the tendencies, desires and ideals which nature (or God) has implanted in it. What satisfies these is what is called good, or right, or proper or fitting, and to strive for this is the leading of the rational life, and the reward for success in doing so, relative or absolute, is the degree of happiness appropriate to the degree of such success.

A criminal, like all creatures, seeks his own satisfaction. In a harmonious universe such satisfaction cannot frustrate the equally proper satisfaction of other beings; to suppose that one's satisfaction consists in inflicting gratuitous pain, or causing other forms of wilful damage, is to misunderstand the nature of the universe; such misunderstanding (which inevitably argues a maladjustment, on the part of the person involved, to the nature of things) will inevitably end in depriving him of that satisfaction which only a correct adjustment, flowing from a right understanding of what the world is like, or, at any rate, the portion of it relevant to his finite function in it, can give – and so will end by rendering him unhappy somewhere, sometime, in this world or the next. If the world is a tight, harmonious system, the only way to secure satisfaction in it is not to offend against the laws of the system. The very notion of such a system presupposes that everything in it has a unique place and function. To usurp these – let us say by stealing something, that is, depriving somebody of the possessions necessary to him for the performance of his own proper function, and for this very reason not necessary to the stealer in the performance of his *ex hypothesi* uniquely different function – is to misunderstand the system to which one belongs. Any offence against the system – the laws of nature or the laws of God – inevitably leads to the injury of the life both of the offender and of others. An omniscient being who understands the laws and the material over which they reign could never suppose that he would derive lasting satisfaction from something which disturbs the system, frictionless functioning within which is the sole guarantee of happiness. The laws of the universe coincide with the rules of right action. Hence crime is always ignorance, hence virtue is knowledge, hence values are facts, and *de jure* and *de facto* coincide.

This was an intelligible doctrine so long as the view that nature and everything in it pursued less or more clearly discernible purposes remained relatively unquestioned. When Grotius talks of natural law, he still thinks that to make unjust wars, or to perform acts of unprovoked aggression against individuals, is contrary to a law by which human beings not merely should be, but in some ultimate sense *are*, governed: that 'law' bears not two clearly distinguishable meanings – in one sense a generalisation of what happens, and in the other a rule bidding that this or that be done whether or not it is in fact done – but is the two in one, since what ought to be – how to live – can be logically inferred from what, in some metaphysical sense, is the universal order. Grotius lived in a world in which to explain something, and to give the rule obedience to which makes it as good an example of its kind as it can be, is still to say the same sort of thing about it. The customs, rules, laws which most men, in most places, at most times, are seen to follow are imperfect earthly realisations of some more perfect schema which according to their lights they willy-nilly find themselves expressing in their acts and thoughts. This schema is the law of nature, which can indeed be disobeyed, but not for long and only at our cost – for to commit crimes is to behave 'unnaturally', to fly in the face of things, a process which cannot be sustained by anyone for long. When Montesquieu, with what is justly considered to be an attitude of sober, observant empiricism, collects evidence for his thesis that men behave differently in different environments, that their laws and customs vary as soil and climate, institutions and temperaments and historical traditions vary, he is engaged in demonstrating that those laws are good laws which correspond to, or spring from, 'the necessary relations of things'.[1] In other words, men are acting well where they are obeying rules which derive from their differing situations – and because situations are so unlike one another, one cannot expect Persians to have a scale of values similar to that of the French, nor does the validity of either scale prove the other wrong, because each suits – expresses the spirit of – its own peculiar circumstances. But this very notion that values – the validity of scales – can be said to follow, derive from, the natures of men and of their situations, that values can be deduced from facts, is plausible only if we suppose that knowledge of men or peoples, and knowledge of their history and environment and physique and mental endowments and the interplay of all these, that is, knowledge of facts, is a knowledge which must automatically reveal to us what is the right life, that is, the right purposes or ends for such individuals or peoples to pursue; in other words, knowledge not of what is but of what ought to be: not of facts but of values. And we think this only if we think that all things are as they are and have been and will be because thereby they have been and are and will be fulfilling this or that purpose, which is discernible through observing their history and the causes of their spiritual and material development. Whereas the theological writers believed these causes to be spiritual in character and to do with the relations of God and man – the Fall, the Crucifixion, the Resurrection, the Redemption – Montesquieu inclined towards more material explanations. But the celebrated opening sentence of *The Spirit of the Laws* makes it quite clear that he thinks that what *should* be – what it is right or reasonable to do – can be elicited from the 'necessary relations of things', that is, from what *is*, and is what it is and as it is because it cannot help

[1] See p. 40 above, note 1.

being so; that one can deduce rules for action – the right laws, the good constitutions – from what is there already, because that which exists is either identical with, or at any rate good evidence of, what is meant to be, that is, what should be. And this is Platonic, Aristotelian, Christian. It may be a materialistic interpretation of such doctrines – a deviation, a heresy – but it is a heresy within the Church: it accepts the major premisses of what it seeks to modify.

But since Helvétius and Holbach and their followers, and Hobbes and Spinoza, revolted against the teleological principle itself and taught that while individuals had purposes, the world had not; and that men and women wanted to do now this, now that, but the earth and the sea and the trees and the winds wanted nothing, and strove for nothing, and had no ends to fulfil – where, it may be asked of them, did they derive the answer to the questions 'What should a rational being do?', 'Whom should a man obey?'? After duly denouncing teleology as absurd anthropomorphism, they proceed to speak, quite blandly, of being given the answers sometimes by nature, sometimes by reason; and the two often seem almost identical. But what does this mean? Who is nature, and how does she make herself understood? And if she does not communicate in some quite literal sense, what is meant by saying that she speaks at all? Often almost all that Helvétius seems to mean is that he rejects most of the assumptions made by earlier thinkers. He thinks – he knows – that there is no God; the writings attributed to him are not sacred and have no authority; there is no mystery in the heart of things whence divine or any other kind of inspired knowledge can flow. He must have evidence of everything that he believes; he wants to be shown either by rational argument or empirical data why this or that rule of life should be followed, and nature and reason are largely negative symbols indicating rejection of authority, and of revelation and of scholastic metaphysics, or of all the voices which have spoken to the prophets and the saints. And he wishes to convey an equally vigorous rejection of the opinions of the unenlightened mob, which are but debased versions of the nonsense taught them by their stupid or vicious instructors, mingled, it may be, now and then, with a little common sense, but seldom enough of it to outweigh the cloud of darkness and confusion.

Helvétius knew the answer to the questions of morals and politics because he had discovered that men by nature seek only pleasure or happiness, and would obtain it too, if only they had the time and inclination to find the most efficient ways of arranging their lives, which in their turn can be discovered only by adequate scientific training. Human beings are not, however, as a rule so made as to understand, without much previous education, what in fact will render them happy; nor, often enough, even when they do know, have they sufficient strength of character to pursue such courses, being prey to many distracting passions. The wise man, the specialist in psychology and the sciences, who knows both what will make men happy and what means to use to procure it for them, will not succeed by merely preaching to his less enlightened brethren; for even if they believe that what he says is true, they will not have sufficient self-control to follow his advice. Consequently, the only method of rendering them happy is by legislation: by establishing an elaborate system of material rewards and punishments, by playing, in short, on their passions – by what is nowadays called adjustment and conditioning – for only in this way can men be caused to act in such a way as in fact to become happy, without necessarily intending, or even understanding, any such goal or how they come to reach it. By dangling a sufficient number of carrots and applying a sufficient number of sticks, the human animal can be made to follow any path which his trainer chooses for him. The average human being is neither strong-willed enough nor rational enough to reach the goal of happiness by his own efforts; but he can be driven thither by a judicious combination of temptations and penalties: that is the task of legislation for those who understand men and their wants. They must institute a proper education to obviate the need for such perpetual pushing and dragging; but a minimum of legislation and conditioning will always be required. Once men are set on the path to happiness by laws imposed by clear-headed and all-powerful governors – enlightened despots or democratically elected rulers – they can be educated into understanding why it is good for them to be so treated, until all elements of coercion disappear, and men's characters, for which education is in any case almost entirely responsible, are, under the new system, transformed: endowed with new characters, they will be enabled to make themselves and others happy, by the practice of a few simple, easily intelligible rules, the purpose of which will be increasingly understood, appreciated and accepted. On this basis Helvétius develops the entire theory of utilitarianism – the reduction of all human purposes to the pursuit of happiness, and the discussion of the best means, in the light of the increase in scientific knowledge, of how this may most painlessly and permanently be secured.[1] With the precise development of Helvétius' ideas we are not concerned any more than with the exposition of the details of his doctrine. The central point is that all men by nature seek happiness, and should be provided with the most effective means towards obtaining it, and this, as we said above, is best done by legislation, which causes even the vicious and ignorant, whether they intend it or not, to work for their own or others' happiness; and by education, which gradually improves the health of both their bodies and their minds. The sciences provide us with a means towards such mental and physical hygiene.

At this point someone may well enquire how it is that Helvétius knows so well that happiness is in fact the only end which men desire. And even if it is, how does he know that it is good or right to give men what they desire, even what they desire most

---

[1] Bentham had virtually nothing to add to this theory. When he acknowledged, as he freely did, his debt to Hélvetius, he could have added that he had adopted his theory with scarcely any modification. So far as theory is concerned, the scattered reflections of the previous thinkers, notably Hutcheson and Mandeville, not to speak of Hobbes and earlier materialists and Epicureans, were developed by Hélvetius into a lucid system to which neither Bentham nor James Mill added anything save practical suggestions about how the system might be realised. Bentham indeed spent much time and many pages of remorselessly tedious prose on elaborating the various 'dimensions' of pleasure, its intensity and duration, its security and remoteness, its fecundity and purity, made (absurd) suggestions about how such dimensions might be multiplied one by another, and how a calculus could be established whereby the maximum quantity of pleasure obtainable by a given person in a given situation could be determined. {NB He was more individualist – did *not* want vivisection – 'Each man his own best judge of happiness' [loc. cit. (p. 52 above, note 1)] – consult Robbins.} There are fatal objections, both logical and empirical, to Bentham's proposals – indeed he offers a curious example of a thinker whose views on practical reforms were notable for their sober and clear-headed and incorruptible good sense, accompanied, as soon as he comes to theory, by the very vices he castigates most sharply: casuistry, pedantry, a reckless fantasy, a passion for elaborate particulars unrelated to the facts, as well as an almost uniform absence of the capacity for abstract thought of the most primitive order. Hélvetius, in an age of writers as fascinating as Voltaire and Diderot, composed with difficulty, and despite his lucidity and earnestness cannot be read with much enjoyment; but what he says is immeasurably more original than Bentham's discussions of the same topic; and as a classical exposition of utilitarianism his two most famous works are far superior to anything to be found in any other author.

passionately of all? After all, there are cases in history where it is not so very evident that happiness is the sole end of men's wishes – the martyrs and the fanatical self-tormentors, of whatever faith, and for whatever motive, seem to bear testimony against the view that no one has ever desired anything but happiness, although sometimes they may have concealed this fact from themselves; nor are there lacking moralists, from the days of Moses onwards, to thunder against happiness as a sufficient goal, and to be acclaimed by later generations for saving them from so egregious a fallacy. Helvétius scarcely troubled to argue against all this. Fanaticism, austerity, the vows of poverty and chastity, seem to him mere aberrations, a perverse 'unnatural' turn of mind. Those who would deny the psychological law that men's sole motive is the desire for happiness, or doubt the moral or political truth that only that life or political order is best which leads to the maximum happiness of the community, are simply mistaken. What does their mistake consist in? Misunderstanding nature. What kind of nature? Not the nature – that is, character, attributes, laws governing the acts or thoughts – of a particular person or group or time or institution, but nature herself – that which, if rightly viewed, returns true answers to all genuine questions. No one in the eighteenth century but seems to speak of nature in this way. No one, that is, save Hume, who half saw the obscurity and the fallacies which flowed from it, and Bentham, who almost alone saw it very clearly and accepted the conclusions of the *philosophes* while deriding their metaphysical premises, which he scarcely troubled to analyse. Nature to Helvétius, to Holbach, to Diderot, to all the great French liberators is the great teacher of mankind. Dame Nature, Mistress Nature, 'supremely great and sovereign fair',[1] the great voice of nature is the great oracle whose true interpreter every eighteenth-century radical claims to be.

And yet she speaks with altogether too many voices. Montesquieu notes her variety, Helvétius her uniformity. Diderot sees her as a superb machine, with wheels and cords, pulleys and springs. Hume admires her contrivances, and Holbach perceives in her the source of all the arts and the sciences, of all that is best in civilised men of refined taste and in great and enlightened rulers. Rousseau is told by her that all that is civilised is corrupt and evil, that the arts and sciences destroy the capacity for discriminating

---

[1] [Untraced.]

between good and evil, that goodness is in simplicity and vigour and a pure heart unobtainable in cities dominated by commerce and the arts of civilisation. She preaches austerity to Mably and communism to Morelly: but defends tradition to A. Müller and renders property sacred to the Jacobins. She creates men wholly virtuous for Condorcet, but neither good nor bad for Helvétius: she is benevolent in Thomasius and misanthropic in Reynal and murderous in Maistre. Condorcet and Paine are convinced that she confers rights upon individuals which, because it is she who confers them, cannot be alienated by human means; Bentham alone fails to perceive any of this and denounces this insight as ludicrous fiction. To some she preaches liberty, to others, adherence to tradition; to some, equality, to others, the acceptance of the rule of the enlightened and the best. Saint-Martin sees her filled with evidences of God everywhere; Holbach regards the very notion of her as incompatible with God's essence. Pope, Shaftesbury, Rousseau, Mably perceive in her the divine harmony in which sinful man alone is the discordant note. Maistre and Hegel see her as a field of battle on which men and beasts and plants struggle continuously in an agony of mutual extermination, an unceasing slaughter fraught with violence, blood and suffering, every such evil being necessary to progress and freedom.

Sometimes nature is identical with reason and sometimes she is not. All those who believe that the world obeys a rational plan must of course believe that whatever happens is evidence of this plan. Some believe that this plan is a conscious purpose on the part of a deity which transcends the world which it has created, and which it governs; others believe that this divinity is 'within' – 'immanent' in – the world, as reason and will are 'within' – 'immanent' in – men, or desires in animals; still others do not believe in the existence of or deny any meaning to the notion of any such divine presence, whether within or outside the spatio-temporal world. And there is another division which cuts across all these categories. Some have a priori reasons for believing in the divine order – whether within or outside the cosmic plan – founded on revelation, or innate knowledge, or truths perceived by 'rational insight', or the utterances of some unquestioned authority. Others believe all this upon empirical evidence, that is, attempt to construct an argument from analogy or an induction upon the data of observation, from which a merely probable or plausible or reasonable conclusion follows. Still others believe in the existence of God or of a plan without reason, by faith, or because they wish to believe it, and perceive no compelling evidence against it, or ignore such evidence. But what unites all such thinkers is that the universe is in some sense 'unintelligible' to them unless there is a plan and a purpose, whether imposed by an agent or unimposed – part of the structure itself of all things and events. To be intelligible is, for them, to be part of a system, and a system, for them, is a planned activity. Those who think in this manner can even today attach some meaning to such phrases as 'the dictates of nature', or 'the voice of reason', for by this they mean either literally that what happens is evidence of the intentions of the engineer of the universe, or else that the universe is its own creator and engineer – a kind of animated purposive engine whose behaviour expresses its purpose much as the behaviour or words of a man express his intentions or outlook.

But all this is denied to empiricists such as the extreme *philosophes* supposed themselves to be. For them nothing can exist save what is given to the senses or can be inferred therefrom and described in terms of it. This rules out all transcendent entities automatically, and because they realised this, Holbach and Helvétius and their followers sternly denied the existence of eternal, non-temporal entities such as immortal souls, to which the less thoroughgoing and scientific among their contemporaries – Voltaire, Rousseau, Diderot and the extraordinary semi-atheistical priests whose influence was so great in the eighteenth century, Meslier, Condillac, Galiani, Reynal, Mably, Morelly – in a half-hearted, mild and inconsistent fashion tended to cling as a natural mode of thought and speech. Nor was the concept of an immanent purpose – let alone an immanent God – any more compatible with strict empiricism, inasmuch as the notion of the world as a single living thing, or a person with purposes, that is, will, reason and the rest, was on empirical grounds scarcely defensible and indeed scarcely conceivable at all.[1] This was duly perceived in the

[1] The argument as often as not came down to saying that the world resembled a purposive instrument like a watch rather than a purposeless one like a stone. But since the very difference between watch and stone rested upon the existence of such contrasts in the world, whereby one distinguished what had been made for a purpose and what had not, it was impossible without logical absurdity to apply those contrasts to the entire universe, and maintain of it that it resembled those of its contents which were purposive more than those which were not; for both the purposive and unpurposive ingredients of it were equally parts of it; and what applied to parts of the whole in contrast with other parts of the same whole could

nineteenth century, and Hume, of course, saw it very clearly in the first half of the eighteenth, and it was expressed in an obscurer if more interesting way by Kant. But the French thinkers of whom we speak either did not notice this, or blandly ignored it, and continued to have things both ways, and built great and memorable constructions upon the basis of this inner contradiction. For on the one hand they maintained that what was not derived from experience, that is, observation of the external world and psychological data, was not knowledge; that to know how to live you had to know how things occurred in the world, and for this only patient observation and study were needed, which would yield sufficient evidence, both observational and experimental, to test the truth of any general laws the scientists chose to conceive of. Anything whatever could, with a combination of sufficient care, honesty and genius, be described, and its behaviour past and future discovered, by means of such observations and laws; only in this way could life animate and inanimate be controlled in accordance with men's wishes; intuitions, dogmas, the isolated flashes of insight embedded in the various religious, metaphysical and ethical systems of mankind could now be dispensed with, as haphazard, unorganised glimpses of the truth, rules of thumb, a chaos of unrelated memories, conjectures and ideas, since all that was of value in them would take its proper place in the new, lucid, orderly, logically coherent, all-embracing system of universal science. This new science would, in principle, as the more optimistic hoped and preached, describe all there was and is and will be, would predict the future, 'retrodict' the past, and so start man on the road to omniscience. Once he knew what position he occupied in the great systematic whole he would thereby acquire the power of compassing his ends without being surprised and

not be applied to the entire whole without conspicuous absurdity. To say that the universe as a whole had a purpose had meaning only if there was something to contrast it with – say, an imaginary universe which had no purpose. But since the very notion of purpose was intelligible only within the universe, as distinguishing some constituents of it from others, and the notion of something outside the universe had no meaning, because *ex hypothesi* the universe was all there was, nothing empirical was conceivable with which the universe could be contrasted. Hence the proposition that the universe as a whole had a purpose, treated as an empirical statement, was the identification of the whole with one of its own parts and therefore founded on a glaring logical fallacy – it was much like saying that there were many colours in the universe but that they were, in the last analysis, all blue.

overwhelmed by destructive, because undetected, and therefore uncontrolled, forces. Power, enlightenment, virtue, knowledge, happiness, benevolence, rationality were necessarily consistent with one another, for they were all aspects of understanding the cosmos and one's place in it. Ignorance alone led to maladjustment, adjustment to happiness. Ignorance was, therefore, the mother of all vices and of all the miseries. Hence the view which seemed so self-evident to the noblest of all the *philosophes*, Condorcet, that the advance of the sciences and of morality, of individual freedom and social organisation, of justice and of benevolence, were necessarily interconnected; and the triumph of them all sooner or later inevitable.

On the other hand, these same persons seemed also to believe that this advance of the sciences meant not merely the accumulation and organisation of information about the world, which would save one from error about how to compass one's ends, but also somehow revealed the best way of using this information – best both for individuals and societies, best not as means, but as ends. Science, in short, told you not merely how to get what you wanted, but what to want. This was a very unempirical idea, as Hume indeed duly pointed out in his characteristically mild but devastating way. For mere inspection of what happens in the world reveals no purpose, dictates no ends, establishes no 'values'; facts remain facts, and what is does not entail, either strictly, or even in some vague and indirect fashion, what ought to be. What is will entail what ought to be only if what ought to be is itself part of what is – is given to the human observer as a datum. The metaphysicians and theologians of nature profess to discover in her not only facts but ideals. Nature speaks to them and commands them as well as merely revealing itself as so much matter – events, things, persons, actual and possible, to be catalogued, having a past to be reconstructed and a future to be predicted. The *philosophes* may have scarcely been aware of the degree to which they were children of their age and, for all their brave talk, far from emancipated from its metaphysical ideas: they preached naturalism indeed, but a metaphysical one, whereby they at one and the same time reduced nature to material bodies in space interacting with each other, and yet continued to hear voices bidding them to do this and that, those very same voices with which nature had spoken when she was still a living spiritual cosmos – embodied reason, the divine will – when material objects were the lowest of her constituents, either the crudest order of reality, or, some thought, mere shadows and illusions – a reality which 'transcended' sensible awareness, for ever hidden from those who approached her in a crudely empirical, stubbornly fact-gathering and fact-arranging frame of mind.

From this profound contradiction the *philosophes* never escaped. It dogged the steps of their followers in the two centuries which followed; and all talk of the scientific ideal of life – rationalist ethics, naturalistic values – suffers from this fatal ambiguity. The task of destruction is plain enough: if scientists ever show us that God does not exist, his commandments lose the force of his authority; and the same effect follows for all refutations of metaphysics, and with it of ethical or political systems founded thereon. But how should scientific knowledge supply us with purposes to follow? How is the advance of science connected with moral advance? What *is* moral advance? What are its criteria, how does one distinguish objectively valid moral or political goals from the play of individual feeling or caprice? On this the *philosophes* throw no light. They have not made good their promises. Their temper and general attitude may be sympathetic or not; but of reasoning there is none that is worth thinking of.

Let us look again: what were the presuppositions so familiar as to have been unnoticed, yet so deeply bound up with earlier views as to make impossible a consistent empiricism on the part of even the ultra-radicals among the great enemies of theology and metaphysics?

(1) The notion that nature is not merely what it is, but embodies an order and a purpose which is somehow discoverable, although none but empirical methods of investigation are employed.

(2) That this order and purpose is not merely a brute fact about the universe, but something which, once it has been observed by a man, cannot remain merely noted by him, but reveals to him the proper purposes of his own life and that of his fellows; that unless he derives from perception of his own place in the universe also the notion of what this place makes it proper for him to do, he is not rational; that rationality consists not merely in making correct deductions, as mathematicians or logicians do, or correct inductions, as those who study nature do, nor in the acquisition of everyday knowledge and the semi-instinctive grasp of what a given situation is like, and how it is likely to develop and how much it can be altered by his or others' intervention (which is often called

common sense or shrewdness or good judgement), but consists also in grasping what, being who and what he is, is the most 'natural' thing for him to do. In the case of eighteenth-century France and pre-Benthamite British utilitarians, what nature enjoined was the pursuit of happiness; but this is only what the utilitarians said of her. As I said above, Rousseau or Maistre thought that nature enjoined something very different; the point being that however different the ideals of various thinkers of this period, they all justified them by reference to what is 'natural', and thought that one of the functions of human 'reason' is to recognise what is 'natural' to us in this sense.

(3) A further presupposition is that nothing that is good can conflict with anything else that is good, much as no one true proposition can contradict any other true proposition. False propositions can and, of course, often do contradict each other; but no truths of fact which describe what there is, nor truths of mathematics which are deduced from the same set of axioms by the same set of rules, can normally be in conflict. If nature is a harmonious system, not merely of facts, but of values (whatever this may mean), no one good thing, being part of nature, can be incompatible with any other – equally natural – good thing. Consequently happiness can never be incompatible with fairness, liberty with equality, the true interests of any one individual with the true interests of any other or group of others; duty can never conflict with interest, mercy with justice, altruism with egoism. If there is any appearance of conflict between these prima facie divergent values, this can be due only to the fact that one or other or both, in a given situation, must have been insufficiently thought through, for we *know* (know a priori, for there is no escaping this conclusion now) that nature is a harmonious whole and cannot contradict herself. If the worst comes to the worst and the contradictions cannot be explained away, some qualities or modes of behaviour previously thought virtuous must be rejected, as survivals of ingrained habits, mistakes due to an uncritical faith in tradition, systematic mishearings of the voice of nature, a congenital philosophic deafness, obsessive delusions. Indeed this drastic course was taken by various eighteenth-century perfectibilians – Holbach, Volney, Godwin – with regard to such putative virtues as austerity, self-sacrifice, self-abnegation and the like, which were clearly incompatible even on the most casuistical interpretation with other more life-enhancing and full-blooded dispositions,

more obviously conducive to the maximisation of happiness by the richer development of human faculties. That no truly natural inclinations can conflict with one another is the a priori axiom; all virtues, ultimate values, worthy purposes, ends worth pursuing for their own sake are objectives of such inclinations; hence tragedy – the classical conflicts of values, between love and public duty, human feelings and the eternal laws – and all situations which appeared to involve agonised choices between incompatible yet prima facie equally stringent purposes, were due to insufficient understanding, just as paradoxes in mathematics or the sciences could not occur in the mind of an omniscient being, but must be due to insufficient knowledge or insufficient mental power. Enough knowledge – enough understanding – and all problems are solved, a cloudless and eternal happiness reigns for ever more.

Some *philosophes* thought that progress – the advance towards a condition in which all these interlinked values would be wholly realised – was inevitable: after many painful crises humanity must surely attain to perfection. Condorcet, in the most eloquent and moving of his writings, written in hiding, asks himself whether that darkening of human minds which caused him in 1793 to have to conceal himself from the fanatical violence of the Jacobins was not perhaps the last station in the martyrdom of man, after which the gates of paradise would be opened for him for ever. Other, more sceptical, thinkers – Holbach, Volney – do not believe in a historical providence, and think that unless a sufficient group of enlightened persons is in control of human affairs, the millennium may be deferred for an infinite length of time. But both sides think that perfection is within human grasp, and the tragic element in life can be eliminated for ever, since suffering is due always and only to imperfect understanding, for whatever is good is at least compatible with, and perhaps unrealisable without, everything else that is good; and nature tells us what is good, by planting a desire for it within us: values are objective after all.

(4) And there is another paradox involved. For the *philosophes* think that man is wholly the product of material factors – environment, institutions, perhaps inherited psychophysical characteristics, education, legislation. So that while some stress environmental factors more than man-made influences such as education, others consider that social influences have greater force than geographic or climatic ones. Again there are those who are beginning to say that modes of production are of decisive

importance, as against those who think that education by itself can mould a human being and make anything of him – a hero or a scoundrel, a martyr or a rake. There are those, again, who think that man is by nature good – that is, always benevolent, sympathetic and just – and those who think that he is at birth neither good nor bad, but may be made one or the other by the influences which play upon him, whether human or non-human. And there may have been those (for all I know) who agreed with the Roman Church that man is born wicked but, as good empiricists and modern psychologists or sociologists may have thought, that education or other forms of conditioning could cure such defects and deformities, very much as sound hygiene can cure the physical deficiencies of a new-born child. For these same people who believed that man was the complete product of one set of forces or another also tended to believe in the immense power of education and legislation – the free activity of the educators and legislators. But if man in general was what he was because of the climate in which he lived or the food which he ate, or the influence of his nurse, or the effects of public opinion or religion or this or that form of social or political life, were not the educators and legislators subject to the same dominant influences? Did they not live the lives that they lived and think as they thought and educate and legislate as they did without being able to help themselves? Were they too not players of parts not invented by them but instilled into them by their own environment and education – mere speakers of lines and performers of duties which they could no more help speaking and performing than the human beings whom they ruled or educated were thought to be able to help becoming what they became as a result of what the rulers or educators did with them? How could one at one and the same time maintain that we are what we are because we have grown under the influences which have beset us from the first moment of our conception, and yet that we can put an end to all the follies and vices and miseries of mankind by an act of will – by changing our methods of education or political life or diet, and so creating conditions favourable to the development of our children; creating these freely as if we – be we never so powerful and enlightened and conscious of our responsibilities – were not ourselves doomed to act as we did, because we were what we were, and could not help being what we were, because of the history of our family and group and race, and the physical and moral and social conditions in which we and our forebears were born and came to maturity and died?[1] And yet both these strictly incompatible views were maintained by the majority of the *philosophes*, some stressing one aspect, some the other, some speaking now with one voice, now with another, now both simultaneously. On the one hand it was fashionable to stress the power of physical nature or institutions, if only in order to discredit rival theories that the soul was immortal and free; or that God or angels or devils or our own inner spirit were causal factors in history – which was the meaningless patter of the Schools. On the other hand there was much talk of the vast opportunities which scientific advance, or an enlightened morality, or our new knowledge of history with its record of past errors, and the moral which they pointed, suddenly opened for human beings armed with reason, and no longer able to blame occult forces – God – or innate tendencies or mysterious and inscrutable powers for their crimes, vices and misfortunes. But the contradiction remained. It remained concealed only so long as the determinists who thought of physics and the perfectibilians who speculated about the triumphs awaiting education were fighting a common enemy – obscurantist priests, vicious or dissipated kings and courts, stupid or corrupt administrators, superstitious and brutalised peasants. Hence, as so often among those brought together by a common enemy, there was an illusion of agreement and solidarity where there was in fact a fundamental divergence of views and ideals. No sooner was the alliance dissolved – as it was in the nineteenth century – than these latent incompatibilities duly emerged into the open, and converted former comrades into rightly antagonistic opponents.

(5) Just as the same persons saw no conflict between complete determinism – as taught by the new natural sciences – and complete freedom of action as required by the new enlightenment, so the same persons believed at once in rational planning and extreme *laissez-faire*. The great purpose was to remove those restraints upon trade, upon production, commerce and all forms of human intercourse – economic, moral, social, intellectual – which were due to bad motives, greed on the part of individuals or minorities, or illicit love of power, or malice or prejudice, or else

[1] {Insert something on Frederick the Great noting this: also on determinism as a purely anti-obscurantist, secularist theory: also Jacques le Fataliste [ *Jacques le fataliste et son maître* ('Jacques the fatalist and his master'), 1796 novel by Diderot].}

mistaken beliefs due to the evil effects of religion or metaphysics. Once that was done, men could plan their lives rationally; that is, in accordance with scientific knowledge and the purposes of nature, which for the most part were identified with happiness and, as often as not, with an even vaguer concept, loosely denominated the common good, the relation to which of individuals was never made clear. There could be no conflict between the desires of any rational man and the desires of any other rational man, since reason could not oppose itself. Hence a rational plan, however rigid, however detailed, however all-embracing, regulating in the minutest particulars every thought and act of every living being, which might appear despotic to persons who did not like to be so remorselessly provided for, could not annoy a rational being, since it would provide him with everything which he would have thought of and wished for on his own account, with the additional advantage of saving him the trouble of having to impart his views to other rational beings who, *ex hypothesi*, play that part in his life, as he in theirs, which the plan, being rational, assigns to all those who wish to live their life according to reason. A rational man cannot have irrational – for example, self-defeating – thoughts or desires; if the social schema which regulates his life is rational, it anticipates his thoughts and wishes; to protest against it, indeed to be dissatisfied with it in any degree, is *pro tanto* a trace of the lingering force of incompletely eliminated unreason. Consequently to plan the life of a rational man completely, and to let him do exactly as he likes with no let or hindrance, is precisely the same thing. The plan is necessary only against unreason, against weaknesses, against the possibility of relapses into earlier, less enlightened states. If all men were wholly enlightened, they would not need a State or any other organisation. Complete *laissez-faire* and complete social organisation are thus, far from being incompatible, in fact identical. In the case of rational men total anarchy coincides with maximum obedience to law. Freedom is perception of rational necessity. It must, of course, be remembered that 'reason' here is not being used to mean that which enters into induction, deduction, common sense, but rather to mean the pursuit of rational ends; which means not merely ends which do not conflict with one another, or defeat themselves, or are not incompatible with available means, but ends which are rational in the very special sense of the word in which some ends are more rational than others, that is, occupy a specific place in that 'objective' hierarchy of ends the whole of which is offered, held out, almost thrust at us, by an active agency which shapes them – nature, reason, the divine order, under whatever name we choose to worship and obey it. The entire rationalist programme of the eighteenth century revolves round this central notion that reason discovers ends as well as means, that to call a ruler enlightened is to say that he is an expert on ends as well as methods, that Hume is mistaken in regarding ends as psychologically given, insusceptible to rational criticism. If Hume is right, the entire edifice built on the assumption that there is a form of life which all rational men would automatically embrace – that this is why they are called rational – collapses like a house of cards. And so far no one has brought any valid argument against Hume's position – none certainly which any *philosophe* could use as a means of escape.

John Stuart Mill wrote an honest, painstaking, characteristically lucid, and bleak essay on the subject of nature. He is puzzled by the way in which philosophers of the eighteenth century have employed this concept. He begins by observing that the maxim 'naturam sequi' is part of an ancient European tradition. But he cannot understand it. What can possibly be meant by saying we ought to follow nature? There are only three possibilities.

(*a*) 'Nature' means all that there is, governed by the laws by which it is governed, which includes human beings and all that they are and do and suffer. In which case it is virtually meaningless, and certainly otiose, to advise them to conform to laws from which they cannot in any case escape, or learn from an order of which they are inevitable constituents. What then can be meant?

(*b*) Nature is also contrasted with the arts and sciences, that is with everything that men have invented or added since they emerged from the condition described as primitive. But if man is being advised to follow nature in this sense, this is tantamount to an invitation to throw away everything with which, by painful effort, men have furnished themselves for the purpose of leading lives which they approve of or enjoy. Nature in this sense (in which it is the subject-matter of the sciences but has no history) is by no means a harmonious organism or mechanism to imitate which would promote the ends which human beings seek or ought to seek: for the most superficial acquaintance with the world of natural 'phenomena', in the sense in which they are contrasted with civilised existence, reveals them as often involved in a most violent and apparently meaningless process of destruction and waste.

Floods and earthquakes, and indeed any natural events which lead to the infliction of pain on sentient beings and the destruction of beautiful natural or human objects, or for that matter of plants or animals – the seemingly blind behaviour of brute matter – are precisely that which every human resource, moral, technological, intellectual, aesthetic, is directed to minimising, rendering harmless, or putting to use in serving human ends. To imitate nature in this sense is to import chaotic violence, meaningless waste, utter purposelessness into human life, and surely it is not this that the wise and benevolent moralists who encouraged us to follow nature can have had in mind.

(c) Finally, Mill continues, there is the somewhat narrower sense of the word 'natural' in which it is contrasted with the affected and the artificial, that is, modes of human behaviour designed to deceive someone or conceal something. This Mill identifies with respect for the truth, which he favours, but points out that this sense of following nature is not sufficient to cover the doctrines involving the whole of human life, which adherents of the 'natural life' must have intended to propagate. It is, no doubt, useful to warn men against excessively mannered behaviour, and to praise spontaneity, truthfulness and warm-heartedness, but this seems to have little to do with organising life in the light of the findings of the natural sciences, or the condemnation of this or that form of government or economic order as being contrary to nature. Surely it is not artificiality of manners or lack of sincerity that the great economic innovator Quesnay or the sternly communist abbé Mably supposed themselves in the first instance to be attacking.

Consequently Mill admits to being puzzled, as well he might be. To tell us to follow what we cannot help doing in any case seems foolish; to tell us to imitate pointless destruction and savage customs, and so make our lives as nasty and as brutish as they can be, seems unreasonable; and to tell us to be more sincere and direct is commendable, but seems not far-reaching enough to have been regarded as a central moral and political principle for over two thousand years. At this point Mill turns his back on the entire idea of nature in disgust as nothing but a sorry confusion, and dismisses it from the list of topics worthy of the sustained attention of serious persons.

There is surely something odd here. If John Stuart Mill, who was born so soon after the close of the century in which the discussion of nature occupied so central a position, abandons the analysis of this political or social concept in despair; if Mill, who so deeply adored the poetry of Wordsworth, finds the concept of nature irrelevant to moral or political thinking; if Bentham, from whom he derived his mode of reasoning, claimed to be equally puzzled by this obscure notion, we cannot, perhaps, be blamed too much if in our turn we find it far from clear. Yet there is no doubt that the doctrine of scientific naturalism – the ideas of observation of nature, knowledge of and advance in the sciences, and perhaps now and then the added idea of 'living close to nature' – means something to us even now, and it is merely disingenuous to pretend that it is nothing but a great muddle which can be made to vanish with a little clear thinking. All the propositions enumerated above have been believed explicitly or implicitly by those very thinkers by whom modern rationalism, liberalism and scientific enlightenment were created. Great and beneficent reforms have been undertaken by men who believed this complex of ideas. The struggle between progressives and reactionaries has been precisely a conflict between those who believed such propositions and those who were held to be appealing to authority or tradition or dogma or prescription, or some other criterion not discoverable by the ordinary empirical methods of acquiring information.

Clearly, then, the notion cannot be dismissed as wholly opaque and meaningless. And it is not: but it is made to appear so by disregarding the one major premiss upon which the entire foundation rests – namely, the belief in the possibility of discovering purposes as well as facts in nature, the possibility of detecting not merely a direction, not merely consistent laws which govern human experience, though that is questionable enough, not merely patterns in history or in the relationships of human beings to one another – but ends, purposes, the march towards which is not only inevitable or possible but 'rational', that is a fulfilment of some total cosmic schema, the partial realisation of which in different fields of thought or art or action is called rational in those fields. It is called rational precisely because it functions within each of these fields, however differently, in an analogous manner. For when all the fields are viewed together it is maintained that they will be revealed to be complementary to each other; and to form one harmonious whole; and reason is the faculty which at once explains how everything is interrelated as it is, and points to the goal towards which everything either must or, according to some, should, if we are to be rational, strive. To say of an activity that it is rational is then to say that it has an intelligent goal; to say of a society that it is rationally organised is equally to say that it has a goal. To ask what this goal is, if this is to be a valid question, must presuppose the possibility of an answer resting on objective evidence, open to inspection by any impartial, intelligent observer; such an answer is that which is meant by a rational goal.

Since the sciences have provided us with the only reliable information we have about other matters of fact, they must provide us with an answer to this enquiry too; and all the political and social doctrines which have claimed to be 'based' on science in this sense, like the systems of Spencer or Comte or Marx, have acquired prestige with persons who believe in rational methods of investigation, and are suspicious of or hostile to religion or metaphysics, or popular superstitions and unthinking assumptions of every kind, because the rationality which they value in methods of enquiry has here been surreptitiously transferred to the ends themselves. But unless we accept a teleological interpretation of the universe for which there cannot be any empirical warrant, and which the sciences therefore abandoned as a sterile and cramping category long ago, at the beginning of the seventeenth century, the proposition that some ultimate ends are more rational than others has no clear meaning. Ends may be bad or good, immediate or remote, social or individual, hallowed by tradition or bold and revolutionary, mutually compatible or incompatible, normal or abnormal, attainable or Utopian, fruitful or self-defeating, variable and subjective or invariant and accepted by entire societies or cultures, or the whole of humanity itself at all times, but they are not rational or irrational in the usual sense in which the word is used. The statements in which we enunciate or appeal to them, because they do not describe facts or events, are not true or false, any more than commands, behests, vows, acts of self-dedication, which they resemble, are true or false. Historical statements to the effect that individuals or groups or societies do or do not pursue particular purposes or systems of purposes – forms of life, ideals, and lives constructed around such ideals – these are of course true or false, and are arrived at by acts properly described as rational or irrational as the case may be. But the words which themselves express or embody or convey such attitudes and ends and ideals are arrived at by methods neither rational nor irrational, nor can they properly be said to be rational or irrational in themselves. Whether Hume was right in saying that they embody (although he mistakenly thought they always described) passions, by which he meant feelings, impulses, transient emotions, appetites and other evanescent states or processes of our emotional lives, may indeed be questioned, and indeed with some confidence rejected as being untrue to the facts of how we come to acquire, retain, pursue, or reject or abandon and oppose, various ideals or ends. But the root of the matter is indeed where he found it: rationality is a concept which applies not to purposes, but only to methods of enquiry or adaptation of means to ends. If our individual ends were all means towards some universal end, pursued by all that exists, nature and man, things and persons, then the degree of their adjustment as means to this universal purpose could indeed, in some transcendental sense, be described as effective or ineffective, and in this sense rational or irrational. But this is precisely what Helvétius and Holbach so strenuously denied; and yet the political doctrines which emanated from the *philosophes* spoke of the organisation of society along rational scientific lines, and advocated that education and legislation should be concerned with the production of citizens capable of being fitted into a single coherent pattern, the validity of which is guaranteed by reason and sanctioned by the sole ultimate authority – the natural sciences. That policy rested on the gigantic presupposition of a teleological universe. And if this premiss is mistaken – as it is certainly confused – the entire vast edifice built upon it lacks a basis. It does not, of course, follow from this that the opponents of this view whose concept of reason or rationality is of some other kind – a priori, theological, Aristotelian, Thomistic, Hegelian, Buddhist – derive any advantage from the fallacies and contradictions of the eighteenth-century empiricists, for their solution to the question has not even the advantage of an intelligible if false premiss, but takes refuge in regions altogether opaque to the normal techniques of discovery; and the remedy is far more dangerous than the disease which it claims to cure.

*At the end of this chapter Berlin has written the following notes for revision:*

More on *planning* and notion of scientific planning of life: and expertise. Also: retention of inconsistencies: behaviourism with (1) natural rights (2) equality (3) free will. But main thing: science is cure for all evils: provides *ends*: questions it cannot answer are *not* questions: empirical or nothing: everything deduced from 'nature' or 'man': who *quod semper, quod idem, et quod omnis ubique* [sc. *quod semper, quod ubique, quod ab omnibus*: see below, p. 164], variations ignorable: Condorcet (and all the Encyclopaedists in a sense) thought *that* to be the ideal to be striven for by all rational means *which omniscient* man *would want*: omniscient man would understand past and future by *calculation*: since world is a deducible body of facts, though empirical: he cannot but desire happiness (all else is induced by error and faulty education – happiness alone is *natural*: dogma). Therefore he would desire it within the framework of the possible: indeed by wanting to do *that* which harmonised him most with universe and made for his and its freest functioning: assumptions (1) that universe *is* a harmony though misunderstood by us (quote Pope) (2) that there *is* one human nature and one human ideal: an order which suits X *must* suit Y, the variety of unconnected ends itself proof of error – for universe is coherent whole: nature is one, needs tying up (3) that this is discoverable by science – chemists know more about what is *right* than poets: and understand nature's ways – and her goals (4) that once men are moulded, whether by rational persons (Condorcet) or legislation (Helvétius) or by social conditioning (Rome: Fascists: Communists), into *not* hampering their own central impulses – implanted by Nature – automatic happiness results. We *know* what is end – what the omniscient want – and we know means – science tells us. So Avanti! ['Forward!']

# 2

# THE IDEA OF FREEDOM

FREEDOM, both social and political, is one of the most ancient, and, prima facie, one of the most intelligible human ideals. The desire for freedom is, in the first place, the desire on the part of individuals or groups not to be interfered with by other individuals or groups. This is its most obvious meaning and all other interpretations of it tend to seem artificial or metaphorical. Human beings have wishes, inclinations, impulses, and anything which stops them from realising these is called an obstacle. Such obstacles may be animate or inanimate, human or non-human. There is a sense in which we speak of someone as 'not free' to do this or that when he is prevented from fulfilling his wishes by non-human obstacles – such as the nature of the physical world, which prevents me from gravitating upwards, instead of downwards, or living for long without food. There may be psychological obstacles, too, as when a man becomes aware that he cannot count beyond a certain number without becoming confused, or is unable to love his enemies or understand the works of Hegel. But as we do not in fact (rightly or wrongly) believe in the laws of psychology quite as firmly as we do in those of physics, the psychological sort of unfreedom seems to us, perhaps, not quite so clear as the more obvious physical sense in which I cannot fly to the moon or see the back of my head.

But neither of these are the senses in which those who speak of political or social freedom mean to use this term. One might say that every sense in which the words 'can' or 'cannot' are used indicate the presence or absence of a freedom of some sort. But when we speak of the lack of social or political freedom, we imply that somebody, rather than something, is preventing us from doing or being something we wish to do or be. We are, as a rule, implying the existence of interference or oppression, whether deliberate or not. When, for example, socialists distinguish 'economic' from 'political' freedom, and maintain that it is useless to provide men with opportunities for choosing forms of government when they are in fact too poor or ignorant to be able to acquire or enjoy the goods which this or that government permits to be obtained 'freely', there is a genuine – and dangerous – ambiguity in such a way of speaking. If they mean merely that if a man has not the means, or is too undeveloped morally or intellectually, to be able to purchase something which in fact would please him if he acquired it, that need not, in a strict sense, always constitute a social or political demand: there may be many other causes which stop a man from getting what he wants (or would like if he was enlightened enough to be able to want). He may be afflicted with physical disabilities, or be born at a time or in a place in which such things are physically unobtainable, and this makes him unable to satisfy a specific need. But the sense in which this makes him *unfree* is not necessarily social or political more than it is physical or biological or historical or geographical. When his lack of freedom is conceived as distinctively social or political what is implied is that he is prevented from getting, or doing, or being, something specific by social or political factors, that is, by the relation to him of other human beings. It is they who in some way are stopping him from behaving in a certain way – and that not simply as three-dimensional creatures in time and space, not in the sense in which a man may prevent me from reaching my destination by accidentally stumbling against me and breaking my leg (in this respect he is behaving like any other piece of matter in space – a log, or a stone), but by themselves behaving in some way in which we believe that they could, if they wished, avoid acting. I complain about absence of personal liberty only when in some sense I think that I am being prevented from doing what I want by other human beings who might, as far as the laws of material nature are concerned, be behaving differently. If I complain of lack of liberty although those who stop me are not, perhaps, intending to stop me, but are pursuing quite irrelevant purposes of their own which merely have the effect of stopping me, I may not blame them, but I still feel my lack of personal liberty; and I do so because in some sense I vaguely realise that I am failing to get what I want not because of physical or biological or other 'natural' factors, but because other people's intentions (though not necessarily directed against me) frustrate my purpose. In short, I complain of the absence of personal liberty when I am prevented from acting as I wish by the realisation of the conscious or semi-conscious or, indeed, unconscious purposes of other beings – and not merely by the mechanical behaviour of their bodies. And when I believe that these intentions are specifically directed at stopping me, and making it impossible for me to do what I want, I feel that my liberty is being deliberately infringed; and when I believe these intentions to be unjust or unreasonable, I complain of oppression.

Freedom is thus in its primary sense a negative concept; to demand freedom is to demand the absence of human activities which cross my own; and the general discussion of this topic has always consciously or unconsciously presupposed this meaning of the term. Theologians and philosophers have used the word in many other senses: in particular that in which a man may be said to be unfree when he is acting 'irrationally'; for example, when he is said to be 'a slave to his passions' or 'a victim of his own delusions' – the sense in which men are said to 'free' themselves from errors or an obsessive infatuation, or hitherto irresistible physical or social inclinations. Whatever the value of such a use of the word – and it is by now virtually an intrinsic part of the normal usage of modern European languages – this meaning of the terms 'freedom' and 'slavery' is still felt to be somewhat analogical or even metaphorical, and rightly so. The sense in which Uncle Tom was the slave of Simon Legree is the literal sense, which nobody would dispute. Whereas the sense in which Cephalus in the first book of Plato's *Republic* claims to have freed himself from slavery to the passion of love – 'a cruel master' – is distinctly different from the former. The struggle against a man who wishes to impose his will upon other human beings, and on the other hand what is called an inner struggle within myself – whether between my passions themselves or between my less worthy inclinations and my 'better nature' – are not struggles in the same sense of the word, and the second is given that title by what is felt to be a quasi-metaphorical extension of the term. Similar emotions may accompany 'liberation' from both; nevertheless one sense is felt to be more basic than the other.

And yet a great deal has, of course, been made of the secondary – metaphorical – sense of freedom, which has, notably with the Platonists, Stoics and Christian philosophers, and later with Spinoza and certain German Idealists, been made to include the first. The well-known Stoic argument that to understand and adapt oneself to nature is the truest freedom rests on the premiss that nature or the cosmos possesses a pattern and a purpose; that human beings possess an inner light or reason which is that in them which seeks perfection by integrating itself as completely as possible with this cosmic pattern and purpose; that the passions are disturbers of this inner reason, and at once darken its perception of what the universal pattern is, and tend to 'drive' and pull it away from its appointed path. Man is a rational being; and to say this is to say that he is able to detect this general pattern and purpose and identify himself with them; his wishes are rational if they aspire after such self-identification, and irrational if they oppose it. To be free is to fulfil one's wishes; one can fulfil one's wishes only if one knows how to do so effectively, that is, if one understands the nature of the world in which one lives; if this world has a pattern and a purpose, to ignore this central fact is to court disaster, since any action undertaken either in ignorance of, or without attention to, or, most foolish of all, in opposition to, the plan of the universe is bound to end in frustration, because the universe will defeat the individual who ignores or defies it. If freedom is a fulfilment of wishes, and such fulfilment depends upon understanding of the world plan, freedom is inconceivable without submission to the plan. Freedom, therefore, becomes identical with a certain kind of 'rational' submission. This paradox is regarded as being explained away if only we remember that the universe possesses a purpose; that to be rational is to understand this purpose and one's own part in it; that wishes may be rational or irrational, and since the universe is what it is, and will be what it will be, only those who seek ends the fulfilment of which is in harmony with the world structure are rational. Hence true freedom, being true self-fulfilment, is a capacity for self-adaptation to the universal harmony; it is submission only in appearance, for the only opposition to such a course can spring from unharmonised or unharmonisable desires, which, being unrealisable in any case, are, *pro tanto*, irrational and cannot lead to freedom – that is, effective self-fulfilment. Hence, to be free is to understand the universe – and that leads rational beings, not intent on self-destruction (which is tantamount to irrationality – for how can reason seek to defeat itself?), to submit to its laws and purposes; and conversely all disobedience to its purposes – which takes the form of sins, crimes, errors (and the differences between these depend on whether they are committed deliberately or involuntarily, and to what degree) –

must be due to, be an expression of, ignorance – ignorance of how the universe 'works', of what reality is.

This is the heart of the doctrine that virtue is knowledge, that the criminal, the sinner and the fool are what they are only because they seek to satisfy their wishes in ways in which these wishes cannot in principle be satisfied, given the fixed nature of the universe. Since such persons will not be satisfied, they will not be happy; and since they will be frustrated, they will not be free; since they will be departing from the norm set them by nature, they will not be virtuous. Freedom, happiness and virtue thus coincide; to fail in any of these is to fail in them all: and to fail means to be in conflict with, and therefore liable to be destroyed by, the universe; if not immediately, then in the end – in the longest run.

This is the doctrine of the principal schools of Greek philosophy, of Platonists, Aristotelians, Stoics, Epicureans and their successors. The Christian philosophers substituted the divine order for that of nature, and the service of God, whose will the universe embodies, for that of impersonal nature; but the doctrine of freedom remained substantially identical. Man is a compound of conflicting elements, bad and good, and the fulfilment of God's law liberates him, that is, fully satisfies the soul, which yearns for the good, which is alone capable of full satisfaction – if not in this world, then in the next – when it has shed its temporary habitation, the body, with its incubus of evil passions which distract his mind and will and darken his understanding (so far as any is vouchsafed to him on earth) of the nature of God and his commandments. The love of God, and the fear of God, take the place of the doctrine of adjustment to the natural purposes of earthly things. In substance, the view remains unaltered: liberty is fulfilment of a universal (divinely enacted) law; the less resistance a man is tempted to offer to this law, the happier and the freer he will be; only the angels and perhaps the saints experience no such temptation – in them true love and fear of God and his universe are fulfilled. Only those who are without temptation to sin are wholly free. Christian Platonism, Christian Aristotelianism and Christian Stoicism are fully intelligible doctrines for this reason; they may be involved in metaphysical heresies about the person of the deity, or the nature of the universe, but in the conception of human freedom there is here no fundamental difference. There is no radical disagreement about this issue throughout the Christian world. There may be passionate and profound differences about how knowledge of God's purposes is to be obtained – whether through the teachings of the Church of Rome and its priesthood and its tradition and its sacred writings, or through the interpretation of the Bible alone; through the pronouncements of the individual conscience or the accepted doctrine of this or that body of men, now or during a long period of time. There may be violent disputes about the emphasis to be placed upon the doing of good works or the acquisition of a peculiar state of soul, about the part played by appropriate devoted study or discipline and by divine grace; about the degree of illumination permitted to mortal men, and about what portion of it is expressible in articulate speech, and how much must remain a mystery or be revealed only in moments of mystical illumination – all that may be and has been a matter of violent dispute, and has led to much reciprocal persecution. But the central principle remains inviolate: the universe is guided by God, and to understand its nature and direction is to know how to live, and to know this is to know how to be free – that is, to avoid the frustration of one's innermost wishes and inclinations and purposes.

In Spinoza's doctrine, which denied general purposes to the universe, the doctrine suffers a certain modification, but remains in essential respects unaltered: freedom is still a satisfaction of our wishes. The universe is a rational whole; that is, any part of it can be deduced by a person of sufficient insight and power of reasoning from any other. When we realise what a thing is, and that it is what it is for logical or metaphysical reasons (and for Spinoza they are identical), namely because of the necessary relations which all things have to one another and which make whatever is necessarily what it is – thus and not otherwise – then we cannot wish it to be otherwise; for what would such a wish ask for? When we realise that two plus two equals four, we realise not only that it is so, but that it must be so, because such is the 'necessary' nature, the essence, of number: if it were not, two would not always be two, nor four be four, nor plus be plus. No one in his senses could grieve that two plus two never was – never would be – five, and nobody in his senses could feel his freedom curtailed by the necessity which prevents it from being five. If he did feel this, we should, for that very reason, hesitate to call him rational: or even sane. But what holds true of number holds of all reality. To understand what a thing is is to understand its relations to other things (and for rationalist metaphysicians this means the inner necessity which binds its elements), that is, to understand why it cannot be otherwise: and to understand this is to accept it as rational, that is, to realise that the opposite is inconceivable or self-contradictory – and what is self-contradictory is unintelligible, and cannot be the object of anyone's true desire. To wish things to be other than what they must be, to lament because they are what they are and not something else, to complain that one is constricted by their being what they are, is to fail to understand the rational pattern which makes all alternatives logically inconceivable. It is the passions – as always, the villains of this piece – that alone produce the illusion that things could be otherwise and make men desire the impossible – the impossible which turns out on examination to be unintelligible, contrary to reason, meaningless. The intellectual love of God is that illumination whereby things are shown in their true reality, determined by rational connections in an order which is perfect, for none other is rationally conceivable; to understand this is to be free, free from pseudo-desires – desires for what, when examined, turn out to be self-contradictory chimeras, impossible objects of desire. And science – the use of unclouded reason, the demonstrator of why objects are as they are and events occur as they do – is thus the great liberator of mankind, the remover of obstacles, the dispeller of mysteries, which dissolves those misunderstandings and confusions which alone cause us to ask for the impossible and to fall into terrors and despairs when we are duly frustrated.

This is a concept of the role of the sciences which many adherents of scientific progress have maintained, often with moving eloquence. Only ignorance plants the fear which makes us unfree. When a disease racks us and we do not know its causes, we – and those who love us – are terrified and fall into despair: once we understand how it arises, what the inevitable, intelligible causes of it are, our fear is dissipated and we accept the inevitable whether it is curable or not, 'philosophically'. Since it is inevitable, part, that is, of the necessity of things, we are at peace with it, as we are with a mathematical theorem. It confirms rather than shakes our faith in the rationality of the universe, it 'liberates' us from the sense of frustration induced by harbouring an irrational desire, for example that the universe remain as it is and must be, but the pain – in defiance of the system – disappear. To ask for this is to ask for 2 + 2 to be 17; the pain is necessary, therefore it is as it should be – good, for good is what fulfils the demands of a rational nature; it is necessary, therefore it is itself a demand of our mind, to the degree that it is rational, that is in tune with the universal harmony; and though we suffer it, we are free – self-fulfilled. We persecute a thief because the motive for his stealing is imperfectly understood by us: but when we call him a kleptomaniac his action has been scientifically attributed to its right place in the universal system, and we cease to fear or hate him. To understand, in this sense, is to accept, and to accept is to rule out alternatives; the absence of what cannot be, of an effect for which there is no cause, of a number which is not coherent with the mathematical system, of a situation which, the world being what it is, cannot arise, cannot any longer be a source of embitterment to us, or a fetter upon our freedom. The universe is a harmonious system of entities linked to each other by ties which cannot be otherwise, a logical schema translated into concrete terms, a rational order, to understand which is to understand oneself, one's own true wishes and what alone will truly satisfy them – and that without the need to postulate a personal deity either to create or keep in being the universal harmony. This noble and serene vision is common to both sides in the great rationalist–empiricist contentions of the seventeenth and eighteenth centuries. It animated the impious Spinoza no less than the devout philosophers whom his luminous and vigorously argued atheism so deeply and genuinely horrified: the *outré* materialist Holbach – a behaviourist *avant la parole* – as much as those more tender-minded thinkers, Voltaire and Locke, not to speak of more traditionalist figures, who were revolted by his grim and 'corpse-like'[1] system.

The early German romantics were perhaps influenced by this notion of rational liberty most powerfully of all. Herder and Goethe, Schelling and Jacobi, Schleiermacher and Hegel conceived of this notion of freedom, freedom from superstition, ignorance, the passions – the identity of total rationality with total self-fulfilment – as the deepest revelation vouchsafed to them in their lives. As Voltaire had liberated so many of his contemporaries in the West from the dark and asphyxiating world of ecclesiastical dogma and ancient prejudice and feudal prescription, so this calm and rational system liberated the Germans from the opposite nightmare: from a scattered, disconnected society in which the majority of educated men were condemned to moral isolation and

[1] Goethe, *Dichtung und Wahrheit*, book 11: vol. 28, p. 68, line 17, in *Goethes Werke* (Weimar, 1887–1919).

political impotence, and political and economic weakness and disunion condemned the noblest enterprises and the purest characters to bitter frustration and ineffectiveness. This spectacle of the apparently haphazard play of blind forces without discernible origin or intelligible direction – a combination of dreary political inertia and moral and intellectual pettiness – was largely, if not entirely, the consequence of the Thirty Years War, followed by the economic, and to some degree intellectual, decline of Germany in the early part of the following century. The luminous and coherent word of the rationalists – whether metaphysical or scientific – acted upon some of the German intellectuals as a vast liberating force, and rescued them, at any rate personally, from their agonising perplexities and sense of solitude and purposelessness in a hostile and capricious world.

The movement of German enlightenment – the *Aufklärung* – is a set of variations, metaphysical and literary, deist and mystical, some of them of great depth and beauty, upon this central theme. Leibniz's metaphysical system set it in German-speaking countries, and Leibniz taught that everything in the universe is not merely connected by those necessary relations which make of it an intelligible pattern – the concept of a static, as it were a geometrical, system of timeless entities in timeless relations, or continuing in a kind of eternal, unchanging present – but also develops or evolves in accordance with internal logical laws. The universe is a hierarchy of entities, but the frontier between the animate and the inanimate is only relative; everything evolves or grows or develops its nature, or fulfils its 'inner' pattern (all these are alternative descriptions of the same process), and metaphysical intuition (as well as the revelation vouchsafed to the great Christian doctors and saints) discovers the principles by which this is regulated. The inanimate 'seeks' to become animate, to become sentient; the sentient to become rational. Everywhere there is an ascending order. To understand something is thereby to make oneself more rational, and to make oneself more rational is to make oneself more real; that is, nearer the ultimate purpose of all that is, that which is wholly intelligible to itself; and whatever is wholly intelligible to itself must understand its relations to everything else; for unless it does so, it cannot wholly understand itself[1] – and that kind of total

[1] Leibniz's peculiar reasons for supposing that no entity can perceive other entities directly but only by means of a kind of complicated system of mirrors need not concern us here.

understanding is possible to God alone, who, in this sense, is not only the creator but the purpose of the world, all of which potentially 'strives' towards him. To realise – in the sense of understand – is therefore ultimately identical with being realised – in the sense of being made actual from something merely potential; and this great pun is the centre of the system. This play on words, whereby to realise, to grasp something intellectually or emotionally, makes one more real in the sense of raising one above some previous level, in some endless ascent, comes to bind its spell more and more upon the imagination of German thinkers, and culminates in the vast cosmological fantasies of the romantic movement, and in particular of its ethical and political visions. But all this is not yet.

One of the cardinal metaphors used by Leibniz is that of an orchestra in which each instrument or group of instruments has its own part to play. The playing of its part is its whole function; the actualisation of its purpose is the inner principle which, since the days of Plato and Aristotle, philosophers have affected to be able to find in all created and uncreated things. The player plays better if he 'understands' – perceives the pattern – of the part assigned to him in the cosmic orchestra.[1] He need not, indeed he cannot, hear the totality to which his activity contributes – only the conductor, only God, can do that. Nevertheless, there is such a totality and we understand it as much – and thereby are of it as much – as our finite natures permit.

Everything moves, and moves according to laws which are in principle intelligible. The empiricists think they can discover them by observation and experiment, theologians and metaphysicians only with the aid of special rational or intuitive or mythical insights. Political and moral life is no less part of such a pattern

[1] Leibniz lived in an age of polyphonic music where each voice or instrument played a distinct tune or melodic pattern of its own, which it could grasp without necessarily hearing or knowing its relation to the other voices or instruments with which it was in harmony or counterpoint. Hegel, writing at the time when symphonic music was composed of sounds which, whatever the effect of their combination, were no longer divided into independently intelligible instrumental or vocal melodic wholes, can use the metaphor of harmony without implying that the player need 'understand' the sounds which history compels him to contribute to the symphony as a whole. We should not overstress the importance of this evolution of the metaphor, but it is nevertheless a significant pointer to the shift in meaning of 'harmony in the rational plan' which had occurred in the crucial half-century which divides Bach from Beethoven.

than any other human activity. Christian Wolff, who systematised
Leibniz – that is, reduced the imaginative writings of a man of
genius into an artificial schema capable of being turned into
philosophical textbooks and primers – was responsible for imbuing
German thinkers of the mid-eighteenth century with the concept
of a tidy, intelligible, law-abiding cosmic order. Science and
religion were to be 'reconciled'. Miracles were due only to a
superior power or knowledge, in line with, though greater than,
that possessed by ordinary mortals. Christ when he turned the
water into wine naturally showed a knowledge of chemistry
greater than any possessed by Robert Boyle, and Joshua made the
sun stand still by means, presumably, not indeed known, or
perhaps knowable, to us, but certainly intelligible to anyone with a
superhuman grasp of celestial mechanics. And so too with politics:
those rulers alone were truly good and wise who grasped as much
as possible of the natural order of which the sciences, theology and
natural reason were but so many different instruments of discovery, whose findings must necessarily harmonise; for the truth is
one, and the function of man is to possess himself of as much of it
as he may from whichever direction and by whatever means his
physical or mental or social endowments make possible. Bishop
Butler, who thought that rational self-love, the rational moral
faculty he called conscience, and the harmonious development of
our natural inclinations must all necessarily conduce to the same
end – the 'natural' self-development of our true inner self in
accordance with the purposes and principles implanted in us by
Providence – was in effect saying precisely this. Lessing, the most
sensitive, imaginative, humane and scrupulous thinker produced by
the German nation, in his celebrated parable of the three rings in
his play *Nathan the Wise*, gave the noblest formulation to this
ideal: all religions, so far as they are true, seek to say the same
thing, and urge men to strive for the same ultimate purposes and
live morally and spiritually equally valuable lives, however different the media, the historical circumstances, the individual personalities through which they work. There are many paths to the great
goal of human perfection, and their differences need not be
contradictory if the unity of the goal is kept in view; each true
human activity has its own unique value; no true values can come
into collision with each other if they are properly understood; for
the good cannot conflict with the good, nor right with right, nor
one form of beauty with another; humanity is one and its ideal is

the universal harmony of distinct but mutually enhancing and enriching elements. Intolerance springs only from misunderstanding of one value in terms of the too narrow pursuit of another. Toleration – that is, a mutual guarantee of freedom – is indispensable if men are to fulfil each one his function; to fulfil one's function is to contribute all that one can contribute to the great concert of the world; and to do this is to be free. Freedom is that true, unique order in which every human soul is fully realised, and cannot occur so long as there is misery, or frustration, or any form of oppression or ignorance – forms of non-fulfilment, imperfection – among men. Progress is the gradual elimination of such gaps between striving and fulfilment. If the metaphysical premises of Leibniz and the rational theologians are not wholly fallacious, this development is surely guaranteed by God; there may be temporary setbacks, or diversion of energy into blind alleys, but in general, and in the long run, progress is inevitable, for all change is in the end improvement, the growth of spiritual self-development on the part both of men and, if Leibniz is right, of all the ingredients in the world, for there is life and spirit and movement in them all. This is the doctrine which Voltaire so mordantly caricatured in *Candide*; the Lisbon earthquake was too cruel a reminder that human happiness is not dependent on education, reason and humanity alone; nevertheless Voltaire too was at times disposed to accept this optimistic and generous view of the world and its purpose.

Hume almost alone among the great thinkers of the century did not believe this.[1] He did not, that is to say, believe in any cosmic guarantee of universal improvement, because he did not perceive any meaning in propositions which affirmed that purposes could be discerned in things in the way in which their natural properties could be perceived. But even he offered a kind of empirical substitute for the divine harmony: men's opinions differ, no doubt, and so do their temperaments, and when they appeared to believe or act in opposition to each other, this was not necessarily due to ignorance, and their disagreements could not necessarily be reconciled by exhibiting a common purpose which, if they but

---

[1] Nor in a sense did Helvétius or Bentham: Helvétius thought that interests clashed genuinely and could be integrated into a single policy only by social pressure. But he often speaks as if such pressure is ultimately inevitable. Bentham followed Hume in supposing that 'nature' guaranteed nothing: but was a good deal more radical and optimistic in his faith in human self-interest and reason.

knew it, animated them all. Differences were differences, and genuine enough. But because men were endowed not merely with passions and tastes and ambitions which divided them and set them against each other, but also with an equally instinctive and inborn sense of 'sympathy', and benevolent pleasure in each other's pleasures, and pains in each other's pains, a harmonious form of common life was organisable, not founded indeed upon pursuit of rationally guaranteed 'natural' goals, but upon common ideals which many of them embodied in customs, traditions and other *de facto* institutions, and in social and individual habits, not all of them by any means defensible in terms of any single artificially applied principle. This was the spring of human association – this and experience of the benefits of division of labour – rather than the grim utilitarian *pis aller* – the only means of avoiding the precarious life of brutes, ever threatened by violent death – of which Hobbes had spoken; or for that matter those 'natural rights' which are implanted by God or nature in all individuals, and which were involved in the notion of the social contract, whereby some portion of them was freely ceded to the ruler, and the irreducible minimum was kept by the subjects – the rights of which Locke had spoken, but which to Hume seemed an unintelligible metaphysical fiction. It was the fortunate sense of solidarity among men, the product of common conditions, common interests, a mixture of reason, emotion and imagination, and the influence of time and circumstance – very like the factors discussed by Montesquieu – that made possible, and even realisable in normal times, a working compromise between egoistic inclination and the minimal demands of social coexistence, such as a reasonable amount of personal liberty, peace, security and property.

Hume's method was strictly empirical, that of the German Enlightenment a good deal more metaphysical: but both perceived the solution of political problems in the discovery of a harmonious pattern, inclusion in which realised men's natural tendencies and so made them happy, secure and free. Doubtless a total lack of restraint would make men even more free, but it would diminish their security; no doubt a severer organisation would guarantee security, but it would gravely curtail freedom. Hume, therefore, inclined to a working compromise, which allowed something of each, and more of either than could be secured under a tighter system. The German thinkers of the Augustan age – like the Hegelians half a century later – wanted a more metaphysically satisfactory pattern: and perceived obedience as submission to the pattern set by God or nature, and thereby a coincidence of freedom with perception of an inevitable necessity; and this, in empirical terms, was echoed among both the French *philosophes* and the British moralists. The more independent spirits, Voltaire and Diderot, were oppressed by certain doubts about this mysterious pre-established harmony between freedom and rational organisation; but by and large, because the advocates of scientific organisation and the advocates of civil and political liberty fought the same enemy, defended the same secular cause against the same obscurantists, the same despots, small and great, feared the same dangers – ignorance, cruelty, irrationalism – they did not question the compatibility of the various elements of their own ideologies too closely. It was not until the zealots of the French Revolution attempted to put into practice some of these conflicting elements that the sharp incompatibilities between them came into full and violent play, and led to the divergent, sharply conflicting movements of the nineteenth century, which exaggerated now one, now another, of the elements which had subsisted side by side, in apparent peace, in the minds and books of the eighteenth-century friends of reason and humanity. And yet the notion of moral freedom from which all this developed – or which it assumed at least as a vehicle of expression – remains a metaphor: and the dethronement of the great Idealist constructions perforce had to take, and still takes, the form of exposing it as such.

Virtue is knowledge. Knowing how to live is not different in principle from other kinds of knowing – theological, metaphysical, scientific, aesthetic. It is impossible to think correctly and yet proceed in a direction contrary to the conclusions of such thought: impossible not psychologically perhaps – men can be perverse or weak or temporarily blinded by feeling, in other words irrational – but impossible for a reasonable being, incompatible with the right interpretation of the universe; logically impossible for an omniscient being and therefore progressively impossible as we gradually attain to that perfect condition. If you know that you are going to be drowned, you do not plunge into the water because you are thirsty or fond of swimming; and to want to drown is self-frustration, unreasonable. This is the sense in which laws, in the sense of that which governs the behaviour of men and things, or even records observed uniformities of such behaviour, ultimately coincide with laws in the sense of moral or political rules.

Montesquieu and Hume were cautious empirical observers and sceptical and enlightened conservatives; Voltaire and Diderot were bolder reformers; Helvétius and La Mettrie, Holbach and Condorcet were revolutionary innovators and condemned everything that would not pass the 'bar of reason', and spoke of building a new world out of the ruins of the old; but they all proceeded from the common assumption that the rightness of a rule of conduct, whether political, ethical, public or private, could be demonstrated only by appeal to 'the facts'. Some may have spoken as if the rules were logically deducible from the facts, and Hume showed that this was a fallacy; but even Hume defended his semi-utilitarian morality by appealing to ascertainable facts – human propensities such as desire for security or pleasure, or feelings of sympathy or aversion from the results of such instability as too frequent or radical reforms might produce. However wide the disagreements about what men were in fact like or what should or should not be done by them, or for them, there is in the mid-eighteenth century no clear distinction between laws as generalisations about facts and laws as rules or injunctions. When therefore J. S. Mill, writing a hundred years later, expresses amazement that Montesquieu should have been so foolish as to confuse the two when he expressed surprise at the fact that the laws of the material world were seldom or never infringed, whereas those governing human action were so often disobeyed, he showed a characteristic lack of historical insight. To Mill it is of course perfectly clear that the laws of nature clarify what happens, whereas moral or political laws describe or ordain what *should* happen or be done; and that to break the first is impossible since this very impossibility is what the words 'natural laws' are intended to assert, whereas the second can of course be, and often are, broken, since they do not assert matters of fact but only express commands which would scarcely have been needed if they were in fact always automatically followed. Mill is perfectly right about the two senses of the word 'law', and his criticism of the misidentification of the two senses has been a commonplace since his day and Hume's. But this fallacy, which he exposes so easily, turns out to be one on which almost the whole of Western European moral and political thought had rested for two thousand years (all or almost all except what came from the early Hebrew tradition and the non-scholastic, non-rational strands of Christianity). The fallacy can scarcely consist in a crude confusion of two senses of the homonym 'law', which once it has been pointed out disappears for ever and can no longer take in even a dim-witted schoolboy. What in fact occurred was a change in the entire conceptual framework of reflective human beings in the eighteenth century, from a view of the world in which the two kinds of 'law' blended into one another, to a view in which they were distinguished with increasing sharpness, until Mill with his clear, but not very imaginative, mind can no longer understand how so acute and distinguished a mind as Montesquieu's could possibly have fallen into so childish an error.

We cannot here even so much as indicate all or indeed any of the many complex factors, economic, social, religious, which led to this change of outlook, let alone trace it to such obvious causes as the influence of the Protestant rebellion against the single Roman world, or the rise of individualism and the spirit of private enterprise and faith in individual energy, or the corresponding value placed on achievements of isolated great men, the cult of heroes, of inner voices calling for individual self-expression, as opposed to the contemplative life. It will be sufficient for our purpose if we consider the role played in this evolution by the most central of all great influences upon the development of thought and sentiment in the eighteenth century – that of Rousseau. For Rousseau's thought is the true bridge between the old and the new. He left moral and political thought in a condition profoundly different from that in which he found it. And the central concept whose nature Rousseau transformed was that of human freedom.

## ROUSSEAU AND KANT[1]

According to all the histories of thought, the writings of Rousseau had a more inflammatory effect upon his contemporaries and on the generations which followed than those of almost any thinker who had ever lived.[2] Lord Acton thought this,[3] and although the

---

[1] [Berlin's subheadings, especially in this chapter, are somewhat provisional in form and (fail to) appear somewhat erratically; also, they do not always closely match the text that follows them. Attempts to improve on them proved frustrating, since it is the text that stands in need of reorganisation as much as the headings; so it seemed best to leave things as they were, but with this warning attached.]

[2] 'He invented ['découvert'] nothing, but set everything on fire,' said Madame de Staël with characteristic malice. Madame de Staël, *De la littérature considérée dans ses rapports avec les institutions sociales* (1800): [vol. 2,] pp. 280–1 in the edition by Paul van Tieghem (Geneva, 1959).

[3] 'Rousseau [ . . . ] produced more effect with his pen than Aristotle, or Cicero,

statement has been rightly condemned as exaggerated, nobody has wished to deny it too strongly; nor is there any doubt that some of the most influential trends of thought of the next century – romanticism, democracy, naturalism, socialism, nationalism, Fascism – appeared to have originated or been transformed or at least violently affected in the vast and turbulent mixture of light and darkness, pedantic argument and fervid emotional eloquence, envious philistine resentment and moving indignation with cruelty and injustice, persecuted puritan fanaticism and disarming childlike fantasies which jostle each other page by page and sometimes line by line in Rousseau's writings. It is therefore neither easy nor profitable to examine Rousseau's views, as many of his critics have done, as if they form a coherent and logical whole, or even as if portions of them do so, or as if he (or anyone else) believes his own conclusions principally in virtue of the logical validity of his arguments, or as if the plausibility, or truth, or historical effectiveness of what he said is in some way connected with his powers of ratiocination or grasp of history or of the principles of law or economics or philosophy. Nor is it enough to explain, as some writers have attempted to do, the secret of his influence by his appeal to, or rehabilitation of, the feelings, the logic of the heart, as against the cold rationalism of his predecessors.

No doubt his eloquence greatly depends upon the fact that he addresses himself to the emotions and that his style is nervous, sentimental, magnetic and at times charged with violent intensity. He has the gift of being a demagogue in print – his prose, more perhaps than that of anyone else who has ever written, creates, when read, something approaching the illusion of actually hearing the words of a man, now addressing himself to the emotions and above all the nerves of a large assembly, now giving vent to suppressed hysteria in a passionate diatribe directed at an individual listener. All this is so; nevertheless something else is needed to account for his stupendous influence. Shaftesbury and Hutcheson, Hume and Adam Smith, Lessing and above all Diderot had not neglected the emotional nature of man; but whatever their part in

or St Augustine, or St Thomas Aquinas, or any other man who ever lived.'
Herbert Paul recalling Acton in *Letters of Lord Acton to Mary, Daughter of the Right Hon. W. E. Gladstone*, ed. with an introductory memoir by Herbert Paul (London, 1904), xii.

the progressive sentimentalisation of the outlook of the eighteenth century, there is something which strongly divides the quality of their thought and writing from that of Rousseau's. He knew this well, and so, at times, did they. In some sense, his friends and contemporaries were aware that they were harbouring an inhabitant of a totally different world from themselves. This has sometimes been expressed by saying that Rousseau was the first man of the nineteenth century, born out of his time in the century before it. When in a fashion which struck his acquaintances as somewhat eccentric he went for his celebrated long strolls in the country, communed with nature, and professed to find in these experiences answers to tormenting problems of social and individual life, he was saying only what a very large number of poets, philosophers and, after them, journalists, politicians and other professional spellbinders, as well as persons of a genuinely romantical or sensitive nature, then proceeded to say throughout the nineteenth century, in every country of the West. When he invited Diderot to go for a walking tour with him through France for an entire year, Diderot thought him a little mad; when he declared that he was suffocated by the corrupt sophistication of large cities and the clever patter of their intellectuals and appealed to the wisdom of simple people – peasants, children, remote aborigines – against the professors and their brilliant talk, he was repeating what many a Christian preacher before him must have said – something which became a commonplace piece of political claptrap in the nineteenth century and our own. His violent and genuine hatred of intellectualism, refinement, subtlety, the elaboration of manners of the rich, the aristocratical and over-cerebral intelligentsia of Paris or Berlin, his extreme primitivism, his appeals to the simple against the complex, the poor against the rich, the rough against the smooth, the oppressed against the tormentor, his poems to the uncorrupted natural man, the homely peasant, the pious unspoilt goodness of the small Swiss commune, his abomination of all that is superior, elegant, detached or connected with any form of fastidious, scrupulous, super-critical individualism – worst of all, of any group or élite of intellectuals or artists or scientists, or any others in any sense set apart from the teeming multitude – and this, as so often, together with moodiness and misanthropy and a passion for solitude – all this springs from no wounded proletarian instinct, nor the sense of personal outrage characteristic of the victims of the social order, to which his revolutionary temper has so often and so charitably been ascribed. Rousseau was not a proletarian, he was not a victim of the social order, he was a characteristic member of the respectable Swiss lower middle class who broke away from his milieu, and became a Bohemian adventurer of no fixed occupation in revolt against society, but still with the temperament and beliefs of a provincial *petit bourgeois*.

This outlook and these opinions in their abraded, inflamed and morbid condition took the form – as so often both before and after him – of a violent, piously philistine attack on all that is refined, distinguished and unique in society, against that which could be considered in some sense withdrawn, esoteric, the product of exceptional elaboration or unique endowments, not immediately intelligible to the casual observer. Rousseau's furious onslaughts upon the aristocracy, upon refinement in the arts or in life, upon disinterested scientific enquiry, upon the lives and characters of all but the most immediate purveyors of objects useful to the average man – all this is not so much the cry for justice or understanding on the part of the representative of the insulted and injured helots, as something far more familiar and less respectworthy: the perennial distrust of moral or intellectual independence and freedom on the part of those suspicious representatives of the middle class who found their voice in Rousseau, and who became progressively more influential in the nineteenth century – the believers in a solid, somewhat narrow, morally respectable, semi-egalitarian, privilege-hating, individualistic ideal, with its respect for work, success and the domestic virtues, its sentimental materialism and intolerance of differences – in short the great middle class of the nineteenth century, which becomes the enemy and the butt of all the *révolté* writers of that period, and which has survived so much more powerfully in America than in Europe today. Rousseau, so far from being the protagonist of the artist or the sans-culotte or the preacher of moral freedom, turns out to be an early and indeed premature champion of the lower middle class – the common man of our century – against not merely the aristocracy or the masses, but against the upper sections of the middle class, with its artistic and intellectual aims and demands and ideals, which prosperous peasants and industrious artisans – the 'common' men – obscurely feel to be a menace to their own more conventional, more deeply traditional, more rigidly set moral and intellectual values and decencies, with their solid protective crust of prejudice, superstition and faith in the sound, the kindly and the commonplace, concealing beneath a solid surface an elaborate network of social sensibilities and snobberies, passionately clung to, and a jealous consciousness of precise status and position in a profoundly hierarchical society. Rousseau is a poor, or rather deliberately self-blinded, sociologist, who threw dust in the eyes of many generations by representing as a rustic idyll or Spartan simplicity – the immemorial wisdom of the land – what is, in fact, an expression of that small-town bourgeois and class-conscious outlook, admittedly in an abnormal and diseased condition, which made him peculiarly aware of the vices and errors of the last days of a collapsing feudal order, and peculiarly blind to the deficiencies of that social outlook and those ideas which his own fiery genius did so much to enthrone in their place. In short, he was a militant lowbrow and the patron saint of the enemies of intellectuals, long-haired professors, avant-garde writers and the intelligentsia – the advanced thinkers – everywhere.

## Liberty [1]

Rousseau is always fighting for that limitless liberty which men may once have enjoyed when they were in the state of nature. Liberty, at least in his early writings, is what it has always been for all liberals, all those who have defended or fought for it – absence of restraint, removal of obstacles, resistance to forces of oppression. It does not matter for our purpose whether his concept of the state of nature was a consciously fanciful myth, or an attempted reconstruction of a past believed to have actually taken place. In the state of nature there are no men seeking to put restraints upon one another or harm one another; there is no despotism; there is no private property; there are no oppressive customs or irrational taboos to hem in the free activities of men; there is no blind obedience to persons or institutions or a sacred past; men are in a state of natural harmony; they fit into a pattern in which they complement each other's characters and activities. This concept of natural harmony, whether conceived as lying in some remote past or as a golden age which men, if they are good and rational, may yet construct, is part and parcel of the older view of the laws of nature of which we have spoken. Men's customs in that blessed condition are good because they are intrinsic to the 'necessary relations of things' which are Montesquieu's criterion of a 'good' rule or social habit or law. But this blissful condition, in which man

is born free, does not last. *Society* arises – whether through some
law of natural development which cannot be arrested, or some
avoidable error, Rousseau does not ever quite tell us. At any rate,
man deteriorates; as his worldly goods grow, and the arts and
sciences and comforts of life develop, oppression and exploitation
set in. Sometimes Rousseau attributes the evils – the miseries,
injustices and follies – of society to the invention of private
property, when one man set up a boundary to divide his fields
from another's; sometimes to natural inequalities of talent and of
demand, to natural growth of wants no longer capable of being
satisfied by each man or each family by itself. At any rate civil
society is set up for reasons not unlike those provided by Hobbes,
that is for mutual self-protection, mutual defence of the many weak
against the fewer strong; and also in order to achieve a division of
labour with its far greater efficiency; in short for utilitarian reasons.
And perhaps the creation of society is also partly due to the natural
'social propensities' of man. At any rate, however this state – civil
society – arises, a return to primitive conditions is now neither
practicable nor possible, and to make life tolerable, specific
conventions are entered into; reciprocal promises are made, the
heart of which is the celebrated Social Contract whereby men (in
the manner more or less correctly stated by Locke) formally give
up some of the unlimited liberty of the state of nature, in which
anyone can do whatever he wishes, and which is restricted only by
physical or psychological limitations, for the sake of new specific
benefits to be derived from life in society, and from the institutions
in terms of which it is to be conceived – an elaborate complex of
social and economic and political arrangements, which may not
indeed give to men all they want, but does give them, wherever it
works at all adequately, more than they would otherwise obtain,
exposed to the fury of the elements and, once the state of nature
begins to decay, of one another. Nevertheless the reason for
submitting to such institutions is not that they exist and are
powerful – that they cannot in fact be successfully disobeyed
because they punish disobedience harshly – for that may record a
fact, but gives no reason. Might is not right: one may not be able to
avoid yielding to it, but it may still be injustice that triumphs. The
reason for obedience is that there is a compact, a promise, an act of
mutual trust, a voluntary agreement made by them or by their
ancestors; and to break a voluntary act is to contradict one's own

intentions, and destroy the purpose for which this transaction was undertaken and which, presumably, is still valid.

So far Rousseau's thought is not very different from that of any other eighteenth-century moderate liberal, who regards the social arrangement as a kind of utilitarian compromise: we lose something of our freedom of action – the full freedom of the savage roaming the virgin forest – but we gain something else. The compromise is worth maintaining because we gain so much more than we lose; complete liberty – non-interference – is very desirable, but order, too, is necessary, if we are not to fall into a chaos in which the strong destroy the weak with impunity, and there is not enough mutual confidence for any cooperative undertaking. We cannot have everything, hence we strike a mean, and hope to get as much as can be preserved, as good a bargain as is feasible, given that things are what they are, human nature is what it is, events have occurred as they have occurred. And this indeed was the view of all those men of sense, mild conservatives and mild reformers, who formed the heart of moderate opinion in the eighteenth century, and perhaps in all ages.

But Rousseau was a man of very different temper and this kind of reasoning could not satisfy him. Firstly he believed freedom to be an absolute good.[1] As for the reasons for thinking this: all men want as much of it as they can have, and ought so to want it. Slavery is not merely detested by most men, but ought to be detested, and this 'ought' cannot be reduced to something utilitarian – to an estimate of how much we are getting for how much. This utilitarian calculation – the compromise – will differ from age to age, society to society, and indeed individual to individual; good utilitarian reasons of public interest can and have been given by thinkers like Machiavelli or Hobbes for crimes – crimes d'état – against human beings. Such thinkers, Rousseau declares, deserve well of us because at least they describe what is, and do not confuse it with what ought to be, or what they would wish to be; nevertheless, because what is differs from what should be, it does not follow that what should be can be reduced to what is – to mere de facto human inclinations, to the actual motives which impel men to act, sometimes abominably. Everything that is Protestant, révolté, outraged in Rousseau makes Rousseau deify liberty as something such that to tamper with it is ultimate self-

[1] {Quote Liberty = the Man himself. To lose liberty is suicide.}

stultification; any attempt to curtail it, to touch it, is sacrilege; the value of liberty is absolute; we must not deprive men of it even if they wish us to do so, and whether happiness flows therefrom or not.[1] Some things are intrinsically right and others are wrong, and moral justification or condemnation must invoke something more sacred – some more absolute standard than what some men happen to feel or think useful in this or that situation.

At the same time, Rousseau is clearly aware of the necessity of some kind of social order – of something which will establish the right way of living, the right ruler, the definitive, morally absolute solution flowing from the need for society, which itself derives from the ineradicably social nature of man and creates those problems which a man who is alone – Robinson Crusoe – does not have to face. Thus on the one hand liberty is an absolute good, for it makes men men: on the other hand there must be a moral order, a correct solution to the problem of how to live, the true answer to the questions 'What am I to do?', 'Whom am I to obey?', 'What are the proper ends of life, of society, of humanity?', which enacts that relations between men should be thus and not otherwise.

Previous thinkers have tended to sacrifice either liberty or order or something of both; Rousseau does not formulate the problem in this way, but nevertheless it is this dilemma which obsesses his entire thought. He cannot sacrifice either. Hobbes sacrificed liberty to security and founded right upon might. But to say that we *ought* to do this or that implies we have freedom of choice between alternatives; to remove these alternatives by imposing an authoritarian order is to destroy this freedom, and thereby the significance

---

[1] [ The following passage appears here in the original text: 'Liberty to him is the essence of humanity, of being a person at all; if you are not free, you are nothing at all, a chattel, a material object, a piece of historical flotsam and jetsam; if you cannot will, cannot struggle for what seems to you true or right or noble, you are not at all the immortal soul, the sacred, inviolable repository of morality and faith, the source and criterion of all earthly values, whose rights and duties, whose sufferings and agonies and ideals and bad and good acts matter. And if men do not matter, what does? And if they are at the mercy of external forces, how can they matter? If you are passive – a slave of other men or circumstances – you are not a person, but a thing. What makes you a man, responsible, a focus of problems and values, is not your contemplative intellect, but your will, your indestructible right to realise yourself, to say your word, to do something, be something – live, suffer and create.' Against this Berlin writes: 'repeated on p. [114 below]. Choose one or the other. *Later*: Other better.']

of the 'ought'; we gain security perhaps, even a limited contentment, but we lose liberty and therewith the possibility of a moral life, which must proceed from our voluntary decisions.

If Hobbes sacrificed liberty, the extreme libertarians – the English Diggers, or all those who, unable to bear the pressure of society any longer, renounce it: the travellers to distant lands escaping civilisation, the hermits and the anarchists – sacrifice the possibility of a social order. Out of such, society cannot be composed; and yet we are parts of one another and cannot live alone. That too is contrary to nature. Rousseau is only too powerfully attracted by those who wish to leave the corrupt and sophisticated society of the great cities in order to seek peace of soul in solitary contemplation; but equally he believes in human ties, personal, social, spiritual, which unite men in families, communes.

Somehow the ideal of liberty and the ideal of order must not merely be united in some awkward and precarious compromise, but must be made to cohere in some single, authoritative, global solution of the problem. If the question is a genuine question then surely there must be a true solution of it; if liberty is absolutely good and yet there are rules that are absolutely right – such that to transgress them is absolutely bad and wrong – then liberty is curtailed by authority: yet liberty is indispensable because without it a man cannot be a moral being, that is, a man at all; and authority is indispensable because without it he cannot be a social one; how can they, then, conflict with one another?

Rousseau, in the *Discourses*, in the *Social Contract*, in *Émile* and *La Nouvelle Héloïse*, is a curious combination of violent emotional imagination, together with a passionately romantic humanistic morality which casts away all but perfection – all that falls short of absolute spontaneity, sincerity, generosity, freedom – and in terms of this ideal constructs vivid visions of the glories and miseries of this or that condition of man; and at the same time a pedantic, narrowly logical capacity for abstract reasoning, something perhaps inherited from his Calvinistic upbringing, a power of rigorous casuistry of an unhistorical sort. Both gifts come into play in what he conceived as his final solution, and have made of it a compound of logic and imaginative art which, however confused, inconsistent and at times absurd, have given it a power over men's minds greater than the more coherent or more concrete constructions of less inwardly divided thinkers.

Rousseau's solution is very bold, so audacious that its inherent unplausibility and absurdity is sometimes concealed by its power and sweep. He proceeds like an engineer or like a fanatical geometer. There are two lines: that of absolute individual freedom, and that of social authority; that which a man would do if nobody could or did stop him from doing whatever he wanted; and that which it is right for him to do in a society with certain needs and demands for its preservation, its security, its progress as a whole – needs which often seem to conflict violently with the quest for absolute freedom of any given individual. If these lines never meet, the problem, with its two unknowns, is insoluble. At some point these lines must intersect: there *must* be a central point, one and one only, at which the desires of the individual and the needs of the society precisely coincide; at which the individual, acting with complete freedom, is engaged upon doing precisely that which is aimed at by all other men acting equally freely – a point where the freedom of one man does not conflict with the freedom of any other; a point where the good of society – the common good, that for the sake of which the original contract curtailing individual liberties was concluded – somehow turns out to consist of wholly voluntary activities on the part of the individuals who compose the society, each pursuing his own individual ends – a point, in short, where men freely and voluntarily choose (and are therefore wholly free) a rigorously determined order (and are therefore wholly obedient to the laws), their choices forming a set social pattern from which they do not deviate because they do not wish to deviate. Total liberty must somehow be made to be identical with total conformity. One point, if one only, *must* exist: Rousseau looks for it with the fanatical cunning of a maniac. How is this sleight of hand to be achieved? How is this geometrical point of intersection to be determined?

### Liberty and authority

Let me make the predicament more explicit. Rousseau's problem is genuinely different from that of those who have as a rule been cited as his forerunners. For Locke, Hume, even Hobbes or Bodin, as well as Hooker or Luther, as well as the great Catholic theorists, the task was one of striking a compromise between the individual claim to liberty and the social need for authority. The solution was usually along lines dictated by realistic considerations – what these thinkers conceived to be practically possible. Human beings, for most of these authors, were neither very good nor very bad – for Locke, more good than bad, for Hobbes more bad than good – but, on the whole, an amalgam of various imperfectly harmonised properties. And the social schemas offered as solutions to the problem, the problem of reconciling individual freedom – civil liberties as they came to be called – with sovereignty, or the claims of kings or Churches or States or societies with those of private and personal life, were designed to solve it as satisfactorily as imperfect human nature allowed. The frontier where individual liberty ended, and interference by constituted authority was permissible or legitimate, was therefore necessarily a shifting one; some political theorists allowed more, some less, to either of the contending parties. Favourable circumstances might make a grant of wide liberty to the citizens compatible with their security and happiness; other circumstances – due to physical or spiritual or social causes – might necessitate a temporary, or indefinitely long, restraint upon men's free activity. Theories differed not merely in the theological or moral or historical premises on which they rested, or the view of the individual and of society which they implied, but in what really mattered – their practical conclusions – in the kind of frontier drawn, the tightness of control on either side of it, or the relative extent of territory it left to the two rival interests. But it was always a matter of the adjusting of claims, of compromise, of the best solution given the imperfections of human nature and the world in which men live.

Rousseau differed in two material ways from this point of view. Firstly he lived in an age when the possibility of a perfect solution accomplished by purely human means had been believed and propagated by the *philosophes* and their allies inside and outside France, since they took literally and seriously the perfect analogy between definitive Newtonian solutions of problems in the natural sciences and mathematics on the one hand and those of politics or individual morality on the other. However deeply Rousseau may have revolted against the temper, outlook and beliefs of the *philosophes*, no one – unless he wished to brand himself as a religious obscurantist or an incurable sceptic or a fool or knave – would fail to make any other assumption in the mid-eighteenth century if he was to gain a hearing in Paris or Berlin.[1] Rousseau's

[1] In England matters were somewhat different. A greater caution was displayed – Dr Johnson did not believe in human perfectibility or the possibility

disagreement with the scientists and rationalists was very deep. As
we said above, he detested the sciences, scientists, intellectuals,
coteries of civilised persons and their salons – the whole notion of
enlightened élites – with all the violence of an outraged member of
the lower middle class, and opposed to them the narrower and
homelier values of family and simple bourgeois virtue and the
decencies and solid respectability of the unspoilt 'common man'.
But he did accept, whether or not he was aware of it, the
proposition that whatever the solution to a social problem, it must
be a proper solution, that is, wholly true and demonstrable and
final, as good as something triumphantly produced by d'Alembert
in mathematics or Holbach in botany, and not empirical, tentative,
elastic, blurred and adapted to altering circumstances.

He believed in freedom in a way very different from such
passionate defenders of it as Voltaire or Diderot.[1] For Rousseau
freedom was an absolute value – it was what made men ethical
beings with rights and duties. His concept of freedom was not at all
clear, but it was very passionate: human freedom was to him what
the possession of an immortal soul was for orthodox Christians,
and indeed it had an almost identical meaning for him. To rob a
man of freedom was to treat him as a chattel – as someone not
capable of spontaneous activity – to deny that he was responsible
for his acts, capable of good and evil, deserving praise and blame,
that he was the kind of being whose spiritual activity alone made
whatever had been or could be done worth doing. To rob a man of
his freedom was to refuse him the right to say *his* word: to be
human at all; it was to depersonalise him, to degrade or destroy his
humanity, in other words those characteristics to maintain and
promote which was the sole justification of any action; justice,
virtue, duty, truth, the morally good and bad, could not exist
unless man was a free being capable of choosing freely between
right and wrong, and therefore accountable for his acts.

This might well not be consistent with the kind of materialistic

of radical solutions of social problems, or noble savages or enlightened despots
educated by scientists, any more deeply than the great religious controversialists
of the seventeenth century; Hume permitted himself a scepticism which led to a
kind of conservative empiricism that was forgiven him only because he resided in
Edinburgh and not in Paris, and because his country still symbolised enlightened
common sense and successful resistance to despotism.

[1] [This is the paragraph that duplicates the passage given in note 1 to p. 110
above.]

determinism developed by Holbach or Condillac. Rousseau was dimly aware of this, and it merely added to his bitter disapproval of what seemed to him blind, narrow empiricism, which by representing man as a material entity in nature did such monstrous injustice to human spontaneity, the passionate impulses of the soul seeking to realise itself in a spiritual unity with nature – with some principle which lay at the heart of all that lived and breathed. And because Rousseau believed in freedom in this absolute sense, the notion that it could be curtailed in response to this or that social exigency – the original theory of the social contract, according to which man began with the full liberty he possessed in the state of nature, and either gave the whole of this away in return for security (as Hobbes had taught), or gave away a portion of it in return for equitable government, retaining certain 'rights', that is, ingredients of the original unbroken liberty, even against his government (as Locke had taught) – a curtailment of this sort was wholly unacceptable to him. A genuine curtailment of liberty, even though it be voluntary, was a curtailment of personality, a diminution of that in man which made him man – a moral agent, the source of all morality, the being whose rights were worth fighting and, if need be, dying for, the only goal to which total sacrifice could be justified. Consequently, whatever the solution to social and political questions, it must include the total preservation of absolute human freedom – the freedom from invasion of one human personality by another, the prohibition of all coercion and violence, of the crushing of one human will by another or the maiming of one will to make it serve another's egoistic purposes.

It is this passionate individualism which is the source of one strand of Rousseau's complex personality, his life-long fanatical love of liberty – his hatred of all despotism, of all bowing to a stronger force merely because it is stronger – and his passion for equality; and, fed as this is by purely social resentments and what are nowadays called 'inferiority complexes', there is the pure belief that all human beings are sacred repositories of the immortal human soul, conceived in thoroughly Christian terms, so that for one man to exploit another or even to subject him to arbitrary orders is to treat him as a slave or a thing, an act of blasphemy against the divine spark, and a stifling in the victim of the original source of all morality – of the impulse to do what is right, which is the activity of the inward, the free and immortal, spirit. Yet side by side with all this there is in Rousseau a thoroughly Calvinistic belief in the need for rules whereby to conduct one's life, a set of principles which are demonstrably true, and the only true answers to the tormenting problems, a set of narrow paths along which men must walk, if they are to keep themselves from error and vice and misery.[1] If he did not believe in the authority of persons, he did most strongly believe in the authority of rules – moral laws – in their most rigorous application, and therefore in institutions, like Calvin's community of saints in Geneva, which existed in order to interpret and apply the right rules of life.

How was all this to be reconciled? How were we to give up not an iota of the freedom – of our souls – to remain unsurrendering, defend to the death the basic rights with which 'nature' had endowed us; and at the same time do what is right, obey the moral law and indeed continue to live in society? For it was undeniable that nature has made us not merely free but gregarious and social – and that we are parts of one another (and affect each other's lives very sharply), and the material and moral conditions for perfection are inconceivable outside the framework of society, of organisation, of the network of relationships in which alone the fullness of our natures can develop to its richest extent.

Rousseau's solution is the celebrated paradox contained in the *Social Contract*, the celebrated doctrine of the general will, compounded out of the 'real' selves of all the members of society. He preaches it with the peculiar fanaticism with which a man propounds a solution which he has discovered for himself, and with the almost lunatic intensity of a somewhat crack-brained visionary who has demonstrated some cosmic solution to his own satisfaction, by some peculiar private arithmetic. Man must both retain his freedom intact and he must obey that authority which bids him do what alone is right. How is this to be achieved? In one way only: Rousseau has found the mysterious, the unique point of intersection of the two scales of value. Men must freely want that which alone is right for them to want, which must be one and the same for all right-minded men. If there is one and only one proper course of conduct for a man in a given situation, Rousseau believed in common with the rest of the eighteenth century, then in some way, by using reason, by following nature, by listening to the inner voice of conscience, which is but nature speaking from within; by doing what your innermost heart – nature's vicegerent – ordained, you *could* discover what this unique course was.

[1] {Not sure of *this* [applies to this sentence and the next].}

Ethics and politics for Rousseau are still descriptive disciplines, concerned with revealing and reporting moral or political truths – facts in nature – to be discovered by the special technique of moral vision. Every man is in principle in a position to put himself into the right state to discover what to do, by avoiding that which obscures the inner vision – the turbulent appetites and passions, the corruption and distractions of cities, the snares and delusions of the arts and sciences and other forms of sophistication in civilisation which might render him blind to the dictates of the inner vision which is the voice of nature. Moreover, what is right for one man cannot possibly conflict with what is right for another in the same situation, for if they do the solution is no solution, any more than two mathematical propositions can, if they conflict, be accepted as both being true, since one of them at least, and perhaps both, must be false; but genuine questions *must*, in principle, be answerable, and questions of an ethical or political kind are solved by that particular inner contemplation – that listening to the inner voice – whereby nature speaks to all but those too decrepit or corrupt or diseased to hear her. It follows therefore that if everyone obeys his inner vision the results will tally, social harmony will be guaranteed. An order will be preserved which will be a moral order, compounded as it will be of the mutually compatible – indeed mutually entailed – individual decisions and acts of men thinking and doing what is right, in accordance with their knowledge of right and wrong, obtained by that species of insight which, Rousseau tells us, all men possess within them. Most important of all, liberty remains intact and indeed becomes capable of the richest development; for liberty is the untrammelled self-development of a soul in that direction in which it wishes to go, free from artificial obstacles or coercion exercised by others. A man doing what he deems to be right, because the inner voice of conscience tells him to do so, is acting freely, doing what he wishes, fulfilling his nature, behaving not under the pressure of fear or ignorance or the threat of violence, but because his whole being strives in that direction; he is, as we say, 'at his best', 'most himself', when so acting; it is when he is acting under coercion, or is blinded by emotion, or some more purely physical cause, that 'he is not being truly himself', that he declares afterwards that he had not been at his best. When a man does what is right he is certainly obeying rules; and yet he is free because he does what he most of all wishes to do.

So the great coincidence is achieved: he is free, as free as a moral being can desire to be, free from his own unworthy impulses, his self-interests, his sectional or accidental or ill-considered aims; he is expressing his innermost self as richly as an artist in a moment of creation. Yet in this very act he is obeying the rational rules embodied in the laws of his community, the purpose of which is to generalise his intuitions of what is right, punishing him and others if later, through an access of weakness or egoism, they disregard them. He is at once free and he obeys; he fulfils his nature and at the same time submits. How is this paradox, which Rousseau feels to be the solution which all humanity has awaited since Plato, who advanced it, though in an imperfect form, to be explained? A man is free because the rules which he obeys are not imposed upon him from outside – for then, however righteous, obedience to them would still be a restraint upon his freedom – but he imposes them *himself* upon *himself*; he obeys them because he believes them, because he has discovered them in his own breast.

Rousseau does not provide analogies, but we can, perhaps without doing too much violence to his thought, interpret his doctrine of the free self-imposition of rules as being analogous to the way in which, say, a child may learn arithmetic. So long as 2 + 2 = 4 is a rule learned by heart it is a curb and an obstacle – a truth to be accepted on trust and to be blindly applied. Once the child grasps the logical nexus in arithmetic, 2 + 2 = 4 appears to be the logical consequence of the axioms and the rules. To *want* 2 + 2 *not* to equal 4 seems irrational and almost meaningless. The proposition '2 + 2 = 4' is not a dogmatic interposition of an insuperable obstacle in the path of free human reflection, but a truth which we accept because we freely choose to use numbers in the way in which we do: arithmetic is a weapon which we employ voluntarily and its theorems are our own. Their discovery is one of the ways in which we make our own thinking clear to ourselves. Rousseau obviously supposes that moral or political theorems are demonstrated in such a way that their truth follows from premises the truth of which we view as part and parcel of what we are, and want, and strive towards, when we are at our clearest and best; that is, when we hear at its clearest the voice of nature which speaks to us within us.

So again we arrive at the central paradox: it used to be thought that absolute freedom and total conformity were incompatible, but, at most, loosely combinable in some uneasy compromise, with uncertain frontiers between the two, moved afresh with each new historical change, in accordance with the differing temperaments of peoples, lawgivers and material conditions; persisting in a condition of unstable equilibrium, precariously preserved by legislators and their advisers groping in the dark, a perpetually collapsing empirical makeshift, liable always to collapse into the opposite extremes of despotism and anarchy. But this is a false view of liberty and authority: they are not merely not incompatible, but in their pure state totally coincide; they are one and identical. All men at their best seek what alone will make them happy and free – the ideal self-realisation, the fulfilment of the behests of the inner voice, which is identical with self-adaptation to the great teleological march of nature. The more they seek to realise themselves, the freer they are; their freedom is uninhibited realisation of the most central tendencies within the personality. The social conformism previously held to be barely compatible with individual liberty is in truth only a conformism with the inner ideal, which, being the same for all men who hear the voice of nature, is the pre-established harmony of all those who choose what is right. They are not forced to choose it, they do so because it is right and because they are free to choose otherwise, and freely avoid doing so. In so far as collisions occur between human beings – and human beings clearly do get in each other's way and coerce one another and commit crimes and need strong government: if this were not so there would be no political (or any ethical) problems – they do so only because they do not perceive the truth, do not know the right rules, do not understand what they ought to do, what will develop their natures, what will alone therefore make them happy, and therefore in some sense do not know what it is that they truly want, and are filled with discontent and inner contradictions. They are like persons quarrelling about some topic in which each side holds false views which contradict the equally false views of the other; if both sides knew the truth no disagreement would arise. Virtue is still knowledge: what Helvétius or Condorcet expect from the development of the natural sciences, Rousseau expects from the wisdom of the heart, the inner vision, the profound understanding of nature and man, of which the simple and unsophisticated have a greater degree than those ruined by the 'unnatural' life of urban communities.

Several extraordinary corollaries follow from this. Despite all his turbulent confusion, the vagueness of his rhetoric and his many inconsistencies, some such view as the following emerges from the body of Rousseau's mature writings. The good is what a man desires; it is not the objective property of objects or persons or situations, but what will satisfy sometimes an individual craving, at others a long-term coherent policy. If I do not understand myself, that is, ignore nature, which speaks to me in a voice which I can hear when I let myself do so, then what I think I want, and what I do to secure satisfaction of this want, will not, in fact, satisfy me, for I do not understand the *true* cravings or desires of my own nature. Therefore my first task is to seek to understand myself, and that wherein a permanent satisfaction of my desires will lie.[1]

## The notion of the real will

The assumption throughout is that the good is that which is in some sense desired, or, if 'desire' is not the right term, in some sense a goal, that is, the object to the attainment of which human effort can be conceived as being directed. Good is defined either in terms of, or at any rate as presupposing the existence of, a specific kind of wishing or wanting on the part of conscious agents. It is not an objective characteristic existing independently of agents, but is to be defined in terms of desire: the good is equivalent, in some sense, to the desired.

There are then at least two ways of discovering what this good is. The first is to find out what people actually want or have wanted in concrete historical circumstances. This is a method common to all empiricists, for whom the description of a property entails its being encountered or being capable of being encountered in somebody's experience. Hence this was the method adopted by, for example, utilitarians, whether of the Humean or the Benthamite kind, who defined the good in terms of that towards which certain emotions are normally directed, or that which would, if produced, cause (or be an attribute of) human feelings or attitudes or outlooks or whole patterns and forms of life. For example, 'good' is said to be identical with 'pleasant' (which qualifies states of mind); or with objects of, or causes of, emotions of approval, or with states of happiness or satisfaction. This means that we

---

[1] {Appendix on Real Will here?} [This refers to the section that follows, typed on separate sheets in the original typescript, and marked '(to be included in section on Rousseau?)'.]

discover what is good by some species of historical or psychological investigation, by finding out what men actually want, or have wanted, and inferring by ordinary inductive methods what they might want (or avoid) in specifiable concrete circumstances.

But there is also the converse method, whereby I may start the other way round, and first, by some means or other, discover what is good; and from this logically deduce that if it is good then it must necessarily be the object of someone's wish. But then experience may confute me. I have grounds (I may suppose) for calling a certain course of action or a certain state of life good, and then fail to find anyone, or any appreciable body of persons (or anyone at all), who do in fact want it, either now or in the past. When this happens I am liable to say that, although it may be desired by no one now, it will be so later; or alternatively that, although people may not appear to desire it, yet in some special sense they *do* desire it – not their superficial or apparent selves (which seem indifferent or even hostile), but something which I now call their 'real' selves. The real self is an entity which I have to postulate as the subject of wishes for that which is really good. For I both assume that I have a special method – independent of finding out by ordinary empirical means what people like or go for – of discovering what this real good is, and refuse to abandon the proposition that nothing can be good unless it is the object of a wish, or at any rate something which will satisfy a wish. If I insist on holding both these propositions I find that I slide insensibly into the position of saying that if to be good is to be wished for, then if a thing is good, and yet does not, prima facie, seem wished for by anyone, it must be being wished for, despite the appearances, in some not apparent, 'deeper', 'more real' sense; and if a thing is indubitably good, and yet does not satisfy a particular set of persons whom I examine for this purpose, then since there is nothing wrong with the object there must be something wrong with them. They themselves do not realise what their true wishes are; there must be some very special sense, which they may themselves never understand, in which they do truly wish for it, though they may strenuously deny it if asked. This is not the sense in which we sometimes speak of wishes whose existence is not apparent to the subject himself – the sense in which psychologists speak of subconscious or unconscious or semi-conscious wishes (though even that is queer enough) – for whatever may be meant by such terms as these, subconscious wishes are allegedly inferred to exist on the basis of some empirical evidence, and not a priori. Whereas those philosophers who begin by first being clear about what they consider good, and then deduce that corresponding to the things or states or acts that are good there must be subjects who wish to realise them; then, failing to find overt wishes, infer that the wishing, if it is not conscious, must exist in some other sense; and if it is not an empirical phenomenon then it must be non-empirical in some way – such philosophers as these are, of course, claiming to be making metaphysical discoveries about the existence of real selves on the basis of an a priori syllogism; namely that all good things are necessarily wished for, and that $x$ is a good thing, and therefore wished for, whether there is empirical evidence for such wishes or not.

The same process of reasoning occurs when what is good is defined as being that which a sane or rational man wants. If the concept of sanity or rationality is defined inductively, as a characteristic in fact empirically discovered to be common to a number of persons and defined in terms of certain empirically observable symptoms, then no metaphysics is involved, and all I am found to be saying is that the good or proper end of action is that which certain persons or groups of persons described as sane or rational in fact want. There is no pretence that those who are not adequately sane or rational also want it, if not overtly then in some secret, occult fashion: or in some peculiar sense of the word 'want'. If I then say that that, and only that, should be realised which is good, I am in fact saying that the wishes of the sane and rational should be imposed upon everyone else, whether the sane and rational are a minority or a majority, and whether the rest want such courses of action imposed upon them or not. Many political thinkers – the *philosophes*, Plato, some of the cooler pre-Fascist prophets – have advocated oligarchies of this type – the rule of the foolish by the wise, or of the inexperienced by the expert, or of the mass of the people by persons with certain hereditary characteristics (biological, psychological and so on) – and have defined the properties of the ruling minority in an empirical fashion, for example in terms of heredity, or election by some specific method, or knowledge of certain acquirable arts or skills. But in such cases there is no pretence that the rulers do not in fact coerce the ruled. They may coerce them for their – the rulers' – good, as Thrasymachus maintained in the first book of Plato's *Republic*, or for the good of the ruled, as Socrates would prefer, or for the sake of service to some abstract ideal, as in theocratic societies; but whether it is justified or not, coercion is conceded to occur.

But there is a metaphysical method of trying to have it both ways – of at once permitting and denouncing coercion by denying that it is in any important sense coercive. This is done by claiming that sanity or rationality – or a special kind of will, or whatever is the criterion of authority entitled to exact obedience – is something present in every individual, if not actually, then potentially. Let us assume the rationality and the required characteristics, good being defined as what the rational man wants. Then to command a man to act or live in this or that way, in the name of reason, when the command is issued by someone certified as rational himself, is to command him to do this or that in the name of his own possibly undeveloped, but nevertheless 'real' and present, reason. It is regarded as being tantamount to ordering a man to act in a way in which he would order himself to act, if his reason were fully developed; and that, in its turn, by a series of insensible steps, is interpreted to mean that which the 'real' man 'within' him in fact – through the ruler who represents this inarticulate entity – orders him to do. In this way, by identifying the will of the ruler with the 'real' will of every individual in a given society, I obtain the desired result: the identification of coercion with complete self-government. For freedom is after all only doing what I want; what I want is that which will satisfy my nature; and what I 'really' want is what will satisfy my 'real' nature – my rational nature – for satisfying my irrational impulses will not 'really' satisfy me, but leave me distraught and hungry for further sensations. My rational needs, *qua* rational, are those needs which any rational being would have in my condition, and to the extent to which I am not wholly rational, I know what these needs are less well than someone else more rational than I. Therefore his prescription for me will do more to realise my true, that is, rational, nature than anything I may conceive as a proper course of action for myself or others. Therefore his dictates liberate me more than my own. Therefore my freedom consists in obedience to him. Hence freedom is obedience – a secular version of the great religious view that God's 'service is perfect freedom',[1] since God knows what is best for me and for the world.

---

[1] The Book of Common Prayer, Order for Morning Prayer, second collect (for peace): 'O God [ . . . ] whose service is perfect freedom'; cf. Augustine, *De quantitate animae* 34. 78: 'in cuius servitio placere perfecta et sola libertas est'.

From this follows the proposition that enlightened despotism is not despotism, that coercion by reason is not coercion, and that to force people to obey its dictates is to force them to act rationally, to provide for the satisfaction of their true or real needs (even though they may in their conscious moments violently reject this), and therefore make them free. To object to this kind of liberation is only to prove oneself irrational, incapable of knowing what would in fact make one free.

This is one of the most powerful and dangerous arguments in the entire history of human thought. Let us trace its steps again. Objective good can be discovered only by the use of reason; to impose it on others is only to activate the dormant reason within them; to liberate people is to do just that for them which, were they rational, they would do for themselves, no matter what they in fact say they want; therefore some forms of the most violent coercion are tantamount to the most absolute freedom.

This, of course, is the great justification of the State despotism advocated by Hegel and all his followers from Marx onwards. The crucial step that needs to be taken to establish this monstrous paradox is that what is good for me is independent of what I find that I in fact most ardently desire, that what is good for me is what my real self desires, though my everyday self may be wholly unacquainted with any such entity, and that in forcing me to pursue the ends of my so-called real self the authority of the State or the Church or the dictator is only 'forcing me to be free',[1] acting on behalf of, and in complete harmony with, my occult but all-important 'real' self, the only self that seriously matters.

This is the doctrine which Dostoevsky exposed with such genius in *The Devils*, where it is expressed by the revolutionary Shigalev when he says, 'Starting from unlimited freedom I arrive at unlimited despotism.'[2] The fact that Dostoevsky's own solution, or what emerges of it, makes use of assumptions no less metaphysical and no less paradoxical is irrelevant to the issue: what is important here is that the entire doctrine is incompatible with any form of empiricism; it needs the assumption of empirically unverifiable 'real selves' and empirically unfindable 'rational ends', wherein all rational men must agree. If these assumptions are false

---

[1] For Rousseau on the right of society to force men to be free, see Jean-Jacques Rousseau, *Oeuvres complètes*, ed. Bernard Gagnebin, Marcel Raymond and others (Paris, 1959–95), vol. 3, p. 364 [hereafter thus: OC iii 364].

[2] Dostoevsky, *The Devils*, part 2, chapter 7, section 2.

the doctrine collapses. There may be good and valid reasons for coercion, for example, on utilitarian grounds, but the utilitarians, in permitting the use of force, at least do not maintain that the persons against whom force is applied are using it against themselves – that their 'real' selves are thereby coercing their 'empirical' selves. It is this last assumption, identifying as it does liberty with coercion, and democracy with despotism, which has made the political views of the idealist philosophers seem such a caricature of the normal notions of liberty and democracy, and such a mockery of human suffering in the eyes of morally sensitive, or for that matter moderately clear-headed, critics.

It may be objected that all education is founded on some principle as that outlined above and ascribed to the idealists – that children, for example, frequently do not wish to go to school and are in some sense made, coerced, to do so; that the tutelage exercised over them by parents, or guardians, or schoolmasters entails a good deal of coercion; and that this is done quite properly, in the name of these children themselves, in the name of what, were they mature, they would be doing for themselves, and which, if it is not done for them in childhood, they will rightly, when they are adult, blame their educators for withholding from them when they were not in a position to judge for themselves what they truly needed. And (the argument continues) a great many so-called adult persons are in fact, from the point of view of moral or political maturity, no better than backward children, persons whose judgement cannot be accepted, so that in their case coercion is simply political education, action undertaken not merely in their interest, but on behalf of their un-grown-up but potentially adult personalities.

All education would indeed be immoral, as well as dangerous, if this piece of thoroughly specious metaphysics were its only justification. Fortunately there is no need to invoke it: there are enough good empirical arguments for education. Here no more need be said than that the most obvious reason for compelling children to go to school is that unless it is done, they may never attain to a condition where they have sufficient knowledge, or sufficiently well-developed personalities, to enable them to perform those acts of free choice between alternatives, bad choices as well as good, stupid as well as wise, in which a substantial portion of happiness and freedom consist. In other words, we coerce now in order to make personal freedom possible at as early a stage as possible. If coercion is an evil as such, then the coercion involved in education is certainly *pro tanto* evil and nothing is gained by denying this truth; but it is a necessary evil, and in a world where everyone was born fully equipped morally, physically and intellectually would not be required. Its justification in our society is that the probable good results justify the means. There is a balance of good, calculated on the basis of the past experience of the human race, which indicates that in this case temporary withdrawal of freedom may be the only means of ensuring a wider use of it at a later none too distant stage. But such coercion becomes patently destructive only when it goes on too long, or the promised fruits are too remote or improbable; when for example great populations are kept in chains for the sake of some condition of future freedom or bliss, when the goals are too remote, or past political experience does not justify us in supposing that they can be attained at all by such means.

The justification of education is that it works; that the educated actually enjoy some, at any rate, of the blessings which it is the purpose of education to provide, and that this has been shown frequently enough to justify an experiment which does involve this much temporary loss of freedom. The evil of political and economic despotism, however enlightened they may appear to themselves, is that the available historical evidence tends to show that, so far from moving their subjects nearer to the attainment of liberty or happiness or peace, whatever the end pursued may be, they appear to make them psychologically and socially more remote from these ideals. This is a matter of empirical judgement; the proof of the pudding cannot be obtained from an a priori insight; and the analogies between education and political tyranny are therefore as specious and fatally misleading as the biological or aesthetic similes in terms of which organic or irrationalist theories of the State have in the last century and a half been presented by their violent and sometimes highly effective advocates. The large number of persons who are prepared blandly to acquiesce in the identification of that which someone declares to be good for them with what they actually want – who are prepared to be told that what is being done to them is done not merely because it is good for them, but because it is they who really demand it, although the notion of it (let alone any conscious desire for it) has never entered their heads – is curious and melancholy food for reflection for those who believe that men know what they want, and can distinguish, at any rate at a crude, empirical level, right from wrong, truth from chicanery, sense from nonsense.

Rousseau in his educational writings enlarges upon the conditions under which alone I am able to hear the sacred voice which tells me what to do and be. Theoretically his appeals to the natural life, simplicity, candour, spontaneity, love, emotional warmth, purity of heart are concerned only with the best conditions for the discovery of the truth about how to conduct my life, but naturally enough what begins as a means becomes for him inseparably connected with the end. Irving Babbitt reasonably complains[1] that Rousseau puts sincerity and emotional relevance above truth – and thereby originates that long European tradition of romanticism, which stresses the value of goodness and purity of nature and warmth of feeling above that of accuracy or intelligence or penetration or the intellectual virtues generally. He begins that great tradition of advocacy of the good will – of the right kind of moral or social character as against intellectual capacity or the ability to discover the truth by the employment of purely cerebral methods. Rousseau of course tends to identify the two – for him sincerity *is* itself the kind of penetration below the crust of outer appearances, the kind of delving in the innermost recesses, whereby alone the truth may be found; so that if one asks what is his conception of the man who knows the truth – the original sage, the possessor of wisdom with whom European philosophy has been so much concerned – Rousseau replies copiously and eloquently but not very clearly: what it seems to come to is that all will be well, provided one has one's heart in the right place. I think, though he does not, of course, use it, that this phrase – the very words which compose it – conveys something very like that which lay at the centre of Rousseau's outlook, and springs from the belief that when we seek advice in moral or political matters – advice about conduct – we trust those whom we believe to have a certain kind of character, a certain moral outlook, a view of things which we find congenial or confidence-inspiring: a scale of values in which we trust. And we trust it, perhaps, simply because we trust it – because it seems authoritative: 'true', 'real'. At any rate, unless

---

[1] Irving Babbitt, *Rousseau and Romanticism* (Boston and New York, 1919), especially chapter 3, 'Romantic Imagination'; see also pp. 160–7. [In the typescript Berlin's note is placed at the end of the previous sentence.]

we believe it to exist, unless we believe that the heart of the individual in question is in the 'right place', believe in him and his moral insight and authority in some way, mere intellectual distinction or width of information or honesty or taste or learning or sharpness of logical power is not sufficient for our purpose.

Rousseau supposed that we trusted such persons not simply because we liked them or felt them to be sympathetic or had been taught to look up to them, but because we realised less or more consciously that their inner world – their faculties and values and habits and dispositions – was of such a kind as to enable them to see clearly in regions where we were ourselves in doubt. He believed in short that what mattered was a certain kind of moral personality – a certain kind of inner spiritual pattern – and that only to this kind of personality was the truth vouchsafed. He did not make it clear what precisely such a personality was or how it was to be achieved – although the celebrated outpourings of indignation against cleverness and elaboration and the vices of civilisation, and the paeans to nature and rustic wisdom and the uncorrupted heart, leave us in no doubt as to the general trend of what he was saying. We can, perhaps, venture to assert that he confused the conditions of insight with its contents; that his concept of the insight itself is highly metaphysical, and in the last analysis not very different from the a priori knowledge of theologians and pre-Kantian metaphysicians; and that its content, as so often, indicates only too clearly the kind of world for which he felt a nostalgic desire. For he discredited the intellect to make room for a view of life compounded partly from his father's social world in Geneva, partly from his own emotional aberrations; and for the particular idyll he paints in *Émile* or *La Nouvelle Héloïse* he offers no serious argument, only passages of magnificent rhetoric, which contrast a life founded upon this kind of outlook with the cold-hearted calculation, bleakness and injustice of the aristocracy and the intelligentsia of Paris. Nevertheless, he did make articulate a new factor in the European consciousness – the notion that infallible solutions to moral and political questions must be sought not in the sciences nor by philosophic speculation, nor by the contemplation of Platonic essences, nor by reading sacred texts, nor by the careful empirical introspection together with social observation recommended by Hume, nor by the study and formulation of general laws of social life advocated by the utilitarians, nor in the pronouncement of any organised religion, nor in the illumination of exceptional mystical natures in abnormal conditions; but in the pronouncements of persons with a certain kind of inner moral adjustment – living in conditions propitious to the development of such constitutions, which almost automatically gave the possessors a semi-instinctive sense of what was right and what was wrong, true and false, beautiful or ugly, because they had an inner faculty for seeing the heart of things and persons and situations – insight, intuition, wisdom, moral superiority. Their hearts were in the right place and they had an ultimate moral and intellectual reliability – in exceptional cases, moral genius – which could be obtained in no other way.[1]

Rousseau praises certain ways of life and the characteristics they breed for the same reasons as those which are to be found among the Stoics or early Christian advocates of austerity and the mortification of the flesh – because these alone create conditions for that unique state of mind and body in which it is possible to perceive what is true and what is right. The Stoic precepts about the best way of attaining *ataraxia*, the motives which led to the prodigies of self-mortification among the Anchorites of the Theban desert and other ascetics, and later to the rigours of the austere monastic orders, are similar to those which inspire Rousseau's hymns to simple virtue, poverty and natural piety as against wealth, ceremony and elaboration – because only simple souls can see the light. This preoccupation with salvation and the dangers of spiritual sightlessness and corruption (and even the rootlessness of the intelligentsia as opposed to that of the Bohemian, who, being naïve and warm-hearted, is saved), which Rousseau inherited from Puritans and Calvinists, and with which he himself infects the entire nineteenth century – novelists and poets, historians and practical men – tends to exalt the opposite virtues of purity and sincerity and natural goodness, the divine flame which burns more brightly in the hearts of publicans and sinners, of the social outcasts of Hugo and Dostoevsky, the rebels and humanists of Schiller, the solitary heroes of Büchner and Ibsen, the peasants

---

[1] In 1791 a Jacobin at Nantes writes: 'To be a good elector, it is not necessary to be rich, it is not necessary to be learned; it is enough to have pure intentions, to be a good man, and above all a good *Patriote*.' *Journal de la correspondance de Paris à Nantes*, No 25, 17 June 1791, 400; cited by Alfred Lallié, 'Les sociétés populaires à Nantes pendant la Révolution', *Revue de Bretagne et de Vendée* 4 (1890), 345, who is cited in turn by Crane Brinton, 'Political Ideas in the Jacobin Clubs', *Political Science Quarterly* 43 (1928), 249–64, at 253.

and converts to the simple life of Tolstoy, the innocents of Henry James; and identifies the great enemy in the nineteenth-century humanistic novel: the rich, the powerful, the official – the important people.

Rousseau's doctrine marks a climax in the Christian revolt against the morality of the pagan or the Renaissance worlds, and indeed the morality of the Enlightenment whether in France or in Germany, a revolt which is a translation into secular terms of the return to the inner life, as against the shows and vanities of the world and of Rome alike, praised by Luther and Calvin, the Puritans and the Jansenists, Pascal and the pietists. The preoccupation with the *état d'âme*[1] – although it is never wholly absent in any of the great religious traditions – is by Rousseau made the focal point of human life; his theory of education is concerned with it to the exclusion of almost all other considerations. The purpose of education which for the great heralds of the new approach to it, Helvétius or Bentham, is the artificial adjustment of men's natural egoisms to serve carefully conceived, [ . . . ]

\*[2]

[ . . . ] with this ideal in view, to which Calvin's community at Geneva is a closer approximation than the huge kingdom of France, with its inequalities and its great population, incapable of being gathered into a single whole, which by living the appropriate kind of communal life together – by the reciprocal influence of

[1] 'State of the soul'.

[2] [At this point two leaves (about 900 words) are missing from the original text. For an indication of what Berlin may have gone on to say about Helvétius, see FIB 18–19. It is uncertain what other material has been lost here, but the following educated guess by George Crowder (personal communication) may be useful: 'In the rest of the missing passage Berlin probably links Rousseau's emphasis on the ethical authority of the real will with his political conclusions. One possibility is that Berlin returns to Rousseau's identification of the real will with the general will for the common good. It may also be that Berlin describes the kind of social and political conditions that, according to Rousseau, are necessary to ensure that citizens remain focused on the common good rather than on their selfish personal interests. Those conditions include the intimate scale of the political community, the avoidance of large-scale economic inequality, the rejection of "partial associations" or interest groups (or their multiplication so that they will balance one another), and the profession of a shared "civil religion".' For further clues to what Berlin may have written at this point, see his lecture on Rousseau in FIB.]

good, simple people upon each other – can produce the appropriate spiritual condition.

Normally, when Rousseau speaks of the common good and of the general will which wills it, he speaks of it as that which each individual wills when he is at his most disinterested – when he hearkens to the voice of nature without being deflected by the influences which obscure the truth, when his sole purpose is to understand his true self, his own true nature, and what will fulfil it in accordance with the immutable laws which govern all things for their good. But sometimes the necessary coincidence of all these disinterested wills seems to him to constitute one vast single act of will occurring within a kind of super-personality – the community acting as one being. Sometimes he speaks as if he is using a metaphor, but a metaphor so pregnant as to make of it more than a mere vivid image, as if there really were something which he calls the *soi commun* – the single social self – an entity in some sense different from and certainly greater than the sum of the individuals who compose it. The *soi commun* can never hurt any of these individuals, any more than the physical organism can hurt one of its own limbs.

Is this merely a vivid simile to convey the truth in which Rousseau so violently believes – that all good men with pure hearts always see everything in the same way and cannot possibly come into genuine conflict? Or is it something more than this, more than an image, the postulation of a genuine metaphysical entity – the super-personal self, which comes into being by the magic of the Social Contract, a genuine organism whose attributes and activities cannot be reduced to the sum of the attributes and activities of its parts conceived by themselves? Is Rousseau, because he speaks throughout as if my or your good were defined in terms of my or your volitions, half-consciously supposing that the common good, since it must be defined in terms of some agent's volitions, and cannot be defined in terms of yours or mine alone – is he assuming that corresponding to the common good there must be the common self to will this good? Society is in some sense continuous in time; and the emotions which a patriot feels towards it are not emotions felt towards this or that member of it, but towards society as such, a complex of persons and institutions, of sights and sounds, soil, climate, memories of common experience, a great enveloping whole compounded of common traditions, common language, common ways of thinking and feeling, as well as blood or political unity or racial homogeneity.[1] Because this is so, is Rousseau thinking that there must be a real entity – something which exists as persons or things exist and are met with, and cause material effects – towards which such feelings are directed, which people can believe in and are prepared to die for as well as with? Does he suppose that it is this super-personal communal self whose will is the general will, that the wills of individuals are general only in so far as they are 'elements in', or expressions of and perhaps actually ingredients of, this larger entity, as living cells compose a body – an entity whose overwhelming presence they literally feel whenever they are solemnly gathered to record not their personal inclinations, but their collective purpose, to exercise their individual functions as part of the life of this entity, whose total function 'transcends' and 'absorbs' the constituent selves of which it is compounded?

This is how he has often been interpreted; and this is certainly the form which his doctrine took in those later writers whom he so powerfully influenced, the German Absolute Idealists, and their prophets and disciples in all the countries of Western culture to this day. It is part of the spellbinding quality of Rousseau's style that he never speaks clearly enough to make a definite decision on this point possible. Sometimes he speaks as if his words about the social organism are only an analogy – a very important and illuminating one, but still only an analogy, as Hobbes's mortal God – the Leviathan – was nothing but a simile: individuals are individuals and, no matter how united and coherent and 'parts of one another', remain particular human beings, so that the authority of their united pronouncements is still no greater than the authority of the pure heart and lucid mind of a single individual. This is the sense in which Kant understood him and assimilated his influence to his own doctrines. At the same time, there is a strong strain of the Christian notion of the mystical body of Christ, the Church as a spiritual whole, particularly in the very formulation of his doctrine, as applying to the Calvinist communities of the faithful – a strain which is never far from Rousseau's thought or language.[2] And when he talks in this strain, he certainly seems to come close to conceiving of the single self and will of the community as actual

[1] {Too historical for Rousseau. This is pure Burke.}
[2] {'forcing to be free' = Church's doctrine of heretic punished for sin against his own immortal soul, by Church = his own soul.} [For 'forcing to be free', see p. 124 above, note 1.]

phenomena in the real world – supernatural entities literally created by the human spirit.

It is an idle enquiry, since all language is in some degree metaphorical, to ask, in the case of so poetical and unselfcritical a writer as Rousseau, where the literal use of language ends and metaphor begins, and at what point if any Rousseau leaves the solid ground of empirical observation and ordinary social data, and when and where he returns to it. His real discovery – as it may have appeared to him – was that there was one unique situation and only one in which complete liberty was identical with the good life, led according to strict rules enforced by the laws and regulations which rigorously embodied and applied them; and that was when what was truly good for men – what nature prescribed – was freely willed by them. All the problems and conflicts of social life appeared to him to arise from the fact that what men wanted, or believed or did, often did them and others harm; and to restrain them from doing this harm led at its worst to blind despotism, and the enslavement and warping of human beings; but even at its best to the deprivation of liberty by social control. Yet a man's acts appeared to him morally worthless unless performed voluntarily as acts of free choice, conscious choices of one among at least two possible alternatives: their moral worth depended on their not being determined mechanically or under coercion or as the result of unalterable habit. But then men's choices often proved fatally disastrous, and led to the very enslavement which the very notion of choice contradicted. Men must be free to choose what is good – that good which is discoverable in the State, and by the means described by Rousseau in so moving a manner, but which must be freely willed, else the pursuit of it is worthless. There is only one alternative in any given situation which is right, which nature bids us choose, which fulfils our true self; and therefore, in order to guarantee our happiness and virtue, circumstances must be created which guarantee that we shall choose that particular alternative, and no other, and yet leave us our freedom of choice, our untrammelled liberty. It is whenever he reaches this central thesis, when he discusses the unique geometrical point of intersection between liberty and authority, that he becomes assertive and dictatorial. He ceases to appeal to the heart, and lays down the solution with a dogmatism which brooks no criticism: he treats the great discovery as a kind of philosophers' stone discovered by himself, which transmutes all things to gold, and he clings to it with fanatical intensity.

### Liberty [2]

On the one hand we must have absolute liberty: unless man does what he does absolutely freely, it is not he who is acting; there is no action, only mechanical behaviour – the movement of bodies in space as conceived by materialists like La Mettrie – and therefore no praise or blame, no duties, no rights, no morality. On the other hand, there must be rules – the true way of life, the uniquely true answer to each problem as it arises, for there is only one true answer to any problem, and many that are false; and what is true – that is, right – we must do, for that is what duty, that is to say morality, means. The ancient conflict is to be resolved by breeding a race of men who will choose absolutely freely only that which is absolutely right. If there were saints, they would not even be tempted by what is wrong; there would be no conflict, no agony, no choice. But, being human, we must be faced with alternatives and be entitled to praise for our virtue, that is for choosing what is right, choosing it freely, in other words without compulsion either on the part of other human beings or on the part of irresistible natural forces. We must have both freedom and the chains of duty: not chains chosen by others for us – which the poets in the past have too often strewn with flowers, so concealing their true na-ture – but chains freely chosen by ourselves, and freely imposed by ourselves on ourselves, not imposed upon us from outside. For then we are at once bound and free, we retain unimpaired the spontaneity and fullness of human nature, but instead of sacrificing it on the altar of some jealous divinity exacting obedience from outside, we ourselves, rationally and freely, mould our own nature to the ends which we perceive to be alone the right ends for men. It is as if a man *wished* to go to prison because he felt at his best there: then he would be at once in gaol and free – this is the solution.

Rousseau both enunciates this doctrine and assumes it in his writings of the last decade of his life. He writes with the peculiar quality of a highly consistent monomaniac, possessed by what he regards as a unique discovery – the key which opens all the doors which others before him had vainly tried to open by force or skill, and at times merely passed by. He belongs to that special category of inspired fanatics who have superimposed upon a disordered, imaginative, violently impressionable nature the straitjacket of a rigid logical apparatus, in terms of which they pretend to formulate arguments of a deceptively clear, systematic and rational kind. He is a madman with a system, which set on fire many cool and sober intellects, by clothing his most violent and incendiary feelings in lucidly deductive arguments, apparently deriving his most startling and visionary conclusions by rational methods from commonly accepted truths.

How is this race of 'free' men to be brought into being? Not by dangling rewards and punishments to canalise evil as well as good impulses, as Helvétius had wanted, because that would make man unfree – determined by psychological rather than purely physical causes, but by material causes nevertheless. The major premiss of Rousseau's entire construction is that all men have within them the capacity to discover the objective truth about what to do morally and politically; that all that is necessary is to liberate these capacities by removing the obstructions which society and its leaders, in their blindness or vice, have created; that once the obstructions are removed, all men will inevitably seek the good; that the good of one man cannot conflict with that of another; that only that is good which men seek, and good because they seek it, because it responds to their needs; and it will make them happy because it will satisfy the yearning for it implanted in them by nature; and that since what is sought by free and no longer blinded or warped natures cannot lead to conflict, it follows that the common good is identical with the individual good of individual men, provided they are rational (that is, morally clear-eyed) and free; and that when men deliberate about what to do freely, that is, rationally, their wills, because their objects coincide, are as one will, like an orchestra playing in unison.

Sometimes Rousseau speaks as if these wills do not merely work like one will, but literally are one will, willed by one being – the society as a social whole, the organism, the great society, the super-personal, all-absorbing unity of mankind, the Leviathan – no longer a tyrannical power pressing from without, but a harmonious confluence of liberated wills, burning in a single human flame.

From this premiss, which he does seriously seek to prove, everything else follows by deductive reasoning. Rousseau seeks the light not from empirical observation, nor from revelation or dogma or the infallibility of priests or prophets, but from a metaphysical insight about the nature of man, which in principle does not differ from the a priori propositions put forward by earlier metaphysicians, from Plato to Leibniz; and he owes his success to the fact that, in his day and time, his analysis of human nature and its capacities and goals, particularly the freedom of self-imposed discipline, the submission to freely adopted organisation – a team, an assembly, an army even, above all a Church or sect – touched a responsive chord in men, who felt that he was describing something which they had themselves experienced, and described it with deeper insight than other theorists, both empirical and metaphysical, whom his contemporaries read or had heard of.

Yet the presuppositions of this view are more than doubtful, although it has taken the vicissitudes of the nineteenth century and our own to shake them, or utterly expose them. The proposition that there must be a generally accepted 'objective' truth about behaviour, which is attainable, as there are generally accepted truths about the external world or in geometry, presupposes that ethics and politics are descriptive sciences, which is far from self-evident; and Rousseau, however unconsciously, himself did much to upset this view; his assumption that men in some way own two natures – the higher and the lower, of which so many religions and philosophies have spoken – and that the suppression of the lower nature 'liberates' the higher for the performance of its sacred task, is a piece of mythology – if taken literally – about human beings which may, like many revealing myths, like those of the poets and the Marxists and the psychoanalysts, have played a useful part in bringing out truths less eloquently stated by more pedestrian means. But it remains a myth, nevertheless, that there is in man literally an entity to be called the pure will, working in accordance with rules set for it by nature, as against, and capable of ordering and subduing, passions, emotions, inclinations and other 'lower' tendencies which are parts of an 'animal' nature, that is, quasi-mechanical elements played upon by material forces, incapable of purpose or freedom. It is an equally optimistic and equally unfounded supposition that one good purpose can never clash with another, because there is a natural harmony of which they form part; so that their conflict, therefore, cannot ever be 'real', but must be due to a misperception of their nature, a subjective ignorance on our part, and not an incorrigible incompatibility on theirs; and that therefore all tragedy – all conflict between apparently irreconcilable values, love and honour, public and private loyalties, liberty and equality, individual genius and society – cannot in the end be serious or final; and must in some ultimate analysis be resoluble into some rational schema which allays all apparent strife, yet satisfies all genuine claims, and preserves all values in their completeness, in peaceful coexistence and perhaps some transcendent harmony; since all conflict must ultimately be an illusion – for do we not know, on a priori grounds, that reality is a coherent and harmonious whole?

But do we know this a priori, or in any other way? Is it so certain that all tragedy is due merely to error, fallibility, that all questions are answerable, that all ills are in principle always curable, that everything *must* come out well in the end like some immense puzzle of which we know that the parts must – have been created to – fit together, so that the miseries and evils of the world are no more than a passing phase, evil dreams that will fade before the real dawn? There have of course always been metaphysicians who have known that this was so; who have not hesitated, in the face of the 'hard' empirical evidence, to pronounce it systematically delusive, and have thereby reduced tragedies and shipwrecks, both individual and collective, to the results of avoidable (or unavoidable) weaknesses, errors, miscalculations, misapplications; and – in the course of contrasting them with the victorious perfection of true reality – incidentally, as it were, trivialised them and taken all dignity from human experience and human ideals. And Rousseau's theory presupposes more than this: it presupposes a teleological ontology in its least acceptable form – the discovery of purposes in nature by contemplation of her divinity in movement and at rest, of which we hear the echoes in our own breast. Hume, if he did nothing else, had shown conclusively, more than two decades before Rousseau set sail upon the turbulent sea of his own imagination, that such anthropomorphism is untenable, that what we mean by purposes – ends, values which we strive to realise – is not intelligible save in terms of specific persons seeking for this or that, and that we understand what we mean by purpose or by value only when we contrast it with what does not have it, namely the world of natural objects – sticks or stones or even trees and animals (though we might feel less certain about these). Therefore to endow the whole of nature with a hierarchy of purposes is a gratuitous and obscure assumption which, however much it may have meant to the Greeks, and however deeply implied it may be by a religious or metaphysical interpretation of the appearances, we have not gained directly from our normal view of things, and our normal use of language. Still less can it be taken quietly for granted that societies as such have wills or purposes in any but a vague and metaphorical sense, as if societies were genuinely persons capable of birth, maturity and death, with purposes 'transcending' that of the individuals who compose them, entities subsisting in some non-empirical realm, immortal, and moulding the empirical men and women who compose them, like a pattern which has acquired a life and substance of its own, a metaphysical being, a transcendental force at once affecting human beings, compounded out of them, and embodying itself in them in some ineffable fashion, a mystery foreign equally to science and common sense. Rousseau did not indeed say as much as this, although many thinkers in the nineteenth century so interpreted him, but he talked in a fashion which made such interpretations all too plausible.

Rousseau never looked back from the vast construction of the *Social Contract*, at the heart of which is, of course, the celebrated general will. What *is* the general will? 'As long as several men in assembly regard themselves as a single body, they have only a single will' and 'perceive' 'the common good' by 'good sense'.[1] 'The constant will of all the members of the State is the general will'[2] – 'the body politic is a moral being, possessed of a will'.[3] It wields absolute authority, namely that 'which penetrates into a man's innermost being, and concerns itself with his will no less than with his actions'.[4] By what right? Because the State governed by it is 'a form of association which will defend and protect with all the common force the persons and goods of every associate, and in which everyone, uniting himself with all, still obeys only himself and remains as free as before'.[5] Well might Mill protest that if I obey the majority – however necessary this may in fact be – I am not obeying myself: that the word 'all' taken collectively cannot be substituted for 'all' taken distributively. Rousseau would make short work of that. I obey myself because my will coincides with the general will: and to do what I should have willed even if there

---

[1] *Du contrat social*, book 4, chapter 1: OC iii 437. [Berlin's wording of the quotations in this paragraph suggests that he used, at any rate sometimes, G. D. H. Cole's translation of works by Rousseau: *The Social Contract*; *Discourses* (London, 1913), at least two reprints of which were in Berlin's library.]

[2] ibid., chapter 2: OC iii 440.

[3] *Discours sur l'économie politique*: OC iii 245.

[4] ibid.: OC iii 251.          [5] *Du contrat social*, book 1, chapter 6: OC iii 360.

had been no decree passed by the assembly *is* to be uncoerced, to be free. The coincidence is all. But still, it is *freedom* that is paramount. If I am to be truly free I must be free to leave the assembly, renounce the Social Contract and wander off on my own. And Rousseau concedes this right: provided I have discharged certain commitments which my membership entails, I can leave my society. But, by the same reasoning, it – the society, with the State embodying its general will – must be absolutely free and untrammelled too. Nothing must bind it: its sovereignty must be absolute. The *soi commun* cannot be less free than its constituents. Hence sovereignty is one and indivisible: there is nothing on earth which can rightfully resist the sovereign when it is exercising its true will; its authority derives from its identity with the wills of its members, and their rights derive from 'the law of nature, the sacred imprescriptible law which speaks to the man's heart and his reason',[1] which are one. This is the only ultimate authority there is – man as a sacred vessel bearing nature's commands – and to resist the union of men collectively embodying nature's will is to sin against all that is holiest in the universe.

It is idle to ask, as many of his subsequent critics have done, whether this general will is general because what it wills is general – namely takes the form of general propositions admitting of no individual exceptions, applicable to all persons in a given situation – or general because it is willed by a 'general' entity – the community, men in general. For Rousseau this must be mere hairsplitting: the will is general because it is the willing of what is right by men acting as a single whole, to secure its good, since all the objects of the true willing of the true self coincide – and the conclusions bind everyone because the whole process of collective willing has been entered into freely, and that is binding and that alone which people freely impose upon themselves. The will is general because its objects are generally binding and proceed from men acting together, there being no differences, except in space and time, between them as rationally willing agents. And from this it follows quite logically that if I will truly – if, that is, the will is an act of my real self in its right state, emancipated from all disturbing influences – then I can argue that, provided I am quite sure that I *am* willing in this way (and the whole of Rousseau's theory collapses unless I, or someone, can sometimes be sure of this, otherwise how has anyone ever arrived at the true difference

[1] *Considérations sur le gouvernement de Pologne*: OC iii 973.

between right and wrong?), I can be certain that everyone else willing in this manner must reach the same conclusion; and that if they do not they cannot be willing properly; therefore whatever seems to me to be right in the circumstances can be quite safely imposed upon others almost without consulting them;[1] for if they are rational they will have reached the same decision themselves, and nothing will be imposed upon them which they are not already freely imposing upon themselves; or they will feel coerced, that is, my decision on their behalf does not coincide with what they wish severally for themselves, but that is a sure sign that they are not thinking rationally and I can therefore safely ignore their resistance. When I compel them to submit to my rational decision on their and my behalf, I am merely compelling them to be rational – that is, to do what they would have done for themselves if they were rational – that is, to be free. Thus Rousseau reaches the celebrated paradox that there is compulsion and compulsion: the irrational compulsion proceeding from the caprice of tyrants, whether individuals or oligarchies or even assemblies; and compulsion which is not compulsion, because it proceeds from a rational judgement – is that which all truly free men will do spontaneously and to which resistance is irrational and therefore wicked. For, after all, our so-called self is not our true self, only its reflection.

When Kant, Fichte, Novalis – all the German romantic philosophers and poets – developed this great religious thesis, they were political heirs to Rousseau. For this is the heart of the doctrine which gives unlimited power to any person or body which feels itself in possession of the right rule for the government of men. Provided I am willing correctly, the authority is absolute: and this applies to institutions and individuals. The State or Church can coerce, imprison, punish with impunity, for it is acting on behalf of men's rational or 'real' natures, like a guardian or teacher, not to impose its own will upon a child or an imbecile, but to make it do that which it itself would be doing if it knew what its own inner voice (which it is too immature or too deranged to hear) would be – almost is – telling it to do. A commentator sums up the view of a Jacobin of a later day all too succinctly: 'No man is free in doing evil. To prevent him is to free him.'[2] This is very pure

---

[1] {Appendix [i.e. section headed 'The notion of the real will', inserted above, pp. 120–7] is improvement on this?}

[2] Crane Brinton, op. cit. (p. 129 above, note 1), 257.

Rousseau of the *Contrat* period: and the fate of the word 'liberation' since his day has added to its sinister significance. This is the inner certainty about what is right which justified the despotic rule of Calvin in Geneva, and of all dictators everywhere at all times, who were inspired by conviction of their own moral superiority or of having unique access to the voice of God or nature, governing and punishing and destroying not merely for the good of their subjects – for that still leaves them slaves – but for that good which their subjects, if only they truly understood themselves, would themselves be desiring, and therefore (it is only a very short step) are in a sense already desiring – not overtly, perhaps, but within their true selves, buried under the weight of their unfortunate empirical natures – mutely, potentially desiring already.

It is a short step, but a truly fatal one, for there is every difference between what in fact I wish, and what someone else thinks I ought to wish; between what I do wish, and what, because I ought to wish it, I am said to be wishing already in some deeper sense, though I may not know it. At some stage I am bound to protest, as oppressed minorities and majorities have always protested and always will protest, that to be free is to be in a position to secure the satisfaction of one's actual wishes, not of those 'potential' or 'ideal' wishes which spring from our occult 'ideal' natures, and which happen to coincide with those of our masters, but which we, rightly or wrongly, do not happen to feel, and, indeed, at times most vehemently reject and revolt against.

In theory, in any given society, there need be no more than one individual in whom this will is embodied. Rousseau does not indeed say that the general will would in theory be embodied in the one 'free' man in an assembly of morally benighted persons, although his notion of the legislature comes very near this – the great Lycurgus, the great Solon, stood in almost this relation to their peoples. Rousseau was to some degree a democrat by inclination and inclined to pursue majority rule, if only because among those whom he disliked were not only the well-known butts of the Enlightenment – the kings and governments and Churches of the eighteenth century – but the enlighteners themselves – the thinkers and celebrated scientists in the Paris salons who openly distrusted the voice of the people, rightly supposing that it was as often raised for reactionary as for progressive causes. Rousseau, with his faith in and sympathy with the social ideals of the common people and their unspoilt attitude to life, preferred to think that the general will, founded upon perception of the true purposes of nature and man, was more frequently to be encountered in the deliberations of village elders seated in the shade of some ancestral oak, or at any rate in small assemblies of persons bound by ties of sentiment and mutual respect, than in vast and heterogeneous assemblies, or in the breasts of individual sovereigns or administrators. There was therefore no inconsistency or betrayal of the ideas of their master in the thought of those who, like Robespierre or Saint-Just, claimed in their own persons to embody the general will against the false advice of the multitude. For although the general will can never be *wrong*, it can be misled; and sometimes, when men are obsessed by personal or sectional interests, the mere coming together of the governing assembly fails to generate the unity of the general will, just as Quakers did not always generate 'the sense of the meeting'. Rousseau says that differences often cancel out, leaving the common ground intact: but this is a lame substitute for the positive unity of the Athenians and Spartans in moments of crisis, which he loves to quote.

All Jacobin or other totalitarian theory which allows single individuals or groups to bind their wills upon others, whether these others like this or not, not in the name of a contract in which the others have had a conscious part, nor for utilitarian reasons, nor in the name of abstract principles wholly independent of human wills, but in the name of the true selves of these others, whom in the very act of coercing they claimed to be liberating – 'forcing to be free'[1] – are the true heirs of Rousseau. There may be many valid reasons for coercion, and in exceptional circumstances even for the methods of terror (though it is difficult to think that such circumstances have ever in fact arisen), but to maintain that the use of force and terror is actually willed by those against whom the terror is directed seems a hideous abuse of words. The fact that this act of will is conceived as springing, not indeed from their empirical selves, which is all these unfortunate persons may be conscious of, but from some inner 'real' self, of which they are conspicuously unaware, but which lives its occult 'real' life within them nevertheless, merely has the effect of obviating any need for listening to the actual wishes of those whom the burden of their errors prevents from seeing the truth, and therefore talking or

---

[1] See p. 124 above, note 1.

understanding sense, and lightens the conscience of the oppressor who is engaged in the sacred task of liberating the inner real personality of his victim from the grip of its hideous outer empirical integument.[1]

No doubt all sincere inquisitors who have punished and destroyed in the name of principles have believed something of this, and have surprised later generations by the total absence of qualms with which they hanged and burned (apparently innocent) men and women in the name of the victims' own immortal, but inarticulate, souls. But so long as something so occult as the soul, which is not a part of the natural world, was invoked, together with the rest of the language of a transcendent theology, the question whether their actions were cruel or unjust was ruled out as irrelevant, since the reasons – the justification – were supernatural and a divine mystery and not open to human reason. But once it was maintained that man was to be conceived as a natural being, that his good was not to be defined in supernatural terms, and was to be realised here on earth, as prescribed by the Great Book of Nature, open for all to read, the doctrine became much more fantastic. A position which enabled some men to torture and kill others not because it was objectively right or useful to do so, but because the tortured and the killed themselves were said to be demanding this, because, however unbeknown to them, their natures demanded it, seemed to add a peculiarly repulsive form of mockery to the last torments of the victims of this 'liberating' process.

From Robespierre and Babeuf to Marx and Sorel, Lenin, Mussolini, Hitler and their successors, this grotesque and hair-raising paradox, whereby a man is told that to be deprived of his liberty is to be given a higher, nobler liberty, has played a major part in the great revolutions of our time. For its modern form the author of the *Social Contract* can certainly claim full credit. This

---

[1] There is no doubt about the theological tone of Rousseau's doctrine. It is a form of the medieval doctrine about the extirpative heresy: the heretic is forced by the Church – the keeper of his innermost self – to expiate his errors against his own immortal soul. The Church's right to cure, or in the extreme cases to cut off, the offending limb derives from its identification with the sinner's own better nature. In this regard no one is less liberal, more violently at odds with such genuine believers in toleration as Voltaire or Condorcet, than Jean-Jacques. And the German political romantics as well as later French Catholic reactionaries found him an unexpected ally against the Enlightenment.

monstrous political farce bears every mark of its origin: a rigid logical schema forcibly imposed upon a deranged version of the notion of moral freedom; the proclamation of a reign of liberty so absolute and universal that it keeps everyone everywhere in chains; adding that this harsh oppression is what all free men would wish if they truly knew how to realise the liberty which they so truly wished. The later versions of the true nature of the good, common man – those of Maistre, Nietzsche, Dostoevsky's Grand Inquisitor, of Mussolini and Hitler and many Communist leaders – are only grimly sardonic variations upon this theme – variations which would perhaps not have astonished or dismayed Rousseau himself as much as they ought – if he on his part truly knew what he was truly saying.[1]

Man must be free – uninterfered with, acting by his own volition, pursuing ends which are his, and solely his, for motives which are his own, in ways in which he perceives to be best – otherwise he may be happy as slaves are but is not a moral being, not an immortal spirit, not man at all; man must live his life according to the right rules laid down eternally in the mind of God and the bosom of nature. These rules have, in various imperfect guises, always been felt to be the true moral and political law in all societies, at all times, called by some the divine law, by others the law of nature, conceived as the law of reason by Stoics and as the law of the nations, the foundations of the general beliefs of mankind, by the Roman jurists; equally accepted as the foundation of law and morality by St Thomas and by Grotius; and indeed more widely than that, by Christian and Jew and Muslim, and even enlightened heathen; a set of general rules which the rationalists

---

[1] {Put in: majority rule; double allegiance (Roman Church, civil religion); Will of All; Corsican Const. oxen etc. and conservatism of manners; Vollmer's phalanstère is patriarchal ('good morals and happiness more important than employment of possible talents some of which are harmful and best neglected' (Vollmer, Nouv. Héloïse)); mass and psychology; team spirit and afflatus; flash and thunder of revelation. Karl Moor [hero of Schiller's play *The Robbers*] is Naturmensch: Humanity v. corrupted: 'Woe to us if masses start reasoning' Voltaire [perhaps a paraphrase of 'when the masses get involved in reasoning, everything is lost', *The Complete Works of Voltaire*, ed. Theodore Besterman and others, vol. 114 (Banbury, 1973), 155]. 'In intellectual questions its [the masses'] voice is full of malignity, stupidity, inhumanity, perversity, prejudice. Beware of it in moral questions: it is ignorant and idiotic; hedonism in its eyes in madness. It is incapable of noble or strong deeds.' Encyclopédie on 'Multitude' [for more accurate version, see FIB 21]. Mandarins of China an enlightened minority skilfully piloting mass of fanatics and fools.}

claimed could be discovered only by those who conceived everything in terms of clear rational ideas connected with each other by clear deductive reasoning, while others, Vico or Herder, claimed to discover these not by rational Cartesian analysis, but by an act of intuitive insight, needing imagination almost more than reason, embedded in the traditions and myths and languages of peoples, in their poetry and their myths, their arts and their religions, and all the widely varied ways in which men sought to express their attitudes and feelings and ideas, born of the interplay of the human spirit with its natural environment. But whatever the path, the true answers to the great problems lie only in these great laws, discoverable in faiths, in philosophies, but best and most clearly of all in nature and its mirror, the heart of men.

Rousseau added to this three notions destined to play a growing part in later thought: (1) that freedom is an absolute value and may not be curtailed, for there is no morality without it; (2) that morality is discoverable not in the *de facto* activities of men in accordance with this or that pattern (an assumption common to philosophers otherwise as diametrically opposed as, say, Plato and Helvétius) but in conscious acts of will whereby men dedicate themselves to this or that goal independently of and, if need be, against other 'pulls' and 'pushes' exercised by their physical nature – the gravitational force of the passions, the appetites, everything which makes men mere objects in nature, seeking only their own preservation, and ruled by natural laws, as helpless as a plant or a stone; and finally (3) the uniqueness of the right rule, distinguishable from mere inclination by the fact that a man can discover it only when he is in the special state of mind in which the truth is revealed to him – and this for Rousseau consists in a peculiar *état d'âme*, a peculiar sensitiveness to the patterns of the universe (what Vico found in the contemplation of history, Montesquieu in that of the social scene, Rousseau finds in absorption in the bosom of nature). Following such truths, obtained in this semi-mystical condition, on the part of the individual cannot conceivably bring him into conflict with other individuals following similar rules, since the following of the rules is automatically a self-adjustment to the goal of the universe, which is one of harmonious development, involving no collisions.

The philosopher upon whom these reflections, on his own admission, made the deepest impression is, of course, Kant. In Kant these elements become united to two further principles: (*a*) that whatever is true must be so universally and always take a general form; and (*b*) that man possesses something which he calls a rational nature, such that true moral rules are discoverable in virtue of this rationality as such, although Kant never quite clearly states precisely how this is achieved. We cannot here go into the nature of Kant's philosophy in general, or of his theory of knowledge. Suffice it to say that he believed the laws of nature as revealed in natural sciences to be compounded of general propositions that record those uniformities which in some mysterious fashion man's non-empirical self imposes upon the 'given' of experience, and without which he would not be conscious of the material world at all; but ethical truths are in some way commandments which his non-empirical nature issues forth as an expression of its own inner reason – moral rules whose essence is that they are commandments, that is to say not statements of fact, however general, which both the rationalist and empiricist philosophers among his predecessors regarded as the sole form proper to all true knowledge. For Kant they are orders, maxims, which earlier thinkers attributed to the Deity, and which Kant, somewhat obscurely, derives from what he calls the rational nature of man – an ideal of perfect harmony which impinges upon the moral consciousness in the form of a set of moral rules accompanied by a unique attitude – something different from a mere emotional feeling – which he calls 'respect' or 'awe' before the moral law.

What is interesting and relevant here is that only that conduct is moral which proceeds from a free act of will, whereby a man obeys a commandment which he perceives to be of the ethical, that is absolute, kind. Merely to do something because one wants it, because one finds it agreeable, or considers that it would lead to pleasure or happiness, is a mere empirical discovery that certain means lead to certain ends, or that certain ends do in fact have the power of attracting one – the first a piece of ordinary empirical knowledge, the second a specifically psychological but no less empirical piece of information about one's condition. For Kant, moral conduct, founded as it is upon the realisation of moral principles appearing as commands, is very different from this. It is the direction of one's will to the actualisation of a unique rule – a commandment – which only a rational being conscious of its freedom from the wholly determined causal world of space and time can achieve. The old metaphysical dualism between the rational and 'animal' nature here reinforces Rousseau's vague distinctions. The self is conceived no longer as a being identical with, or resident in, a spatio-temporal body subject to natural laws, but as a unique entity outside time and space, generating in some non-empirical sense acts of will free from the trammels of the material world, acts which are ethical only if they conform to maxims which again it itself in some mysterious sense generates, in accordance with its inner rationality, and which in virtue of this unique nature awaken the peculiar awe which the pronouncements of reason alone carry with them.

Kant's moral law – the celebrated categorical imperative – is the special possession of every being which is human, and therefore, in Kant's peculiar sense of the word, rational; not an object in the material world, but a subject. A subject is an autonomous entity, something which rationally perceives and freely chooses to obey or disobey the voice of its (non-empirical) reason, bidding it do this or that. The first mark of reason, in whatever sense, is that its pronouncements are *general*. In the material universe they take the form of general laws like those of Newtonian science, which brook no exceptions. In the mysterious sphere of non-empirical reason, moral laws are no less general; they are not, however, general statements of facts, but laws, commandments – not truths of fact, however profound and universal, but behests which one does not verify or falsify, but obeys or disobeys. The volitional element is, in a sense, already present in much of Christian and the whole of the Hebraic tradition. It is the element which most clearly marks off the Lutheran revolution against the Hellenic elements in Catholicism, and asserts the notion that to be truly moral one must not merely *be* or understand something – be adjusted to, through comprehension of, some universal scheme of things, in harmony or communion with a self-developing pattern, static or moving (as the Greeks and the rationalists and to some degree the Thomists taught) – but issue commands to oneself, assert one's will, act, bend the world to its demands. It is present in Rousseau, with his stress on the disinterested will that wills the Common Good; and it is immensely strengthened by Kant's doctrine, with its affinity to the pietistic tradition of German Protestantism, according to which moral rectitude and spiritual salvation depend on absolute obedience to the inexorable dictates of the individual conscience, which is the voice of God speaking from within.

But the Kantian doctrine is bolder and clearer than this: it lays down for the first time, in uncompromising language, that the sense of duty – the state in which alone knowledge of what to do and what to avoid is clear to a man – is utterly different from, and on no account to be confused with, desires, wishes, yearnings of any kind – the many springs of action which cause men to behave as they do, as the forces of nature cause things or plants to be as they are and change as they do. The hearing of commands of duty is a unique condition immediately recognisable by all moral beings (as all men potentially are) as something 'higher than' or 'transcending' the currents of the appetitive life upon which men are tossed when they are not listening to the inner voice, whose presence in men alone makes them capable of idealism, of disinterestedness, of 'rising above' their animal natures, of moral goodness; of what in its purest form has always been recognised as a spiritual disposition which sets men off as saints, of which Rousseau had some inkling when he maintained that not worldly knowledge, not cleverness, not erudition or skill or intellectual genius revealed moral truth to men, but a special purity of heart and will, to be found more often among the simple and humble and unspoilt than among men admired for power or wealth or success. In Kant the dualism of the two natures is quite explicit: every man is, as it were, two selves – on the one hand an empirical self, subject to the ordinary influences of the physical world, an entity properly studied by such natural sciences as physics, biology, psychology and (save that it was not called so in the eighteenth century) sociology, as rigidly determined by the laws of nature as all the other objects in it; and on the other a transcendent, self-directed, non-empirical self, not 'behaving' at all, but acting, capable of freely obeying or flouting precepts which it issues to itself, and which it follows because it wills to follow them, because they are what they are – ends in themselves, something to be fulfilled for its own sake, for no other reason at all, absolute purposes. That is Kant's specific contribution and the basis of the romantic doctrine of man, who stands, in Herder's words, intermediate between nature and God, beasts and angels, touching at one extremity the mechanical world of the sciences, and at the other the spiritual realm revealed only in moments of the special illumination peculiar to spiritual beings.

There is no doubt that, whatever the extravagant metaphysical implications of this view, Kant in the course of stating it said something which no one has since altogether wished to deny, even though they might not accept the theology or ontological implications which Kant himself evidently drew from it; namely, that to conceive something as one's duty is not the same as merely to wish it, however strongly, or to think it likely to lead to pleasure or to happiness or to avoidance of pain, or to a strengthening of some natural or social pattern whose value resides in some psychologically identifiable satisfaction which men find themselves naturally pursuing. It was never plausible to say, as the rationalists and empiricists were both compelled to say, that the great acts of self-abnegation, the acts of heroism and martyrdom that occur when a man is prepared to sacrifice his worldly possessions and indeed life itself in the service of some ideal goal, in the pursuit of the truth, or the saving of a life, or the many other ends in whose service men have been prepared to perish with no thought of the consequences – that these states are, as Bentham insisted, so many disguised forms of the pursuit of happiness, the satisfaction of natural appetites, common indeed and 'natural' to all men, but perverted and distorted by centuries of error and obscurantism into seeming utterly different from the normal rational pursuit of personal or social well-being. It was not merely that the emotional afflatus, the compelling quality of the 'sense of duty', with its uncompromising fiats, had been ignored or reduced to something very different from itself by analyses of rationalists such as Spinoza, or of empiricists such as Hobbes or Hume (however different their views about the empirical nature of man), or of those who reduced morals to aesthetics like Shaftesbury or Lessing; but that a sufficiently careful contemplation of what men in fact experience when they choose to do what they conceive to be their duty leads inevitably to the conclusion that they are in a state very different from that in which they are said to yield to the strongest desire, even though that desire may be for self-mortification or self-sacrifice.

The celebrated Marquis de Sade had already, before the romantics, declared that if nature is what we are meant to follow, the conclusions of the optimistic rationalists were far from realistic; the desire to give pain and to suffer it was no less natural than the desire to give or suffer pleasure; Rousseau and the Encyclopaedists bade us be kind, reasonable and studious; but to say that inclinations to do the opposite, to seek violent sensations which might involve cruelty, pain, inequality and a life very different from that of the virtuous statesman or the scientific researcher, were 'unnatural', was a merely dogmatic interpretation of the concept of nature; the man who lusted after power or found satisfaction in disharmonies – turbulent emotions, or perverted experience of every kind – was merely following his natural appetites, which, *qua* appetites, had as much claim to fulfilment as the milder and more 'reasonable' inclinations of the idealised beings of the *philosophes* – following the line of the 'tough-minded' philosophers Hobbes and Mandeville. And this was a genuine criticism of the identification of what is natural with what seems satisfactory or worth pursuing to this or that school of virtuous philosophers. Kant cut out the ground from this argument by maintaining that the content of duty had nothing in common with the object of desire, and the fact that duty might often be difficult or painful was neither here nor there, since conformity or non-conformity to human wishes and likes and dislikes was irrelevant to this notion; duty was that which man, not as a desiring being, but as a being willing the fulfilment of the moral law, commanded himself to do, and it was determined in accordance with the special faculty of non-empirical reason. A man might obey or disobey such inner orders. But whether or not he did so, if he was acting as a being conscious of the voice of duty, he was not acting as a mere desiring being pursuing happiness or pain or whatever his education or environment caused him to do, but as a transcendent entity – an immortal soul free from the world of causality, psychological or otherwise. Because this represented a genuine insight – because if good and bad are defined in terms of what men like or dislike or calculate as likely to lead to happiness, then right and wrong are inevitably felt to be different from and to possess an urgency and an authority and an imaginative quality very unlike good and bad; because to wish to do one's duty is a desire generically different from the desire to compass one's happiness, in any form – Kant's doctrine made a profound and lasting impression upon mankind.

Kant more than any other man impressed upon the consciousness of his generation and posterity two basic notions which had indeed been obscurely perceived but never so unequivocally emphasised. The first was that of disinterestedness – the proposing of specific acts for their own sakes; not because they were useful, nor because 'nature' inclined one towards them, but against nature if need be, because they were what they were and ends in themselves; and, following from this, the nobility of a life spent in the pursuit of a purpose which was its own justification, irrespective of whether it made the doer happy or miserable, and irrespective of what might be thought about it by other men, past, present or future. The concept of integrity, purity of heart, moral independence, 'autonomy', the sacrifice of oneself upon the altar of some activity whose absolute worth resided in itself, without hope of reward or fear of punishment in this world or the next, which dominates the nineteenth century, largely derived from Kant's highly original and articulate moral doctrine. And secondly, the notion of men – individuals – as ends in themselves, because they were the sole authors of moral values, because moral values were not to be found in empirical nature, qualifying it like so many attributes, as colours or tastes or shapes qualify objects in space, but were goals, ideals – and therefore something which men – or rather that which was transcendent in them – venerated. Because of this men were sacred. To harm or destroy a man was to harm or destroy the sole author and source of absolute values – that for the sake of which whatever was worth doing was worth doing, the end or purpose of all existence or activity. Purposes and ends did not subsist in worlds of their own, they were only what human wills willed. Human beings conceived as sources of acts of will, creators of values, could not be sacrificed to anything other than such purposes without stultifying the absoluteness, the end-in-itselfness, of these absolute values.

Rousseau's attitude to individual liberty and to the unimpairable sovereignty of the general will already has this flavour; but Kant is far more clear, unequivocal and devoid of the vague sentimental glow of Rousseau's eloquence. Men as such are sacred because their consciences, their wills, are the only absolutely good, absolutely valuable things in the world. Kant's celebrated doctrine of men as ends in themselves – his stern words about the wickedness of using men as means – flows from the notion that the sole, absolute reason for doing anything or being anything in particular is the absolute idealised image of what to do and be – of acts worth doing and lives worth living, in and for themselves alone – which each man carries in his own consciousness; and any denial or diminution of it is the only absolutely bad act in the world; and from this it follows that all men are morally equal, because all men are equally the sole creators, carriers, fulfillers of these internally conceived, self-imposed absolute ends. To deceive a man, or to exploit him, is to treat him as if he were an object in nature, a means towards something other than his own absolute ends, and this is in effect a denial of the sacredness of such ends.

Human equality is a commonplace in the eighteenth century. Bentham for instance said that every man was to count for one and no man for more than one,[1] but gave no convincing reason for this egalitarianism. He maintained that happiness is in fact more likely to be produced if equality rather than inequality is promoted; but this is an equivocal hypothesis which is not necessarily true or plausible: unequal, feudal, hierarchical societies have not demonstrably been unhappier than the democracies; slaves have been known to be not discontented in their servitude. And although the eighteenth-century philosophers by and large denounce privilege, and there is much talk of natural rights and appeals to nature's purposes as intending men to be equal, it is only when Rousseau angrily cries out that men may wish to be slaves, but that it is a degrading wish, that men ought not to wish to be slaves whether they do so or not, that it is an insult to human dignity to wish to submit irrationally to a tyrant, that we recognise the new note: too universal to attract attention in the nineteenth century, but one Kant had done more than any other thinker to instil. The notion of human pride, dignity, the immorality of slavery or any form of human exploitation, rather than the fact that it is unprofitable or inefficient, or led to diminution of human happiness, is due very largely to the effect of his ethical doctrine. There is a point in his argument where he says that I may not lie, even to a man coming to murder my friend about my friend's whereabouts, because I thereby use the murderer as a means – I cause him to behave in a manner which serves my friend's or my own purposes but not his – I deprive a man of the right of determining himself freely, in this case to murder or not to murder, which is his right since he is a human being entitled to generate and pursue his own ends, right or wrong, virtuous or wicked. No doubt Kant is exaggerating, as it may seem to some to the point of absurdity. But at any rate his thesis is clear: ethics and politics are not sciences or arts which instruct men in the attainment of happiness. Ethics is concerned with explaining not what a man must do in order to be happy, but what he must do to be worthy of happiness; this worth is bound up with the way in which, and the motives for which, an individual acts or would act in any situation involving choice. This worth –

---

[1] Attributed by J. S. Mill in *Utilitarianism*, near the end of chapter 5: vol. 10, p. 257, in *Collected Works of John Stuart Mill*, ed. J. M. Robson and others (Toronto/London, 1963–91). Mill's version runs: 'everybody to count for one, nobody for more than one'.

which Kant calls the Good Will – is the only absolute value that exists. All vice and sin and crime is such only in so far as it 'contradicts' this – denies the reality of or obstructs the free exercise of moral personality, that is, of the individual freely obeying the moral law, which thunders at him with all the force of a commandment in the Bible; and obeying it not blindly, not with that faith divorced from reason which Luther and his followers demanded, but because it is the demand of his 'rational' nature, which is respect not merely for the consistency of his logic, when he is describing the world or doing mathematics, but for the consistency and indeed the content of the rules or commands whose fulfilment is the realisation of himself as a rational being.

From Rousseau, and in particular from *Émile*, Kant obtained the notion that rules, so far from being forces severely inhibiting the spontaneous impulses of men, could themselves spring from the depths of common human nature and be filled with emotional content. He began by contrasting the necessarily small minority of enlightened, autonomous, self-controlled, superior beings – philo-sophers – liberated by their own morality, which has subdued their chaotic impulses or craving for happiness – contrasting these with the mass of humanity, helpless and at the mercy of desires and circumstances, heteronomous, more objects than subjects, unable to lift themselves to this austerer and freer sphere: and claims to have been taught by Rousseau that the moral impulse, and therefore the categorical imperative, so far from being shrunken by rules, gives them life, springs more pure in the overflowing heart of common man – Vollmer – than in palaces or lecture rooms: hence a renewal of faith in the morals of humanity, in democracy, in equality. Since the human personality is the source of these rules, and thus of all ethics and all politics, all that is right and just and equitable, all rational happiness, all freedom, every moral and aesthetic value, the individual has, as in the Christian interpreta-tion, 'infinite value'.

Kant has translated the mystical doctrine of the sanctity of the human soul of man as the carrier of a spark of the divine flame, of all men as sons of a father in heaven and brothers in the spirit, into ethical or metaphysical terms, and declared men inviolable because they alone give birth to the ultimate ends of life; man's self-perfection is the only ultimate end, and the infringement of the right to pursue it is the ultimate sin against the only light which exists. Man is unique, and the sacred vessel of the absolutely good and right and true; and to use him, exploit him, deceive him, degrade him, diminish his status in any way is the most terrible wrong that anyone can commit. The whole ethical content of nineteenth-century democratic doctrine is here: the emphasis on the preservation of the right to develop one's individual capacity, the hatred of anything likely to derogate from it, to lower human dignity; the liberal protest against any form of despotism, however benevolent and rational, not because it diminishes human happiness but because it is intrinsically degrading, a falsification of what human relationships between equal and independent (and ideal-pursuing) beings ought to be, a betrayal of the ideal which humanity exists to fulfil; the notion of humanity as something in the name of which rights can be claimed, crimes punished, revolutions made – this complex of values is inspired not by the utilitarian considerations or the empirical sociology of the eighteenth century but by the humanist idealism of Kant and his successors. No doubt many whose language has this tone (whatever they might think they are saying) and who were inspired by these ideals supposed themselves to derive them from some empirical science of man. Condorcet and Volney (and to some degree Voltaire and Diderot before them), Saint-Simon and even Comte, for all their pretended acceptance of only scientifically established propositions as true in any sphere whether of nature or of conduct, in fact derived their social doctrines as well as their belief in progress and the infinite capacities of men, however unconsciously, from the complex of ideas about the nature and purposes of man which Rousseau had stirred into life and Kant had organised and impressed upon the European consciousness so deeply that it has radically transformed Western language and thought, both private and public. No political proclamation, no statement of purposes in peace or war, none of the conflicts of moral and political ideas which have agitated Europe and America in the last century and a half would be intelligible in pre-Kantian terms; not least the language of those who most vehemently repudiate the individualism and stern anti-naturalism and anti-utilitarianism of his doctrines.

# 3

# TWO CONCEPTS OF FREEDOM: ROMANTIC AND LIBERAL

### *The notion of liberty*

LIKE MOST WORDS which have played an important role in the history of mankind, the terms 'human freedom' and 'liberty' bear many meanings. Nevertheless there appears to be a kind of nuclear, central, minimal meaning which is common to all the many senses of this word, and which signifies *absence of restraint*; more specifically, absence of coercion on the part of specified or unspecified fellow human beings. There are senses in which 'freedom' is not so used – in which it is idiomatic to speak of the free movement of human limbs or of the free play of the imagination or of freedom from pain, or of freedom from the trammels of the earthly life; but when we speak of political freedom, these senses seem to be quasi-metaphorical, and an attempt to bring them into play often merely clouds the issue. The struggles for freedom or liberty on the part of individuals or groups or communities are normally conceived of as efforts on the part of particular individuals to destroy or neutralise the power of coercing them to act against their own wishes possessed or used by some other individual or body of persons. And the party of liberty, as opposed to those who wish to uphold some particular kind of authority – that of a king, a Church, a hereditary aristocracy, a commercial enterprise, a sovereign assembly, a dictator, sometimes disguised as impersonal agencies ('the State', 'the law', 'the nation'), but always in fact consisting of individual persons, living or dead – is composed of persons who are opposing some existing or threatened form of restraint.[1] They may themselves be in favour of some other specific form of authority – say that of a democratic body, or a federation of units constituted in various ways – but it is not in virtue of supporting the form of authority which they

---

[1] {Rewrite sentence.}

favour that they are described as friends of liberty. Although there are many accretions which have grown up around the words 'liberty', 'libertarian', 'liberal', they will always be found to carry a greater or lesser connotation of resistance to interference on the part of someone – some person or persons, and not things or circumstances – in more or less specified conditions. This seems the basic sense of the word 'liberty' as a political term, and is the sense in which it is defended by all the great champions of it in thought and action, on behalf of both nations and individuals, from Moses and Leonidas to the present day.

The classical formulation of the ideal of liberty in modern times is the fruit of eighteenth-century thought, and culminates in the celebrated formulations of it in the Declaration of Independence of the United States and of the 'rights of man and citizen' of the first French Republic. These documents speak of rights, and when they mention rights they primarily have in view the invasion of certain provinces – say those which a man needs in order to secure life and adequate opportunities of happiness; or to be able to own property, or think and speak as he wishes, or obtain employment, or take part in the political or social life of his community – and they intend that invasion of such provinces should be regarded as forbidden by the law. The law is in this sense an instrument for preventing specific encroachment, or punishing it if it occurs.

Political liberty is thus a negative concept: to demand it is to demand that within a certain sphere a man be not forbidden to do whatever he wishes, not forbidden, that is, to do it whether in fact he can do it or not. A cripple is not *forbidden* to walk straight although he cannot in fact do so; nor a healthy man to fly to the moon, although in fact, as things are, he is not in a position to do so; yet we do not speak of a man as not being *free* to fly to the moon, nor of the cripple as not *free* to walk straight. Efforts have been made to speak so: freedom has been equated with power. The sense in which science, for example, is said to make men free is precisely the sense of enlarging his technical capacities for overcoming obstacles offered by nature – and also, to some extent, developing his imagination until it conceives of more possible alternatives than his previous ignorance or mental incapacity, or what is called a narrow mental horizon, had enabled him to do. But these uses of the word 'freedom', although reasonably familiar and clear, are felt, and rightly felt, to be somewhat metaphorical: the fact that I am not able to think of various ways of enjoying myself which occur to a more imaginative person does not make me unfree in the sense in which someone who locks me in a room, and so prevents me from obtaining some pleasure which I may long for, is said to do. If I am unable to rid myself of some violent infatuation or *idée fixe*, which makes me forget the whole world in the frantic pursuit of the goal which obsesses me, I can, no doubt, be described as a 'slave' of my passions; but I am not literally a slave; and no one thinks of me as a slave in the sense in which Uncle Tom was a slave to Simon Legree. Something is certainly common to the two cases – there is something that I am not doing, which I might be or have been doing – but the basic or more literal sense of the word 'freedom' and of the word 'liberty' is felt to be connected with the fact that the obstacle which stops me from doing this or that, from following my actual or 'potential' desires, is the deliberate intervention of a human being.[1]

There are all kinds of natural factors – physical and psychological – which prevent a man from doing what he wishes, or from wishing as someone else wishes or might wish. But these obstacles are not, as a rule, felt to be the direct objects of political action, not matters of political principle; for politics has to do with deliberate arrangements by sentient human beings, concerned with the degree of interference with each other's lives which they are to be permitted to exercise. And when sociological obstacles are said to arise – for example, the influence of education, or social environment, upon the development of a man, which is said to thwart or maim him in some way – we are not quite certain whether the resulting frustration is or is not a deprivation of freedom in the relevant sense. We are uncertain because we are not quite so strongly convinced of the facts of sociological causation as we are of psychological or physiological, not to speak of physical, causation; and therefore are not sure whether to regard such frustration as due to natural causes – not human acts, but what is in law called *force majeure*, for which no one is to blame – and so not at all a case of slavery or oppression in the political sense, or due to the preventable behaviour of human beings, and therefore a case of straightforward deprivation of liberty on the part of somebody at the hands of somebody else in the sense in which those who are its defenders are expected to fight for it, and occasionally secure it. We feel a kind of borderline quality about such cases – as when we hesitate whether to blame an individual or a group for acting

[1] {Quote Helvétius on liberty here.}

despotically, because they could avoid doing so, or on the contrary not to blame them, or call their behaviour despotic, because they are 'socially conditioned' and so 'cannot help themselves'; and this in itself indicates that the word 'freedom' has a somewhat different meaning in the two cases, of which the borderline case forms as it were a bridge-instance: it has something in common with both cases, and is puzzling and problematical because it does not sufficiently clearly belong to either.

Liberty in its political, non-metaphorical, sense means absence of interference by others, and civil liberty defines the area from which interference by others has been excluded by law or code of behaviour, whether 'natural' or 'positive', depending on what the law or code in question is conceived to be. This may be further illustrated by taking usages of the word 'freedom' which are felt to be correct but somewhat ambiguous in their force: for instance, the celebrated phrase 'economic freedom'. What those who invented it meant to say was that the granting of civil or political liberties – that is, the lifting of all restrictions from certain types of activity so far as legal interference alone was concerned – was of little use to people with not enough economic resources to make use of such liberty. There may be no prohibition on the amount of food a man may buy, but if he has no material resources, this 'freedom' is useless to him, and to tell him that he is free to buy is to mock at his indigence. Sometimes such freedom is said to be 'meaningless', if the person to whom it belongs is too poor or weak to make use of it. And yet the advocates of political liberty have at all times felt a certain unfairness in this argument: the fact that the law does not forbid the purchase of, let us say, unlimited food is, some of them tend to say, a genuine liberty the withdrawal of which would be a serious setback to human progress. The fact that the poor cannot profit by this freedom is analogous to the fact that a deaf-mute cannot derive much advantage from the right of freedom of speech, or of public assembly; a right is a right, and freedom freedom, whoever may or may not be in a position to make use of it. And yet those who speak of economic freedom are felt to be pointing to some genuine defect in a social organisation which makes material goods theoretically available to those who cannot in practice acquire them, and point out that such persons are about as free to profit by their economic freedoms as Tantalus, surrounded by limitless water, is free to drink, because there is no statute forbidding him to do so.

But this dilemma, like many other arguments where both sides are felt to be saying something true yet mutually incompatible, derives its paradoxical quality from the perhaps inevitable – and not always undesirable – vagueness and ambiguity of words. Mere incapacity to make use of something which others are not preventing one from using – say a biological or mental defect on the part of the would-be user, or inability to reach it for some physical or geographical reason – is certainly not, as such and in itself, felt to be a form of unfreedom or 'slavery'. And if complaints about the absence of economic freedom were simply laments that some persons in society were, in fact, not rich enough to obtain all they needed, in spite of the fact that it was all legally obtainable, that would not differ in principle from laments about other incapacities, and it would be as absurd to describe it as absence of freedom as to say that the possession of only two eyes *eo ipso* constitutes an absence of freedom to possess three eyes or a million, which after all is not forbidden by law. The real plausibility of the charge which the term 'economic freedom' is meant to convey derives from the fact that it implies, without always explicitly stating it, that the economic incapacity of the poor is due not to natural factors merely, nor to 'inevitable' psychological or social ones, but to activity, if not deliberate, at least avoidable, once it is attended to, on the part of specific individuals or classes or institutions. The thought which lies behind it is that the rich have too large a share of the total possessions of society, and this is the reason why the poor have too little and so cannot make use of laws which turn out to profit only the rich. The implication is that the rich can act voluntarily, or be forced to act, in such a way as to cease depriving the poor of resources which they need, and would want if they knew what they needed, and which, according to the champions of economic freedom, they would obtain in a society which was more just, that is, differently managed by its organisers, though not one that was necessarily different in any physical, or psychological, or any other natural respect from the present, less just, society. What gives the word 'freedom' force in the phrase 'economic freedom' is not that it stands for a claim to a missing capacity for action but that it indicates that someone has deprived someone else of something due to him; and 'due' in this context, if rendered wholly explicit, means at least this, that the person or persons thus deprived can be described as being interfered with, encroached upon, coerced, in the sense that a strong man interferes with a weak one or a robber coerces his victim.

Thus 'freedom' usually denotes absence of positive coercion, or the presence of negative restraint, on the part of one set of human beings towards another; and claims or demands for freedom often refer to the particular kind of coercion or restraint which in the specific circumstances in question happens to prevent men from being or acting or obtaining something which at that moment they wish for most ardently, and the lack of which, rightly or wrongly, they attribute to the preventable behaviour of others. This is certainly the classical sense of such words as 'freedom' or 'liberty', in which they denoted the principles or 'causes' in the name of which, since the beginnings of Western civilisation, States, communities and Churches have fought to preserve certain forms of organisation against interference from outside, however greatly they may have believed in interference with lives of individuals within such organised wholes; and individuals, in their turn, have fought against interference by other individuals or bodies within or outside their own unit, seeking to retain, win back or enlarge the area in which they could fulfil their own wishes, without effective opposition on the part of others. Freedom is in the first instance freedom against; liberty is liberty from. Liberty *to* do this, or that, turns out, upon analysis, to mean freedom from obstructors, freedom against individuals seeking to interfere – the clearing of an area against outside pressure – implying, but not asserting, the corresponding positive element: the existence of wishes, ideals, policies on the part of human beings which cannot be realised unless the negative conditions for its realisation are fulfilled – unless they are in fact 'free' in their functioning.

In the best of all modern defences of political freedom – in J. S. Mill's essay on liberty – this is made extraordinarily clear. Mill's objective, like that of all the liberals of his time, is to set a frontier beyond which State interference must not go. He lays down the principle (whether rightly or wrongly is not relevant here) that self-preservation is, in the end, the only valid reason which one human being can ever have for compelling another to do what the other does not wish to do, for to use compulsion for any other end would endanger the values for which Mill principally cares – non-interference with the free self-expression of human beings, the protection of private lives and personal relationships, the opportunity for the fullest and most spontaneous development of men's imagination, intellect and emotions, even positive encouragement of individual eccentricity, provided that this does not obstruct or impinge on others beyond certain set limits, and makes for the richest variety of experience, and encourages originality, temperament, genius, permitting the widest field for personal development.

Freedom, which is for Mill, as for all liberals in the nineteenth century, the central political ideal – so sacred that death is certainly preferable to its total extinction or grave diminution – is nevertheless purely negative, almost more of a necessary condition of the good life than an ingredient in it, in the sense that only when it is made secure can those activities which alone make life worth living develop and flourish and yield their finest fruit. The freedom the price of which is 'eternal vigilance' is a perpetual defensive operation from ramparts which would not be needed if it were not in constant danger. But the ramparts are not an end in themselves; the defensive operation presupposes that there is something to defend, and that something is not the operation itself but the intrinsically valuable activities and experiences of mankind – love and friendship, personal relations, justice and variety in public life, the arts and sciences – all the elements which compose a life which appears as an end in itself to those who live it, as the song itself is the purpose of the singer, not as a means to something further but as a final goal, as the satisfaction of basic impulses and desires, as an element in that still empirical but no longer simple – on the contrary, exceedingly refined and complex and somewhat vague – ideal of happiness into which J. S. Mill developed the all too clear but somewhat jejeune concept of his father and Jeremy Bentham.

As for the elder Mill and Bentham, they were perfectly satisfied in their own not very subtle and thoroughly lucid minds about liberty and why it was desirable: unless individuals possessed it they could not rationally pursue each their own greatest happiness. Adam Smith had discovered the mysterious but most fortunate and wonderfully liberating principle whereby the interests of all men, rationally seeking each his own greatest happiness, must automatically coincide in a universal harmony; providence was in favour of *laissez-faire*; every offence against that cardinal principle was an offence against its beneficent power. Bentham indeed was no fanatical defender of *laissez-faire*; he had accepted Helvétius' original notion, that rewards and punishments must be so arranged as to cause men to seek their own happiness, whether they knew it or not (or consciously wanted it or not; for unconsciously Bentham had no doubt that all sentient beings wanted that and that alone), by a species of ingeniously arranged psychological and sociological conditioning; and from this it seemed to follow that those who arranged society in this way would have to be given more power than those who were being arranged for – for whose benefit the arrangement had been invented – and this might seem to curtail the liberties of the subjects to give greater freedom of action to the virtuous legislators.

Bentham clearly did not much care if this was so: he was concerned, or thought he was concerned, merely with discovering the conditions for the maximisation of the happiness of as many persons as possible. Bentham refused to have any truck with any of the talk of natural rights, moral duties, ethical intuitions, natural law, revelation, the proper ends of man, self-evident metaphysical truths – the entire philosophical paraphernalia of the theologians, metaphysicians, *philosophes*, revolutionaries, with all their many brands of political and moral philosophies, including the ideas which found their way into the tables of human and civic rights and duties drawn up by the makers of the American and French Revolutions. All this seemed to Bentham's stout and uncompromising empiricism so much meaningless rubbish, abuse of language, deliberate mystification or empty patter, an obsolete amalgam of magical formulae which had never signified anything, and were now finally seen by all sensible men to be mere gibberish. However, he approved whatever he thought true even though it was expressed in grotesque phraseology, and the French (or American) passion for life or liberty, or fraternity or equality or the pursuit of happiness, as natural rights, although the formula itself was, in his view, well nigh meaningless, indicated some grasp, however imperfect, of the conditions in which alone the maximum happiness could be secured.

Bentham believed that happiness could be maximised by a rational organisation of society, and that a large measure of individual liberty was necessary thereto, firstly because people on the whole disliked to be coerced, and secondly because happiness could not be maximised so long as vested interests were permitted to pursue their sinister ends against the common good, that is, the state of the greatest satisfaction of the largest number of individual purposes as securely and intensely as possible. But freedom remained to him a means, just as equality is a means (fraternity is a piece of Christian sentimentality which Bentham clearly regarded as scarcely worthy of mention), to the maximum satisfaction of the maximum number of desires. It is in fact all too clear that his maxim about 'Each to count for one and no one to count for more than one'[1] is in fact sheer equality for equality's sake – the principle of fairness – almost Kantian in its strictness. But his reasons for it were, according to his own theory, strictly empirical. It might be that unequal societies produced more happiness per head than relatively egalitarian ones; and it might be that people preferred life in slavery or in prison to enjoyment of political liberties. All this might be the case, but in fact it was not: observation of human nature (Bentham had little love of or interest in history) showed the opposite to be the case. Hence, in the beginning of his life, Bentham did not advocate liberty and political equality too ardently, since he believed that a utilitarian society would be built more swiftly and efficiently by a shrewd and benevolent despot, who might be easier to persuade than an assembly. Towards the end of his life he favoured democratic rule simply because he had lost hope of finding or producing a suitable despot, regarded the vested interests of economic and political and religious minorities as, on the whole, a greater obstacle to happiness than the follies of democracies, and decided for the lesser evil. How to reconcile equality and liberty he does not tell us, but however this is to be done (or left undone), liberty is to him liberty against – against fools and knaves, sectional interests and ambitious or oppressive governments, enemies abroad, and indolent or stupid, or self-seeking or misanthropic, or puritanical or bigoted or simply narrow and prejudiced persons at home.

Liberty is an ideal only so long as it is threatened; like war and economic science, it should have as its ultimate purpose to abolish the conditions which make it necessary; the ideal society would not be conscious of the need for freedom. For freedom is a mere guarantee against interference, and the need for guarantees is felt only where there exists the idea of these dangers, to avoid which they are provided. The fight for liberty is the fight to create a situation in which the very name of it is forgotten; but this is an ideal state of affairs; and few of the sane, empirical thinkers from which later liberals are for the most part descended supposed it to be completely attainable in practice in the sense in which the true

[1] See p. 152 above, note 1.

anarchists – Godwin and Fourier and Stirner and Bakunin – and perhaps, at times, Condorcet, thought of it as a thoroughly practical possibility not at all far removed, and needing only a few readjustments of social foundations to realise it; and are for that reason justly relegated to the category of visionaries, cranks and eccentrics, often gifted and fascinating, sometimes profoundly influential, but always demonstrably deranged.

When the not wholly unmysterious notion of freedom in this negative sense comes in a metaphysical setting – connected, as it often is, with the notion of natural law in the teleological sense of all nature conspiring to a single goal, or with metaphysical or theological beliefs about the nature of man and his function or purpose in the natural or divine order – there comes into play the notion of natural, or inherent, or inalienable rights which men possess innately, that is, in virtue of their immaterial, unalterable, constant, super-empirical or transcendent natures. Rights so sacred that no human arrangements can prevail against them or alter them are clearly of non-human origin: and indeed those who defend them, even when, like Condorcet or Paine or even Rousseau, their belief in any recognisable deity seems dubious, at least agree in recognising in men a power of non-empirical insight – often by them called reason – which discerns a system of relationships between sentient beings (some include animals and some do not; but there is no need to concern oneself with the more extravagant excursions of this school) such that the performance, or omission, of certain actions constitutes failure to satisfy certain a priori claims which, within the system, individuals 'own' vis-à-vis each other.

These claims are usually represented as claims justified by the existence of a natural law which is 'quod ubique, quod semper, quod ab omnibus creditum est',[1] and of which we have a priori guarantees; thus they are a reflection (their champions would say the originals) of claims which are created by positive, man-made laws. Sometimes the existence of this ultimate metaphysical system is forgotten and natural rights are conceived as isolated entities or attributes or relations, somehow 'inherent' in moral agents in an altogether unique and inexplicable fashion: as imprescriptible or eternal 'rights of man', something which makes certain forms of interference or frustration by others or refusal of goods or services by them wrong or wicked eternally, and a priori, though it is not

[1] 'What is believed everywhere, always, by everyone.' Vincent of Lérins, *Commonitorium* 2. 3.

made clear by what logic or cognitive process such conclusions are reached. Such rights, though inherent and indestructible, can nevertheless be 'waived' or even given up, as in Hobbes's theory of the social contract, although all of them cannot – Locke supposes the rights to life, liberty, security and property to be unsurrenderable; and Rousseau is by no means clear on the subject. But whatever the 'metaphysical status' of these odd entities is and however they come to be 'possessed' or 'owned by' or 'alienated from' individuals or groups – even Godwin, who had no objection to thoroughly a priori laws of nature, cannot understand what these entities are, whether 'transferable' or 'inalienable' – what they appear to have meant in political terms is not obscure: assertion of their existence was tantamount to maintaining that the limits of interference were bounded not by *ad hoc* convention between human beings but by some rule or arrangement which was to be preserved as an end in itself. This was one of the ultimate values – however one established what these were – which needed no justification in terms of other values, since they belonged to the upper row in the hierarchy of values in terms of which all else was tested and justified; and minor modifications in this pattern could be achieved only by consent of the persons concerned, this degree of elasticity being justified in its turn by the fact that consent too was an ultimate value, one which did not indeed so far exceed the other values in authority as to be able to abolish them altogether – rights did not depend on consent but were 'absolute' – but could, on occasion, resolve minor conflicts and collisions. But of course the concept of the sanctity of rights owes a great deal to Kant's defence of human dignity – of man's moral nature as the source of all that is valuable, of all that lifts him above nature, and makes death preferable to surrender, to degradation, to denial of what he knows to be true. And to call such attributes a priori seemed one way of emphasising their uniqueness and supreme importance and, to the humanists, sublimity.

But whether conceived in the quasi-mythological terms of the true believers in natural rights like Paine and Condorcet and some, at any rate, among the founding fathers of both the French and the American Republics, or in more positivistic or empirical ways, as by Hume or Bentham or Mill, or within the curious intermediate area between the two in which some of the lawyers and constitutional writers on democracy seemed to be thinking, the notion of freedom remains to the liberals not a positive goal like pleasure or knowledge or the beatitude sought after by Eastern sages or Western saints; nor a positive goal like Kant's duties or Hume's approved states of mind or body. It is only the means which must be taken to prevent these positive goals from being frustrated – the political habits, with laws to prop them up against breakdown in individual cases, which make possible the fulfilment of the favoured purpose. To be free is to be unobstructed, to be able to do whatever one wishes. To be absolutely free is to be in a state where nothing can oppose one's wishes – to be omnipotent. To be absolutely free in the normal social or political sense of the word, both in private and public life, is not to be obstructed in one's desires by another human being. To be relatively free, in Mill's sense, is not to be obstructed within precisely laid down, or less or more vaguely conceived, limits. Freedom is not a word denoting a human end but a term for the absence of obstacles, in particular obstacles which result from human action, to the fulfilment of whatever ends men might pursue. And the struggle for freedom, like the fight for justice, is a struggle not for a positive goal but for conditions in which positive goals can be fulfilled – the clearing of a space which, without ends which are worth pursuing in themselves, remains a vacuum.

## Positive freedom

But this is by no means the outline of the whole story, even of the modern concept of liberty. Throughout the history of the discussion of liberty, which is almost as old as speculative thought itself, there has existed a tendency to speak of something which was called a *positive* notion of freedom, as opposed to the so-called 'negative' one of which we spoke above. One of these notions of 'positive freedom' – the doctrine of self-adjustment to the unalterable pattern of reality in order to avoid being destroyed by it – has been mentioned already; and clearly this sense of 'freedom' is a peculiar one, for it solves the problem of how to avoid interference by recommending acceptance of it as inevitable, and in consequence – it is a very curious consequence – as no longer interference; in other words it reconciles conflicts by declaring them to be always illusory and thus needing no solution at the level at which they occur. Yet to accept a state of affairs as inevitable seems prima facie very different from escaping it; and the identification of the two seems to be accomplished by substituting the notion of adjustment, or happiness, or frictionless contentment, for that of liberty or freedom from interference, and calling it liberty.

A somewhat more plausible version of this peculiar procedure is that Stoic doctrine which has entered so deeply into the texture of Christianity, whereby the wise man is free because no outside factors, least of all material ones, can disturb his peace of mind or soul, wherein lies *true* freedom. The liberal doctrine of freedom certainly implies the possibility that outside forces, whether human or natural, intended or unintended, *can* frustrate an individual's endeavours, and that this is what is meant by saying that he lacks freedom in some degree or other.[1] The Stoic recommendation is not to fight against the invaders of our territory, the interlopers and tyrants, but to make ourselves invulnerable to their activities by getting rid of whatever aspects of ourselves they can, at their worst and cruellest, hurt or destroy. I desire to retain my possessions, and the tyrant, whether an individual or an assembly, deprives me of them. To avoid frustration, that is, loss of liberty, I must kill the desire: so educate myself as not to covet possessions any longer, and thus be indifferent to the prospect of retaining or losing them. Enemies hem me in on every side, they threaten my goods, my family, my life. The only certain guarantee of retaining my liberty is by making it reside in some region where my enemies cannot penetrate; if I no longer feel attached to my goods, my family or my life, their loss cannot affect me. The policy advocated is that of a kind of strategic retreat from territories which could in principle fall into danger from agencies not under my control, a policy of self-containment, autarky (a term which was indeed used in this very sense in the Stoic writers), of self-sufficiency on ever narrower terrain.

In other words there are two ways in which I can prevent my desire from being frustrated: I can defeat those who threaten to prevent me from fulfilling it, and that I do by force, or perhaps by persuasion, for example by public law or by private influence; or alternatively I can rid myself of the desire itself, in which case my opponents will find nothing to oppose. I cannot in the second case be said to fulfil my desires, because there are no longer any desires to fulfil. I no longer need an army, for there is nothing left to

---

[1] {Should contrast this with eighteenth-century optimism: that is, either conquer nature and folly and vice; or say they are *illusory*.}

defend. The inner citadel of the spirit, according to Christian and Stoic thinkers, is the only true freedom, because it is incapable of invasion; if a thing needs defending, it had better be cut off before ever the need to defend it arises; in this way I can guarantee my freedom and independence for ever.

This 'positive' doctrine of freedom has exercised a deep influence on the thought of mankind in both the East and the West. The Buddhist notion of killing all carnal desires or love of things because they produce dependence on terrestrial things, which, whether by accident or design, may be taken away from me and so render me restless and miserable, preaches the same doctrine: the less I am, the less there is to defend; the only true security is retention of what no enemy can reach. There is only one such inviolable territory, my inner spirit, absorption in which renders me insensible to anything which the outside world may do to me. What is precarious is never wholly free; it is always in danger of invasion, always trembling, always armed or wishing to be armed, and preoccupation with danger is incompatible with that serenity in which alone fulfilment of anything worth having for its own sake can occur. Our earthly existence is full of such alarms and wars and rumours of wars. True freedom must lie in some sense outside it: for Christians or Jews or Muslims, in some future state; for Stoics and Spinoza and certain among the German Idealists, in the inner state protected by its metaphysical independence from everything that may happen to upset the empirical self – the body and its senses and appetites and desires – in the course of time and space.[1]

This doctrine, which has been made familiar in our own day by the popularisation in the West of various types of Eastern mystical religions, once again, prima facie, appears to rest on a play upon meanings of words. Peace is one thing and freedom another, and peace may be preferable to freedom and indeed be possible without a certain degree of it, but it is not identical with it.[2] My degree of freedom is measured by the extent to which my wishes are being

---

[1] {mention political impotence as creating absorption in 'inner' life, and giving a curious inner freedom *au dessous de la mêlée* ['below the fray'] – ανω and κατω ['up' and 'down'] being the same. Curious way of meeting[?]. Xtian[?] and Dost[oevskian?] thesis. Also Gandhi-ish non-resistance: and Schopenhauer's: *music*: liberation from treadmill: the determinist world which defeats my wishes through being brutishly what it is.}

[2] {omit: fallacious.}

prevented from realisation. The fewer wishes I have, the fewer the possibilities of being frustrated. If I have none, I cannot be frustrated at all, and if liberty consists in the absence of frustration, I am completely free. But by the same reasoning I am also completely free if I cease to exist. Hence total extinction is the only complete freedom: no man is wholly free until he ceases to be. But when he has ceased to exist it seems unintelligible to call him free or unfree, for he is not there to have such properties – or absence of them – attributed to him.

There is something specious about the reasoning which argues that the freedom of a desire satisfied is freedom in the same sense as that of a desire eliminated. If a man suffers a pain in a limb there are doubtless two ways of ridding him of it: one is to cure the disease; the other, to cut off the limb. There may be circumstances which necessitate the amputation, but only if the pain is likely to be intolerable or the disease to spread to other parts of the body. But this is not normally regarded as the best and most obvious solution of the problem, else it would be done whenever the slightest pain was felt (which would obviate the need ever to worry again about even the remotest possibility of its recurrence). There is no reason why babies at birth, or whatever seems the optimum age, should not have the maximum number of limbs removed which could conceivably be affected by known diseases, while still leaving them capable of life (but threatened with a smaller number of ailments). There is even a case for exposing not merely misshapen, but all infants, and thus putting an end to the human race as on the whole heirs to too many ills of the flesh – and that is what pessimistic thinkers in various ages have come near to advocating, and what has indeed stimulated a good many individual suicides. To contract oneself into the smallest possible compass, in order to leave as little of oneself as possible vulnerable to the forces of nature or the acts of men, is not so much the pursuit of liberty as of security. And without judging between the relative values of these different purposes it is enough to point out that they are different. For liberty consists in a condition where the fulfilment of a man's purposes is not interfered with; while security consists in the elimination of dangers, independently of the question whether there are purposes to fulfil or not. The question of whether it is better to have many purposes, with relatively little defence against adverse factors which might interfere with them, or fewer purposes with better chance of fulfilment, is no doubt a perfectly real, practical problem and arises at all levels. This, though, is not the problem of freedom, but a quasi-utilitarian problem of calculating factors in the empirical world for the purpose of obtaining as much of what one wants as one can. The ascetic solution to this problem in effect eliminates liberty by eliminating desires, that is, the need for it – in favour of something else. Such a solution may or may not be worthy of consideration in itself, but what is certain is that it substitutes a suppositious entity for freedom, and conceals this fact by calling both by the same name.

While any process which seeks to rescue a person or an institution from total slavery, by casting away part of it in order to rescue what remains, does not compass the original goal – the freedom of the whole – it sometimes takes the form of regarding that portion which is saved as being in some sense 'more real' than that which has been abandoned. If I find myself in a world where I am exposed to the iron laws of nature, and, where the sway of nature does not extend, to blind chance or irrational and arbitrary acts of human cruelty and folly and injustice, I may comfort myself with the reflection that a world in which my fate is so precarious, virtue is ineffective, and unmerited sufferings unavoidable cannot be altogether genuine; and that there must somewhere be a region in which my ethical and intellectual and aesthetic and spiritual demands *are* satisfied – in which all that is inharmonious, ugly, unintelligible, all that outrages or perplexes the intellect or the emotions, at last becomes intelligible, harmonious, and satisfying to reason and imagination. Such a world would clearly be superior to the monotonous triviality or destructive catastrophes which cause men to agonise over the purposes of the empirical world; and because it is coherent and provides solutions to the tormenting problems, and because reality can scarcely be conceived as incoherent, it must be more 'real', as well as more pleasing, than the world of ordinary life.

Transcendental religious thought has tended to place this world beyond the material universe, as the life after death, or in the Elysian fields, or in the paradise, earthly or heavenly, of the monotheistic religions, or to describe it as the eternity of which terrestrial existence is but a delusive reflection. Greeks and Romans and the Book of Genesis speak of a golden age from which human history has been a steady process of degeneration; the optimistic believers in the inevitable progress of man – Turgot, Condorcet, Saint-Simon, Comte, Marx – have placed it in a less or more distant future. But in the seventeenth and eighteenth centuries, under the influence mainly of the Protestant doctrine of the inner light contained within each immortal soul, there developed the notion that this world of divine tranquillity, incapable of being disturbed by the storms, or worn down by the failures, of the material world, was to be found neither in the remote past, nor in the remote future, nor among some happy tribe of innocent aborigines described in the real and imaginary travellers' tales of which there were a great many in the late seventeenth and the eighteenth century, nor in some ineffable region at which theology, or the pronouncements of mystics, could only darkly hint, but resided in the realm of the human spirit itself, accessible to every man in the course of his terrestrial life.

According to this view there are two lives lived by men, the life of the flesh and the life of the spirit. The first is subject to all the material laws discovered and classified by the natural sciences, and forms the realm of nature or necessity. The second obeys only the laws of the spirit – which Kant, following Aristotle and the main trends of Western philosophy, called reason – and is the only context within which one can intelligibly speak of moral and spiritual purposes, or of absolute truth and falsehood, or of absolute values of any kind. Spinoza denied that the category of purpose could be applied to nature: nature is mere matter, and its laws are those of a mechanism, the unalterable succession of cause and effect. Since matter neither has desires nor is conscious of itself, it is meaningless to attribute purpose to it. The materialists of the eighteenth century followed him in this and maintained that Leibniz and the Christian thinkers who detected such purposes even in dead matter, by means of a metaphysical insight which they claimed to possess, did not in fact possess any such faculty and were not entitled to make such claims. But what applies to material objects does not apply to subjects – centres of thought, volition, activity. Anthropomorphism is the false analogy which led to the pantheistic spiritualisation of nature, and obscured the deep gulf which yawns between nature and spirit. The material universe is determined by causal laws, and consequently the thought of freedom as applying to it is irrational, in so far as it denies such determination and attributes relations to things which in fact exist only between persons. The material universe is either governed by laws which make it amenable to classification and explanation by the sciences, or it proceeds in a haphazard fashion, in which case scientific explanations cannot be applied to it. The very notion of freedom, implying as it does the notion of choice, and the absence of obstacles to its fulfilment, is inapplicable save to agents, that is, beings with purposes, a category which has no application to material nature. The entire notion of freedom is concerned with the relations of active wills towards one another or themselves, and is intelligible only in terms of a realm to which causal laws do not apply, in which it is proper to speak of means and ends, reason and irrationality, freedom and subjection, creation and destruction, harmony and chaos, justice and injustice, right and wrong – concepts which mean nothing if applied to trees or stones or any of the entities of the natural sciences.

This notion of the two worlds – the material world, causally determined, in which the human body obeys the laws of nature as much as any other material object, as opposed to a moral or intellectual or spiritual world in which a man is free to construct and follow what ideals he wishes, the world of art, religion, and the more abstract sciences, limited, perhaps, but not determined, by the behaviour of matter in space – the distinction between spirit and matter, soul and body, the realm of freedom and that of necessity, active subjects and passive objects, purpose and causality, reality and appearance, is the great dualism which dominates all Western thought, Christian and Jewish and pagan – the very notion which the more sceptical materialists both of the eighteenth and of the nineteenth century set out to destroy. Holbach devotes his most eloquent pages to demonstrating that the world of spirit is a chimera with which priests or metaphysicians, whether by error or unscrupulous wish to deceive, have confused mankind. The nineteenth-century materialists speak of it as the universe into which German bourgeois intellectuals escaped from the impotence and humiliation of the petty but despotic society of their time, and which they peopled with all the romantic properties which they longed for and which had been denied them in Berlin and Weimar and Jena.

The notions of the presence of freedom and its absence are central to both worlds: it is totally absent from the lower or material one, and it is the heart or quintessence of the upper or spiritual one. The free man is the man whose spirit follows its own 'internal' laws of development, that is, purposes, the moral and aesthetic, the logical, historical, juridical principles which it constructs and imposes upon itself in accordance with its own inner ideal. So long as social life is conceived as a set of purely material relationships, political liberty cannot mean anything in it – at most only the creation of such arrangements as make free spiritual development possible. In so far as 'freedom' refers to relations between free spirits – human beings each engaged upon fulfilling his own inner purpose – it is embodied in the Kantian doctrine that free spirits are forbidden, by the very recognition of the existence of one another's freedom, to deny that freedom in action, that is, to treat one another as other than ends in themselves, as authors and embodiments of the only ultimately valuable purpose in the universe, the self-development, according to his own inner reason, towards ideals conceived of as absolute by himself, of the individual human being.[1]

This doctrine was developed with great originality and force by Schiller, who accepted the Kantian division of the world into that of mechanical causation and the inviolably free inner self, and from it developed his aesthetic theory, according to which art – and indeed all human self-expression of the creative kind – is a form of *play*. Children, when they play a game, give full freedom to their imagination, and suspend those laws which may in fact hold in the ordinary world, and create ideal types endowed only with such characteristics and bound only with such laws as their authors choose. They 'posit', and thereby 'create', imaginary worlds in which all the freedom which is lacking in real life because of the 'brute' laws which act rigorously as they do, whatever men may want, is restored. The laws of the children's pretended worlds are not generalisations capable of explaining events, but, being invented *ad hoc*, are norms justifying what happens. So the artist – the only true creator on earth, who stands nearest to the creative power of God or nature – performs the most sacred of all tasks which fall to the lot of man: out of his inner soul, armed only with his own intellect and imagination, and emotional and spiritual powers and creative capacity, he fuses life into the dead material provided by nature, and shapes it into whatever semblance he chooses, and it is convincing, beautiful, permanent, aesthetically valid in the degree to which he succeeds in incarnating within it the ideas, feelings, values, perceptions, attitudes which are the elements of his own 'free' inner life.

[1] {Insert note on two meanings of 'Why' here. 'This may be put in another way, that is, "Why do I act as I do?" ' Socio-psychological explanation versus absolute ends.}

Schiller's doctrine of art as play entails this contrast between the two worlds, one of empirical reality, where we obey laws willy-nilly and are frustrated by obstacles which we cannot remove, and at best can hope only to adjust ourselves to the inexorable pattern which we have neither created nor willed, and which we accept, but of necessity, not of choice, where 'Why?' means only 'What happens after what? Next to what?'; and the other world, for which we are ourselves wholly responsible, in which we are totally free to create as we please, which embodies all that our intellects, imaginations, emotions and powers of creation are capable of achieving, thus building the ideals by which we live. Here 'Why?' means 'For the sake of what? To achieve what purpose?' These ideals are not something discovered either in contemplating nature and attempting to describe and predict its behaviour, nor solely in the course of daily behaviour, in so far as this is confined to resisting recalcitrant nature, or trying to adapt ourselves to the inflexible laws which govern it. These ideals are not discovered at all, but *created* – invented as the artist creates and invents. They are not something which we find but something which we *impose* upon the dead matter which we inevitably encounter, in which we move and live and have our being.

The central thesis is that every human being has within him an active spirit, a personality compounded of desires, passions, capable of intellectual or imaginative constructions, and with a creative impulse to impress these upon the dead world of nature, so as to create something which the act of creation animates, and makes a work of art or history or religion, a philosophy or even a political constitution, which can inspire or repel, evoke love or hatred, and alter the inner lives of men, because it is itself the expression – the free expression – of an ideal, a purpose which some human beings have proposed to themselves as the goal or pattern of their activities. Schiller, while ostensibly merely developing Kant's dark notion of the reason within the noumenal self, in fact revived an idea powerful in the Renaissance, and perhaps older even than the Platonic philosophy whence it issued, whereby the artist is a demiurge, a creator of worlds, repeating on a smaller scale the work of the great Creator himself. Everything that is noble, great, sublime, compelling, worth doing, worth submitting to, worth acquiring or expressing is not *found* but *made*. Ethics is not descriptive – a record of truths embedded in some external sphere, treasures waiting to be uncovered and described – but *normative*.

It takes the form of laws, maxims, commands, battle-cries, which are neither true nor false, since they state nothing, but only good or bad, right or wrong, shallow or profound, genuine or false, creative or destructive. Morality and art are to this extent parallel: they both make, whether out of stone or words or any other medium, myths, ideals, patterns of sound or colour of which it is idle to ask whether they are true or false, in the sense of corresponding to or failing to correspond to some external reality, and trivial to ask whether they stimulate approval or disapproval, or stimulate pleasure or pain. They constitute ends, purposes, commandments, ways of life, insights into the aims of this or that way of life and action that illuminate because they stir the human spirit to a realisation of its own creative possibilities, of what it can do and be. They do not *derive* from inanimate nature, as Montesquieu taught: rather they shape, direct and transform it.

Education – *Bildung* – the shaping of human beings, the central idea for which the celebrated group of German humanists in this period – Goethe, Schiller, Herder, Humboldt – is justly remembered, consists in the development of personality to the fullest extent, the limitless development of every faculty and property as richly and as variously as possible. And in order to achieve that state which preserves a human being from inner contradictions, from the diffusion, frustration and self-destructiveness which results from ignorance of and fruitless battle against the actual conditions of life, or the pursuit, as a result of this, of self-defeating or Utopian ideals, what is needed is a judicious mingling of scientific information about the real world (conceived in the Kantian terms of a Newtonian science founded upon the discovery of the laws of nature in accordance with categories imposed by our own understanding) with purposes and ideals created spontaneously by each man individually for himself – ideal moral, spiritual and aesthetic forms and models. These ideal models are proposed by each man to himself, not 'given' (*gegeben*) to him like an object in experience, but set (*aufgegeben*) like a task, like a goal, a demand, a claim, an order; and in terms of such an ideal a harmonious correlation can be established between the many conflicting desires, duties, claims which seem to press in on him, as it were, from outside – the ends of life. The solutions to political and moral questions of the form 'Why live thus and not otherwise?' are to be conceived as a harmonious, coherent form of life, perhaps embodied in some real or imaginary example, as the lives of the saints – or of Christ himself – were held up before Christians, or the lives of the good or great men of classical antiquity before the Greeks or Romans, or before Hellenists and virtuous republicans in Western Europe from the Renaissance to the French Revolution. But these need no longer necessarily be conceived as historical persons, actual individuals whose example we are commanded to follow for historical or theological reasons, but as timeless ideals, made vivid by being incarnated in lives of real or imaginary persons, or myths, or romances, at once revealing the ends pursued by nature and by men (as parables or fables reveal truths more vividly than more discursive methods) and imposed upon themselves by the free intellect, imagination and will, fired by the realisation that they too are part of this pattern, unconsciously yearning for these same ends; and by this very act giving shape and direction to all our activities, whether in the sciences, in the arts, or in the different situations created by the exigencies of the vast variety of private and public life.

This way of thinking led to the emergence of two relatively new concepts which thereafter dominate the next half-century of European philosophy. The first is the notion that the ends of morals and politics are not discovered but invented; not found in some region different from, but external to, the individual, in the sense in which the realm of nature in which he discovers the data for the knowledge of facts, notably scientific knowledge of them, is external; but imposed by a man upon himself in a curious reflexive act, or if not in a conscious act, at any rate by behaviour justifiable only in terms of some such imaginary act. So that when seeking to explain why it is right to obey the government or go to war or liberate serfs, I appeal neither to revelation nor to authority, nor to the Book of Nature, nor to intuitions which yield true premises for ethical or political deductions, nor to decent respect for the common opinion of mankind, but to the fact that in doing so, and advising or compelling others to do so, I am fulfilling, making it possible for them to fulfil, an ideal or goal, which is the right ideal or goal because therein I am fulfilling my true nature or self. And fulfilling my true nature is imposing upon myself laws and purposes which I have discovered as inner demands of my own self, and which I have therefore myself created, and follow only as the artist follows his inner inspiration; of which it is not true to say that he has discovered it as a ready-made entity, but that it – the inspiration – is but a name for his own continuous creative, that is inventive, activity. And the laws he follows are not laws which he discovers and which have a certain form and validity whether he discovers them or not; but they are the principles according to which he finds himself acting when he is at his best, when he is most 'fully himself'. They are a way of being and acting, and not objective, independent entities inspectable in isolation, by themselves.

This leads to the second notion that belongs to this way of thinking: the concept of the real (or, as it is sometimes called, ideal) self, that which imposes the goal or the form of life, not an entity so much as a kind of process, a special activity involved in all conscious experience as such. This notion, apart from the Christian metaphysic which plays an obvious part in it, derives mainly from Kant's theory of the self as an organising principle, which in some occult way superimposes upon the mysterious ultimate stuff of the world those forms and relationships (which he calls categories) which make it susceptible to human awareness. This active organising self is plainly not that self which is 'given' in experience itself – which is the subject, for example, of physical pains or emotional pleasures, which psychology treats empirically in the case of individuals, and sociology also empirically, but taking groups or masses of men as its subject-matter. This latter self – the empirical 'I' – is on a par with the rest of that which the sciences and common sense find in the everyday world, and is itself one of the products of the mysterious organising ultimate self, which is responsible for making normal experience possible at all. This ultimate self, since it is the act of force which generates the world we perceive around us, is not itself part of that world, nor of the time or space which are the dimensions of that world, and cannot be apprehended by any normal act of inspection. And it is but a small extension of its powers to make it generate not merely normal cognitive experience, but purposes and ideals, moral and political principles as well, no longer indeed by performing mysterious acts of synthesis upon an unknowable something called the 'given' or the 'manifold', but simply in virtue of being the active principle that it is, by the presentation to 'itself' of its own principles of operation, which Kant, because to him they seem to demand inner consistency and harmony, likes to call reason.

Fichte, who takes this final step, conceives this entity as a kind of super-self, a transcendental entity embodying itself in finite centres of experience, a universal will responsible alike for the creation of

those objects of experience which form the material world, and for
the creation of the goals and ideals which are the principles of its
creative activity. This self, which he in effect identifies with God
(although it is obviously not personal enough to be compatible
with Christianity, and so earned him a reputation as an atheist,
which he did not wish to deny), is the creative principle of the
world, embodying itself, at times, in heroic individuals who
transform society by violent revolutions, obedient to the creative
impulse within them. This impulse vis-à-vis the dead stuff of the
world which the spirit or self shapes must now and then take a
destructive form, in order to sweep out of the way in its irresistible
creative advance whatever is superfluous or obsolete. In this frame
of mind Fichte is Jacobin, a violent upholder of the French
Revolution, a mystical visionary, seeing the world like a phoenix
renewed from the ashes of its outworn dwelling. Then in his later
thought the creative impulse takes the form of social organisation,
to which individual human beings are in some sense subordinate,
because man is by nature social, and only in the storm and stress of
social cross-currents can true creation, that is development of
personality, occur. Hence the self tends to be virtually identified
with society, and then with its most organised, self-conscious,
articulate form, 'the State', and a very socialised and collectivist
State at that; and finally it is embodied in the nation, conceived
partly as race, partly as culture, owning a common language,
habits, institutions[1] – the Germanic tribes bound together by
impalpable ties, not exhaustible by any empirical analysis, ties
which create them, or rather are created by them, and unite them
with each other and with the generations past and future, forming
together with them a timeless mystical body expressing, in the
pattern which runs through it (and perceptible only to the inspired
gaze of the seer – metaphysician or poet or theologian or man of
action), the working of the absolute will, the self, which in forms of
greater or lesser intensity expresses itself in all the scattered
empirical selves which are individual men and women as we know
them in our hours of normal experience.

For all its claim to be a rationally argued philosophical position,
this is a poetical or theological version of life: the world is
conceived as the life and activity of a super-person, to which
normal human beings – as well as, in their lower degrees, animals,

---

[1] {isolationism: tariffs: planning: *dirigisme*: self as *directeur*[?].}

plants and inanimate things – stand as tongues of flame to the fire in which they play, or reflections in a glass, or sometimes as matter to form, or the subjective to the objective, or appearance to reality – or according to many other metaphorical and fanciful analogies. The nearest terrestrial analogue to this central world-force is the creative individual, whether artist or general or statesman or thinker, who knows how to will, that is, how to shape the less or more recalcitrant materials with which his life provides him to the pattern which is demanded by the real self whose presence he feels at his most exalted and most self-conscious moments, when he transcends the mechanical day-to-day routine of bourgeois life, and hears the inner voice, the dynamic will attempting to alter and create – feels himself to be a centre of a creative force, stronger and more authoritative than anything he has experienced. Freedom for him consists in dominating the matter which obstructs his free self-realisation, according to those principles which the creative force within him in fact dictates. Ethical and political ideals are the demands of this force, of the real self, when it recognises its own true reality, knows itself for what it is, the sole principle of action and source of authority – the creator of all things and all values.

Two ideas are discernible here. One is that the self knows itself not by tranquil contemplation, for in that state a man does not feel his self at all. The more clearly he observes the object, the deeper he is absorbed in its contemplation, the less aware of himself he is, for in any case the self, being the subject, cannot be the object of knowledge. A man is aware of himself properly only when he comes into collision with something not himself, another person or a thing which in some way obstructs, causes friction, perhaps altogether frustrates his activity. In the impingement (*Anstoss*) of what Fichte calls the not-self on the self, in the conflict, the self becomes aware of itself as the active, thrusting, forward-moving entity or activity made self-conscious by its collision with something other than itself, aware of itself not as an object alongside other objects, as it is aware of bodies or sounds or even mathematical truths, but aware of itself in the peculiar sense provided only by a *volitional* experience; feels itself (assuming the word 'feel' not to be confined to sensations) in the very act of being stopped or driven or pushed by forces foreign to itself, and therefore causing it to differentiate itself from them.

Mere contemplation yields only objects. The more successful and perfect the contemplation, the more frictionless the perception

of the object, the more the contemplating self diminishes to
vanishing-point, the more it approximates to a mere Kantian
relationship – the unity of the horizon within which the contem-
plated objects are related to each other. But the more imperfect his
vision, the more obstacles there are, the more conscious of himself
as a self, hemmed in and pressing against the obstacles, the observer
becomes. Now he is no longer lost in contemplation of the objects,
aware of the finest differences between them, oblivious of his own
existence; now he is struggling to obtain a better view of them, to
destroy the obstacles; and in this struggle he is aware of himself as a
self; for the struggle is activity, an attempt to impose something –
himself, his way of vision, his methods of operation, his ideal, his
purpose – upon the foreign and indeed hostile outer world of
matter or other persons, nature or man. And this activity, in which
every man is engaged to some degree throughout his life, is, when
seen in all its vast universality, the struggle towards self-perfection
of the entire universe, of the great super-self against the great
super-not-self, of form against matter, of consciousness against
nature, of will against the recalcitrant medium, of reason against
brute fact, of light against darkness, of good against evil, of rights
and laws and duties against blind force, chance, mechanical
causality.[1]

Connected with this megalomaniac vision of men as the self-
conscious centre of *natura naturans*[2] is the notion that freedom
consists in the hewing of the dead lumps of reality according to any
shape imposed by the spirit, that creation and freedom are
identical, and are but another name for that force – the super-
person, the absolute self – which alone is responsible for all change,
all progress; both for the intelligibility of the world shaped by the
patterns which it sets upon itself, and for the works of human

---

[1] The French philosopher Maine de Biran said much the same thing when he
criticised Descartes' principle 'cogito ergo sum' and said that he should have
declared 'volo ergo sum'. ['[P]ar *"je pense"* j'entends, *"je veux* ... donc je
suis...["]': *Notes de M. de Biran sur l'idée d'existence* (1824), Première Partie,
Les Principes, 2. L'idée de substance et l'idée de force: pp. 50–1 in [part 2 of]
Pierre Tisserand, *L'Anthropologie de Maine de Biran* ... (Paris, 1909); also in
*Oeuvres*, 14 vols (1920–49), vol. 14, p. 63. Henri Gouhier, *Maine de Biran par lui-
même* ([Paris], 1970), p. 125, writes: 'il explique pourquoi revenir à Descartes et
jusqu'où le suivre: je veux serrer le poing, donc je suis.']

[2] [The somewhat obscure Thomist and Spinozist concept of *natura naturans* –
'naturing nature' – picks out, very roughly, nature's active aspect, as opposed to
*natura naturata* – 'natured nature', its passive aspect.]

imagination and reason, which in fact embody human progress in an endless process of imposition of the self upon the not-self, and the bending of it to its indomitable will, in accordance with its own inner principles, which because they are its own are absolute and sacred, beyond which there can be no authority more final or powerful. It is this notion of endless creation taking the form of domination of something by something else which is responsible for the theory of freedom among the romantic philosophers.

The free personality is conceived by the romantic writers as one which imposes itself upon the world outside it. It is conceived not in bodily but in spiritual terms, as an activity seeking to shape all else – the matter of the external world, its own body, other selves – to its own purpose, an 'objective' self-subsistent ideal the realisation of which is the activity, conscious and unconscious, of the supreme agent – the self. This may take various forms: political domination – the shaping of peoples and societies by a single mighty spirit – Alexander the Great, Charlemagne, Frederick the Great, Napoleon; and on a smaller scale every imposition of patterns on other human beings by a single individual or body of individuals, who, in doing so, for a nature-mystic like Fichte or Herder or Schleiermacher, represent the progressive development of the world spirit imposing order on chaos through a specific manifestation of itself in the form of a dominant individual or group. Or it may take the form of the scientific subjugation of nature by the understanding of its laws, which is again the recognition of the spirit (the ultimate animating force which causes all things to occur as they do) by itself, as realised and active in the mind of the scientist. But this consciousness by an agency of itself as dominating matter happens most obviously in the world of the arts and thought and religion, where creation and understanding, discovery and invention, the realisation of the true essence of the subject-matter, and the articulation of such understanding in external forms, as is done by the artist, the thinker, the prophet, the religious teacher, cannot be separated.

Objectively, freedom is the imposing of my purpose, the realising of my nature in terms of the external medium. Subjectively it is the absorption into my own system of what begins by being a foreign body outside myself. I begin by being inevitably faced with a world which in some sense hems me in: inanimate matter which limits my physical movements; the laws of physics or mathematics, which seem to be hard, immutable, objective realities not flexible to my will; everything, in short, whereby I distinguish the external world from the 'free' world of my own imagination and fancy, my own unhampered thoughts and beliefs and likes and dislikes and ideals and emotions – the inner citadel into which the Stoics proposed that strategic withdrawal which would rescue the individual from the uncontrollable vicissitudes of the outside world.

The development of freedom, then, consists in the gradual conquest of this outside world by assimilating it into the inner citadel. So long as I think of, let us say, a law of mathematics as a schoolboy thinks of it, as a hard brute fact which is as it is whether I want it so or not, which has to be taken into account because to ignore it would involve error and possibly practical damage and even danger – which, therefore, has to be learned by heart as an isolated lump of recalcitrant fact – it remains outside myself as an obstacle and a limitation upon my opportunities of action or thought. But if I understand it – once I grasp the axioms of mathematics and the rules whereby deductions from them are made – then I perceive the *necessity* of any given mathematical proposition; not, that is, its necessity as something inexorable, not to be wished away out of the external world, but as something which follows from the axioms which I myself have freely recognised, as being part of my own rational thinking, and by rules which I have myself freely adopted, such being my rational nature – the adoption of the rules and the axioms being part of what is meant by having a rational nature.

Fichte appears to adopt what is in a sense a very modern view of scientific thought, whereby its structure is not something made valid or invalid by its resemblance to a world for ever external to myself, which thus forms the rigid, unalterable outside standard of truth and validity; but is whatever I choose to make it, and is the same for all scientists and thinkers not because they all perceive the same fixed outside structure, but because there is something called a rational nature which is common to them, and which consists in the similarity or, at its purest, complete identity, of the acts of this nature, in particular the imaginative, constructing activity which gives birth to axioms and rules, scientific laws and the concepts of history, art, religion – in short, to all those activities whose results are capable of being measured in terms of some publicly accepted standard. For Fichte the outside world is absorbed into my 'inner' system when I understand it, that is, realise that the laws which it obeys are identical with those which are expressed in my own freest activities – when I imagine or invent or act. In other words, freedom consists in perceiving the outside world as the fruit of the creative operation of one's own creative self, and what had seemed before to be brute facts or inexorable objective laws forced upon me by the granite necessity of the world are now seen to be the results of my own free choice, and therefore no longer obstacles, parts of the non-self. It is as if I were to say to myself that two plus two need not equal four, but once I accept the proposition that two plus two equals seventeen, I find that too many other propositions upon which I had relied, which were woven into the texture of my innermost thoughts, expectations, volitions, are upset by this; whereupon I realise that it is I, and I alone, who am ultimately responsible for the validity of 'Two plus two equals four', it is *I* who wanted to have it so, and if I rejected other alternatives, it is because the consequences of their adoption would frustrate *me* in some way, lead to the opposite of the way in which I – Fichte would say my rational nature – found that I functioned and, being as I am, wished to continue to function.

This sense of the consonance of the objective laws with the demands of my nature – not indeed with my casual, fleeting, evanescent whims and tastes and thoughts at moments when I am ignorant or uncontrolled (or 'not at my best'), but with me as I am at my most philosophical, most profoundly self-conscious (which for Fichte is equivalent to the most intense awareness of myself as a finite expression of the ultimate, infinite, all-creating and all-understanding super-self) – is the romantic bridge between personal freedom and the apparent inflexibility of nature. The chasm which divides freedom from nature – the will of the subject from the fixed constitution of the object – is bridged and finally abolished by the realisation that the laws which the object obeys are identical, although 'unaware of themselves', with the principles according to which the free subject consciously acts when he is at his freest. Of course, the majority of mankind, living semi-mechanical lives, are incapable of perceiving this. It is only in the most intense moments of illumination on the part of the most developed minds, whether they are artists or prophets or philosophers or statesmen or scientists, that this unity reveals itself. But to those to whom it reveals itself the world is seen as *one*, and the lack of freedom which most men experience in their daily lives is seen to be due solely to that ignorance of the identity of the principle of subjective action with the laws of external objects which makes the object seem an obstacle to the free self-realisation of the subject. This is the pantheism of such romantics as Schelling and the Schlegels – in the sense of the unity of principle of all action, thought, feeling, and ultimately of all existence, of change and identity, motion and rest, which in one form or another has dominated the human imagination in India, in Palestine, in Greece, in the Middle Ages, and in the visions of the poets, culminating in our day in the romantic imagination of the philosophers and poets of nature in Germany and England, and to a certain degree in the symbolist movement in European poetry and among the transcendentalists in Russia and the United States.

Freedom here means identification of the ends for which one strives, and of the ways in which one most rationally seeks to realise oneself, with the apparently mechanical march of the external world; identification, in Fichte's case, by the creation of that external world – not ideal empirically but in some transcendental realm – by the self of which we are all parts. This automatically makes that world part of oneself, no longer alien, obstructive, no longer a frontier, a field of force which hems one in, but on the contrary that which one's own free activity would have made it, if one had been the demiurge, the Creator; and therefore, by a slight but fateful step, that which one *has* made it – in one's capacity as a finite element in the great super-self. The world is the answer to one's unspoken questions, the fulfilment of one's inner wishes, which become plain to one only by contemplating it – metaphysically, through the eye of the super-self – the response which is, as it were, already real before the yearning for it has become explicit and aware of what it wants. Freedom is not achieved by escaping from but by 'integrating oneself' with the apparently antagonistic element: by 'transcending' it.

What do these dark words mean? Perhaps an example will make this clearer. If I am a musician, let us say a player in a quartet, what is it that I most wish to do? If to play in quartets is my genuine purpose, I wish to translate into sound the symbols offered to me by the score and to achieve a most precise coordination with the other players. If I am a true musician, I cannot be said to be truly playing unless I 'understand' the score – unless, that is, I see the relevance of one sound to another, unless I grasp the pattern which the relationship between the sounds is intended by the composer to produce, unless I fulfil the 'purpose' of the score and make it *my* purpose, my free and personal purpose. In a sense, of course, I obey 'external' instructions: the score was not written by me in any circumstances which I can remember; nor do the other players obey my direct wishes as communicated expressly to them; nevertheless, nobody *forces* me to obey the score, nor to coordinate my playing with that of my fellow players. Yet it is certainly the case that the more precisely, fully and faithfully I translate the notes of the score into sound – the more I make myself the faithful, undeviating, almost impersonal vehicle of the pattern of the ideas, or the sounds (or whatever the general design and purpose of the score may be) – the more I realise my function as a musician, the more creative I am being, the more freely my capacities as a musician are allowed to develop, the more deeply I satisfy my craving to play; and although there is no formal contract between me and the other players, and although I exercise no coercion upon them, the closer the collaboration, the more undeviating the adherence to the rules for concerted playing, the more fully satisfied the players feel, the fewer obstacles at that moment do they find in the universe about them.

In a sense this is a paradox. I obey a law, in this case a specific set of musical instructions, yet I claim that only in so far as there is a law, a specific rule which in my activities I obey, can I be free. If the score breaks off or is obscure, or if some inner physiological accident or psychological impulse causes me to abandon the pattern dictated by the score, and produce a haphazard collection of disconnected sounds, I feel not free, but confused, *désoeuvré*, and in a state of chaos, bombinating in the void without rule or measure, no longer realising a purpose but veering idly and helplessly. The romantic explanation is that to desire at all is to desire to fulfil a plan, to realise a pattern, to obey a law; the absence of law or pattern destroys any possible end or purpose, and leaves the world aimless, in an uncharted sea, at the mercy of every gust of passing wind. If the plan is imposed upon me by force from outside, I complain of coercion, slavery, the inexorable force of an outside reality, pressing upon me whether in the form of other persons or of nature; but if this plan corresponds to some 'inner' desire on my part, then and then only am I free, for freedom is freedom to do what I wish, and what a rational being wishes is to fulfil some plan, express some pattern. If there is no plan or pattern, I am not rational, and my wishes are not, in the normal sense, wishes, but blind impulses, and then there is no sense in speaking of freedom or slavery; but if I am rational, I am fulfilling a plan, that is, something rational, of which the means are subordinated to ends, in accordance with discernible rules; and if I understand the world, I understand the rules according to which it is constructed. All things are intelligible, therefore all things obey rules, and all the rules must be interconnected by being subsumed under wider and wider rules, else they would not be connected at all, save in a mere brute way – that is, not be intelligible. Therefore to understand the world is to understand its rules, to understand myself is to understand the rules of my own wishes and ambitions. These two sets of rules would, in a perfect understanding, coincide. Freedom – the following of my inner rules – would coincide with the outer rules, for it is in some ultimate sense I who make the world, as it is I, the player, who by playing make the music, by being 'one' with the pattern of the score. In this sense, freedom is obedience to laws, understanding of necessity. The conflict between mind and nature is dissolved: nature, from being a brute reality, has been analysed into a set of rule-obeying entities; the object, that is, has been analysed as potentially part of – an element in – the freely self-developing subject.

Thus, once again, we arrive at the celebrated and paradoxical conclusion that freedom is awareness of necessity, but by a somewhat different route from that taken by the rationalists. Their position rested on maintaining that to understand the world was to understand the necessary relations which connected all its elements, and made them what they were; and that this inevitably involved comprehension of one's own situation as being necessarily what it was, and therefore its acceptance as part of the inevitable scheme of things, satisfying to reason as perception of mathematical truths was satisfying to reason. According to this argument, when I realise that everything is as it is, and I am as I am, in virtue of laws rationally deducible from self-evident truths, forming a closed, coherent system, it becomes senseless to ask for anything, whether in my own life or outside it, to be otherwise than as it was, or is, or will be, since that is tantamount to asking for a suspension of the rules of logic, whereby conclusions necessarily follow from their premises, and constituents of systems are what they are, for the sole and sufficient reason that they are elements in such systems. Freedom in this conception represented simply the disappearance of distorting factors – emotions, irrational impulses and other causes of darkness and ignorance – which kept men from the clearest perception attainable to a being with finite faculties of the world as a system of necessary relations. Once I saw it as it was, I should cease to wish for it to be otherwise, since such wishes would be a desire for conclusions not to follow from their premises, and this cannot *ex hypothesi* be desired by a rational being. Nevertheless, this argument has never carried full conviction, particularly to those who note that the view rests on premises and arguments of a metaphysical or theological character, and which they reject because they see no reason for believing that no events in the universe are contingent, that is, could have happened otherwise (indeed most empiricists believe such a contention to be almost meaningless). Indeed, the greatness of Hume's discovery consisted precisely in driving home this cardinal point against all possible forms of metaphysics.

Moreover, even those who have in some sense accepted the proposition of the 'block universe', in which everything is rigidly determined to be as it is by everything else, may think it irrational to protest, but have never fully convinced themselves that freedom consists in refraining from protest because it is irrational. It may be wise to accept the inevitable, and it may be foolish to wish for the contrary, but this is not felt to be quite equivalent to a condition where the contrary cannot have been wistfully wished for. Freedom reduced to its narrowest terms is at the very least freedom to choose between alternatives: it cannot be *less* than that. If the very notion of logically possible alternatives turns out to be an illusion – which is the rationalist case – then freedom in this sense is an illusion, too, and neither the term itself, nor the confused notion for which it turns out to have stood, should any longer darken the thoughts of a rational being. But to exorcise the notion of freedom altogether is not the same as to say that to recognise the omnipresence of necessity is itself a superior kind of freedom. Freedom to choose turns out to be an illusion; we have learned better, and it no longer deludes us; it is a confusion, a lingering superstition, and must be eliminated from the list of respectable concepts, like other mysteries exposed by the clear light of reason. A rational man will have no use for it; least of all will he be tempted to call its very absence by its own discredited name.

The sleight of hand whereby the rationalists, from Plato to our own day, have tried to substitute for the essence of freedom its exact opposite, while preserving the hallowed name for this opposite, has always worn an air of paradox: we were invited to contemplate the majesty and beauty of the logically flawless structure of the world, and forbidden to sigh after the lost illusion of freedom which sprang from the gravest of all misconceptions of what the world was like. Still, it was only within the framework of this 'misconception' that the concept of freedom was intelligible: and the splendour and symmetry of the new vision might or might not make up for the original belief in the possibility of freedom to choose between alternatives, but was certainly not identical with it. We might be compelled by reason to face the facts and face the truth, but in the course of this something had certainly been lost. We might be told that what had been lost was irrational, a figment founded on confusion and muddled terminology. This might be, but we certainly felt deprived of something: the notion of freedom might be delusive but it was irresistibly attractive to some; if it was irrational, it was no doubt right to divest oneself of it, but it was idle and cruel to pretend that what had been put in its place, however superior, was identical with it, that it was the very same notion, albeit purified and made deeper or wider or clearer, as that which had for so long been the comfort of the immature days of our youth.

The approach of the romantics is a different and far more plausible road to the same paradoxical conclusion. The necessities of which the universe is composed are no longer 'given', no longer imposed upon us as an objectively necessary reality whose laws are either recognised for what they are or else ignored to our cost. Man is not for Fichte or Schelling a passive observer who can accept or reject a world which is what it is, whether he likes it so or not. He is in virtue of being a 'subject' wholly active. His 'activity' consists not in contemplation, but in imposing principles or rules of his own making upon the *prima facie* inert mass of nature. He begins to do so in Kant, where he imposes categories in some precognitive condition; in Kant's successors he does so at more and more conscious 'levels'. Sometimes he moulds reality as the all-powerful will; sometimes he discovers in reality laws which are identical with those rules and principles which guide his own purposive life, because both he and nature are, at different levels, emanations, embodiments, of the absolute spirit which 'realises itself' in him and in it, in various less or more intelligible ways.

Without examining all the vagaries of Absolute Idealism, we may draw attention to its principle of activity, whereby what the earlier rationalists represented as being necessary connections, discovered by some metaphysical intuition, now turn into a form of activity, whereby I do not so much observe something, as *do* something with it, or at it, or through it. If I am a musician, I do not contemplate or intuit the structure of the music which I compose or play, I compose or play it, I act according to rules or principles, I bring them into being. If I am a statesman or a general, I legislate, I command, I impose my will upon bodies of men. I do not first contemplate the nature of the world, go through the process of understanding and learning – memorising – a set of interrelated propositions about it, and *then* put them into practice, as Aristotle or St Thomas sometimes seem to say. Skill in action was not a mysterious transposition of thoughts into acts, it was a certain kind of acting itself, an action which could be said to have form, purpose, to embody will-power, imagination, grasp of the circumstances, understanding.

This was Fichte's conception of how we arrived at ethical or political purposes: not by finding them as ingredients in the data of contemplation or of that inner activity of which the eighteenth-century psychologists had spoken, some kind of empirical intro-spection; not by deductive reasoning or any other form of logical or scientific inference; but in the very act of creation itself, which is a pursuit of ends in accordance with rules, and therefore, for him, rational; in the act of moulding or assimilating the medium of our activity to our own souls, whether in music or metaphysics or legislation or the handicrafts – at all possible levels – always with the same sense of striving to fulfil a purpose; the fulfilling of a purpose being the imposition of a pattern, a pattern not previously conceived as an independent entity to be impressed upon a plastic medium independent of it, but itself the form or attribute of an activity, realised only in the activity itself, internal to it, as it were – as the song is realised in singing, and does not exist apart from it as a set of rules hovering in limbo, waiting to be brought into operation; as walking consists in the act of walking and is not an entity which occurs by itself, dormant until awoken into actuality by the act of willing which releases or realises it.

This kind of imposition of laws, forms, patterns, is a good deal more plausible as an interpretation of 'freedom' than the self-prostration and self-identification with the inevitable pattern of the universe of earlier rationalists. Here at least – although I am driven to create as I do by some inner necessity, by principles and rules which spring not from my casual, superficial 'empirical' self, but from those alleged inner sources of my being, whatever these might be, which unite me with the spirit of the world, which in its turn is responsible for everything whatever being as it is, and developing as it does – I am at least active, I am doing something, which presumably releases some inner spring within me, allows 'free play', as we should say, to some capacity which might otherwise remain inhibited and atrophied. I am now being represented as an active being, carried along, it may be, in some universal stream, and not merely floating upon its surface, but determined by the very fact that I am part of it to thrust forward, to identify myself with a perpetual forward motion in which my faculties are strained in various degrees in the pursuit of goals, whether in the ordinary round of daily life, or in those more obviously teleological and purposive activities which are the continuous effort of the artist or the games-player or the man of action at the time when he is at his most active, and binds his spell upon others, to whom the very consciousness of such a spell acts as a stimulus and a goal, which in its turn releases something in them, heightens their consciousness of what they want, makes them increase the conscious output of energy in the various directions to which they are half driven, half self-impelled.

To apply the term 'freedom' to this kind of activity is no longer absurd. I may be obeying a universal law, but I am obeying it in the act of doing something, and in doing what I desire to do, what everything in me urges and impels me to do. Reason is no longer interpreted as some kind of necessary relation holding between the elements of a system, but as the principle which 'informs', shapes, directs, adapts action to the realisation of goals, which themselves are not conceived as something external to, but as part of, the action itself, which is its own purpose, its own goal, as the song is the goal of the act of singing, as a specific form of political life is the purpose of a specific political policy, which is itself not an external means to, so much as an element in, the kind of life conducted in accordance with it. The paradoxical phrase 'Freedom is the awareness of necessity'[1] now no longer conjures up the image of the prudent self, adaptable to natural necessity, but rather more that of the musician who, having penetrated the nature and

---

[1] [cf. p. 186 above. This Hegelian tag (not apparently a direct quotation from Hegel, or indeed from Engels, to whom it is sometimes attributed) has Spinozan origins.]

purpose of the score, which another may have composed, finds his fullest self-realisation in the playing of the music so as to convey all that the score is meant to express. So far from conceiving freedom as some kind of release from outside pressure, he may declare that the more closely he adheres to the precise structure of the score, the more faithful he is to it, the more rigorous the discipline which he imposes upon himself, the more scrupulous and undeviating, the more self-absorbed his performance, the more he allows himself to be wholly dominated by a pattern to whose realisation he is now totally committed, which now represents for him all which at this moment he stands for and believes and wishes to be, the *freer* he is; and the more disciplined the correlation between various players, the more sensitive the interplay, the more absolute the pattern which binds his fellow musicians – provided always that this is a voluntary submission on their part – the more they realise their natures, the freer they feel; and *per contra*, if the pattern is broken, if they forget it or it becomes interrupted, if the bond which holds them is loosened,[1] the common enterprise in which they are engaged stops and each is left to his own resources with no plan of action, no single goal to unite the players and magnetise their energies to that condition, at once intense and harmonious, which any concerted action requires – that now constitutes not an increase but a decrease in freedom, the irruption of an element of haphazardness, a brute obstacle without purpose, pure chance, absence of purpose and direction, which, so far from liberating people, leaves them puzzled, solitary, exposed to the buffetings of external forces, which they no longer understand, and of which they feel themselves to be blind victims.

We must conceive the entire universe as a kind of immense concert, of which every portion is active, and free in the exact proportion to which it realises, by its own activity, in the degree to which it is capable, that is, rational, the rules and principles the total realisation of which is the general end of the entire concert of players; as a vast and various whole, in a condition of ceaseless activity of all its elements, each in accordance with its nature and relative purpose, but all sensitised in some degree to each other's activities, and seeking to attain a kind of total interrelated perfection, and gaining freedom in the precise degree in which they approach this perfection, that is, as their activities become more frictionless, more nearly expressive of the goal which determines

[1] {See earlier passage [pp. 184–5 above]: either/or.}

the inner rule the conscious realisation of which is the definition of purposive activity – of becoming what one's inner nature seeks to be. In this image we have something like Fichte's notion of the universe.

Fichte's vision is that of the entire world as a single gigantic act of the absolute self (sometimes identified with God). This act is rational because it obeys its own inner, self-imposed rules and these rules are the rules of the harmonious development – the coherent mutual interrelation – of a system of necessary connections wherein everything is determined to be what it is by everything else in the whole. Within it, finite centres – individual human beings or groups of them – occur at various levels of development. Development means the imposition of the forms of harmony, the realisation of which is the realisation of themselves, upon the relatively less harmonious, more haphazard (relatively to them) external world. The process is one whereby mere 'togetherness', mere 'side-by-sideness', is 'developed', by being made conscious of its own potential inner harmony, into networks of no longer merely *de facto*, but progressively more and more logical – *de jure* – and therefore more and more *explicable* relations. Freedom consists in the satisfaction of the irresistible wish to unravel this dormant harmony of what at first is felt to be a mere accumulation, without much shape or purpose, with which a man begins a sentient life. Coercion, yielding to necessity, whether imposed by human beings or things, is always a sign of the imperfect penetration of matter by spirit, of acting without understanding the reasons for action, of allowing oneself to behave like a natural object, instead of functioning freely, that is, doing as one does to achieve conscious ends satisfying to one's reflective or moral self. We need not continue with this vast metaphysical fantasy, which does more credit to Fichte's poetical imagination than to his sense of reality or power of reasoning. But there are certain consequences or by-products of it – or if not of it, then of the general trend of ideas of which this is only one of the most vivid and uncompromising expressions – which are both interesting in themselves and have had decisive influence on the thought and practice of their own and of later times.

To begin with there is the notion of 'positive' as opposed to the old Benthamite or liberal 'negative' freedom – the notion of freedom as not merely removal or absence of interference with the activity of individuals or groups or nations by persons outside the designated unit, but the notion of freedom as an attribute or constitutive principle of the imposition of will upon some malleable medium. I am free not merely when no one is preventing me, but when I am acting, altering things, imposing a pattern, impressing my personality upon persons or objects, and from this follows the notion of volition as central in the determination of ends or purposes, of what is good and bad, right and wrong. The rational will, of which Kant had stressed the rationality more, perhaps, than the volitional aspect, now becomes identified with the dynamic principle of all creation, creation of things and values alike, even in my normal everyday life. Even in peaceful contemplation my will is at work: the furniture which I see in my room is not something given and independent of the observer, it is the product of the clash between the ever-active subject and nature, which is but his own self unconscious of its potentiality as a subject. The natural sciences are impositions of patterns, forms, categories by those activities – imagination, invention, reflection – which *are* the subject. But above all, moral ideals are those ends which the subject invents for its inner self, and proposes to itself – they are absolute for him, for his own self is the only absolutely independent entity in the world. There can be no independent values in terms of which ideals created by the central creative principle of the universe itself can be tested – for to call something an end or a value is to say that a creative being, a portion of *natura naturans*, is acting and desiring and being as it does and is for the sake of it, that it – the value – is its guiding light, that which it is trying to realise, in all that it is and does, at once the pattern and the purpose of its creative activity, for its pattern – it itself – is its own purpose. The purpose of creative activity is the act of creation itself.

This notion of the value of an individual consisting in the degree to which he is capable of imposing his will upon his environment is something relatively new in the consciousness of Europe. Previously, the admired figure was the sage – the wise man who knew how to obtain answers to the questions which most agitated other men, whether practical or ideal, intellectual or moral, political or theological. What was admired was, in a sense, success: strength and courage and steadfastness were admired because they were needed in the attainment of human purposes, and wisdom, honesty, knowledge were valuable because they provided a man both with the right ends and the right means to attain these ends.

Certainly it was right to fight against odds, but only if one's cause
was just, only if what one fought for was a true end, as against the
false purposes pursued by one's possibly stronger opponents.
Martyrs – Leonidas, Socrates, the Maccabees, the early Christians –
did right because they testified to the truth and, if need be, laid
down their lives in its service. But if their ends had been false, if
patriotism or the service of God as conceived by Christianity were
founded on some vast moral or spiritual error, then such self-
sacrifices, if not actually foolish, were pathetic, capable of inspiring
pity or sympathy for the sad victims of their own ignorance, like
Iphigenia or the poor Muslims who were said to die bravely for the
sake of the beatitudes of the paradise which their Prophet had
promised them if they died in battle against the infidel. It was a
sorry although it was a moving and even heart-rending spectacle to
see fearless and upright men so sadly deceived; to lay down one's
life for an illusion was not an admirable thing as such.

But almost suddenly in the nineteenth century it did become
admirable, and more admirable than anything else whatever. The
new romantic hero of the nineteenth century is someone – anyone – who is sufficiently disinterested, pure-hearted, incorruptible
to be able to lay down his life for the sake of his own inner ideal.
The truth or falsity of the ideal becomes comparatively irrelevant.
What is admired is not the truth but the heroism, the dedication,
the integrity of a life devoted to and, if need be, sacrificed on the
altar of an end pursued for its own sake, for the sake of its beauty
or sanctity to the individual whose ideal it is. Whether the ideal is
true – that is, conforms to some 'given' nature of things – is neither
here nor there.

This attitude takes many forms. The artist as hero is perhaps the
most familiar of these. The artist is a man who has an inner vision,
and this he must at all costs realise, translate into sound or paint or
some other medium, neither in order to give pleasure to others, nor
for the sake of profit or glory to himself (although these were
respectable enough motives so long as the artist was a craftsman,
and like all other craftsmen was expected honestly to ply his trade
for the sake of the delectation of others, and his own livelihood and
reputation), but purely and solely because of the overwhelming
duty to utter what is within him, to testify to the truth or express
his vision in concrete form. The artist, conceived in these terms,
must above all not sell himself for success or money or power or
anything whatever. He must remain pure, in order to remain

independent. He is permitted, almost expected, to have eccentricities of dress, behaviour, manner; he may be as rude and fierce as he wishes, provided he never temporises, provided he always speaks the truth in the highest places, respects no man where his ideals are concerned. The image of Beethoven which dominates the entire nineteenth century – the poor, dishevelled genius in the garret, diseased, unhappy and violent, a rebel against all convention, incapable and unwilling to adjust himself to any of the normal requirements of polite society, the sacred dervish, a man chosen, and dedicated to the fulfilment of a holy mission – was something very new in the consciousness of Western mankind. No doubt it begins with Rousseau, as so much of what was new in the nineteenth century: but of course he is also Karl Moor in Schiller's *The Robbers*, the wicked and violent and almost criminal outlaw, hunted and living dangerously, who has broken with the conventions of society because its falsehoods and compromises are intolerable to him, because a free man cannot submit to a framework imposed upon him by others, or by the dead hand of the past, because the mission of a man is to proclaim the ideals which possess him, if possible within his social environment, but, if this is forbidden by it, then outside it and, if need be, against it.

The emphasis grows gradually to be less and less upon the truth and validity of one kind of life or moral system over another, but on the supreme value of generating, worshipping and sacrificing oneself to ideals as such. What is most noble and deeply admired is the spectacle of a man alone, unsupported, with all the conventional values and forces against him, hurling himself into battle because he can not do otherwise, because a man must live for his ideal, whatever it may be, and if need be die for it, but above all never sell himself to the Philistines, never betray his cause, never permit himself any comfort which would make him depart an inch from that narrow path which the vision within him directs him to follow. David against Goliath, Luther against the hosts of Rome were models impressed upon the imagination of Protestant mankind; but they were heroic and noble because they had the right on their side, because Goliath worshipped the gods of Philistia, who were false gods, because the priests of Rome had betrayed its heritage. The great heretics were admirable only to those who thought that they were right, and the Church wrong, that they knew the truth and the Church was deceived or a deceiver. But with the secularisation of religion in the eighteenth century, these religious values became translated into moral and aesthetic terms. It was not because Beethoven was in some sense *right*, and his musically orthodox detractors wrong, that made him a hero. It was the unbending independence of his moral personality, the vehemence and incapacity for compromise upon what to him were ultimate issues – in his case issues of music, but it might occur in any province. It was having ultimate issues – serving principles fanatically, without reckoning the cost – that made his image linger so long in European memory. Carlyle cared very little whether Muhammad or Dr Johnson or any of his other heroes correctly answered the great human problems. Heroism was not a matter of intellect or wisdom or success, that is, adjustment to the rational scheme of reality, but of will-power, of violent, continuous, irresistible expression of the inner vision, a matter of bowing to the absolute principle – the categorical imperative which meant utter defiance of all that obstructed and opposed a man in the worship of the inner light.

It made no difference whether the odds were great or small, whether the prospect was victory or death. Once the inner voice had spoken, there was no turning back; or rather any compromise, any evasion was the ultimate sin against the light, was ultimately the only contemptible and vicious act of which a man could be guilty in this world. The inner voice no longer needed to be supernatural or to tell the truth, as with Socrates or Joan of Arc, still less to be rational, as with Rousseau or Kant. It was sufficient for it to be the voice that it was. Those men, and only those, were good and admirable who, if need be, threw away all they had without counting the cost, spoke the truth, created beautiful objects, resisted injustice, or in any other way behaved in a disinterested, uncalculating, dedicated way. Such words as 'integrity' and 'idealism', with all their ethical connotations, as well as the various schools of thought which offered now one, now another, absolute end for human worship – the State or the human personality, religious dedication, or the cult of friendship and personal relationships – the immense respect paid to everything which entails heroism and martyrdom, whatever the cause in which it is done: all this is development of this attitude of mind. Similarly the worship of powerful personalities as such – Napoleon and Frederick the Great – derives from the same general conception of the purposes of life. Napoleon is *l'homme fatal*,[1] the Corsican

---

[1] [The origins of this phrase are obscure. It occurs twice in the works of Jean-

adventurer coming from nowhere, with no clear purposes except domination for its own sake. He is admired precisely for this reason, because he is the culminating point of will-power raised to its highest point – of the possibility of binding one's will upon others, as an end in itself.

Nothing is more admirable than the ruthless realisation of whatever burns within one, at all costs – at the price, it may be, of the lives and happiness of others, at the price of the fear and hatred of one's subjects and one's victims – because this is the function of a man, to act as the expression of the great creative principle of nature, which destroys obstacles in its irresistible advance; for self-expression, self-realisation, is the goal of man, as of everything in the universe. The universe increases in perfection through awareness of their true natures on the part of its constituents; but since everything in it is less or more active, such a self-awareness must take the form of self-imposition of the aware and active upon the relatively unaware or passive. We are back to the indestructible inner citadel, now conceived as the source of power. Freedom is independence, of everything save the inner ideal, whether it takes humanitarian and benevolent forms, as in the case of scientists or composers, or brutal, violent and destructive ones, as in the case of conquerors and captains of industry; but it is always a disinterested self-realising activity the goal of which is not discovered, but generated or made by, identical with, the activity itself. This romantic doctrine of the early nineteenth century takes both anarchistic and authoritarian forms in its second half and dominates both aesthetic and political theories to an increasing extent until our own day.

For if freedom is a kind of disinterested self-assertion, an act of creation, out of the stuff with which the self finds itself confronted,

Louis Guez de Balzac (1594–1654). In his *Socrate chrestien* (1652), Discourse 8: 'Il devoit perir, cét Homme fatal (nous le considerasmes il y a quelques jours dans l'Histoire de l'Empire d'Orient) il devoit perir des le premier jour de sa conduite, par une telle ou une telle entreprise; Mais Dieu se vouloit servir de luy, pour punir le Genre humain, & pour tourmenter le Monde: La Iustice de Dieu se vouloit venger, & avoit choisi cét Homme pour estre le Ministre de ses vengeances.' And in his *Dissertations critiques / de critique* (1654), Dissertation 26: 'Denis fut ainsi deschiré, en la personne du Cyclope Polypheme: Et comme Tibere a esté, apres sa mort, l'image de l'Homme fatal; durant sa vie, Agamemnon estoit l'image de Tibere.' See *Les oeuvres de Monsieur de Balzac* (Paris, 1665), vol. 2, pp. 237, 679. Among its later uses is that of Wellington by Chateaubriand, *Mémoires d'outre-tombe* (1849–50): vol. 2, p. 474, in Maurice Levaillant's edition (Paris, 1948).]

of something modelled on a pattern imposed upon it by the creator
in accordance with his own inner purpose, whatever that may be,
then the kind of pattern will depend upon how the notions of self
and of creation are conceived. Anyone who holds a doctrine
according to which the self is a 'rational' entity, and all creation is
the adoption of a plan or policy capable of being described as
rational, will conclude that free activity (and all activity is free,
since if it is conditioned by 'external' factors it is no longer activity)
is necessarily rational, obedient to laws, conforming to a pattern. If
the self is conceived as a timeless entity, freedom is whatever is
done by this metaphysical agent, and empirical human acts
performed in time and space are free only in so far as they issue
from, and correspond to, the demands of this self-sensible
personality. If, on the other hand, the self is something which is
born and dies at definite times – a pattern of events, as Hume
supposed, a series of states of consciousness each swallowing its
predecessors, as William James thought, a succession of psychophysical events in time susceptible to normal scientific observation
and description, as psychologists or physiologists treat of it – then
freedom is the imposition of whatever patterns this empirical self
conceives and imposes upon the equally empirical material which it
encounters in the way of material objects or persons. If, again, the
self is conceived as a mere fragment of a wider whole, a group, a
Church, a society, a State, a race, a nation – history itself – which is
the only true unified whole deserving the term 'self', then freedom
consists in the activity of this larger organisation, credited with
quasi-personal attributes, and the individuals who compose it can
be called free no more and no less than the limbs or organs of a
complete organism, a human body, in close analogy with which
such wholes are conceived.

And indeed many of the social and political doctrines of the
nineteenth century do employ the concept of freedom in these
various ways. The inspired artist or prophet who is the centre of
Schelling's world is a being who in moments of inspired insight is
conscious of the presence within him – of himself as part – of that
world spirit the self-development of which is the life of the
universe. The sense of illumination, of understanding the connections which hold, below the level of ordinary vision, between the
ingredients of the world – the unity and harmony which lie
concealed 'behind' the world of conflicting and chaotic 'appearances' – is the awareness on the part of the self of itself as part of

this inner stream which creates all that is and occurs. Therefore the inspired artist at the moment of creation, the inspired statesman or soldier or philosopher, is justified in acting as he does by his intuitive grasp of these inner connections. He cannot, perhaps, explain it by the kind of reasoning employed in everyday argument, or by calculation, which is but a stylised and deeply inadequate mechanical set of logical patterns invented for practical purposes and unenlightened minds in need of a ready-made discipline. The 'reasons' for which a man of genius creates a masterpiece are not explicable in terms of inductive or deductive logic as it is employed explicitly or implicitly in the sciences or in ordinary life. No more should the inspired statesman, who by his creative power advances a country or a civilisation towards a greater degree of freedom, that is, consciousness of itself as part of this non-empirical, 'divine', creative process – an emanation of the world 'spirit' – be accountable for his acts in terms of everyday middle-class reasoning; for his act is as self-justified as that of the gifted painter or inspired poet who does what he does at the moment of the highest tension of his faculties, in other words when the vision which is but the perception of the inner harmony, the inner relationships not perceptible to the naked eye, 'takes hold of him', and he becomes the sacred vessel through which the creative spirit makes its advance. Freedom consists, then, in a kind of intuitive, non-discursive, perhaps semi-conscious self-identification with the divine afflatus. It is a 'transcendent' act, that is, it is not intelligible or analysable in empirical terms. It is the outburst of energy transforming dead matter (which is potentially filled with such creative fires, too, but only potentially and therefore needs to be worked upon from outside), and this is what is meant by saying that the highest freedom is in the creative act, in the self-identification with the great creative river, the overcoming of the obstacles of the flesh, and of space and time, which are at once a process of transforming them and – because the self knows, in this almost mystical sense of knowing, why it is acting as it is – of understanding the true essence of the universe, its texture and its goals.

It is worth remarking here that what Schelling appears to mean by 'understanding' is the precise contrary of what this means in the empirical sciences, and much more what it means in the arts. In the sciences, to understand is to be able to bring under general laws or rules, to be able to classify the thing to be understood in such a way as to be able to perceive it as an instance of the operation of a law; that is, to see it as one of an indefinitely great number of other cases similar to it, all of which behave as they do 'because of', fall under, one and the same general law, namely a statement describing uniformities or functions, how any entity, E, behaves in circumstances, C, when it has been preceded by some antecedent circumstances, A. To explain why water boils at 100°, or why a bullet through the heart puts an end to a man's life, is to formulate a set of general laws, each of which applies to the regular and uniform behaviour of all the analysable ingredients in the situation, such that according to these laws this is what normally would be expected from a specific conjunction of them. But to explain 'why' a particular patch of colour is 'necessary' in a given painting, 'why' a given sound 'must' occur in a symphonic pattern, which without it would be not merely different but *utterly* different – transforming the entire pattern, destroying the unity of the whole, making what would otherwise be a work of art into, it may be, a mere succession of sounds or a juxtaposition of lines and coloured surfaces, no longer intelligible or 'beautiful' – to talk like this is to imply that 'explanation' is no longer a matter of general laws which summate uniformities between events. To 'understand' a work of art is in some sense to grasp why all its ingredients are indispensable to one another, uniquely so, without being able to frame laws which apply to other less or more similar situations: a patch of blue, a chord consisting of C, E and G, is uniquely indispensable here, in this particular work of art, and not necessarily anywhere else ever again.

This artistic 'necessity' is either perceived by a flash of insight or not at all. Such flashes equally illuminate the characters, personalities, of individuals, as when I suddenly comprehend the character of my friend or of an historical personage long dead. This comprehension is not arrived at by a process of inductive reasoning, although without such reasoning at some stage the flash may never occur, or if it occurred might reveal something delusive. Similarly the 'sense of history', the sense of occasion, the perception of what is, and what is not, a critical moment in the lives of human beings or nations or cultures, of the peculiar characteristics of peoples, or institutions – of what makes certain combinations of characteristics come together at certain moments of history, because of a certain inner relevance not to be explained on the basis of inductive generalisations – *that* is the use of the aesthetic 'because', the use of aesthetic 'explanation', which employs the concept of artistic 'inevitability', of the kind of connections which make a pattern something other than a mere collection of isolated bits and pieces, which is not causal, not inductive, not, in the strict sense of the word, logical, which governs the imagination as much as analytical intellect. Schelling called this 'reason', and identified it with purpose, with whatever it is that guides the creative artist and the inspired preacher, the statesman in a moment of fateful action, and the historian who grasps the essence of some remote period or culture, where others see merely a collection of separate facts or events, juxtaposed loosely in time or space, and leading to the bleak and mechanical records of archivists and antiquaries, as opposed to the creative reconstruction of historians gifted with insight into the 'inner' structure of the universe, with some glimpse of it as a growing work of art created in accordance with an inner non-scientific logic by the Divine Artist in the unbroken act of eternal creation.

Freedom is the state in which the artist creates. The deeper his inspiration, the closer he is to the heart of the inner power which makes all things to be as they are, the source of all movement, all change, all that is new, unique and irreversible. Here we find the beginnings not only of the worship of the artist as the only entirely liberated personality, triumphant over the limitations, the fears, the frustrations which force other men to follow paths not of their choosing, but also of the fear of democracy as simply a conjunction of the enslaved wills of such earth-dwellers, and the worship of the leader as the inspired being in communion with the world spirit, the source of creative power, the inspired visionary who, in virtue of his superior insight (not to be obtained by those normal scientific methods or skills which any competent person can learn), can discern and bring into being (for the two, as in the case of the artist, blend indissolubly) the next stage in the self-assertion of his society against nature or other societies which is progress. Freedom then consists in trying to catch fire from the sublime prophet or teacher, to perform with him, to the extent of one's ability, that audacious leap into the future which only a combination of faith, imagination and a general dynamism – capacity for action without too much critical reflection – can achieve.

This is the celebrated act of liberation from the bonds of dreary everyday concerns which the semi-divine leader promises his followers, the embryo of that notion of the superman who rises

above, and mocks at, the petty vision and sordid calculations of
men and women bound by the senses, by attachments which
spring from conventions or methods which they practise without
understanding and cannot 'free' themselves from, because they lack
the capacity for 'transcending' the empirical level upon which the
sciences so impotently do their menial mechanical work. And now
it is not difficult to understand why the notion of freedom as
necessarily rational is gradually melted into its opposites. If
freedom is the imposition of one's personality, the destruction of
all that resists one in the name of an ideal which is absolute because
it is one's own end, one knows of no other authority; and if
rationality is identified either with the operations of some kind of
logic, whether of the strict formal kind, or some transcendental
discipline, or even with the search for the realisation of some
coherent or harmonious system, might it not be that the self will, in
its victorious self-fulfilment, reject this too, as a mere obstacle to its
progress, a mere bridle which hampers its total freedom? If
freedom consists in altering what I find, as a sculptor moulds clay,
or a composer shapes sound, irrespective of the condition in which
he finds his raw material, and if an individual seeking liberty must
transform the conventions of his society or perhaps break them
altogether, if they confine his turbulent spirit in a manner contrary
to its 'inner' goals, why should any rules, any laws, remain sacred?

Anything that is finite confines and kills; freedom is freedom
from all chains, freedom to act and do whatever one wills. The
possibilities of action must be infinite, or we complain that our
freedom is not complete; and any of these infinite possibilities must
be realisable, or it is incomplete again. Hence the irrationalist
notion of freedom as developed by the extreme romantics at the
turn of the century, for example in Friedrich Schlegel's (or his
wife's) novel *Lucinde*, in which an infant kicking and screaming is
suddenly presented as a symbol of absolute freedom, totally
unconfined by laws, conventions, social bonds – and in which
marriage is denounced, and freedom of association between the
sexes is advocated, not as fulfilling some harmony the elements of
which are represented as in some way rationally related to each
other, but as the free self-realisation of the unconfined human
spirit, bursting from its bonds, leaving the earth to be nearer the
eternal, infinite flame which knows no logic and no rules, but is the
infinite, not expressible by petty human categories, invented by
small-minded beings who live their lives in obedience to rules

which they accept because they dare not question them. This is the ideal of violent anarchy, of the triumph of the bold, free Gulliver over the knock-kneed rickety armies of the self-enslaved inhabitants of Lilliput. Stirner, Bakunin, Nietzsche: the succession is familiar enough.

The principal difference between these figures and those who find freedom in submission to this or that rigid social pattern lies in their interpretation of what it is that we are realising when we realise the self. Some realise a self that is rational, and seeks to submit to rational patterns, but is still individual. Others conceive the self as rational, but see its fulfilment only in a society of various degrees of cohesion and rigidity of organisation. Still others regard the self as a finite emanation of the central world spirit which proceeds according to laws, but laws not logically deducible so much as obeying some 'inner logic' which guides the creative artist, the prophet, inspired men of action. And still others believe the self to be a violent source of energy following no laws but asserting itself not in accordance with, but against, all that is rational, coherent, therefore finite and confining. Others again see the self realised most truly in history, race or Church.

What unites all these cases is the notion that freedom is some kind of ecstatic self-absorption in an activity. The violin-player is free in proportion as he expresses the score more and more precisely, obeys the rules more and more completely and faithfully, identifies himself with them, eliminates everything which is subjective, attempts to make his personality a transparent medium of expression. Alternatively freedom may take the form of self-obliteration by marching in an army, by identifying oneself with one's team in a game, by feeling oneself at one with a tightly functioning trade union, or a school, or a bureaucracy, or a Church, or a State system. In its hysterical forms it may take the form of violent destruction of others or oneself. In all these cases the freedom in question is the precise opposite of the *liberal* notion of it – the individual left to pursue his purposes without interference, whether the fulfilment of these purposes makes him happy or not, 'realises' him – the negative notion of preventing interference by others which lies at the heart of the notion of liberty as conceived by Locke and Hume, Mill and Macaulay, and which still functions as at any rate the ostensible ideal of modern democratic governments. No two ideas could at first seem more remote than, on the one hand, passionate self-immolation on the

altar of State or race or religion or history or the 'dynamic' pursuit
of power for its own sake, as the only symptom of a free man, on
the part of Fascists and other hysterical romantics, or embittered
anti-liberals; and, on the other hand, the concepts of inalienable
civil liberties, of limitation of interference, and of the sanctity of
certain areas dedicated to private life which form the substance of
liberal individualism as it is defended against encroachment in
democracies.

The freedom of those who, whether they know it or not, have
absorbed the ideas of the idealistic metaphysicians and look upon
the State or the Church as a work of art moulded by themselves or
some transcendent power, and of which they are but the
indispensable though tightly controlled ingredients, happy in the
unique but unalterable function which history or some other
abstract despot has laid upon them to perform, seems a slavery –
happy, perhaps, and even ecstatic, but still a slavery – to those
brought up in a more individualistic civilisation. And on the other
side freedom to live and let live, being abandoned to one's own
resources, the possibility of a choice of alternatives for no better
reason than that a given kind of life, or a given alternative, leads to
an increase in happiness, or appears attractive in itself (and does not
conflict with similar personal and almost casual reasons on the part
of others), seems not freedom at all, but a form of aimless drift, idle
and formless self-indulgence, a feckless pursuit of short-term ends,
an *ad hoc* hand-to-mouth morality lacking in all dignity or
seriousness of purpose, above all a blindness to the vast creative
potentialities of one's 'inner' spirit, which demands liberation and
the right to command – seems trivial and precarious and empty to
those inured to or hankering after some form of collective self-
sacrifice, some Messianic mission. And between these extremes
there are many versions and types of attitude, resembling each
other, and the extreme poles between which they oscillate, in
numerous not precisely definable respects.

There is something paradoxical, surely, in the vicissitudes of a
word used within the same short period of time by Condorcet in a
sense almost the exact opposite to that used by Saint-Just; by
Fichte to describe a form of life which was precisely that which
Bentham or James Mill, under this very same banner of liberty,
fought all their lives to make for ever impossible; which is used by
Mill and Macaulay, Hegel and Nietzsche, Marx and Woodrow
Wilson and Lenin as a central term, the basic concept on which

their beliefs are founded, so sacred as to exact the greatest degree of intellectual scruple and intense feeling of which they were capable, yet which is employed to describe ideals which were conspicuously incapable of compromise, and which collided violently and with consequences of which no one living in the present needs to be reminded. It is evident that the only common meaning which the word bears in all these differing, and indeed vehemently opposed, traditions is concerned with elimination of obstacles to something, which they each believe to be the most important ends of life. Liberty as an end in itself turns out to have scarcely any meaning for anyone. It means something to say that a man should seek happiness and nothing else; or knowledge and nothing else; or even power to gratify his whims and nothing else; but what could it mean to say that freedom and freedom alone would be sufficient? Unless (it seems almost too platitudinous to say) one wished to do or be something in preference to something else, one could not wish for freedom to do or be this; and the difference must derive from differing interpretations of what, according to the different schools and traditions, it is worth doing or being for its own sake.

The notion of 'positive freedom' is certainly founded on a confusion, and a confusion which has cost a great many human lives, for it means no more than that all men have positive goals, and feel unhappy or unrealised or abandoned to cruel fate or cruel masters unless these positive ends do not too violently conflict with one another, or the environment of those who pursue them, or the purposes and behaviour of their fellows; and that to remove obstacles to the realisation of this or that end is of little use to those who do not know what ends they seek, or seek ends incompatible with one another, or ends that are unrealisable, or in too violent a conflict with the ends of others. And the force of the argument of those who speak of 'positive freedom' is that this is so, and that those to whom freedom is given under these unfavourable circumstances do not feel it to be valuable, and do not therefore recognise this for what it should be. But freedom does not cease to be freedom because it is not the most valuable possession under specific and unfavourable circumstances. A blind man may not appreciate a gift of a beautiful painting, but a gift it remains nevertheless, nor does the painting become less beautiful because he cannot see it – the meaning of such terms as 'visual beauty' is derived from the experience of those who can. Civil liberties may mean nothing to the starving and the naked, but because they are not in a condition to want them, or understand what they are, it does not follow that civil liberties are in some sense 'negative', whereas they might be 'positive'. No doubt the concrete content of the kind of freedom under discussion is different in accordance with the concrete contexts in the minds of thinkers with different ideas about human nature, human capacities and the ends of life; and the notion of freedom will duly differ for those who conceive of man as a fragment broken off from some initial, all-embracing whole, to unite himself with which and lose his identity (save as a conductor of some central source of light or power) he seeks above all things, whether he is Hegelian or Buddhist; and for those who conceive of a man as an empirical being in time and space, pursuing such ends as he pursues, for whatever reasons, and requiring, in order to be what he wishes to be, a certain area protected from invasion by others, whether their views tally with his own or not, whether they approve of him or not, and whatever their general attitude towards him and his ends, and his attitude towards them and their ends, may be.

The size of this area, and the question of whether there are any occasions, and if so what, upon which this area may be invaded, may then be disputed. What remains constant is the notion that unless *some* such area is delimited in practice (and in theory too), those ends cannot be attained which, as a matter of common observation, are in fact and have been and very likely always will be pursued by men. And the wishes and ideals of these men are to be respected because in fact (and again as a matter of common observation) such men and such ideals are regarded as sufficiently valuable by those who attach this kind of meaning to freedom to be worth taking into the most serious possible consideration for their own sakes, as such, as ends in themselves, very much as Kant recommended, though not perhaps for one of his explicit reasons – not because they are rational beings (whatever may be meant by that) – but really for his other reason, that men are ends in themselves because they are the sole source of all morality, the beings for whose sakes alone whatever is worth doing is worth doing, because the notion of ends in themselves is one of ends which men invent for themselves, and there is therefore nothing outside them to which they can in principle be deemed worthy of sacrifice.

These conflicting humanistic and non-humanistic definitions of freedom, the latter of many kinds – transcendentalist and theo-cratic, 'organic' (whether in the Hegelian or Fascist senses) or heroic (in some Byronic or Nietzschean sense), ordering men to bow to the demands of history (as Burke or the German jurists demanded) or of class, like the Marxists, or of race, like the National Socialists, or some aesthetic ideal of self-destruction in the interests of some violent eschatology, or a quietism as preached by Schopenhauer or Tolstoy or Hindu sages – all these appear ultimately to depend partly upon the views held of what men are like, how they behave, and what are the results of the interplay between them and other forces. Partly on that, and partly on ultimate purposes about which there can in the end be no argument, only assertion and counter-assertion, and attempts to convert by persuasion or by violence. The use of the word 'freedom' is one of the surest of indices of the user's general ultimate ideal of life, of what to want and what to avoid, whether consciously or unconsciously pursued by him; and the distance which divides the humanist from the non-humanist vision of human society is brought out most dramatically by the unbridge-able chasm which stretches between, let us say, Fichte or Görres on the one hand and Mill on the other. Every one of the great thinkers of the nineteenth century will be found to be nearer one or the other of these poles; the general trend is unmistakable and there is no possibility of neutrality. The two ideals are neither compatible nor capable of compromise and have dominated men's minds (far more than, say, the opposites of collectivism and individualism or spiritualism and materialism) ever since. And the use of the term 'freedom' is one of the most faithful indicators of where a man stands.

# 4

# THE MARCH OF HISTORY

THE NOTION of scientific method as alone leading to objective, that is, dependable, information about the world is sufficiently widespread today not to appear paradoxical in itself. There are three kinds of ways of showing propositions to be true: by direct empirical inspection, as when we discover that roses are red by looking, or have a sweet scent by smelling; by deduction, which we practise in logic, in mathematics, and wherever these disciplines play a part; and by induction – by assuming that the unknown resembles the known, in some respects at least, we infer from what we know by one of the other methods to what is for some reason not directly presented, because it is in the past or in the future, or concealed from us by physical or psychological or other kinds of obstacles to direct inspection.

The systematic use of these methods with a sense of their proper scope, how to apply them, and the way in which they fit in with each other is called scientific, and the various sciences depend partly on their subject-matter and partly on the methods which seem most useful in producing the result desired, that is, the provision of information whose dependability is ultimately checked by actual human observation or a specifiable logical relation – such as probability, consistency and the like – with such observation. In this way we accumulate and organise our knowledge of uniformity, of what happens in company with, or in succession to, or next door to what else. Such information is said to be more and more scientific as the number of unassimilated data grows smaller and smaller and the number of generalisations – laws or rules – grows more and more comprehensive in scope, and the generalisations are themselves organised like a pyramid, the more specific laws being directly deducible from more general ones, and the number of ultimate laws, themselves not deducible from any others, being made as few as possible. The ideal is derivation of all laws, in other words formulae for the description, prediction, correlation and retrodiction of all phenomena – the behaviour of all things and all persons – from one single integrating law or principle from which all else is deducible.

This is the ideal of the unity of all the sciences, the search for which has been a persistent strain in human thought since Thales, and which has influenced both scientific thought and thought about science particularly powerfully since the eighteenth century, when the goal, if not reached, seemed almost in sight. Yet if we ask ourselves what history is about and how it is written, it is not clear how it is to be fitted into this general pattern.

When we are seeking to describe a succession of historical events, the parts played in them by specific peoples or groups or personalities, the effects of this or that historical situation, or the influence of personal or impersonal factors such as the economic behaviour of a given community or the influence upon it of particular governments or particular individual rulers, do we in fact proceed by trying to 'abstract' all the characteristics common to the period or the society or the individuals in question and to other periods, societies and individuals, to extract generalisations about the behaviour of what is common to different periods or persons, and to deduce from these generalisations what must have happened during the period or with regard to the persons under discussion? To some extent of course we do; all words classify, that is, stand for characteristics which categorise more than one entity, automatically compare and contrast things or persons at different times and in different situations. Such historical concepts as 'change', 'revolution', 'political power', 'government', 'popular discontent', 'democracy', 'tyranny' and the like do of course attempt to denote something similar in very diverse situations and presuppose a sufficient degree of likeness in situations widely separated in time and space to enable such common terms to be used profitably. Nevertheless, this is not sufficient. The whole purpose of chemistry is to define the entities with which it deals – say, molecules or valency – in such a way as to eliminate all that is irrelevant, so that each molecule qua molecule has the structural principle of a molecule, or all valencies are identical with each other qua valencies whenever and wherever they may occur, whatever else may be different in those situations. Biology somewhat less successfully tries to define, let us say, 'organisms' in a similarly uniform manner, so that wherever and whenever 'organisms' are said to occur, they shall possess as many characteristics that are as wholly similar as possible, in order to make generalisations cover as many instances as they can. This is plainly not how history proceeds.

To begin with, if we are describing, let us say, the French Revolution, or the character and influence of Robespierre in it, the last thing that we should normally be doing is to describe it in such terms as make it as indistinguishable as possible from other revolutions at other times and among other peoples. It would be odder still if we attempted to describe Robespierre in such a manner as to make him seem as much a Siamese twin of other revolutionaries, French or Italian, or Roman or Chinese, as we are able, in order to demonstrate that in acting as he did he obeyed the same general laws of revolutionary behaviour as make all revolutionists, wherever and whenever they may be, act in a precisely similar manner, given such and such conditions of an identifiable kind. What we seek to do – and no one would be called a historian (still less a biographer) who did not – is to convey what actually happened in a particular situation, whether or not anything very similar occurred under other circumstances. We are trying to convey something which in a sense is altogether unique – something which happened when it did and where it did and as it did, and was what it was precisely because it did not happen at some other time or at some other place or with regard to a quite different set of human organisms. It may be that history is cyclical or reproduces itself precisely, and that every historical situation precisely repeats itself somewhere, sometime. But historians are not concerned with that. We look to them to provide us with as good an account as they are able of what happened, so far as we know, only once, at a particular time, in a particular place – for that alone is what we want to know. Naturally, if we are asking for the causes of what happened, we are in a sense asking for general laws (for that is what causes are), for that element in a given situation which, had it happened elsewhere, would have been – and whenever in fact it did happen at other times or places, was – an instance of some general law which tells us how such elements do in fact behave in varying circumstances. And such general laws are no doubt 'abstracted' from concrete situations by comparison and contrast, by some kind of rough induction. But merely to state these laws and their applications would not be enough, for it would not account for the uniqueness of what happened, for the particular way in which it happened, for the specific characteristics of an event or situation or person, which form the particular pattern which we are expecting the historian to describe and analyse. The character of Napoleon, the course of the Russian Revolution, are not deducible from general laws as the behaviour of bodies is by physical science.

Sociology and psychology, which in so far as they are sciences promise one day to be able to make such deductions, have not yet even begun to do so in any serious fashion; whatever the validity of their claims, history as written by historians does not pretend, indeed, does not wish, to be doing this. It may or may not be seeking to demonstrate general principles, general laws, empirical or a priori, material or spiritual, as they show themselves further in what occurs; and historians are called philosophical or unphilosophical in proportion as they believe themselves to be doing just that. But they would not be historians at all – at most philosophers of history, or advocates of the elimination of history as it is written in favour of some other way of treating the facts – if they did not as an absolute minimum set down in their order the facts with which they are concerned in such a way as to bring out the particular character, the specific qualities, of historical events or persons, thereby alone giving us the impression that they are in fact describing actual events in actual time and space as and when and where they happened, and not hypothetical persons or events in possible times and spaces, which might have happened at any time, anywhere, or not at all – in the way in which, when scientists speak of atoms or even geological formations (for which indeed they claim existence), they mention characteristics which describe them in general terms, that is, whether they exist or not.

It is clear that in some sense history as we know it is not a science at all, but an art, in the sense in which portrait painting is an art, whereby the uniqueness of a personality or an expression is conveyed and not merely that which it has in common with many other men, which is what, say, an X-ray or even a photograph might convey – the success of the painter being to some degree directly dependent upon the degree to which his portrait is a portrait of one unique individual in the universe, so that if there is another who precisely resembles him, this is an irrelevant and peculiar coincidence to which, as a portrait painter, he is completely indifferent.

Moreover, apart from its method, there is at least one other fact which distinguishes history from the sciences, and that is that it deals with human beings, and deals with them as creatures who think, feel, desire and act. The natural sciences are engaged in recording what happens in company with what else and how often and for how long and how widely; it provides answers to such questions as what there is in the world and how it behaves, that is, what it does where and when; and this applies no less to the human sciences – sociology, anthropology, psychology and so forth – than to the natural sciences, so far as the former are properly called scientific. But human beings, as we know because we are ourselves human, are not merely bodies in space, moving and being moved, but have purposes and motives and act as they do under the influence of other than purely physical or biological causes. If it is a fallacy to be anthropomorphic, falsely attributing human characteristics to the gods, or animistic, attributing them to planets or rivers or trees; if the pathetic fallacy is condemned because it attributes human emotions to inanimate objects or animals; it does at least follow that somewhere these categories are appropriate – namely in describing human beings. And if it is a mistake to make false analogies between them and natural objects (or the Deity), it must be equally fallacious to apply the analogy the other way around – to treat human beings as if their attributes were not different in important ways from those of stones or trees or birds or dogs or the solar system, as the eighteenth-century rationalists with their analogies of the societies of 'bees or beavers',[1] and their nineteenth-century and twentieth-century followers, have tended to do.

We assume that Caesar or Robespierre felt emotions or were moved by desires for certain ends and thought and reflected in certain ways not on the basis of such slender inductive evidence as may exist for such hypotheses, but by analogy with ourselves, because we have good inductive evidence for believing that men called by these names existed, and if they were men, there is no reason for confining ourselves to such observations of the behaviour of their bodies as records may make available. We can credit them with, for example, purposes as well, and ask not merely how they behaved but why. 'Why?' is a question which we cannot put to nature unless we believe her to be in some sense animate or

---

[1] Condorcet, *Discours prononcé dans l'Académie Française, le jeudi 21 février 1782, à la réception de M. le Marquis de Condorcet*: vol. 1, p. 392, in *Oeuvres de Condorcet*, ed. A. Condorcet O'Connor and M. F. Arago (Paris, 1847–9).

purposive; and this is one of the great fallacies which we discussed in the first chapter. But we can and do ask such questions of human beings, and since history is concerned with the experience of human beings, their purposes, and thoughts, and feelings, the impact upon their minds and emotions of natural events or of other men – since history is not an account of the behaviour and evolution of human bodies or of the structure of their brains or their senses, which, however relevant, belong to other disciplines – we are not writing history unless we answer such questions as why certain individuals acted as they did, or what they felt about this or that, or what kind of ideas they had in acting thus and thus, all of which are well-nigh meaningless when asked of flowers or fishes or the moon. It may be of course that vegetables or minerals are in some sense, as Leibniz thought, sentient beings, although in a very embryonic and inchoate way, but if so this is opaque to us and too speculative. We can establish that most stones when thrown at windows break them, but if it is suggested that stones like or dislike doing this, that windows wish to be broken or, on the contrary, to resist to the utmost, that tables literally groan under their burdens, that meadows smile and seas grow angry, we have no evidence for it. We can describe only the 'outer' aspect, whatever may be going on 'within'. But in the case of human beings we can quite clearly distinguish between such 'outer' behaviour as bodily movements and 'inner' states or processes, which the whole of our mental and emotional vocabulary is meant to describe. Therefore in a sense we know more, or know in a different sense, about human beings and what makes them behave as they do and be as they are than about inanimate objects. We know, in short, what it is to be a human being, and do not know what it is to be a table or a rock, only what it is to see, touch, taste material objects. Any historian who attempts to deal solely in terms of natural characteristics – as a zoologist describes beavers, or an entomologist ants – would seem to be acting very oddly, deliberately refraining from saying what he knew, artificially confining himself to what is common between men and natural objects, and thus failing to take account of what uniquely distinguishes men, or at least our knowledge of them. This kind of behaviourism is certainly incompatible with any kind of historical description, however fruitful it may be (and even that seems more than doubtful) in such sciences as economics or sociology.

Indeed, what we mean by 'understanding' differs profoundly in the two cases. In natural science it is ultimately reducible to the proper attribution of individual cases or sets of such to the laws, that is to say uniformities, which have the greatest predictive and classificatory power. 'Understanding' here means knowing the place of given phenomena on a map – the most comprehensive and detailed attainable system in which as many different types as possible of phenomena are interrelated; whereas to understand historical facts, whatever causal assumptions are here also involved, certainly entails at least some degree of knowing what people were at – how they felt, what they wanted, what ideas influenced them, how they viewed the world, how they reacted to experience, what arts and sciences they pursued, why they acted and what they suffered; and understanding of this type is obviously akin to the way in which we understand one another, in which we are said to understand what others say to us, gather their intentions, size up their characters, something we perform by an empirical process very different from that of scientific induction; it is a sense in which we cannot be said to 'understand' flowers or stones or protoplasms at all.

Sometimes, indeed, ambitious historians with claims to quasi-intuitional powers may go too far for us in this respect. When a Roman historian claims to understand the individual character of a given emperor by the buildings which he caused to be erected, because these buildings in some sense 'express' his attitude to life, 'speak to us' almost as a personal letter might, we may reasonably doubt whether this is altogether reliable as a form of historical investigation; but our doubts are due to our suspicion that buildings do not 'speak' as letters do, that though they may provide some kind of evidence for the tastes of a culture, for what some men, at any rate, wanted or thought they wanted buildings to look like, yet architecture is not a form of direct communication of thoughts or feelings like speech or writing, nor organised by sufficient conventional rules intended to make such meanings intelligible. But it follows from the fact that such an approach is too imaginative and requires, therefore, in the absence (and sometimes in the presence) of direct information, to be eked out by the normal inductive methods of the sciences (as corrupt portions of manuscripts or little-understood alphabets can be 'restored' reliably only by the use of scientific methods as the natural sciences use them) – it follows from this that if we are not to be too speculative, we must return to the level at which such methods are properly applicable, where 'understanding' is the right method of obtaining information, as when you read books (though these may be written in the past) and understand and believe their contents without inductive tests as to whether written marks on paper were used by the writers more or less as we should use them now. In other words, historical understanding is directly related to that sense of understanding in which human beings understand or misunderstand one another in normal intercourse, or in which the written records of the past are understood, or in which works of art are said to express something without conveying descriptive factual information. This is not understanding in the sense in which a phenomenon is said to be understood when it has been scientifically explained.

Clearly, historical explanation includes inductive inferences both in those ancillary studies, palaeography, archaeology and so on, with which much of the evidence is reconstructed, and in the process of actual historical reconstruction of the past as well; but because it involves so large a degree of understanding in a sense other than that which results from the methods of the natural sciences, historical explanation is radically different from scientific explanation. In its categories – the sense in which it uses such terms as 'evidence', 'fact' and even 'truth' and 'probability', such words as 'because' and 'therefore' – it deals with the unique situation rather than with general laws (it may presuppose such laws, but it does not and is not required to formulate them). It does not proceed from the particular to the general or from the general to the particular, but, like any other form of story-telling, from particular to particular. It seeks to reproduce the actual situation, not to abstract characteristics common to it and others like it. Its claims are verified as common-sense conjectures and beliefs are verified and not as those of the special sciences are. It asks questions to which the sciences are not intended to provide an answer. To say that they do or should do so, as the proponents of 'scientific' history have done since the days of Holbach and almost of Hobbes, is, as Tolstoy once remarked, like causing a deaf man to answer questions he cannot hear – he provides answers which the questioners do not wish to know since that is not what they are asking.

*Vico*

The proposition that history in this sense is unique, and the celebrated and important distinction (which has cast alternate light and obscurity on its subject-matter) between the natural and historical sciences, or more broadly still, the sciences and the humanities, was formulated with astonishing insight by the Italian philosopher Vico, and was thereafter wholly ignored for more than a century. It was rediscovered independently of him, and when his immense originality was revealed to a world wider than his native Italy, in the early nineteenth century, others – Herder, the historical school of jurisprudence in Germany, Saint-Simon and his disciples, and the Catholic counter-revolutionaries and other romantic theorists – had discovered these truths virtually for themselves. Nevertheless, it is in Vico's writings that the central issue is most clearly and boldly stated. It is he who, in protest against the prevailing method of Descartes, denies that the models of the mathematical and physical sciences, for all their triumphs in their own sphere, are applicable to the study of mankind. And his reasoning takes the form of saying that only that can be perfectly understood by a man which he himself can make. Mathematics is indeed perfectly intelligible because, Vico maintains, it is not a description of something found in the external world, but an activity of the mind in accordance with its own rules, upon material provided by itself. Physics is less intelligible to the extent to which there is here more than mathematics, namely the behaviour of matter – brute matter which man has not invented and whose behaviour is therefore something given – thrust upon him by nature in accordance with her own laws, which govern his body as a natural object, but which he has not thought out for himself or had as an inward experience in the sense in which his thoughts or emotions are his own and not part of the external world.

The Cartesian method seemed to assume that while the 'inner' world of emotions, desires, purposes was turbid and uncertain, it was the 'outer' world – with which physics and mathematics dealt – that offered the best sphere for the discovery of those clear and distinct ideas out of whose necessary concatenation alone true knowledge could be constructed. Vico opposed this with all the poor eloquence at his command, and in his characteristically confused but nevertheless vivid fashion maintained that the processes of nature were obscure to us since we observed only a succession of appearances; but ourselves we knew by introspection. Only God, who made nature, could understand her processes in the way in which we understood our own creative acts. For only he understands something perfectly who creates it bit by bit – since to make and know what one is making, and how, is the most pellucid sort of understanding; I can explain mathematics perfectly because I make the moves myself. Later generations of 'historicists' give instances of games such as chess or cards where I understand everything, where everything is clear because I make it happen in accordance with my own will, as I choose – I or others like me with whom I can identify myself, who have themselves invented the rules – and I understand perfectly only that which I myself invent, make, or could have made.

It is at this point that Vico takes his boldest and most original step. History is intelligible as material bodies – nature – are not, for history is an act of human experience. Trees and stones may persist in time but are not said to have a history. And the experience of one body of men is something homogeneous with the experience of any other, for that is what is meant by calling men by that name – that their experiences cannot be totally different. I understand my parents' or my ancestors' reactions, thoughts, desires because I am a thinking, desiring, reacting being and can imaginatively place myself in the situation of other men. When, therefore, historians speak to me of the past, they are describing what men did and suffered, thought and willed, and I understand how it might have been so, for I might myself have been in the place of the men described. But I can never have been in the place of a rock or a tree, and so nothing Descartes can tell me about their constitution is intelligible to me in that intimate sense in which the thoughts or passions or ambitions of others are intelligible.

Vico now goes further. Men are made what they are not merely by the influence of physical environment, although he recognises the strength of this, but by their relations, conscious or semi-conscious or almost totally unconscious, to other members of their group. It is a sophisticated thing, and late in human development, to be able to articulate one's thoughts into wishes in clear words adapted to the purpose. In previous ages, before human languages had become as differentiated and specialised as they later became, men expressed their hopes and fears, their desires and images of reality, in myths, in works of art, in dances and religious rites and social customs. Instead of looking upon the fables and customs of the ancients as so much unintelligible mumbo-jumbo on the part of primitive or savage peoples, the true historian will perceive in them the richest possible source for the understanding of the psychical states, hardly perhaps to be dignified by the title of views or opinions – the attitudes to life of primitive societies.

It was not only in mythology and ritual that this evidence lay buried, but in language itself. The words, the symbols which men used, the ways in which they formed them, the structures of their sentences, the types of sounds, the morphology and grammar, which have hitherto formed the object of dry, mechanical, antiquarian accumulation, expressed, because they were the vehicles of – and more than vehicles, identical with – the thoughts and wishes and attitudes which men entertained towards themselves or one another. The early languages – epics and folk-tales – were fantasies which conveyed the ways in which men pictured life to themselves and others. Men sang before they spoke and spoke rhythmically and poetically before they spoke in prose. Songs and poetry, rhythmical movements for the dance, the syntax of a sentence, the similes and analogies, the metaphors buried in language and in primitive rites, in stylised behaviour of every kind, were not merely evidence for, but themselves the direct expression of, the *Weltanschauung* of the time. We understood what our ancestors were trying to say because they were our ancestors and we were their descendants, not merely by some kind of organic development (that, rather than evolution, was Vico's central concept), but because there is a single, continuous consciousness which belongs to the human race taken as a whole, as a particular consciousness belongs to an individual, and each generation of men represents the growth of this total human consciousness as the different ages of an individual represent his growth, and we understand the past of the human race as a man understands his own individual past, by a kind of collective cultural memory, by an awareness more or less dim, but capable of being stimulated by the use of imagination and the discovery of concrete evidence, of the condition from which we emerged, stretching into the most distant past, to the moment when, as Vico, being a pious Catholic, believed, the Lord first breathed life into the body of the first creative man.

It is difficult to overpraise Vico's originality when we remind ourselves of the time at which he lived. Descartes was condemning history as incapable of precise deductive formulation, and therefore in the end nothing but a collection of old wives' tales. Grotius and Pufendorf were trying to formulate those permanent a priori principles of indestructible natural law which were the same for all men at all times in all places, and from which all rational legislation should be deduced, as the physicists were deducing the constitution of the world from self-evident propositions revealed by natural light to natural reason. Even so relatively historical a theologian as Bossuet expounded a vision of history as a gradual unfolding of his divine plan by a rational deity, all parts of which were interconnected by logical relationships and occurred in time only because of the finite nature of man, who could perceive them, at an empirical level, only as an illusory succession of events whose inner pattern was a timeless whole in the mind of God – a doctrine of rational development similar to that of Leibniz, save that Bossuet emphasised the medieval doctrine of an actual hierarchy whereby everything in the universe belonged to an order subordinate to the next highest order, and kings were mortal gods set over the social order with the same authority that God exercised over the universe. Hobbes tried to derive the principles of politics from those of physics and to explain institutions, without regard to historical change, as ever-recurrent identical effects proceeding from identical causes. Spinoza regarded history as largely a product of human failure to grasp the permanent rational principles which could completely explain why everything was as it was, a science which could have been attained by anyone of sufficiently powerful intellect at any time, but owing to human fallibility and vanity and emotional instability was revealed, and that very partially and fitfully, only to the great philosophers, isolated from each other in time and space, all of whom perceived aspects of the same truth. Even such enlightened men as Bayle and Saint-Evremond looked to history at most to provide examples to encourage or deter the men of their time from this or that belief or way of life.

In this atmosphere, so deeply unpropitious to historicism of any kind, Vico, apparently by his own efforts, in the course of a thoroughly unsuccessful career as a Neapolitan literary hack and lecturer, humiliated by his patrons and appreciated only for his most trivial accomplishments, managed to formulate a view of history which he presented clumsily and obscurely but himself knew to be derived from an insight of genius. This insight consisted in perceiving that the institutions and thoughts and acts of a given generation are the products of the interplay of specifically social forces; that nothing in the lives of men is wholly unrelated to every other element in the lives of these men and of other men who form with them an organised human society; that from grammatical forms it is possible to gain an understanding of the economic life of a country, because certain words are likely to come into being only in response to certain social needs, which in their turn arise only at a certain stage of political or economic or social growth on the part of a given society.

Vico was, of course, not born fully armed from the head of Pallas Athene. He was a child of his time; he too spoke of history as useful because of its moral lessons, because it taught us what to do and what to avoid, and stressed the spiritual as against the material factors which affect men, to confute the materialists and the atheists to the greater glory of the only true Church. In these respects any pious Christian theorist seeking to refute the new materialism and atomism used the same arguments, whether he was a Cambridge Platonist or an Anglican teleologist or a Jesuit logician. What is truly original in Vico is the notion that to understand something is to understand the way in which it came to be what it is, and the way in which it is related by relations other than logical necessity or mere compresence with other developing things, together with which it forms a single evolving pattern; that this is more easily grasped in the case of human experience, because the student, who is himself a human being, can imaginatively grasp the course of the evolution, both social and individual, of other human beings better than whatever it is that causes changes in nature; that the system of causal connections which we attribute to nature is something with which we are not directly acquainted in the way that we are with motives and intentions and policies, which are the springs of our actions; and that therefore history, which is the product of human attitudes and motives, is transparent to us in some sense in which nature remains opaque; that human history is made by human beings by their voluntary and involuntary relations with each other and with nature, and that we are, as it were, on the inside of this process, ourselves the makers; that such monuments and antiquities as we possess by way of records of ways in which men spoke or thought or served their gods or celebrated, took their pleasures or solemnised various public and private undertakings, should be studied not as geometry or astronomy must needs be studied – inductively, which is but second best, a long way round where direct acquaintance cannot be had – but as we would try to discover facts for our own autobiographies or the biographies of others, where our criteria of and methods of establishing truth and probability, what is possible, important, trivial, permanent or ephemeral, come to us from our intimate knowledge of ourselves, of what it is to be a human being, to know, to want, to feel, to learn, strive, suffer, to love and hate, and engage in all the various activities in which the lives of families or sects or towns or countries or entire cultures consist.

By way of illustrating the depth of Vico's conception, we need mention only his treatment of mythology as a symbolic way of representing the world, both facts and values, to ourselves, which grew insensibly among primitive men; his adumbrations of class struggles as a major factor in historical development, and the evidence for these in the religious practices or etymological structure of language; the emphasis on language as perhaps the most characteristic example of a social institution dependent for its growth on nothing so artificial as the Social Contract, and reflecting in its very formation the complex, semi-conscious life of cultures taken as 'organisms', of which individuals are almost – Vico does not go so far as this himself – abstractions, limbs separable in thought but not in reality.

Whether Montesquieu read him or not, his own historical relativism and view that men are as they are because of differences of material conditions or education or national character, sensible, original and interesting as it is, is greatly inferior to Vico in depth and boldness of conception. The contrast between the intelligibility of history, because we make it – for we can understand thoroughly only what we make ourselves, and not what is thrust upon us from 'outside', ready-made, as it were – and the impenetrability of nature is an imaginative step far removed from the sober and milder metaphysical Montesquieu. Yet the mysterious 'relationships of things' to which human institutions must be made to correspond if they are to work is certainly something akin to the spiritual progress of mankind, the collective experience of an entire society – of which Vico speaks so eloquently – as its members develop not only technological weapons but arts, sciences and 'ideologies' in response to both environment and one another.

Vico conceived human history as a process whereby the immortal souls of men sought to attain unity with their Creator

and Great Prototype, but his theology need not concern us. It is
not this any more than Herder's similar view that is the foundation
of his great claim. We need perhaps add no more than that Vico
laid the foundations not merely of modern comparative ethnolo-
gical, anthropological, philological and related sciences, but discovered something about historical method – about the difference
between the way in which botanists and historians or philologists
reach their most illuminating conclusions – which has transformed
thought about these subjects.

Vico's *New Science*, in its several versions, lay unread until a
Neapolitan Jurist, Cuoco, brought it to the attention of the
philosophical world towards the end of the eighteenth century. It
is possible that Galiani brought it to the attention of his friends
among the Encyclopaedists in Paris some decades before that, and
that Herder derived something from it – and perhaps even that the
great Greek scholar Wolff owes his view that Homer was not a
single author but the epitome of a mass of popular epic poetry, the
fruit of a culture rather than a single individual, to Vico's
remarkable suggestions on this subject, and that Niebuhr and
Savigny owe more than they care to acknowledge to the echoes of
Vico's views on Roman history and the historical development of
laws. But these are merely conjectures. Vico's nineteenth-century
reputation was made by Michelet, who derived from him the
notion of history as something made by man for himself out of and
against recalcitrant nature, and he saluted him in a celebrated essay
as the first of those who perceived history as the story not of the
fate of men as passive entities played upon by external forces, but
of the active endeavours of men, united in classes and nations and
civilisations, to create their life in the light of ideals which they
have themselves fashioned for themselves in the long process of
struggling to realise themselves in accordance with an inner force –
an energetic impulse of self-assertion which cannot ever be
extinguished.

However, long before 1825, when Michelet published to the
world his remarkable discovery, the conception of impersonal
forces – history, 'the people', humanity, national or religious
tradition – as being factors more powerful than individual wills or
artificial compacts in influencing human lives, and as alone
justifying as well as causing human actions, began to grow and
dominate Western thought.

## *Herder*

The greatest name in the history of this movement is that of Herder, who in vague but eloquent and at times moving German prose spoke of the history of humanity as being not a mere causal sequence of rigidly determined events, each external to one another, but as a process similar to that of the creation of a work of art. Vico was a pious Catholic professor of rhetoric and Herder was a Lutheran pastor, but both were deeply devout men and believed in God as the personal creator of the universe. For Herder, history was similar to the planting of seeds in the ground by the sower, or the painting of a picture by an artist. The laws which determined these processes are the laws of the 'inner' life. Anyone who has ever engaged in any creative process knows what it is to be dominated by the inner ideal to the realisation of which everything is subordinated; to be in that inspired condition in which the elements which combine into the final work of art do so not in obedience to some mechanical law nor in a haphazard manner, obeying neither blind necessity nor blind chance, but because of the peculiar principle whereby each element is seen to be indispensable to every other, and to the pattern of the whole, which cannot be reduced to explicit, logically organised categories. Herder rejected Kant's dualism of the causally determined world of appearance and the world of freedom and rational purposes, of which Schiller had made so much, because it offended against his vision of the universe as a single growing whole in which the seeds planted by God – individual souls, the spirit of human institutions, societies, Churches, artistic movements – all developed in accordance with an inner purpose for which it had been created.

Herder's originality consists in denying human uniformity. He maintained that the diversity of human individuals and societies, which no one could deny, could not be explained on the assumption that an entity existed in nature called man which could be taken as sufficiently uniform to afford data for a natural science which could in theory deduce every fact about the past, present and future, social and individual alike, given sufficient factual evidence – evidence as adequate as, say, that which chemists or physicists possess or would clearly one day possess in their field. The data from which such would-be sociologists sought to explain human diversity were relatively constant – neither climate nor soil, human organs or material needs, had altered appreciably during the millennia of human existence, yet the differences between human societies were great, and the history of, say, art was scarcely deducible from anatomical or geographical data. Herder maintained that anyone with eyes to see could perceive morphological differences between cultures, could see that there was something that was common to German music, German painting, the political outlook and general attitude to life of Germans of any given period – a common spirit which made it recognisably German and different from everything which was characteristic of the French or the Italians; just as everything that was typical of the eighteenth century differed in certain sharp recognisable ways from what was typical of classical Greece or Rome or Judaea.

The ideal of the German Enlightenment, whereby anything that was good or true or beautiful could be discovered by anyone at any time and introduced into any society simply in virtue of its own intrinsic value – so that the Roman art discovered by Winckelmann (for all that he supposed it to be that of classical Greece) could act as a suitable model for modern men – was instinctively recognised to be false. Every people had an inner spirit of its own – its own *Volksgeist* – which moulded its outlook and conditioned the expression of that outlook into the concrete shape which it assumed. What is so dear to a German about the sounds and shapes of German words and letters is not merely the fact that they are familiar, that his ancestors before him have expressed their thoughts in them, but the fact that they uniquely convey the German attitude to the world – the very handwriting, the accents upon the words, and in a far larger way the early poetry and art of a people are what they are because they flow from and are the outer expression of a feeling and a vision which are the peculiar contribution of each historical people to the sum total of human civilisation. The customs of a people, its primitive poetry, all that is the 'natural' expression of its inner spirit is never vulgar, always moving and true, because it is felt to convey a genuine vision of life, to be the genuine fulfilment of the personality of a particular people – a personality which is sometimes called its culture.

Cultures differ much as individuals do. They have a peculiar physiognomy of their own, and when we unhesitatingly attribute a particular song, philosophical thought or building to a particular nation, it is because we are classifying not in accordance with some abstract theory invented by the French philosophers – the *philosophes* – whereby such and such material conditions cannot but produce such and such works of art or thought or action, but because we have a sense of inner relevance which relates everything which flows from that common outlook which is the historical pattern that makes peoples what they are – gives them their individual flavour – and at once shapes and justifies what is best in everything they do. It is idle to explain one's feeling of loyalty to one's community by maintaining that it is a utilitarian calculation of mutual benefit; and to attempt to eradicate it in favour of some utilitarian arrangement unconnected with a particular past and with the memories and outlook of a given society is at once unpractical – and will not survive – and shocks the moral sensibilities of the patriotic members of the society.

What is loyalty? What is patriotism? For Herder it is neither the expectation of benefit from the mutual aid given to each other by members of a community, nor a mere blind impulse towards solidarity which cannot be explained at all except, it may be, by physiologists or zoologists. It is the conception of the fact, on the part of an individual, that he 'belongs' to a particular culture and past and place and time and tradition; that he is part and parcel of a network of relationships which is not a haphazard heap, a mere togetherness of elements which might but for some causal accident have occurred in some other order or in no order at all, but stands to his surroundings in some such relation as that which a note in music has to the total harmony, the creation of which alone makes a given sound significant and necessary. Loyalty for Herder is the recognition that one's purposes are an intrinsic element in a larger pattern, the other constituents of which are the acts and purposes of other human beings in the present and the past and the future. Only when I know how far and in what way my life and acts and words 'hang together', contribute to the total stream of the social life of my community, can I ever discover any value in them for myself; and upon deeper reflection I find that I want what I want and am what I am because in my nature I express – and cannot but express – aspirations, hopes, fears, attitudes to life which are intelligible – which I can justify if challenged – only because I know them to be bound up with the past of the society from which I myself emerge and which has made me as I am. This emergence from and continuity with the past, this feeling that I am an intrinsic member of a specific culture and not of all the other cultures, however much I may admire them, is not the perception of some *de facto* causal relation so much as the kind of connection which one part of a work of art has with another, which the stages of an organic development have with each other, the kind of unity which only patterns have, the relation not of cause to effect but of means to ends, of the potential to the actual, which men experience, for instance, in the process of learning, when the gradual increase of knowledge and understanding at once conditions and justifies the particular steps through which the learner goes in the process of illumination.

It is this sense of direction, which only the sense of purpose can give – an inner purpose which the sense of belonging to a movement or a religion or a society gives to its members – that can explain such phenomena as loyalty, devotion to a cause, or pride in one's city or nation or civilisation. A German can develop only along German lines, a Frenchman only along French ones. No doubt they can be transplanted, but the sense of being on alien soil which a man born in one culture has if shifted to another cannot be explained by mere absence of knowledge on his part of his new surroundings, easily cured by a course of instruction. A plant can flourish only in a soil peculiarly native to it; the full development of the faculties of an individual can occur only in surroundings in which those faculties interlace with what is cognate with and congenial to them.

Herder denounces cosmopolitanism as a false ideal and man in general as a hollow abstraction. The course of history cannot be explained except by those who understand that the peculiar sets of characteristics which serve to define cultures and peoples and to distinguish them from one another are related to each other by intimate bonds and can be understood only when they are seen to form a unique harmony, to be realising in their totality a unique purpose. Each piece has been endowed by history or by God with a particular function to perform, and its characteristics are those characteristics which enable that and not some other function to be performed with unique success, and the duty of a man is in the first place to understand to what place he has been assigned in the world, to what people he belongs, combination and cooperation with what men will bring out most fully his and their natural endowments.

For Herder every *Volk* has a mission, a peculiar contribution which it is uniquely equipped to perform. He is a patriotic German, but still sufficiently a child of the eighteenth century not to indulge in nationalistic megalomania. Every people has its own sacred task to perform and can afford to respect the special values and ways of life of one another, even if it cannot share in them: the goal is the self-realisation of all the peoples on the basis of mutual respect, and above all love for one another, for it is love alone which reveals the inner ideals of others, ideals which have as great a right to consideration as my own. For Kant's individuals, Herder substitutes peoples or cultures; values, ideals, ultimate aims are the patterns of life whose realisation is a continuing historical culture. They are absolute and sacred because they represent the aspirations of cultures, because they are the goals which the spirit of the people has generated, has proposed to itself, and the only absolute duty is that which develops the true potentialities of human beings.

The notion of an isolated human being is a vicious abstraction, for all human beings are as they are and act as they do because they are children of a historical process and find themselves from birth already involved in certain concrete relations to one another which are but the translation into material terms of the inner spiritual forces which create the great units of history – the peoples. As for great men, they are those who understand their situation best, those who understand the purposes of the society into which they have been born; partly by a species of inspired vision granted to very few, partly by the knowledge which can be gained from studying the antiquities of a society – the roots of its life, the ancient traditions, the social customs and religious ceremonies, the songs and poetry, the painting and thought, above all the language of the early days – the youth of the people – which are the most revealing expressions of its deepest tendencies, of its purposes and its temperament, of its outlook and its ways of life, which form one seamless whole, for that is the pattern of history, the ways in which in fact the human character is moulded, human ideals born, the process which at once supplies the conditions and the ideals which make and always will make men what they are.

This *Volksgeist*, the ultimate difference of pattern between social wholes, audible only to the spiritual ear, which alone perceives the differing historical tones which are the differences of human cultures, sets a limit upon the malleability of human nature. A Frenchman cannot be made to do what a German does by nature, and should not be. Besides natural characteristics – physical strength, intellectual acumen – there are national ones, which if anything are even more ultimate. Hence the faith which social planners place in the possibility of changing human beings by changing their environment or education is Utopian. The pattern of the orchestra prevents a flute from being transformed into a violin – to each culture its own tone, its own range of possibilities, its own type of musical composition. One group of instruments may be as valuable as another and as indispensable to the harmony of the whole, but the differences are at least as important as the similarities.

The specific quality of all that members of one culture feel and know and do comes out most vividly in contrast with the very dissimilar products of another. This contrast need not result in tensions or wars. In Herder's benevolent and optimistic view everything is reconcilable. God in his goodness has so created men that if they only realise themselves along their own inner natural grain – within the framework of their own tradition or their own native soil, responding to the voices of their own unique past – they will fit into that ultimate harmony which is taken for granted by him as much as it is by Condorcet or Adam Smith or the other thinkers who suppose that true values cannot in principle ever contradict each other. Nevertheless, to each people its own unique and separate function, which the whole of its history progressively reveals and hallows.

This view differs from that, for example, of Burke, in that it lays its principal emphasis not on the facts themselves of growth and uniqueness but upon the goals, the valuable results, of adapting oneself to the patterns innate in a given culture; and attempts to create a new science of history by insisting in far more explicit language, and with far more empirical evidence than Vico, on the light to be obtained, in the study of one manifestation of the national genius, from the study of other manifestations of the life of the same people, or of the interconnection of all the manifestations of a single society. The moral of this is to lower the barriers between the various arts and sciences. If the study of French music has less to teach us about the development of German music, the study of German painting has more to teach us on this topic than the cosmopolitans had supposed. For Burke, the justification of this or that form of political life lies in the very fact that it has grown by insensible stages from some earlier form, that it is the product of the many minute causes obscurely combining to produce a particular form of development – in the very idea of growth itself, of spontaneity as against artificiality, of instinct against reason and calculation, of faith and a sense of the past against the fanciful inventions or petty reckonings of narrow specialists blind to the real wants of peoples, the strength and value of their non-rational natures. Herder worships spontaneity, growth, the past no less passionately, but sees the ultimate source of justification, both moral and political, not in the mere fact of growth or spontaneity *per se*, but in the fact that they exemplify the untrammelled pursuit of that ideal which is native to separate civilisations or peoples, and towards which the bursts of spontaneity and inspiration which inform the works of genius of conscious artists and anonymous popular art equally are so many steps – so many stages in the inevitable ascent to universal freedom and universal good.

Politically Herder's ideal is a free association of spontaneously born associations, the expressions of the 'folk spirit' as it embodies itself following its own inner laws in this or that institution peculiar to the genius of a particular people. Herder is the founder of the worship of ancient rites and customs, of folk-dancing and popular ballads, of the free, unfettered expression of the inner national spirit with which Schiller became so strongly infected, and which led in its turn to the typically German youth movements and various, sometimes grotesquely exaggerated, attempts to commune with the ancient Germanic spirit wherever that dark force might be thought to be still discoverable. But he also gave a very powerful impulse not only to the careful study of all social institutions, and in particular to comparative philology, but also to that form of romantic nationalism which looked everywhere for the sources – the most vivid expressions – of its inner essence. The lost paradise was sought everywhere: in the Middle Ages and in classical antiquity, in the bosom of nature and in mystical experience, in popular festivals and in Masonic lodges, in the early experiences of childhood and the art of primitive savages, in the sacred wisdom concealed in fairy tales or ancient legends or exotic languages – everywhere but in the artificial constructions of men, whether the enlightened scientists congregated in Paris or the rigid bureaucrats who were conducting the affairs of the German principalities.

Politically Herder's philosophy was hostile to State authority because the latter was a mechanical confining of the free human spirit, because it enacted laws and enforced obedience to rules which did not and could not take account of the rich differings of the human spirit in all its multitudinous aspects, because it presupposed a uniformity among men, treated them as if their legal or political purposes were similar, at least within the confines of the estates or ranks into which it graded them. And this was in itself a falsification of the facts, since the productiveness of a culture rested upon the greatest possible diversity of those who carried it within them, within the unifying pattern of the culture. No doubt laws were indispensable for the conduct of life among men who were imperfect, and through folly or vice might do each other harm and break each other's powers. Doubtless also the particular forms of government, unless crudely imposed from outside by a regardless conqueror, were themselves the outgrowth of the national spirit, like every other institution of the people. Nevertheless, in so far as the laws and their execution were rigidly enforced and not allowed to develop further in that spontaneous striving after the inner ideal which was alone creative and valuable, they were a chain upon human effort, an imprisonment of a free human being; and their authority should therefore be reduced to the minimum compatible with the preservation of public order and security.

Burke was sympathetic enough to Herder's anti-utilitarianism and anti-cosmopolitanism, but reached very different conclusions. For Herder, revolution might be a spontaneous outburst of creative energy, a flash of the genius of the *Volk*, an immense leap forward in the direction of self-realisation, the attempt to make concrete some binding moral and political revelation which the people from the depths of its 'folk soul' had nurtured unconsciously during many years of apparent calm or political oppression. For Burke, any break with the past was wrong as such and meant the gratuitous rejection of all the accumulated wisdom of the race, all those prejudices and superstitions which were but beliefs tested in the furnace of actual experience, a blind opposition to the only final political authority there could be – the inheritance of the past, the bonds with our ancestors, the indissoluble union between the quick and the dead, the great society which, because the future was not yet, could look only to the past for light about how to live.[1] Burke detested French theories not only because they were revolutionary, but also because they were a priori, because they had no foundation in actual human experience, because they took no account of how human societies lived and changed, paid no

[1] See p. 6 above, note 1.

heed to those actual values by which men lived and, being organised as they were and descended as they were, could not but believe in.

In Herder, there is a powerful element of the a priori – the passionate conviction that exceptionally gifted persons can discern not merely the voice of the past, for which perhaps only piety, historical erudition and sensitiveness to the contour of the culture are sufficient, but the voice of the future, too, of history about to burst the bonds of the present, take a new direction. Always and everywhere he looked for evidences of new social forms developing from the old, of the inexhaustible creative spirit taking on new and astonishing and, to his enchanted eye, more and more perfect guises. Hence, while Herder in one sense laid the foundations of romantic conservatism, with his hostility to anything that went against the pre-established pattern of the spirit of a given people, and his doctrine of self-immersion in the intellectual climate of your town or country, of your own times, your own place in the scheme of things, in order to be identified with the social currents which, if you were a true son of your people, echoed in your own heart and soul too; yet, on the other hand, he inspired the desire for romantic self-assertion, for the breaking down of obsolete barriers, for the spontaneous self-realisation of uncorrupted human nature, for the bold imposition of one's German will, if one is a German, even as Caesar was great because he imposed his Roman will upon his environment; and thus led directly to Fichte's early Jacobinism, his rhapsodic acceptance of the great act of liberation constituted by the French Revolution, which most truly expressed the deep French passion for liberty and equality and fraternity – the historic mission of the Gauls or the Franks.

Herder's sermons led equally to the apolitical attitudes of those German romantic poets and artists who found freedom only in some region free from the fetters of daily life and the arbitrary oppression of kings and governments and legal systems, in mystical self-absorption, in the pursuit of the blue flower which the common eye cannot see, the worship of night and death and destruction which alone frees the soul from its earthly bonds and alone cuts through the Gordian knots, the moral and intellectual contradictions, which torment the artist and compel him to fly for freedom to distant regions – the remote ages, or the exotic lands of the East, or unearthly fantasies whereby alone he can say his word and find peace. Ultimately, too, of course, his doctrine led not

merely to the anti-political attitudes of those anarchists – both
pessimists and optimists – in whom Germany appeared particularly
rich, who defied and denounced all authority, and in particular all
political and religious authority, as a monstrous tyranny over
human freedom, and called for the unleashing of the elemental
forces confined, as Bakunin held, in the dormant popular masses,
or of the will to power of the superman whom Nietzsche described
in language which has roots in the German tradition so genuine
and lasting that even the mild Herder could scarcely denounce it as
either artificial or of unwanted foreign origin.

Herder also influenced Schelling and the doctrine of the creative
individual expressing the world spirit in its national form.
Schelling's doctrine of religion as mythology, and true precisely
because it is a mythology, because only by myths can esoteric
truths far above the level of natural science and common-sense
facts be made to attack the individual consciousness with the
proper violent afflatus; his irrationalism, too, and heroic theory of
government – romantic Fascism, according to which the State is a
work of art, and the leader as its fashioner justifies his acts like the
artist, who is beyond and against conventional morality or the
concepts of good and evil, by the light of which less gifted men live
out their lives, and seeks to raise the people to his own level and
not to be blamed if in this process his subjects, unused to and
resisting such vivisection, cry out against what *prima facie* appears
violent cruelty and oppression – all this proceeds from Herder's
nationalism and 'spontaneity' also.

Once more the concept of freedom as Herder appears to use it is
very remote from anything meant by it in the Anglo-Saxon
tradition. The theory of the profound differences of cultures and
the unique meanings which words acquire in a national tradition is
borne out by the distance which separates the meanings of this
fateful word. Certainly the liberty on the lips of the demonstrating
bands of students and bourgeois whipped into patriotic fury by
Father Jahn or the poet Arndt may have sprung from some deep
layer of German feeling which Herder had incautiously uncovered.
It bore little recognisable resemblance to the ideals of civilised men
in France or England or America of this time. But apart from their
importance in stirring the emotions, Herder's ideas have had a
decisive influence in the development of critical thought in Europe,
both historical and aesthetic. His conception of human development has as its centre the metaphysical notion of the *Volksgeist* as

the active source of the entire material and spiritual life of the individuals who compose the *Volk*, and who are effective or ineffective in direct proportion to the adequacy with which they express and understand this central force. The notion of impalpable causes of observable effects – of the objective inner spirit, not perceptible to the senses or the normal methods of investigation, whether as practised in science or in daily life – is a notion more readily accepted in an age when theology was becoming secularised but, in the form of metaphysics, retained all its non-empirical attributes, than in the present time, when the tendency to account for the content of the external world by invoking intangible but omnipotent entities, neither describable in terms of, nor capable of being inferred by, any normal methods of inference from the characteristics of the external world, is no longer taken seriously as a method of explanation by scientists or philosophers.

Nevertheless the rejection of metaphysical explanations as such has tended to blind modern thinkers to the depth and originality of the fundamental ideas, often expressed in obscurely and wildly fanciful terms, of the German metaphysicians of the romantic period. Herder was virtually the first thinker to draw attention to the fact that what might be called group patterns existed and were discernible in human behaviour: that it is possible to identify works of art or political and social forms or the habits of entire communities as possessing certain common patterns which belong to the behaviour of groups and not of individuals; that to say, whether truly or falsely, of the Germans that they were a young and vigorous people with a peculiar genius for spontaneous spiritual self-expression, which took the form of music and philosophy rather than painting or epic poetry, could not be analysed into statements about individual Germans, but was a description of the collective properties of the German people as a whole, historically surveyed. Similarly, when the historical jurists[1] – Hugo, Savigny and their disciples – declared that law was neither on the one hand an approximation to something called natural law, discernible by a special a priori type of vision alone, for that was clearly a figment; nor based upon the arbitrary commands of individual rulers, for that, once natural and divine rights had been seen through, no longer carried authority; but that it derived from the evolving historical relationships which men in fact had with

[1] {Hist. School.}

one another – from the actual ways in which men behaved, and thought it right to behave, both within communities and as communal wholes, vis-à-vis each other – and that this elaborate network of relationships was neither something analysable into conscious utilitarian arrangements nor behaviour deducible from what could be discovered about the physical and physiological and anatomical habit of individuals, but could be understood only in the way in which a member of a family understood the pattern of family life of which he was himself a part, and accepted the rules of such a life, neither because of its deducibility from abstract principles nor because it had been ordered by a specific superior, but because to accept these rules in some measure was to lead that kind of life, and this was part of the natural habits and outlook and morality of those who constituted the family; when this was said, ideas were uttered which can scarcely be conceived but for the transformation of the entire field of history and social relations by Herder.

The historical jurists, the metaphysical philosophers, the critics of art and religion spoke of the varieties of human experience as the self-expression of the infinitely various spirit of the nation, or of the people, or of history, or of the universe. And this has misled many into rejecting this entire way of thinking as a worthless metaphysical fantasy. But whatever its vices as a piece of metaphysical architecture, the vehicle in which the romantics expressed their thoughts must not blind us to the fact that they used such terms as 'the spirit' or 'the absolute', to some degree at least, to convey the unity of social and historical patterns, the interconnection between apparently widely different aspects of human life, the existence of characteristics which apply not to individuals but only to collections of them, and whose presence makes us speak of such collections as wholes or systems or organisms rather than mere heaps or aggregates. Because there was no vocabulary to express such notions as those of the emergence of patterns in the lives of individuals or groups analogous to those to be found in works of art – or of interconnections between the characteristics of processes or activities which, while widely divergent in purpose, appear to throw light upon one another, such as those of, let us say, music and architecture of a given period – they tended to express them by speaking of emanations of the world spirit; tended, that is, to attribute the only type of unity which to them was relevant – that of the human personality – in order to express the idea of unity at all. But because they did this we must not lose sight of the fact that it needed doing; that the eighteenth-century canons of reason, either inductive or deductive, either a priori or a posteriori, failed to explain the march of events; that analysis of everything into its uniform constituent atoms, as recommended by Descartes and later by Helvétius and the German Enlightenment, a method of analysis which did indeed lead to magnificent triumphs in the natural sciences and mathematics, and did expose and refute a great many confused metaphysical and theological claims to territory in which they spread only darkness, did on the other hand prevent description and examination of the arts, of social life, of history in the terms which alone fitted these inexact disciplines – in terms of patterns of growth, differences of regional, national and historical characteristics, the occurrence of re-lationships between human beings and their environment of which they might be scarcely conscious, but without the assumption of which the emergence of primitive art and institutions – the anonymous epics or social, judicial and religious arrangements later attributed to mythological founders – could scarcely be accounted for.

If the metaphysical language of Herder and Schiller and Fichte and Schelling and the historical jurists, in so far as possible, is translated into a clearer and more empirical language, in terms of which it is possible to describe the world in language more sensitive to its contours than the over-simple, militantly crude analyses of eighteenth- and nineteenth-century materialism, it will be found that these thinkers showed critical and historical insight of great depth and range. Because everything which can be touched and seen and weighed should be so treated in the interests of precision and science, and because dark metaphysical generalisa-tions were too often substituted for these careful labours, with disastrous results, it does not follow that there are not in the world imponderables and impalpables and that these do not need to be spoken of in terms whereby their existence and importance may be brought out; and because societies are in fact not independent entities over and above the individuals which compose them any more than symphonies are independent entities over and above the sounds of which they consist, and to attribute independent personality to them, as Rousseau began to do, and as Hegel certainly did, was not merely a fallacy but one which has done a great deal of damage both to the thoughts of men and to their relations with one another, it does not follow that societies do not resemble symphonies in that both possess collective characteristics which the individuals or isolated sounds do not possess – pattern qualities, Gestalts – and which are perhaps their most essential characteristics, in virtue of which alone they are of interest and importance. The deliberate denial of these by fanatical or self-blinded positivists causes their audiences to feel that something familiar, important and valuable – the heart of the matter – has been left out of their analyses, and makes them fly to the nearest metaphysical or theological practitioner who does at least seem to understand their need and minister to it as best he can. Certainly those who read in the works of Herder or his many conscious and unconscious disciples that the community was an indissoluble whole of persons seeking to serve a common goal, bound by impalpable relations of language and kinship and blood, and a common soil and common experience for many centuries, seeking to realise a form of life which alone they understood and loved and felt to be their own, for the survival of which they were prepared if need be to die, cannot be blamed if they found that such formulations came closer to their own experience than anything they might hear from Bentham or Spencer or Russell about the rational purposes of society, its use as an instrument for the provision of common benefits and the prevention of social collisions, miseries and injustices between individuals, each bent on realising his own purposes, beyond which sphere social control should be severely curbed. Liberals and anarchists may well be right, and the romantic metaphysicians may be the originators of the triumph of irrationalism in our day, but the latter did as the former did not – they described the facts of both social life and history, and of everything in the life of the individual which can broadly be called creative or inventive, with a subtlety and depth of imagination, and a use of dangerous but illuminating simile and metaphor, which made them seem, as indeed to some degree they were, profounder thinkers than their opponents. To ignore or decry their achievement is therefore as unjust and philistine as it is and has been unwise and dangerous: the discovery and propagation of knowledge are valuable in themselves, and their supression leads to the satisfaction of the hunger for knowledge in inadequate and socially destructive ways.

## Hegel

If Herder gave a more satisfactory explanation of what it is that moves human beings when they hear the songs of their country or see its flag or feel themselves a part of something which they describe as being larger than themselves – a class, a nation, a historical tradition; if Fichte cast a powerful if fitful light upon the notion of volition – imposing one's will, realising ideals conceived in terms of realising some 'inner' real self, above all the sense of election, of being dedicated to a mission against whatever odds, in virtue of blood or race or tradition or class or intellectual capacity, which gives one a moral right to hack a path against all obstacles, natural or human; if Rousseau first expounded the idea of liberty as the imposition upon oneself of a law derived from premises supplied by reason, which is common to all men and entitles any rational man to act on behalf of all others; if the scholastic tradition on the one hand and Vico on the other continued the tradition of the Greek philosophers in regarding change as development, in other words the gradual actualisation of potential, the coming into being according to laws intelligible to reason of something which had from the beginning been 'potentially' present in the circumstance which is changing – it was Hegel who combined these elements into a vast unitary system, rigid and elaborate in detail, which attempted to account for every aspect both of man and of nature, to give the final answer to every question which had hitherto perplexed or distracted men.

But it is only the political aspects of this gigantic metaphysic which concern us here. Hegel accepted the romantic notion that to explain a thing, to obtain knowledge of it, is to know the way in which it is developing as it is from its origins towards that final culmination which represents the purpose of or reason for its existence. Everything is in this sense to be explained historically. To know a thing or a process or a person is to understand the laws which make it behave as it does, and the proper philosophical insight will reveal that these laws are not those merely of endless repetition under identical circumstances, as represented by the natural sciences, but of a unique one-way progress from some utterly simple beginning – an undifferentiated whole, incapable of being described, because nothing in it can be contrasted with anything else – into differences and even contradictions; these differences split up and differentiate themselves further like cells in an organism. The process is not one of smooth progression, whereby the simple becomes gradually more complex, the bad becomes better, the stupid wiser, the brutal more humane, as represented by the seventeenth- and eighteenth-century liberal optimists. In order to explain why things do not for ever remain the same, why change occurs at all, Hegel adopts an idea to be found in Kant and Vico, an idea as old as the Greeks, whereby it is strife and struggle that cause movement – a perpetual conflict, which occurs at all levels of life, and in lifeless matter too causes each of the elements in the struggle to develop in the very act of seeking to overcome and outdo its opponent.

Every process, for Hegel, may be analysed into this condition of perpetual conflict: any analysis which regards any change as a smooth transition from one state to another is insufficient. A deeper insight will show that in every process there are to be found always two tendencies, one opposed to the other, one working against the other. From this tension of opposites working to destroy each other there is born movement, change, progress. Neither side wins in the struggle, each destroys the other in a kind of Pyrrhic victory, but from their reciprocal destruction there arises a third element in which whatever was needed by either aspect of the process is retained and transformed. This is the celebrated synthesis of the thesis and antithesis of which the Hegelian dialectic consists. The synthesis, however, in its turn, no sooner than it is created, bears the seeds of its own destruction within it in the form of its own antithesis, which enters into a life-and-death struggle with it, and ultimately destroys it, and itself too, in its turn leading to a 'higher' synthesis, and so on indefinitely. This process is not of course haphazard, but tends in a direction, that is, is conditioned to move in the direction it does by the 'inner purpose' of the whole world process – towards the progressive destruction of matter and the transformation of it into spirit.

In order to understand what Hegel intended to convey by this, despite all the darkness of his language, we must bear in mind firstly that he, like the Greeks and the schoolmen, conceived of change as the realisation on the part of the changing object of an inner plan; the plan having a logical structure like, say, the Euclidian system of geometry. Within a logical system it is possible to speak of the relation of ground to consequence. The axioms and rules of the Euclidian system, taken as a whole, logically entail the particular theorems which logically follow from them; in that sense it can be said that the ground is always larger and wider than its consequences, as the Euclidian system is larger and wider than, or logically prior to, the theory of Pythagoras, which is at once a part and a consequence of it, and as a portion of an architectural ground-plan is narrower than, contained in, entailed by, follows from the architect's plan as a whole. It is in this sense that the schoolmen conceived of the universe as the realisation in time of a timeless logical schema, ever present in the mind of the Great Architect – God himself.

One of Hume's most celebrated achievements consisted in divorcing these ideas, drawing a sharp line between a purely logical relation such as that of ground and consequence, and a spatio-temporal one between events such as that between cause and effect – the former being deducible by rational calculation from formally stated premises, the latter being founded upon observation of actual things and events, what happened with what or after what and under what conditions. In this sense the world of abstract theory and that of fact were kept sharply distinguished, and the relations of the former to the latter – of theory to practice, of formal schemata to the actual world as recorded by careful observation – became a separate problem for empiricists.

Hegel, in common with all other metaphysicians, denied or ignored this difference and regarded Hume's sense of cause and effect as a mere superficial classification of events in their temporal or spatial juxtaposition. A true account of the changing universe would represent everything which happens as happening according to logically inexorable laws, would represent them as not merely happening *de facto* but *de jure*, having to happen – as it were, being logically incapable of not happening any more than a triangle is logically capable of not having its angles equal to 180 degrees, given the Euclidian premises or 'grounds'.

Now if history is in this sense to be understood as a kind of logical system in which everything is strictly necessitated by everything else and nothing merely is but always must be what it is, mere observation of events in their casual succession or togetherness is not enough; and what is needed is a profounder insight, a special philosophical faculty for discerning necessities beneath the mere flow of experience. This meant that empirical history, the mere account of events – the lives of kings and great men, of wars and treaties – is a superficial activity which may describe but does not explain why what occurs occurs as it does.

This can be done only by relating whatever happens to the ultimate plan of the universe as a whole, just as an 'explanation' of a note of music or a part of an architectural design can be achieved only by showing the unique and inevitable need for it, and for nothing else, in the specific place which it occupies in the design of the whole, which in its turn is unique and must be as it is. Moreover, Hegel believed with Vico that history is ultimately the history of spiritual activity, not only because only that is intelligible which itself in some sense 'partakes of' the nature of the reason which enquires into it – if history were something other than reason it could not be apprehended or understood at all – but because the explanation of such relations as necessity, the 'must' between events or things, forms a logical category and not a natural one, in the sense of not being discoverable by the senses; so far Hume was right, but what this proved was not, as Hume supposed, that no 'explanation' of events was possible in the sense in which mathematics or logic were 'explicable', but on the contrary that the universe was 'explicable' only in so far as it partook of the nature of logic or other mental activity.

Hegel took as a premiss that all problems must be capable of true solutions and that the question 'Why do changes occur as they do?' is a genuine question, that unless the universe were like thought, like mental activity, like logic, it would not be properly explicable at all – we should be left face to face with 'mere brute facts' which we should have to accept without being able to tell why they were there as they were, what end they served, of what logical premisses they were the embodied consequences. It followed that the universe, if it was a rational system, capable of satisfying enquiring reason, must be mental or spiritual in character, must be the history of an evolving consciousness. This consciousness he calls sometimes the 'idea', sometimes the 'world spirit', sometimes God. In this sense he is a follower of Plato and Spinoza – in the sense, that is, of regarding everything in the universe as describable in rational terms, namely, in those ways which satisfy reason most closely, as a priori logical truths do, which, once known to be true, are true for ever and universally. And because Hume had made his successful attack upon the crude identification of factual with necessary truths, Hegel was forced to conclude that, if what was factual was to be represented as being necessary as well, it must be represented as being the only activity where necessity could be found – that is, as being logical, in other words mental or spiritual.

The universe is therefore a self-developing (for what else could develop it?) spiritual (otherwise it would not be connected by necessary relations) whole (for it is all there is). Its development is what spiritual development always is – self-clarification, progress from ignorance to knowledge, from unconscious to conscious to self-conscious; from darkness to light, from ignorance to observation and acquaintance with what there is, and from that to progressive grasp of why it must be as it must be and why it will be what it will be, why it cannot logically have been or be or be about to be anything other than what it was and is and will be. But just as thought, in that process of gaining clarity in knowledge, goes through the process of dialectical argument with itself or the thought of others, whereby it first frames an inadequate hypothesis or generalisation which claims to be the final answer to a problem, and is then duly opposed by another generalisation which contradicts it, itself claiming, with equal lack of right, to be the final answer; and from the conflict of these two some answer is born which retains whatever was valuable and partially true in the two previous mutually contradictory answers, itself being a more comprehensive and better answer than the two previous partial solutions, but still not perfect or final, and doomed to meet its own opponent and perish in battle with it, giving way to a higher 'generalisation' which in its turn absorbs what was true in the two previous contenders, and so on – this being the process of learning by trial and error, by argument, by disputation, by self-criticism, hypothesis succeeding hypothesis, world-view succeeding world-view, but each successor always superior to its predecessor, a steady increase in light – so in the material world of physical objects, and in the social and political and juridical worlds of human beings in their relations to each other, this is the principle of progress: in nature, the conflict of the elements; in human society, conflicts of individuals, competition of classes, wars of religion and of society.

Hegel believed that the progress from darkness to light, coincident as it was with the spiritual inner core of the universe (material objects, unconscious spirit; plants and animals more conscious, but not always self-conscious; great men conscious of themselves and of their age – of the stage reached in the self-consciousness of the absolute spirit which is identical with the universe), was not smooth and continuous, but punctuated by moments when the thesis and antithesis finally locked in mortal

conflict. At those moments leaps occurred from one level, that of
thesis and antithesis, to the higher level of the synthesis – the
phoenix which arose from the ashes of the previous contenders.
These leaps, when they occurred in the history of thought, were
those moments of illumination, the spiritual revolutions, which
occurred in the souls of the individuals or the outlooks of entire
civilisations. In the material world they took the form of conflicts,
wars, revolutions, which transformed the history of a people or a
continent by precipitating it from the level at which it previously
was to some new level which was a stage – an inevitable stage – in
its progress, in the growth of self-knowledge on the part of the
stuff of which the world is made, the spirit whose finite centres
were individual human beings.

This was a bold and extraordinary metaphysic and appeared to
Hegel and his followers to explain many things which had
previously proved puzzling. It explained the nature of evil, for this
was bound up with the necessity for conflict and destruction.
Unless the thesis which had had its day was destroyed, no advance
could occur, and while the destruction of a mere theory in the
development, say, of the science of biology might not be
accompanied by acute suffering – by more than intellectual
frustration on the part of the obsolete biologists left behind by
scientific innovators – the passing of a political or a social order,
which, being bound up with a certain stage in the realisation of the
spirit, with a particular outlook expressed in the arts, the sciences,
the moral, intellectual and personal habits and customs of a given
stage of civilisation, could only go down in a violent explosion
attending the final conflict of thesis and antithesis, would necessarily cause much bodily and spiritual suffering. The dialectic
necessarily contains 'negative moments' which embody the needful
destructive forces which kill the old to make way for the new.
These destructive moments may take the form of natural disasters –
the Lisbon earthquake which so disturbed the optimistic nature-
lovers of the eighteenth century – or brutal invaders who put entire
nations to the sword, or the destruction of whole classes by other
classes whom history is beckoning to play their allotted part in the
great cosmic drama upon the universal stage.

Hegel conceives of the universe as a kind of performance in
which individuals, classes, groups, nations are each called upon to
play their part before being destroyed by the next necessary actor
to be called in. If they are not philosophers and do not understand

that the 'idea' in its inevitable march towards self-consciousness necessitates these occurrences, they may never understand why it is that they are acting as they do. Hegel speaks of the 'cunning of reason',[1] whereby reason uses men or armies or societies for its own ends, unknown to its agents, who may think that they are acting for various selfish or altruistic motives, who may in their ignorance imagine they are pursuing various goals, but unless it is written in the book of reason that these goals are due to be realised, they will, for all the endeavours of the pursuers, remain unrealised. Hegel speaks of history as the 'slaughter-bench'[2] of humanity – as a process in which much that is considered beautiful, noble and good in its own day is destroyed, apparently senselessly, by forces considered wicked, unjust and brutal, which nevertheless reason makes use of for its own ends. These ends are impenetrable to all but the philosopher, who, because he understands himself and the progress of history, is thereby automatically an agent in its self-fulfilment, for increase in understanding *is* progress. Understanding is not merely a recording of events, for the events themselves are but the outer aspects of a spiritual process, and understanding, which is a spiritual act, by its own development automatically alters material reality – which is but an outer symptom – as well. The real actors of human history are ideas. The outer events – kings and governments, treaties and wars, economic struggles and the daily lives of peoples – are but the outer integument of ideas, the ripening of which, both in the minds of thinkers and in the deeds of men of action, sometimes proceeding smoothly but in the end always performing the revolutionary leap, the catastrophic collision, which marks each stage of progress, is what the universe is – the process of self-recognition.

For Hegel the universe is a pantheistic entity which thinks and feels and wills through its various 'aspects' – the inanimate world, plants, animals, men, communities, Churches, States. Progress is the growing consciousness of the idea of freedom, for reasons much the same as those advanced by Rousseau and Fichte. All change, all action occurs in accordance with laws, and all laws are ultimately, like the laws of logic, transparently intelligible, self-evidently necessary; that is what is meant by calling them rational.

---

[1] Georg Wilhelm Friedrich Hegel, *Sämtliche Werke*, ed. Hermann Glockner (Stuttgart, 1927–51), *passim*, vol. 11, p. 63.

[2] ibid. 49.

Since these laws govern those processes whereby the universe – the eternal spirit – realises itself, obtains what it wills, they are self-imposed as by a player in a game. Therefore progress – the fulfilment of acts of will in accordance with self-imposed rational laws – is growth of freedom. The purpose, the final end of the universe, is total rationality, namely total self-comprehension by everything in it. To understand everything is to understand why everything must be as it is. To act and to act freely is to act in accordance with a will directed to ends to which there are no rational or imaginable superior alternatives. Therefore a totally rational entity is totally self-governed, totally free. This is the goal towards which everything in the world marches and in terms of the distance from which its status, its value, its importance, its interest to the philosopher can be assessed. The universe is thus an army on the march, the advanced portions of it those beings whom history uses for her latest ends, those nearest to the ultimate purpose – whether in the form of conquering generals who destroy some antiquated system, like Napoleon, or philosophers and poets whose genius consists in perceiving the contours of the future and discerning the difference between what is dying and what is to come, and who thereby automatically bring the future nearer.

Hegel traces the ascent of man from the condition where he may indeed be guided by the occult operations of reason, by reason not yet fully conscious of itself, and taking the form, therefore, at first of purely appetitive instincts, and then of those normal feelings and desires whose satisfaction and harmonisation is the function of laws, economic arrangements and the rest of the social and political establishment that constitutes society. 'Civil society',[1] as Hegel calls it, is the normal condition of men not yet enlightened by even the beginnings of truly rational understanding of their own natures and place in the universe. Society at this stage is determined by the empirical ends of individuals, groups, associations and so on, and is designed to provide these agents with as much of what they desire as is compatible with survival and the provision of certain minimal goods. These economic ends are quickly analysed by a utilitarian concept of morality, the purposes of the State, and so forth, and social contracts of whatever kind, whether between the citizens themselves or between them as a body and their rulers, represent this kind of arrangement for mutual advantage and no more.

[1] 'Bürgerliche Gesellschaft'.

Liberty, which for Hegel, as for Fichte, consists in the absorption of that which is external, foreign and therefore an outside force and an obstacle into the system of the self, here takes the form of property arrangements: the possession of property is the acquisition of liberty inasmuch as owning property is extending one's self over objects – means of action and objects of appetites – instead of being dominated by or having the scope of one's action curtailed by other persons or things.

But we are still moving at a level which Hegel calls subjective, that is the satisfaction of individual desires, the domination of pictures which the individual forms for himself of the world and society, the prevalence of conceptions which belong to individuals and sections of society and into which 'objective' reason – the creator and the rational explanation of the universe – enters, if at all, very faintly. But, of course, only what is truly rational is truly real. And by 'rational' Hegel means something much larger than the reason which governs consistent thinking, or the kind of understanding which occurs in normal common sense or the sciences. Reason, moving by dialectical contradictions, sometimes by gradual accumulation, sometimes in revolutionary leaps, is the master of the universe, at once the ground of which all events, states, situations are consequences; the goal towards which all things are tending; the spirit, the recognition of whose inner structure by itself is the world and the developing whole; the pattern in terms of which alone anything has significance, in terms of which its function can be discerned, so that everything is ultimately interconnected and made to be what it is by its unique position in the system which makes it possible to illuminate one aspect of the total whole, say the art of a given period, by accommodating it to other manifestations of the spirit, say religion or political action, which we indeed tend to classify in artificial categories, but which in fact are 'organically' interrelated manifestations of the same ultimate force – reason – in its self-development.

The presence of this power, at once central and all-embracing, is what creates those feelings of loyalty to institutions which may be the confused emotional reflection of what at a rational level becomes rational obedience to the march of history, of which I myself am an intrinsic part, and which, having recognised my part in it, I obey freely since I obey only what is rational in me. The celebrated proposition that the real is the rational and the rational real must be understood in this sense: that only what belongs to the central schema is rationally necessary, is significant, likely to survive, to have influence, to be the key to the understanding of the process itself, and the work of philosophers is to some degree no more than distinguishing what is rational from what is not, to accelerate the emergence of the kernel from the husk, of the advanced liberty which is the goal of the progress of self-consciousness on the part of the rational spirit, increasingly rational as it recognises itself to be such.

This process of recognition is always the perception of the inevitable relationships which make things or persons what they are in terms of some much wider system or context to which they belong and to which they are intrinsic. This is the meaning of Hegel's perpetual insistence on the 'concreteness' of such notions as entire civilisations or systems of thought as opposed to the 'abstractness' of particulars with regard to their context – individuals, for instance, who are mere abstractions if considered in isolation, and can be properly understood or understand themselves (and so be made more 'real') only by perceiving the network of relations of which they form at the most a mere though indispensable crossing-point – the focus of a finite number of characteristics. This is a precise reversal of the normal meaning of concrete and abstract, since in ordinary speech as well as normal philosophical prose 'concrete' means particular – that which can be perceived, experienced, that which is actual, has a specific position in time and space, for instance men, things, events as opposed to general terms – names of qualities or relations or types of situation which do not themselves exist as entities though they are convenient labels for classifying that which does.

Using this sharp distinction between the rational level and merely utilitarian or other forms of pre-rational awareness, Hegel develops his notion of the State and his concept of greatness, both of which have had an influence greater perhaps than that of any of his other doctrines. Since freedom for him is the expansion of personality, a kind of laying on of hands, making free with whatever might be an obstacle to the individual's self-realisation, development of all his faculties in whatever directions these are best developed, the State appears to him to be the wholly rational organisation of the lives of human beings, since they are mere abstractions unless taken in their totality, wherein each conditions the lives of the others and occupies a unique place in the social system. The perfect State is the perfectly rational structure in which men understand fully their inevitable relations to each other and to everything else, and which they perpetuate by freely willing it, since they are rational beings with rational wills – wills, that is, that will only that which truly satisfies their natures.

If this is the perfect State, imperfect States are those in which not all but only some – whom history has appointed to understand and to govern – apprehend more or less clearly the historical process whereby all the miseries, tyrannies and oppressions, when viewed from the point of view of reason, seem to be inevitable and therefore rationally willed stages in the dialectical progress of the universe. Hegel conceives of history not as the empirical accumulation of data and the establishment, by such precarious empirical means as we have, of generalisations and hypotheses – not in the way in which historical enquiry is in fact conducted – but as a rational intuition into the sublime process of the universe, open only to the metaphysician. The rest is mere empirical history and, like empirical law, like all the institutions of civil society, survives no doubt into the rational era, but only as a dying, obsolescent stage of historical enquiry. History conceived metaphysically is perception of the unrolling of the vast rational pattern which all things compose: and not merely contemplation of it, though that is valuable enough, but activity in terms of it, for one of the ways of knowing is action. We know the laws, we understand the social whole of which we are a part, not by contemplating them from some outside vantage-point like a disinterested observer, but by living within them in the fashion which they enjoin – this kind of living being itself the life of the law, the life of the institution, or the life of society; mere contemplation implies, indeed, that this form of life is already dying. The professional historian is in a sense always an obituarist; a civilisation can be reviewed in its completeness only when it is over. We understand the Greeks from 'outside', but ourselves through being what we are, through activity, through issuing orders and obeying them, through the actual fighting of the battle. We do not first acquire and then apply our knowledge: acting is acquiring. To speak of the difference between understanding, being and doing is ultimately an abstraction, a cutting into arbitrary pieces of the seamless fabric of reality.

### Objectivity, praise and blame

If history is understanding the nature of things in general, and thereby automatically a conscious self-identification therewith, there is something trivial and absurd in praising or condemning the process. To be aware of the vast process in terms of which everything is explicable – the objective whole – and then to praise some parts of it because we like them, and condemn others because they seem to contain cruelty, injustice or waste, is a mere indulgence in subjective moods, in the values of civil society – economic, moral, legal – which shallow thinkers like Locke discuss, the values which we have as private citizens, as individuals not completely conscious of the march of reason, living in our own peaceful, limited, bourgeois way, as against the true objective values which are those in terms of which history does her work. To observe a vast human upheaval and condemn it, to condemn something which cannot help being, is something very foolish and contemptible. Who can wish to know what X or Y feels about events of cosmic importance? These are trivial facts about someone's passing feelings. To be truly worthy of the occasion is to rise to its level, to realise that something immense and critical is taking place, to have a sense of historic occasion, when perhaps a new level is being attained by humanity, which will automatically transform contemplation of facts and systems of values alike.

In Hegel there is a sharp distinction, which runs through his entire work, between, on the one hand, the subjective, emotional, personal, utilitarian, middle-class, individualistic, which is no doubt a necessary stage in human development, but a transient and by the early nineteenth century a superseded one; and the objective, the demonstrably rational, the powerful, the inexorable, the decisive, the concrete, the 'world-historical'. He is fascinated by the concept of the great man who is the maker and breaker of societies, the being in whom for the moment history has concentrated her powerful, irresistible strength; who is at once the instrument and the goal of the remorseless march of history. For him such questions as whether the great man, the earth-shaker, is good or virtuous or just are meaningless and petty, since the values implied by these words are themselves created and superseded by those very transformations of which the great man is the Herculean agent. Hegel never ceases to underline the importance of this kind of realism (which he calls being rational), the need to be conscious of what matters, what is important, where the true centre of gravity of the historical situation lies, where the great march or vast sudden revolutionary leap is occurring; beside this any preoccupation with normal moral values – kindness, compassion, fairness, hatred of injustice and suffering – which does not accord with this concentration on power, effectiveness, everything that is large-scale and permanent as against what is personal and ephemeral, is mere evidence of being caught fast in some earlier phase of history, when these values perhaps had some historical significance; a result of historical backwardness which blinds us to the overwhelming importance of the 'wave of the future' through which at any given moment humanity may be living. Above all one must keep in mind the moral necessity of identifying oneself with it, for whatever resists is bound to be overthrown, whatever is subjective, personal is weak, pathetic, is liable to suffer, to be sacrificed in the inexorable march of history; and thereby condemned as trivial, worthless, irrational – the flotsam and jetsam rightly carried away by the current – rightly, because what is right and wrong is what history creates and rejects; because the sole objective source of right is in the 'direction' of the facts themselves, not an individual judgement, not any particular code of laws, not an immutable set of moral principles, but the 'imperatives' of history itself, that which it, being the world in evolution, the divine process itself, enjoins, by proceeding where and as it does, crushing whatever is meant to be crushed, enthroning that whose hour to dominate has struck.

This worship of energy, power, the movement of force for its own sake has penetrated far more deeply into European consciousness than we sometimes suppose. It is to be found not only in Carlyle's heroes or Nietzsche's supermen, or in the openly power-worshipping movements such as Marxism and Fascism, both of which (in their various ways) derive morality from historical success (Marxists more faithful to Hegel find it in classes which carry out the rational behests of history, nationalist Fascists allow greater scope for the imposition of the violent and imperious individual will). It is also at the root of the contrast between great men and ordinary human beings – fighters who hack their way and raise humanity to a new level as opposed to the mere ants of the human ant-hill who perform their task without effectively questioning whether to carry such burdens is necessary. It lies behind the everyday use of the words 'real' and 'unreal', when we speak of

human beings or governments or situations as 'unreal', meaning by
that very much what Hegel meant,[1] that they are artificial,
ineffective, not genuine, historically thin, with the implication that
they should be swept away by the 'real', the forcible, the genuine,
the strong – not only should be, but will be, swept away by the
'real human beings' and the 'real facts' in terms of which such
condemnations are commonly made.[2]

There is something here too of Rousseau's distinction between
the reality of the honest, simple person as opposed to the hollow
artificialities of intellectuals or courtiers. However, Hegel derives
this not from Rousseau's criterion of closeness to nature, but from
the somewhat similar but nevertheless different notion of capacity
for historical survival – history being the sole arbiter, history in the
sense, we must say again, of events not as conceived by empirically
minded historians but as the 'real' process, the unfolding of reason,
as the inner pattern visible only to inspired metaphysicians or
inspired men of action. When he speaks of history, and still more
when he speaks of the State, Hegel tends to regard them as
personalities. The description of the State as God on earth, the
ecstatic references to Napoleon, spring from the notion of the State
authority – or of the men who are the latest and therefore probably
the most perfect embodiments of the vital stream – as that rational
order, that furthest point reached by the self-development of
reason. To worship reason is at once to demonstrate that one is a
serious person who looks for effective satisfaction only where in
fact it lies, in what history will bring forth rather than in that which
it has for ever condemned; and also to be free, because freedom lies
in full self-development, in the realisation of the inner harmony
which human beings cannot achieve individually (for a man taken
by himself is an abstraction), but only as parts of the vast network
which they form between them. This network is realised as one
united whole by overcoming whatever is external to it – external
matter, physical habits, everything that has been imperfectly
rationalised, made imperfectly transparent to itself, emotions,
economic purposes, all the moral values founded upon them. These
are overcome by that which is wholly rational, therefore wholly
harmonious, which provides only one path to be followed, one
solution to each genuine problem, and the despotism of which, in

[1] {Jena.}
[2] {Also 'realism' as disagreeable truthfulness[?], justifying hard-hearted behaviour[?] – brutality[?], slavery[?], etc.} [Cf. e.g. IB's 'Realism in Politics', in SR.]

the form of the State – that hierarchy in which everything has its proper place according to the dictates of 'objective' reason embodied in 'concrete' history – is the despotism of the rational part of a man over the rest of himself, the despotism which forces the mathematician not to break the laws of his science, the artist to create only in terms of the insistent inner vision which is the Divinity speaking within him, the soldiers and the statesman to dictate and conquer in obedience to the voice of history, which has made of them its chosen instruments.

This notion of the chosen instrument is as strong in Hegel as it is in Fichte. Some individuals are 'historical' because they carry within them, and to some degree must know that they do so, a historical mission – the task of transforming things as enjoined by the demands of objective reason. They may perish in the attempt, but they will have risen to their full stature, been 'fully real', liberated themselves from 'subjectivity', from bourgeois morality, from the views and opinions of the herd. Similarly, there are historical nations, and they have been given by history the right to assert themselves, to promote the march of history by subjugating and swallowing up the unhistoric nations, those which have either had their moment and turned into a mere slag-heap of used-up human material, or have never even been called to play a part, and have no role in the cosmic drama.

Civilisation begins in the East, in despotism, where only one man is free – the despot. It develops into the Graeco-Roman civilisation, where only a few are free – the slave-owners and the oligarchies. The historic task of Christianity was to make all men free. This freedom was not to take the hollow, external, artificially levelling form of equality, as demanded by the French or American democrats, which is but some economic category, something connected with civil society, below the level of reason; it was to be that freedom which consists in the fact that every sentient being realises itself in its own proper station, performing its own proper duties with its own proper rights in the elaborately articulated social organism of which every element must perform its task 'freely', realising that thereby it is realising itself without limit as part of the social whole, playing its proper part in the historical orchestra, looking upon those very restraints upon which only yesterday it looked as obstacles – the duties of service to the State, obedience to hierarchical superiors – as the fullest possible freedom, since these restraints, which seemed to press from outside arbitrarily, are now that which every being's own reason demands for the fullest perfection of the whole with which its own perfection is inevitably bound up – of which it is indeed a logically necessary element.

Hegel's world is one of State, laws, discipline, of obedience to those whom history has appointed to be leaders: and he struck a note which then reverberated more and more loudly into the nineteenth and twentieth centuries, of contempt for those who revolt against systems as such, who wish to oppose their private and personal moral sense to the march of history. There is an almost sardonic element which enters his writings, no less than those of Marx, when he speaks of the dreadful but inevitable and thoroughly deserved doom which simple but kind-hearted Utopians,[1] bourgeois moralists, trivial seekers after personal happiness, philanthropists and woolly-minded benevolent persons of all kinds are preparing for themselves when the volcano, condemned by history, upon which they build their foolish, optimistic, pathetic houses duly erupts and history destroys them in her march.

Hegel, like Marx, is on the side of the lava: and contemplates it with malicious joy. Perhaps this was due to the weakness and dispersion of Germany in the face of the more powerful States of England and France; or to a passion for theological authority and unity; or to some innate worship of power for its own sake, and bitter anti-liberalism; but he bitterly detested everything which was spontaneous and undisciplined, whether in the form of individual morality or of the outbreaks of popular feeling to which Herder attached such importance. Certainly it remains true that Hegel was the greatest of those who established that tradition of the worship of what is strong, effective and inevitable – the march of history, the almost sacred character of States and the titans who make them and maintain them, worshipped not so much as objects of aesthetic contemplation – as superior beings – as because they embody the life force, nature in action, whose laws are reason, which is wholly intelligible, wholly rational, and therefore wholly good and free – because good means that which a rational being rationally seeks for his satisfaction, which history, being wholly rational, is therefore bound to bring forth. This, in its turn, has led to the concepts of superior individuals and superior States or nations, beyond the utilitarian laws which bind them *de facto* – for in the process of

---

[1] {Silly people.}

dialectic individuals are bound to break through existing laws and existing conventions in the name of higher values, the next stage which history, in other words reason, is about to utilise. Similarly there will be no advance and no progress, only a bourgeois stagnation, only a world of material satisfactions, if States do not go to war with each other, each in the name of its own morality – the morality which its own historical stage has provided. That State whose morality is in accord with the highest point reached by reason will in fact win the battle, absorbing in the course of its victory those lower stages personified by the defeated State, whose citizens can be benefited only by being made free of the higher culture, by having their faculties heightened – made 'more real' – by the conflict of war, participation in the historical process, identification with the great force which at once is and governs the world.

The metaphysical rules of Hegel have been discredited, and rightly, for many years. His identification of cause and effect with ground and consequence was a logical error. His assumption that institutions could be rational in the sense which persons are, that there is an actual historical spirit – a personality – which embodies itself in courts of law or books or wars as much as in persons, is a piece of mythology which it is today difficult to take seriously. The notion that the good must be defined in terms of desire, and that for this reason the common good must be defined in terms of the desire of what can be described only as a common self, rests as in the case of Rousseau on a logical fallacy, that when we say that England expects every man to do his duty, there is literally a person whose name is 'England' which 'expects' as human beings 'expect'. It is as if, when one says that a community is old, one implies that it may wear a grey beard.

This kind of point is today too familiar to need pressing. But Hegel's general outlook is a very powerful force, more so perhaps in the present than in his own day. His historical categories have certainly led to great advances in the historical treatment of many topics. By representing everything as evolving in accordance with reason and as intelligible only in such terms he vastly raised the importance of the concept of history. He made it seem the most important activity in which a human being could indulge – the process of self-understanding, self-advancement, without which there was no ultimate salvation.

*History*

Hegel's almost religious worship of history, and his stress on the claim that to pick and choose among facts, to think some good and others bad, was subjective, blind and trivial – that all facts were in a sense of equal value, that above all else no moral differences must be made – created that notion of objective history which militated against the historians' personal, moral, social or aesthetic bias and formed the foundation of a great school of German history and historical jurisprudence, and historical criticism generally. A great part was played, too, by Hegel's notion of the spirit of an age, expressed in all its various phenomena, its clothes no less than its laws, its music no less than its politics, which henceforth made it impossible to conceive of history as an amalgam of biographies, antiquarian information eked out with occasional statistics and tentative sociological generalisations. The very notion of the history of institutions as such, and later of entire periods and civilisations, as at the very least frameworks, and at most constitutive principles, in terms of which alone the lives of peoples, the meaning of institutions, the significance of facts and events can be understood, is a direct effect of the Hegelian philosophy.

To apply its categories to itself, it was itself a fruit of the rise of both individualism and nationalism – of the view which individuals took of themselves as free agents seeking to develop and enrich themselves by absorbing and dominating all that they could procure for themselves, and, by a parallel process, of the conception of nations as individuals seeking to develop their lives as institutional wholes both by increasing the interdependence or subordination of their members and by pitting themselves culturally or militarily against other nations. An intellectual and spiritual aspect of this social and political and technological process was its conscious expression in words which, both in prose and poetry, bound their spell over a great portion of a civilised minority of Western Europe, and through them increased the tempo and scope of centralisation, and of the concentration of strength which is believed to be the central force of history, and whose virtues and power these intellectuals preached.

Its consequences produced a transformation of men's attitudes towards themselves and their past and their future, not without exacting a great price in terms of the errors which it bred. It took two generations to dispel the magic of a priori methods of reconstructing the past, of interpreting the facts to fit dogmatic systems, of escaping from the necessity of minute and scrupulous empirical study, on which the new philosophy poured such contempt. Hegelianism led, too, to the fashion of looking on history as proceeding down a great central avenue – that chosen by the all-conquering spirit – which was the inevitable, set direction from which only the foolish or ignorant try to escape; with the result that historians tended to neglect all those unrealised possibilities which at some earlier stage might have come to be if men had chosen otherwise, and therefore to look upon all the casualties and the failures of the historical process – the martyrs and the minorities – as not merely unfortunate but stupid and ultimately immoral as well. Men's values – what was good and right, the true reasons for obedience or for having this rather than that form of government – were provided by the demands of history itself, and to want things otherwise, still more to try to alter their course, was to oppose the wishes of the spirit. Since the spirit – reason or history, nation or wisdom, culture or wherever it was considered to have embodied itself – was the sole creator of the good, of the correct goal (Kant's 'good will' now magnified and perverted into the will of the great impersonal force which shapes our ends), to oppose it was not merely futile, but wicked.

Don Quixote was not merely ludicrous: he was no longer pathetic, no longer the emblem of human idealism vainly seeking to overcome a mean and hostile environment, but at most a blasphemer against the right, a breeder of error and crime, or at the very least a piece of trivial human flotsam swept away or pulverised continuously by the march of the great armies of mankind. Hamlet could no longer be regarded as in some sense embodying a spiritual condition tragic and valuable in itself, but as a man caught in the contradiction of trying to square his own narrow subjective scale of values with the great objective world pressing upon him. His tragedy was not so much an inevitable conflict between genuinely irreconcilable values as a 'moment' in the transcendence of the outlook of 'civil' society by the superior organisation and superior social discipline of reason incarnate in the State. The conflict of good with good of which Hegel had spoken in defining tragedy is not a real conflict, for the wise metaphysician knows that neither Antigone nor Creon understands the world as it ought to be understood, even if at their stage of development neither can be expected to understand it. The Hegelian State will presumably solve or dissolve the conflict in its higher synthesis.

This outlook put so great a premium on strength and success and sheer historical effectiveness – as against unavailing individual protest, or heroic opposition, in the name of individual beliefs, to outside pressure, opposition which was not guaranteed to win, whose value, indeed, for earlier romantics, consisted in the purity of the principles adopted or the disinterested passion with which they were defended, whether or not against great odds – that it inevitably led to political conservatism and conformism and a kind of ecstatic submissiveness to authority, to leaders and spellbinders of every kind, for which the Germans were to become so notorious.

Hegelianism has a revolutionary element in its doctrine of the inevitable conflict by which the dialectic advances, so that the negative, destructive passions had their place and revolutionary action was justified if it fought on the side of dynamic reason against static actuality, if it embodied that criticism of the past, and destruction of it, without which the future could not be born, often with immense pain and difficulty. However, that originality and eccentricity in which Humboldt and Mill saw the very life of a civilisation could not be permitted unless it justified itself by turning out to have been the vehicle of victorious reason, that is, by its success. This emphasis on success and fulfilment as the sole criterion of what was interesting, important, right, worthy of being striven for, written about, while it militated against subjective systems based on passing emotions or inclinations or prejudice, substituted for the values, whether relative or absolute, of liberalism, which allowed some worth to all ends which men sufficiently desired and stressed the imperfections and therefore the lack of universal authority of any one individual or social ideal, the sole pragmatic criterion of actual achievement, whereby the world did good to the formidable for they alone were the true prophets and creators of the future.

This doctrine came to say in the end that values, the proper ends of men, were those acts and forms which the élite in any society desired, not because the élite had a clearer vision of something objective and absolute, but because it was the élite that desired it and, being the power which history had reached in a given phase, were themselves an incarnation of its highest manifestation, and their wills were the life-force itself, directing the way of mankind.

It was of no use for Hegel's defenders both past and present to point out that he did not believe in the irrationalism which is an element in Fascism, that he believed in the *Rechtstaat*, the tidily organised Prussian bureaucracy, that he stressed that respect must be paid to skilled officials and competent administrators rather than to outbursts of elemental passion or religious exultation, to which Schelling in his latter, devout, years seemed inclined. Hegel certainly believed in rational organisation, but organisation in terms of the most advanced ideals of mankind reached to date. But these ideals were derived from the demands of the objective march of events, in the name of which anything and everything could and should be made to submit or be destroyed. The rulers of a society, the earthly embodiment of its immortal institutions, acting in the name of super-personal entities – the eternal order itself, the State or the law – were free to invade any realm. The notion of individual rights, of areas of privacy, of freedom of choice within even confined limits were mere subjective aspirations and could be 'transcended', that is, abolished, in so far as they did not fit in with the objective pattern, the *Weltgericht*, history at once omnipotent and liberating – liberating because liberty is consciousness of necessity, the knowledge that I am free only when all that is private, personal, 'subjective' has been sacrificed to the reason within me, to what unites me with the central pattern which everything obeys.

The choice is between blind obedience, as stones or trees obey, as slaves obeyed in the ancient States, as the defeated obey the victors, as deluded idealistic heretics find that they must obey the arm of the State law, and willing, happy, conscious obedience to the State which embodies in its institutions whatever is rational in me. There is no other choice: to seek for it is to seek for things to be other than they are, to be irrational, or at least childish, insufficiently mature and adult, to need discipline, to invite disregard or prosecution or coercion. This rests upon a priori premisses, which no one but Hegelians need accept, about the existence of objective reason, about inevitable laws of history, about the identity of what is good with what is inevitable and of freedom with rationality in this peculiar metaphysical sense. Since none of these premisses are either self-evident or deducible from either empirical or self-evident data, there is no need to believe them. Indeed, it is not easy to set them out further in clear and intelligible language; but it is clear that they appeal to a strong

conformist strain among human beings, to the desire to submit
rather than choose themselves, to barter freedom for the contentment bestowed only by a thoroughly tight system which solves
problems by abolishing them, and creates conditions in which
those who might ask questions are conditioned into inability to
conceive them, and thus promotes harmony by eliminating those
factors in which the liberals saw the sole value of individuals, but
which prevent the completely smooth and united working of the
social mechanism.

At a humbler level, the Hegelian method influenced thought
fruitfully. While there is no greater nonsense than the attempted
formulations by Hegel and his followers of the 'lower' activities,
natural sciences and mathematics, in the case of the imprecise
branches of knowledge – the historical sciences, criticism of
literature and art, and what might be called the humanities in
general – they have in the first place performed the useful task of
increasing awareness of the interdependence of apparently separate
human activities, of preventing that schematism and scholastic
classification into watertight compartments which had made such
subjects dry collections of unilluminating facts; and of insisting, in
their Marxist incarnation, on the importance of economic and
social factors as well as of the environment in the formation of
intellectual and artistic activities and in explaining the relations of
human beings in the past. Moreover, by insisting that all mechanical deduction of conclusion from premiss – indeed all systems
which attempt to represent events as a smooth transition or
evolution from an earlier to a later phase, each of which is neatly
contained in its predecessor – misdescribed and oversimplified the
turbid stream and inner conflict of actual life and actual history, the
Hegelians certainly served to deepen the treatment of such topics.
They maintained that within every process there is an inner conflict
with some other process seeking to subvert it; and without taking
this too literally, there is no doubt that if, instead of classifying,
say, writers as classical or romantic, one treats such categories as
provisional and formal, and seeks to discover what is characteristically romantic in writings normally described as classical, or
classical in what is conceived as predominantly romantic, a closer
approximation to the perhaps ultimately unanalysable texture and
content of art is achieved.

And so with history. The attempt to classify into neatly labelled
movements, epochs, types of government and so forth with which

Montesquieu had merely continued the tradition of Aristotle often leads to a pedantic schematism which obscures as much as it reveals. In demanding that every process contains its opposite, that every classification necessarily breaks down, that every category is necessarily incomplete and may become paradoxical, Hegelianism greatly increased the critical acumen, the sense of reality of the investigators in those regions in which the idealised entities of science and mathematics are of little if any use, and thereby created the modern approximation to humane and historical studies.

# APPENDIX

## *Subjective versus Objective Ethics*

THE EMPHASIS on nature as a source of moral or social wisdom is of course closely connected with the desire to establish the principles of conduct on an 'objective' basis, that is, to give them the same authority as the laws of nature established by the natural scientists; and this in its turn is due to the belief, present in all discussions on this topic, that unless this is done, the only sanction for this or that ethical or political rule will be 'subjective', that is, built upon such shifting sand as the individual tastes and inclinations of particular persons, in particular circumstances, at particular moments of their lives – that is, liable to change from person to person and moment to moment, and therefore incapable of forming the basis for permanent modes of behaviour either for individuals or for groups or nations.

Such subjectivity and relativity have never been regarded as fatal to, for example, aesthetic views or such codes as those of manners – or social habits adopted in free associations such as societies or clubs, in games, etiquette, and so forth. But the rules of political and social behaviour, and above all of moral action, which are intended to govern men's inner and outer lives, are obviously of supreme importance; and seem to require a more solid basis than the vagaries of individual temperament, or casual whims subject to transient influences. With the collapse of the authority of theology and scholastic metaphysics, and the accompanying disbelief in other such rationalist systems deriving from the Platonic or the Aristotelian traditions (owing to denial by empiricists of the special intellectual faculties presupposed by these systems), the peril of a chaos of conflicting individual opinions, with no criterion to decide between them, was a source of profound uneasiness, and at times alarm, in the eighteenth century, no less than in the nineteenth or the twentieth. When Hume denied that such rational faculties existed, and analysed ethical propositions as recording no more than the sentiments of individuals or groups (he never evolved any clear doctrine which distinguished between these two, nor related them unambiguously to the utilitarianism which he also supported in a general way), this was held in his day as in ours to reduce ethics to a set of subjective beliefs – in contrast with the objective beliefs of the scientists, or even of untutored common sense, about what kind of objects there are in the world and how such objects behave.

It seems clear that one of the principal motives for a search for an 'objective' ethics was the desire to escape from such subjectivism, not merely a desire for the secure knowledge which only the 'objective' seemed to promise – although this was strong enough – but also a perfectly sound recognition of the fact that there do exist sharp and profound differences between statements of personal taste or inclination and statements about the ends of life and the rights and duties of individuals. Such objective systems as those of Kant, of the Idealist philosophers, in particular Hegel and his German, British, Italian and American followers; the evolutionary ethics of the Darwinians, and no less the anti-naturalist ethics of G. E. Moore's *Principia Ethica*, and the schools of thought which followed him, not only in philosophical but in political and literary circles in England and elsewhere; the German phenomenologists and their disciples, and other related movements – all these were concerned to emphasise this deep difference and provide ethics, and by implication politics, with an 'objective basis'.

Whatever the intrinsic merit of such doctrines, they partially stemmed from a profound misunderstanding of the revolution effected by Hume. Certainly he transformed the history of thought by his conclusive demonstration that ethical statements – as indeed all normative statements – differed from statements asserting a priori connections on the one hand, and those describing matters of fact upon the other; that of the two types of statement, the first depended for its validity upon the man-made, or at any rate man-accepted, rules which govern such artificial disciplines as logic, mathematics and the moves in games, that is, which ultimately derive from the way in which we choose to use words, symbols, counters or anything else; while the latter depended upon appeals to normal experience, for which 'verification by the senses' was perhaps too narrow a description, but which consisted in those empirical methods, whatever they might be in various situations, whereby we ascertain whether or not a statement about the world is true or not. But normative statements, according to Hume, differed from both these categories inasmuch as their correctness depended neither upon the ways in which we choose to use the symbols with which we express ourselves, nor upon the kind of inspection needed for the verification of ordinary empirical statements. In the case of both these categories, the distinction between subjective and objective was clearly valid, and it was tantamount to distinguishing between the kinds of evidence upon which conclusions were founded or the kinds of methods by which they were reached. An objective statement of mathematics differed from a subjective one in using methods recognised as proper mathematical methods by mathematicians or other persons using mathematical methods – if they were reached by guesswork or mystical intuition or in an haphazard way, or believed with an obstinacy which repelled efforts to modify it by pointing out that the method used was not that which, by definition, was the sole method of mathematics, these views were described as capricious, irrational or subjective. Similarly, if anyone asserted that the earth was flat or that water never boiled, this was regarded as not merely untrue, but subjective, since it could not be certified by the empirical methods of investigation considered appropriate to the subject-matter, that is, in terms of which truth in such matters was defined or understood.

But although Hume himself in effect tried to reduce ethics to psychology, that is, a branch of empirical fact asserting scientific or common-sense procedure, his argument can easily be shown to lead to a somewhat different conclusion. If one takes him literally, then an ethical proposition would be objective if it correctly described the state of mind of an individual or a group (its approvals or disapprovals, to use his not very happy terms) – that is, by using methods recognised to be appropriate to the discovery of such states of mind – and subjective if it failed to use such methods but employed some illicit, that is to say, not commonly recognised, mode of procedure. But, of course, the objections of those who felt the whole of ethics to be rendered subjective despite this distinction were not thereby removed. If all that was being referred to were passing moods or variable approvals or disapprovals – almost likes or dislikes – whether of groups or individuals, the foundation of ethics seemed dreadfully uncertain.

This rests upon a fallacy. For if what is felt is that this sort of subjectivity of normative statements – the rules and ideals of political, social or personal life – somehow renders them more precarious, less authoritative, weaker, because bound up with the unpredictable fluctuations of the emotional life of the individual, this implies a belief that what they lack is an 'objective' element which could stabilise them; in other words, that whereas the ethical principles of our fathers used to be firm, true for all time, as rock-like as those of algebra, now the basis of all this has been removed, and we are plunged in a sea of doubt and vacillation without a rule or compass. We feel robbed of something, gravely impoverished; something which used to be objective has been degraded to being merely subjective. We may still want to believe that ethics are objective, but Hume's remorseless logic has refuted this belief, and we must have the courage to face the painful conclusion to which our premises have driven us. Given this state of mind, it is not surprising if those who seek for permanent principles of political or social action denounce Humeism as subverting the moral order and leading to disillusionment, cynicism and a heartless and opportunistic pragmatism.

The fallacy of this position consists in the tacit assumption that ethics, which is, alas, subjective, might in principle have been objective, although it has been shown by Hume's cold reasoning not to be so in fact. But if Hume is right, at any rate in maintaining that normative statements cannot be describing entities called values which exist in the world, which have independent being in the sense in which things or events or persons can be said to do – because the notion of such objective values proved, upon examination, to be unintelligible – then he is in effect implying (though he never himself saw this clearly enough) that ethical statements are in principle different in the way they are used from logical or descriptive statements, and the distinction between subjective and objective may turn out to not apply to them at all.

Kant and some among the German Idealists had a glimpse of this in supposing normative statements to be not statements of fact at all, but orders, commands, 'imperatives', deriving neither from an artificial convention, like mathematics, nor from the observation of the world, like empirical statements. And if we follow this line of thought, it becomes clear that normative statements fail to be subjective not in the sense that they might have been objective, but in the sense that they are wholly different from the kind of statements (or beliefs or thoughts) to which the distinction between subjective and objective applies. My view that murder is wrong is merely subjective. Why 'merely'? What could make it objective? What is it that a subjective statement lacks, the presence of which would make it objective, so that we feel justified in applying to it the restricting adverb 'merely', which seems to deprive it of a property which it vainly seeks but cannot have? Can a world be conceived in which normative statements acquired 'objective status'? It is only when we realise that this is a meaningless suggestion – that the note of regret which the word 'subjective' often expresses springs from what has been called a 'pseudo-lament', because it deplores the absence not of something which could be present (although prevented from being so by empirical or metaphysical causes), but of something whose presence cannot be conceived, of which to say that it is present is to utter a meaningless phrase – it is only then that we grasp the unsuitability of such an epithet as 'subjective' when applied to ethical, political or other normative disciplines.

Political statements are not subjective in the sense of not being objective – for the reader must ask himself what it would be like to transform, by whatever species of metaphysical magic, the answer to the question 'Why should I obey the government?' into something 'objective'. When he has failed to do this, he will understand that whatever the truth about how such questions and their answers function, about what the correct questions are and how the correct answers to them are to be obtained, it is not the case that some theories can maintain that the answers are objective – and that this is comforting but false – and that other theories can maintain that the answer is necessarily subjective – and that this may be upsetting but has the advantage of being true. He will realise – though this requires some intellectual effort on the part of those brought up in a different tradition – that value statements, for example the statements of politics, are neither subjective nor objective, but wholly different in kind from the kinds of statements which are so.

A clear understanding of this should dissipate the feelings of insecurity and moral impoverishment which the relation of propositions hitherto considered firm, eternal and objective to the class of uncertain, relative and subjective statements has so often induced. The tendency to call political principles objective derives, as we said above, partly from the correct realisation of their great importance in the conduct of life. This importance is not diminished or altered by a clearer realisation of the confusion

about their logical status. They remain as important or unimportant as before, but are neither subjective nor objective: they are *sui
generis*, to be assessed by methods appropriate to them (as indeed
they always have been, save by those obsessed by a misleading
metaphysical view), and no longer capable of being modified on
the ground that they are merely subjective and therefore lack
sufficient authority. The principles by which men live and act, the
ends for which they fight and die, are what they are, whether or
not they are valid, and whatever constitutes validity in this sphere,
and they lose nothing in sacredness because they are no longer
misleadingly described in terms or categories which do not apply
to them. Scepticism, cynicism and the rest seem to be the
consequences not of a disconcertingly clear view of the facts, but of
the confusions which frequently follow from false analogies with
other regions of experience, such as, in this case, mathematics,
physics and history. That is Hume's abiding service in the history
of human thought: his argument is as fatal to subjectivism and
relativism in ethics as to its equally unintelligible opposite.

# SUMMARIES OF THE FLEXNER LECTURES

*Bryn Mawr's weekly* College News *published the following sometimes somewhat innaccurate summaries of Berlin's Flexner Lectures in its issues of 13 February to 19 March 1952*

## I. DR BERLIN NOTES 'MODERNISM' IN THEORIES OF ROMANTICISTS: STATES THOUGHTS OF HELVÉTIUS AND HOLBACH EVIDENCE OF A 'CENTRAL VISION' SHAKING TRADITION

MONDAY NIGHT, February 11, Dr Isaiah Berlin discussed, in the first Mary Flexner lecture for 1952, 'Nature and the Science of Politics', as revealed by Helvétius and Holbach, early political theorists of the romantic era. The next lectures in the series will also discuss 'The Rise of Modern Political Ideas in the Romantic Age: 1760–1830'. Dr Berlin first explained that he had chosen this era for his discussion because it is more like the modern age than any other. He then proposed the question with which all political theory is concerned. The question is, why anyone should obey anyone else.

The thinkers of this time had a common quality of profound depth. They had a 'central vision' which they imposed on their hearers, replacing the conventional visions of the people. They did not merely answer questions within a framework of the universe, but they shook the framework itself, continued Dr Berlin. The popular theory at the time was that of the 'divine harmony of nature'. The essence of this theory is that every entity in the universe has a function, and must function well to obtain this harmony, which is happiness. According to this idea, obedience is necessary for individuals to fulfil their portions of the divine pattern.

Newtonian physics had a great effect on the thought of this period. According to Newton, everything in nature should be analysed into its constituent parts. Then hypotheses should be formed concerning these parts. Next the hypotheses are reduced to the least number and a universal principle for the explanation of everything is procured. Helvétius and Holbach were extreme exponents of these ideas, said Dr Berlin, and were thus 'extremely lucid' in their explanations. One Newtonian point which particularly affected these philosophers was that a question is a real question only when it is answerable. It is essential to know what type of answer is required and how the answer may be obtained.

Helvétius first declared the need of Newtonian scientific method, rather than intuitive method, in the problems of human sociological action. He thought that human beings are dominated solely by the pursuit of pleasure and the avoidance of pain. Helvétius further wanted to produce scientific morality through education of the people by moral and political experts: psychologists and sociologists. These experts should teach self-interest to the people, 'harness it', and use it for the greatest good. This idea resulted in a clash between the schools of interest in the individual and social interest.

Said Helvétius, legislation must create the greatest happiness for the largest number of people. The educator must mould men in the image of the ideal State, encouraging happiness and punishing melancholy. Enlightened leaders are necessary to uniformise the world and produce the semi-automatic activity of conditioned human beings.

*Dr Berlin expounds idea of nature as proposed by romantic [sic] philosophers: Helvétius, Holbach*

Several of the presuppositions on which this philosophy lies are false, continued Dr Berlin. In the first place, it is concerned with factual questions of politics and morals while the actual questions which should be answered are of value. These questions of 'Why should I?' not 'Why will I?' are difficult to answer factually. Helvétius assumes that nature can answer these questions.

Holbach reiterated and expanded Helvétius' ideas. He asserted that nature dictates the answer to all things. Nature speaks to all men, but in a different voice to different men. This was one of the beginnings of the idea that nature is intermediate between God and man. Holbach's definition of nature is teleological. He asserted that there is a purposive universe in which all good things are in harmony. This indicates a presupposition that good things can not collide and cause tragedy. The universe is in a divine harmony and a scientific enlightened despot can retain this harmony in the communicable peaceful world.

The people who attacked this view will be discussed in the later lectures.

### 2. I. BERLIN EXPOUNDS ROUSSEAU'S CONCEPTS OF POLITICAL LIBERTY: ROUSSEAU'S THEORY CONCERNS FLEXNER SPEAKER; VALUES OF LIBERTY, RESTRAINT EXIST HARMONIOUSLY

Mr Isaiah Berlin discussed 'Political Liberty and the Ethical Imperative, Kant and Rousseau' for the second Flexner Lecture, Monday night, February 18. As it was, he concentrated on Rousseau and said he would discuss Kant in his next lecture.

Rousseau's main theory was that liberty is an absolute value, that man must be educated for freedom, and when he is trained for liberty, we reach a state where absolute freedom equals absolute authority.

Mr Berlin disagrees with the opinion of many Anglo-Saxon countries that Rousseau's theories were not original. He thinks that Rousseau definitely had a new concept of liberty, replacing the negative theory that there were only certain phases of a person's life with which no one should interfere, that a human being should be protected, within certain areas of experience, to do about [sic] what he wishes. The extent of liberty versus restraint has been a constant problem.

Rousseau regarded liberty as an absolute value, not only for specific phases of life. He felt that a man is of no importance unless he is completely free. Liberty is connected with man's personality, his capacity for making choices. It is not reason but responsibility, the will to act, that creates the difference between man and beast.

Slavery is a denial of humanity. Forcing men to act against nature takes away their human qualities. Rather than force men to follow rules and punish them for disobedience, Rousseau believed that people should be educated to recognise what is right; they should be shown the values in justice so that they will want to do right.

His belief in absolute liberty was accompanied, however, by a belief in absolute authority. Certain moral rules exist which govern the universe. According to these rules, there are acts which are right and those which are wrong. The strong are not necessarily right.

Rousseau answered the problem of the coexistence of absolute authority and absolute freedom by explaining that two good things cannot collide, because nature is in harmony. They cannot oppose each other just as two true propositions cannot contradict each other. If they seem to collide, it shows a lack of insight in the person who sees collision.

### Mr Berlin interprets freedom and authority

It was in solving this problem that Rousseau proved himself an original thinker. The two components of this thinking were a rigid, logical reasoning and an intuitive sense of right. His answer to the problem of absolute freedom existing with absolute authority is that maximum liberty and maximum authority are as two intersecting lines. At the point of intersection they are the same. Maximum liberty and obedience coincide; therefore, because of this coincidence there is no need to reconcile liberty to authority. Man's desire for restraint is a Christian philosophy.

Men want to be happy. There are certain rules which make them happy. Once they are aware that laws are beneficial, that they provide happiness, they will want the laws. We must create the kind of laws that men want to impose upon themselves so that they will want to obey those laws; they will desire authority.

Rousseau was conscious of man's relation to nature. He thought that men should observe what is good in nature, its wholesomeness and simplicity, and adjust themselves to the conditions of nature. Peasants were closer to nature because of the simplicity and sincerity in their lives. The natural are wise, and the wise, natural.

People should all want the same qualities in an ideal State. If they do not want the same thing, freedom must be forced upon them. After they have tested it, they will want it. If men possess a rational nature, they will know what is right. If they do not know, they must be educated to what is right; they must be educated for freedom.

### 3. BERLIN EXPLAINS BRIDGE LINKING KANT AND FICHTE: LATER THEORIST APPLIES ETHICAL IMPERATIVE TO STATE

Continuing his discussion of political ideas in the romantic age, Mr Isaiah Berlin delivered the third of the Flexner Lectures on Monday night, February 25, in Goodhart Auditorium. Mr Berlin's lecture was concerned with Kant's concept of the ethical imperative, which was followed by Fichte's extension of this idea to the State.

Beginning with a general discussion of nineteenth-century Europe's concepts of liberty, Mr Berlin explained that the two ideas commonly held at that time had very little similarity. The first was that held by the British and French liberals, who regarded liberty as a negative concept, the privilege of not being interfered with.

The liberals recognised a general pattern of the universe and held that sufficient liberty should be given every man to fulfil his part in the plan. Any attempt to encroach upon this was, they thought, against the plan. Thus, liberty was defined as non-interference.

Kant presented to his followers a different view of liberty. It seemed to him that because men are wicked and stupid and tyrants strong, any attempt to make one's own decisions is frustrated by chance or by other people. Rather than seek vainly to pacify wishes, it would be better to suppress them. If one would seek freedom, it is necessary for him to contract his area of vulnerability by withdrawing within himself, and build an inner citadel which no one can reach. The basis of this concept lay in the 'sour grapes' idea that anything capable of being taken from one did not matter.

### Kant's idea of inner self expands in Fichte

The followers of Kant tried to compensate for their lack of outer freedom by the development of an inner soul, an 'impersonal immigration into themselves' where no one could reach. They held that the true man is the inner man, and that a desire eliminated is a desire satisfied. The use of 'this notion', said Mr Berlin, was 'analogous to the confusion of security and liberty'. In the outer world of the empirical self, freedom was meaningless; only in the inner world of personal ideas could one be free.

In describing the bridge between Kant and Fichte, Mr Berlin discussed the question of the ethical imperative. Prior to Kant, moral questions were considered questions of fact. Kant was the first European thinker to state that answers to ethical questions were not statements of fact, but commands. And by 'command' he meant no external force, for he considered that man commands himself.

Fichte, too, held this theory, believing that one's conduct was justified by ideals which he created himself. This led to an ethical view of morals in which political and ethical concepts were not regarded as propositions, but as evolved, projected attitudes of mind.

The second concept common to both Kant and Fichte was that of 'integrity' and 'disinterestedness'. The ancient world valued knowledge and truth; martyrdom was admired because it defended a principle that was right and true. However, the beginning of the nineteenth century brought a transformation of thought. Integrity was valued as such; people were willing to throw everything away to follow an ideal for the sake of devotion to that ideal, whether or not it was a worthy one. The emphasis was on martyrdom for the sake of martyrdom, not the principle it defended.

With Fichte, the original Kantian inner self became a real demiurge. The non-empirical self was regarded as pure activity whereby human beings generate ideals within themselves, ideals which they proceed to serve passionately. Thus the non-empirical self became superhuman, identified with the basis of everything. According to this idea, liberty became the sole moral or political reason for doing anything, the inner force by which man bends himself to his own will.

The concept of the generation of an inner ideal and the subsequent imposition of this ideal upon the outer world was applied by Kant only to the individual. But the individual was conceived by Fichte as being a fragment of one central unity, struggling to reintegrate himself with the central flame of which he was a spark. Man was not merely an individual but a social product, part of a social network.

From this grew the notion that the German people as a whole possessed an inner soul which was the unifying factor of the people, that the nation itself gave birth to an ideal, and the people were animated by something stronger than themselves, the fact that they, as individuals, were bound by a unique kind of experience, a common ideal.

Thus arose the Fichtean concept of man as a spiritual entity, part of a large divine pattern; and of nations as a 'union of non-terrestrial spirits bound together by the perpetual ties of imposing their ideals upon individuals'. From this followed Fichte's concept of liberty as the capacity on the part of the unit to realise itself, a far cry from the liberalists' idea of liberty as the freedom from interference.

## 4. BERLIN TRACES A PHILOSOPHIC STUDY OF PAST: HERDER, HEGEL MARKED HUMAN VALUES IN HISTORY

What influence did the philosophers Herder and Hegel have on our present-day concept of history? How did our methods of studying history evolve from a strictly scientific analysis of events? These were the questions that Isaiah Berlin sought to answer in the fourth Flexner Lecture presented Monday evening at 8.00 in Goodhart Auditorium.

Mr Berlin began his lecture, entitled 'Individual Freedom and the March of History', with a précis of some remarks made in 1837 by the German poet Heine, warning the French against the coming danger when the German lion, rearmed, would destroy Western civilisation in a conflagration against which the French Revolution would seem like 'a peaceful idyll'. From his own study of history Heine understood the warlike German spirit.

It was the Italian philosopher Vico, an obscure Neapolitan lawyer, who first distinguished between the study of the natural and the humanistic sciences. His idea was that too much import-ance was paid to the scientific and analytic method of studying history. Vico thought, according to Mr Berlin, 'that this was saying rather less than one knew'. The scientific method was quite adequate for external knowledge which demanded only description and classification, but history should be a study of why human beings did things and this internal knowledge demands that the student have insight into human ideals and feelings. Thus a study of history should convey an attitude of life.

The Encyclopaedists could not explain the differences among the peoples because they ignored the inner experience of the spirit. Taking the human spirit as a total of everything we do, Herder said that there was a spirit among the people binding every nation by an imponderable complicated network of similarities. He believed each culture had a unity which expressed itself in different ways from music to politics to shoemaking. Then when these unities, these group-souls, train themselves to look kindly on other group-souls or ways of life, we should have a happy humanity.

Human values are indeed connected, said Mr Berlin, but Herder's idea of a group-soul definitely contained within the limits of every group has been a 'tremendous source of human obscurity'. When this analogy between the human and group-soul is carried further, we come to the fallacious conclusion that every group and nation likewise has its mission to fulfil. Though these ideas of a group-soul have something plausible in them, there is a basic fallacy in Herder's reasoning, since there is no great underlying pattern but rather a great number of patterns within the bounds of one group or nation.

### *Humans need to personify, be loyal to whole: continue in pattern and avoid self-destruction*

There is indeed a need to personify and be loyal to the institution or the 'whole' of which humans are a less important 'part'. Whoever defies the pattern and, as Don Quixote, tilts with windmills, is denying the purpose of the universe, which is 'good', and so, pitting himself against the advance of society, is destined to be destroyed.

According to Hegel, history moves not in a straight line but rather in circles by continual inner conflict according to history's own secret plan for using human beings. He threw light on the fact that what happens in history results from the collision of human plans. (Hegel, said Mr Berlin, is apt to identify himself with the force of history.) For Hegel, history was everything, and through it one is able to see everything in logical relation with everything else.

At that time, concluded Mr Berlin, history first became a study of institutions on the theory that the whole is greater than its parts.

### 5. BERLIN LECTURE EXPLAINS IDEAS OF PHILOSOPHER: SAINT-SIMON REPROACHES ABSTRACT IDEALS OF LIBERTY

Mr Isaiah Berlin chose as his topic for the fifth lecture in the Mary Flexner series, which was given in Goodhart Auditorium Monday, March 10, 'Saint-Simon and his Disciples'. Saint-Simon's most important thesis, said Mr Berlin, was that human society should be reconstructed as a large factory, in the form of a pyramid, with the technocratic dictatorship of scientists, artists, industrialists and bankers.

Every member of society has his place in this great factory, should seek it, and stay there when he finds it. In this way, an overabundance of the necessities of life will be produced, each person will be kept busy, and there will be no cause for contention among men. According to Saint-Simon, liberty, equality and democracy are absurd conceptions which only hamper human existence. Technical clarity should take the place of abstract political theories.

Saint-Simon, a nineteenth-century French nobleman, was nevertheless a great believer in the modern doctrine of historical evolution. The French Revolution failed, he averred, because the people did not understand the laws of history. People should adapt themselves to the human needs of their particular age, which are not necessarily the requirements of any other age.

### Pyramid ideal social order, says Saint-Simon

The evolution of man should be understood in order to perceive what the needs of one's own age are, and these needs should then be fulfilled. Society is in a continual transformation. To Saint-Simon this idea of evolution was the most efficient way of putting heterogeneous beings into a system. Since human existence is always in a flux, no basis of life is valid unless it evolves in response to human needs. For example, Luther was an 'arch-villain' to Saint-Simon since he 'tied religion to a book', the Bible.

To Saint-Simon, the human ideal is the 'richest, broadest development of human faculties in all directions'. Happiness is found in this full development and ceaseless creation in man of his intellectual, imaginative and emotional powers. This can be done only with efficient organisation of society, with the experts of a particular age as the leaders and each person in the job he likes. No one is useless if he is placed in a productive capacity and not allowed to become a parasite. A society of endless productivity, with scientific experts, industrialists and bankers as the leaders, will lead men to the ends they really want, food, shelter and culture, not to rights such as liberty and equality which they really cannot use and do not need. All organisation of society should go for these productive ends.

In the pyramid of society, the classes generally should be aligned as follows: the business class of engineers, poets and painters on the bottom, the critical body of examiners (physicists, biologists and chemists) next, and the organisers (bankers and managers) on top. With this plan, unlimited plenty will be produced, and it will be distributed correctly. The ideal is a vast industrial empire in which politics are of no necessity: an efficient enterprise which works to capacity.

Towards the end of his life, continued Mr Berlin, Saint-Simon saw that he could not preach just this economic and social doctrine. Consequently, he developed the idea of 'Fraternity'. The essence of this doctrine was to instruct the masses by teaching them a different, simpler doctrine from that of the upper classes. In this way the masses could understand and abide by the moralities of the higher classes. Through the notion of a personal God, the great scientific principles on which society is based can be brought within the understanding of the populace. Saint-Simon did become more religious later in life, said Mr Berlin, and his atheist followers thought that he was beginning to believe his own philosophy of a personal God, which he had postulated only as useful.

To Saint-Simon, there were no vices, but only maladjustment. If people will find their appropriate places in the great 'workshop' of life, and if they do not try to leave them once they are there, all will be in complete order and each person will feel self-realised. This tight totalitarian doctrine allowed no room for freedom to 'make blunders'. The evolution of man must always be towards perfection. Said Saint-Simon, the Golden Age is before us with a vast international workshop in which everyone is ideally adapted to his job. These ideas, Mr Berlin stated, were extremely far-sighted and 'have something to do with the twentieth-century ideas'.

### 6. BERLIN REVIEWS MAISTRE ENDING FLEXNER SERIES: IGNORANT GENERALITIES FALSELY LEVELLED BY ACCUSERS

Mr Isaiah Berlin delivered the last of his lectures on the political ideas of the romantic age in Goodhart, Monday evening, March 17. In this close to the Flexner series, he discussed Maistre, a philosopher of the late eighteenth and early nineteenth centuries. Maistre, because of his opposition to the theories behind the French Revolution, is often brushed aside with harsh epithets: a supporter of the 'unholy trinity of dictator, pope and executioner', a fanatic Catholic, a demented, eloquent reactionary. Mr Berlin pointed out Maistre's beliefs, in an effort to dispel ignorant name-calling and to show his influence on the thought of the nineteenth and twentieth centuries, particularly on what Mr Berlin called the 'romantic Fascism' of our time.

Maistre, writing after the bloody, tragic days of the French Revolution, felt that the Revolution had failed because its supporters laboured under 'a grave illusion about human nature in general'. They based their struggle on a belief in the intrinsic goodness of man, a trust in reason as a guide to wise political administration, and an assurance that men could best profit under a clearly defined, free, progressive government.

### French philosopher Maistre refuted reason: believed nature destructive, violent, furious

Maistre, on the other hand, claimed that men were intrinsically 'vicious, weak and undefended', that reason was useless in ruling a State, and that only a mystical, absolute, stable government could properly benefit its subjects.

In quoting Maistre, Mr Berlin gave several examples of the philosopher's theory that 'Whatever is reasonable collapses; whatever is irrational survives.' Maistre showed that the reasonable, logical free elections in Poland, where the best-fitted person was ostensibly chosen for each position, led only to unrest and disorder, while the monarchical system in the rest of Europe, where a man became ruler for the unsatisfactory reason that his father ruled before him, had been able to maintain peace, unity and stability. Here reason fell before irrational policies.

Maistre believed that the laws of nature, too, were lacking in the reason that was ordinarily attributed to them. It appeared to him that nature was destructive, violent and furious. The earth was 'perpetually steeped in blood' and man, by his very nature, was a killing animal; he killed for food, adornment, attack, defence, shelter, and even for the sake of killing. Just as man exterminated animals for these necessities and pleasures, so, thought Maistre, would he kill other men if uncontrolled. Since his instinct was destructive, government must be instituted to control this instinct and to provide order.

Government, then, must be based on certain principles that are offshoots of Maistre's mistrust in man and in reason. Since criticism, uncertainty and freedom of expression and thought are means towards the assertion of the violent individuality of man, such ideals are harmful to the authoritative, powerful State. The only way of exerting complete control over human beings is to base their society on something that they cannot question, rebel against or criticise. The centre of their authority must be mysterious, 'something which is terrifying, something which is dark'. Only complete obedience to such sure, incomprehensible, frightening 'somethings' can prevent reason from taking possession of a man's mind and destroying dogmatic authority.

The government proposed by Maistre is, of course, totally antipathetic to the Social Contract which was the newly accepted theory of his liberal contemporaries. To Maistre, the Social Contract assumed the shape of a series of misconceptions leading to an unrealistic system. He could not accept the proposition that a promise was a natural relationship between men; he could not accept the savage as a man with some habits of as great value as the habits of civilised communities; he could not accept society as a mutual trust and belief in the good intentions of one's fellow men. His view of the social structure was that it was built on man's desire to suppress his very wicked instincts, to sacrifice his individual evil for his own protection. This element of self-sacrifice was combined with man's innate desire to be obedient to some power. By giving man some ultimate power to obey, governments could maintain peace and security.

The power that Maistre thought man needed and wanted was, of course, without reason. One of his most famous passages speaks of the executioner as 'the terror of human society, but ... also the power that holds it together'. The dark, violent punishment represented by the executioner is the bond that keeps government alive. If reason is denied, doubt and refutation cannot exist, and the oscillation that causes the downfall of government is thus done away with.

To the end of absolute, irrational, mysterious power, Maistre advocated the abolition of the testing, examining and questioning of science and literature, and a blind faith in the past, in the mystery of tradition, maintained by 'potential terror'. The enemies of Maistre, as he defined them, were not just those who differed from his basic precepts, but all who would not conform to irrational, unthinking obedience, 'all persons who, in one way or another, question the order'.

For an absolute, immobile, stable society, the reverence for myth, absolute authority and terror provided the best curb on the individual and, according to Maistre, the only practical direction of his naturally destructive instincts.

Mr Berlin closed with a summary of his five previous lectures, and Dr Nahm[1] expressed the college's gratitude for the opportunity to hear them.

[1] Milton Charles Nahm (1903–91), philosopher; professor and (1946–72) chairman of the philosophy department at Bryn Mawr.

# NOTE FROM THE EDITOR TO THE AUTHOR

*1992*

THE TYPESCRIPT that follows is a reconstruction of most of an unfinished book. It is based on what you call in your notes the 'long version' of the Mary Flexner Lectures, afforced by an 'Introduction' [here retitled 'Prologue'] which seems to have been written for the book version of the lectures – it certainly fits.

In the autumn of 1952 (October–December), of course, you delivered another version of the same lectures on the Third Programme under the title 'Freedom and its Betrayal'. I believe Anna Kallin's[1] first notion was that these should be the 1952 Reith Lectures, but that she failed to find support for this idea in the higher echelons of the BBC – I haven't discovered why, or when. The best introduction to the initial genesis of the main typescript takes the form of a letter you wrote to Miss Kallin on 11 December 1951. I quote:

> This is a hurried, quasi-official note to reply to your latest *cri de coeur* about the date of the talks; the position is this. It is indeed true, I am even now in [the] process of hysterical dictation of the rough draft for these lectures, and it is quite clear that there will not be anything like a finished text by the time I have to start delivering them on 11 February. I do not, of course, need to submit a manuscript for publication immediately after the lectures are over in late March, and although I may have enough material – with the help of God and the good will of the lady who will type this letter – I rely on the latter rather more than the former – to make the delivering of the actual lectures possible, this material will be in a dreadful state, without all the historical references which alone will not merely corroborate the wild generalisations contained, but, in fact, check their truth so far as I myself am concerned. You will easily perceive how it is one thing to say a lot of things in a general fashion to an audience and

---

[1] The author's Third Programme producer. (This and the other notes to this item were not present in the original version sent to Berlin.)

a very different one to commit words to cold print even though it may be only the *Listener*. I shall arrive in England only in very late April. With me I shall have (*a*) the rough draft of the lectures, partly in typescript, partly in my own fantastic handwriting; (*b*) possibly a wire recording transcript of the lectures themselves;[1] (*c*) an inchoate collection of odd references picked up here and there which may or may not tally with the text and which will need to be supplemented by quite a lot of Blunt-like research[2] before anything like an approach to a dependable truth can be achieved. Therefore, before I can deliver a text in[to] the hands of the Oxford Press, I shall need to do at least three months' work on all those original sources (what the subjects of my lectures actually said as opposed to what they ought to have said to support my theses about them) and this cannot be ready, if I get to work in May, before, say, August, if then. I certainly do not propose to send a text to the Press here (in the USA) before 1953, though I may be able to achieve this in, say, November 1952. On the other hand, I ought to have an adequate text, if I work properly, by August or early September and from this text condensation for broadcasting will, of course, be feasible. I realise that you perform miracles of cutting, condensing, crystallising etc., but I do not believe that I shall have written-out lectures to deliver even into your magical hands in late April, which, anyhow, will be a little too late. Nor would you or the BBC wish to print in the *Listener* statements for whose accuracy I shall certainly not be able to vouch on topics of which a good deal of exact knowledge exists on the part of benevolent scholars let alone captious rivals. You may reasonably ask why I had not thought of all this before suggesting May. To which the answer is – as it always must be – error, sheer error on my part, miscalculation of the time it takes to write a book and guarantee [the] reasonable accuracy of the statements which it contains. I do not deny that I should be able to produce impromptu lectures of a somewhat speculative kind by May – but that would certainly be unprintable in the *Listener*,[3] which is surely

---

[1] This I have not found – if it ever existed.

[2] A reference to the intensive and extensive research undertaken by Anthony Frederick Blunt (1907–83), art historian, authority on Poussin, former Communist spy, who at the time of this letter was Surveyor of the King's Pictures.

[3] The broadcast lectures were not printed in the *Listener* (or indeed elsewhere). The Editor of the *Listener* said that they were too long. As Berlin wrote to T. S. Eliot on 7 November 1952: 'As for the B.B.C. lectures, they are a semi-impromptu version of my Bryn Mawr talks: & I am under contract to publish these or something like them. *The Listener*, I dare say rightly, refused to have anything to do with talks of such prolixity; I possess the MS. of the text on which the talks are based, even longer, fuller, duller, with an apparatus of notes, &, under the Bryn Mawr contract, dedicated to the Oxford University Press. The lectures themselves therefore seem doomed to perish: & just as well, I should

undesirable. So on these grounds – mainly, that is, of the probable absence of a condensable version of my lectures by the beginning of May – I must, with great guilt and a sense of my incorruptibly Oblomovian[1] nature, beg to be postponed until October or November and promise sacredly to deliver an elastic text into your hands by September. It really is better so; the text will be much better if propped up with solid 'research', even though this may not find its way into the text; I should be terribly ashamed and you would not be pleased to have a rough and chaotic sketch when you can have the finished article, however poor, however dull. In any case, I cannot be home before the end of April and how much time will that leave for the preparation of the text? Imagine the frantic hurry of those last hours, the mistakes made, the apologies subsequently required, instead of which, tranquillity, detachment, harmony, culture and rest in September. Please convey my humblest apologies to Harman Grisewood[2] etc. – I realise that this is an alibi which one is allowed to use only when in the throes of genuine despair.

In this unhappy state I greet you with the last remnant of my failing powers.

This undoubtedly represents a considerable underestimate of the worth even of the unamended typescript! At all events, revisions were duly made, as I explain below, and have been incorporated here.

The typescript lacks its last two chapters – those corresponding to the lectures centred on Saint-Simon and Maistre. Perhaps shortage of time prevented you drafting these, or perhaps they are lurking somewhere. Of the chapters that do exist, the earlier ones in particular have been worked over very thoroughly indeed in your handwriting, in places growing to over twice the length of the original typescript. The decipherment of these excrescences has been a major task (involving, for example, photographing through an ultraviolet filter a sheet that must at some time have been exposed to sunlight, in order to reveal writing that had become all but invisible), but I think that no mysteries of significance now remain. My guess is that a good deal, at any rate, of your rewriting took place after the delivery of the lectures, and thus represents the first stages of preparation of the book version.

think. I shall preserve the B.B.C. transcripts of them wistfully for a month or two, and then lose or destroy them.' Fortunately he did neither.

[1] The central character in Ivan Goncharov's eponymous novel *Oblomov* (1859) is a well-meaning day-dreamer who spends most of his life in his room, clad in a dressing-gown or in bed; he loses any capacity for decisions or action and achieves nothing.

[2] Controller of the BBC Third Programme 1948–52.

The BBC files suggest that the reuse of the Flexner material on the Third Programme had been planned some time in advance; they also show that the conception of the lectures changed between the time they were first mooted at the BBC and their delivery. An internal BBC memo of 19 September 1950 from Anna Kallin to Controller, Talks (then Mary Somerville), gives the titles as follows:

1  De Maistre (and Fascism)
2  Marx
3  The Encyclopaedists – Diderot etc. – and their Nineteenth-Century Followers
4  Hegel and Romantics (which will include all romantics – even Swiss)
5  St-Simon and Co.
6  Bentham (or what Isaiah Berlin calls 'The Calculators')

A (very inaccurate) transcript of the fourth lecture, dated 16 May 1952, entitled first 'Individual Freedom and the March of History: Herder and Hegel', then 'Herder and Hegel and the March of History', presumably taken from a recording made at the Flexner Lectures, marks a subsequent change in the scope of the fourth lecture. An internal BBC memo of 11 June 1952, again from Anna Kallin to Mary Somerville, gives the overall title as 'Political Ideas in the Romantic Age: The Source of Modern Political Ideas'[1] and the contents as follows:

1  Science of Politics – Holbach and Helvétius
2  Nature and the Moral Imperative – Rousseau
3  Two Concepts of Freedom (romanticism and liberalism) – Fichte
4  The March of History – Vico, Herder and Hegel
5  The Organisation of Society and the Golden Age – St-Simon and Fourier
6  The Counter-Revolution – de Maistre and Görres

The titles given in this memo under 1, 3 and 4 are (nearly) the same as those that appear in the typescript for chapters 1, 3 and 4. Indeed, the titles in the memo presumably give a pretty good idea of what was actually delivered in the USA.[2]

---

[1] The title I have adopted for publication comes from a subsequent letter from the author to Anna Kallin.

[2] Now confirmed (though Vico, Herder, Fourier and Görres become less central figures than this list might suggest) by the weekly summaries published in Bryn Mawr's *College News* (reprinted above on pp. 266–78); these I had not seen

By the time the BBC lectures came to be delivered they had been further focused on the six figures named in their titles.[1] (Before the final title was chosen they are referred to in the BBC file as 'Six Enemies of Human Liberty'.)

A word about two conventions used in the typescript: curly brackets – { } – identify your handwritten marginalia (mostly notes pointing to further revision), here presented as footnotes. Square brackets mark editorial comment or intervention.

---

in 1992. There is also a sheet (MS. Berlin 570, fo. 24) in the Berlin Papers (see p. xi above, note 2) on which appears a list of titles for the lectures in a hand other than Berlin's (perhaps that of a secretary?), heavily corrected by Berlin. This seems to be a draft of the list in the letter to Katharine McBride of 20 November 1951.

[1] Helvétius, Rousseau, Fichte, Hegel, Saint-Simon, Maistre.

# INDEX

## Compiled by Douglas Matthews